The Marriage Clinic

Also by the author

Seven Principles for Making Marriage Work (with Nan Silver)
When Men Batter Women (with Neil S. Jacobson)
The Heart of Parenting (with J. DeClaire)
Why Marriages Succeed or Fail
What Predicts Divorce?

A NORTON PROFESSIONAL BOOK

THE MARRIAGE CLINIC

A Scientifically-Based Marital Therapy

John M. Gottman, Ph.D.

W.W. NORTON & COMPANY
New York   London

For information about permission to reproduce selections from this book,
write to Permissions, W. W. Norton & Company, Inc., 500 Fifth Avenue,
New York, NY 10110

Composition by PRD Group
Manufacturing by Haddon Craftsmen

Library of Congress Cataloging-in-Publication Data

Gottman, John Mordechai.
 The marriage clinic : a scientifically-based marital therapy / John M. Gottman.
 p.   cm.
 "A Norton professional book."
 Includes bibliographical references and index.
 ISBN 0-393-70282-0
 1. Marital psychotherapy. 2. Marriage counseling. 3. Marriage—
Psychological aspects.   I. Title.
RC488.5.G68   1999
616.89' 156—dc21   99-18916   CIP

W. W. Norton & Company, Inc., 500 Fifth Avenue, New York, N.Y. 10110
www.wwnorton.com

W. W. Norton & Company Ltd., 10 Coptic Street, London WC1A 1PU

1 2 3 4 5 6 7 8 9 0

In memoriam
To my friend and colleague,
NEIL JACOBSON

Noble Gadfly,
dedicated to Truth,
to accountable
and effective
marital therapy

Relentlessly, he pursued the search for effective marital therapies, doing careful dismantling studies as well as basic research on marriage. When others were publishing self-congratulatory meta-analyses, Jacobson noted that effects were often primarily due to the deterioration of couples in the no-treatment control groups. Maintaining the importance of clinically meaningful rather than statistically significant changes, he reanalyzed his own data and concluded that only 35% of couples were really improving, and that 30–50% of those were relapsing within a year or two. He alone made the field face the truth and continue its search.

Acknowledgments

This book was made possible by continuous research grant support from the National Institute of Mental Health, Behavioral Science Research Branch. The more recent grants that have supported this work were: Marital Discord, Parenting and Child Emotional Development, MH2484, Basic Research on Changing Marital Relationships, MH4776, and Research Scientist Award, The Maintenance of Close Dyadic Relationships, MH0257, which I have been fortunate to have held continuously since 1979.

The book was also made possible by a number of important collaborations that have been a joyful part in my life. These are a collaboration with Professor Robert Levenson of the University of California, Dr. Laura Carstensen of Stanford University, and Dr. Neil Jacobson of the University of Washington.

I have also been blessed with important collaborations in my laboratory. The cornerstones of this collaboration have been my secretary, Sharon Fentiman, who graces my life and keeps me from chaos, Dr. Sybil Carrére, who runs my lab and is a colleague, Cathryn Swanson, my programmer and data analyst, and Dr. Lynn Katz, a former student who used to run my lab, and is now a collaborator who runs her own lab. Sybil, Sharon, Katie, and I are really just four friends who meet regularly to discuss ideas and the everyday management of research, and simply enjoy working together.

My wife, Julie Schwartz Gottman, provided love, friendship, motivation, leadership, intellectual camaraderie, support, and conceptual organization. She made doing the couples' and parents' workshops a lot of fun. She has been a dedicated colleague and friend in the development of our Gottman Institute and in our newly established Marriage Clinic in Seattle. Increasingly, she and I have become partners in applying research to clinical work and I learn a lot from her, both in our joint teaching and in our clinical work.

I have been blessed with excellent students and staff, including Kim Buehlman, Jim Coan, Melissa Hawkins, Carole Hooven, Vanessa Kahen, Dr.

Lynn Katz, Michael Lorber, Kim McCoy, Sonny Ruckstahl, Dr. Regina Rushe, Kimberly Ryan, and Tim Stickle.

At the moment my laboratory is an exciting and nurturant place that Dr. Sybil Carrére has created, in which every staff member has a research project. Sybil has a great gift for managing a wonderful research environment. My current students are Alyson Shapiro, Kim Ryan, Heather Kelly, and Jani Morford. My staff include Donnel Howell, Erika Johansen, Stephanie Jones, Angie Mittmann, Amber Tabares, Erica Woodin, and Dan Yoshimoto. They are a gifted and dedicated crew, and I could not function without them. Tied to this effort are a dedicated army of volunteer undergraduates who take research seminars and do a lot of the unpaid nitty-gritty work of research.

Finally, let me acknowledge the true bravery and dedication of my research subjects. Despite guarantees of confidentiality, it is still remarkable that they are willing to share such intimate parts of their lives with us. Many people do not understand their motivation and think that they are just American exhibitionists. Nothing could be farther from the truth. They form fairly representative samples of couples in the places in which we do our research. Hence, for every couple that does not volunteer for the research there is a couple very much like them who do volunteer. Their motivation is usually not just to earn a subject fee, but to help advance science in the highly delicate and private parts of family life. I will be forever grateful for their devotion and trust.

Contents

Appendices

Tables and Figures

Save a life and you will save the world.

Mishna *Sanhedrin* 4:5

Part **I**

Research and Theory

Chapter 1 &

Myths and Mistakes of Marital Therapy

 In this chapter I share my view of the current status of marital therapy and the question of what is "dysfunctional" when a marriage is ailing or headed for dissolution. There are many myths and misconceptions about this issue, and clearing up these misconceptions is critical in setting the objectives of marital therapy. Our view of what is dysfunctional tells us the goals of therapy.

The divorce rate remains extremely high in the United States, and, in general, the remainder of the world is not far behind. Current estimates of the chances of first marriages in the U.S. ending in divorce (within a 40–year period) range between 50% and 67% (Martin & Bumpass, 1989). The data suggest that failure rates for second marriages are either about the same (Martin & Bumpass, 1989) or about 10% *higher* than for first marriages. Cherlin (1981) presented data that show that this trend is not new in the U.S. The divorce data back to the 1890s can be well fitted with an exponential function. However, it is clear that we are now reaping the results of this long-term trend. Divorce can be said to have reached epidemic proportions in our own time.

There are serious consequences of marital dissolution for the mental and physical health of both spouses. These negative effects include increased risk of psychopathology; increased rates of automobile accidents, including fatalities (Bloom, Asher, & White, 1978); increased incidence of physical illness, suicide, violence, and homicide (Bloom et al., 1978; Burman & Margolin, 1992; Verbrugge, 1979, 1986); decreased longevity (Berkman & Breslow, 1983; Berkman & Syme, 1979; Friedman et al., 1995); significant immunosuppression (e.g., Kiecolt-Glaser et al., 1987; Kiecolt-Glaser, Malarkey, Cacioppo, & Glaser, 1994); and increased mortality from diseases (Bloom et al., 1978; Burman & Margolin, 1992).

Also, there is now convincing evidence to suggest that marital distress, conflict, and disruption are associated with a wide range of deleterious effects on children, including depression, withdrawal, poor social competence, health problems, poor academic performance, a variety of conduct-related difficulties, and markedly decreased longevity. This is not to say that spouses in ailing marriages should stay together for the sake of the children. In our own laboratory we have discovered that the same consequences are experienced by children when parents remain in hostile marriages (e.g., Gottman & Katz, 1989). The active ingredient that hurts children in divorce appears to be continued marital hostility between the parents, particularly if the child is used as a pawn by parents to hurt one another (Buchanan, Maccoby, & Dornbusch, 1991; Hetherington & Clingempeel, 1992).

Hence, it seems clear that we are in a crisis in the United States today in terms of the dissolution of families. Every day America's families and children reap the negative consequences of this crisis. These consequences are now very well researched. We marital therapists are supposed to help solve this crisis. But, unfortunately, in my view, we do not have the tools to do the job.

Not all marriages end in divorce, and among those who remain married there is a wide range of marital happiness. What predicts divorce and eventual marital happiness has been the subject of surprisingly little prospective research. This kind of research is important for designing a marital therapy, because it pinpoints what may be "dysfunctional" in marriages that are ailing.

Identifying what is "dysfunctional" when a marriage is not going well essentially tells us what is broken and what needs fixing. The goals of marital therapy are based on this knowledge. Later in this chapter I will address the many myths that abound in our field and describe the marital research laboratory I created to find empirically based answers to this question.

MARITAL THERAPY EFFECTS: LITTLE OR NOTHING WITH HIGH RELAPSE

More people seek therapy for marital problems than for any other type of problem (Veroff, Kulka, & Douvan, 1981). But how effective is this most sought-after form of help? The largest effect sizes found in meta-analyses were those for behavioral marital therapy (for a review of these meta-analyses, see Bray & Jouriles, 1995). There are two ways to get a large effect size in a meta-analysis. One is by having large experimental group effects. The other is by having large deterioration in no-treatment control groups.

Indeed, when Jacobson (1984) reanalyzed data from four of his behavioral marital studies (which had among the largest effects), he reported that, although 55% of the couples improved after treatment, only 35% were in the nondistressed range at the end of therapy. He concluded that significant effect sizes in controlled marital therapy studies may exist largely because people tend to deteriorate in the waiting-list control groups. Jacobson and Addis (1993) wrote, "The success that investigators have had establishing these effects for their preferred treatments is not as impressive as first thought. The improvement rate in the absence of treatment is so low that even small changes in an experimental treatment are likely to be statistically significant" (p. 85).

Furthermore, a pervasive problem exists for almost all marital therapies that have been systematically evaluated using a long-term follow-up (and this is a minority of studies): a ubiquitous *relapse* effect. Of the couples that make some initial gains in marital therapy a sizable percentage of these couples, about 30–50%, relapse in two years (Jacobson & Addis, 1993). Something like a second law of thermodynamics seems to function in marriage—that is, when marital distress exists, things usually deteriorate (entropy increases). The therapeutic effects of the therapies that have been scientifically evaluated are generally weak, and there is a very high relapse rate.

What effects, in general, does marital therapy have? In our longitudinal research we have typically found a strong positive correlation (about .50) between having been in marital therapy and getting divorced. Is our result representative? The best study we have available on what therapy is "out there," that is, non-university-based therapy, was done by Cookerly (1980). Cookerly conducted a 5-year follow-up of 326 clients treated by a wide variety of marital therapies in the U.S. The separation/divorce rate was 43.6% after 5 years. The highest separation/divorce rate occurred in the first year after therapy. These rates are considerably higher than base rates would lead one to predict. *So marital therapy appears to be a reliable vehicle toward divorce!*

To summarize, after taking a hard look at relapse rates, our current best estimate is that for about 35% of couples marital therapy is effective in terms of clinically significant, immediate changes, but that after a year about 30–50% of the lucky couples who made the initial gains relapse. This means that all we can claim is that in the best studies, conducted in universities with careful supervision, only between 11% and 18% of couples maintain clinically meaningful initial gains when treated with our best marital therapies. What must the actual success rates be in real clinical practice, where the standards of training, treatment adherence, and supervision are generally lower, if not absent altogether? I think that we must conclude that it is likely that *we have an intervention methodology that nets relatively small effects, and we have a huge relapse problem.*

In my view, this is not due to the fact that marital therapy needs just a minor fix; rather, we need a *major* change. If you ask the question Jacobson and Revenstorf (1988) asked about whether the observed changes in marital satisfaction are clinically meaningful, the results of most marital therapies turn out to be quite unimpressive. As I noted, in our longitudinal research we have consistently found significant correlations between going for marriage counseling and getting a divorce. *Consumer Reports* (1995; see also Seligman, 1995) published a survey of their readers who had undergone some form of psychotherapy from various types of professionals. Despite many flaws in the design of this study, therapy generally got reasonable marks for customer satisfaction. However, if one makes the (probably very large) assumption that most of the marital therapy in this study was done by the marriage counselors, then the number who showed major improvement for presenting symptoms constituted only 22% for those who saw the marriage counselors for less than 6 months and 37% who saw the marriage counselors for more than 6 months. Other research (Simmons & Doherty, 1995) shows that the typical number of sessions of marriage counseling is 11, which is about 3 months.

In this area of marital and family therapy we have discovered that anything we do will work to some degree, as long as the therapist is highly active and the intervention has some clear rationale that is articulated to the clients. Otherwise, people terminate, against professional advice. That is a pervasive finding in our field—that nondirective approaches lead people to quit the therapy. So it seems that in the family therapy field anything that makes sense will have some degree of effectiveness if the therapist is directive and active—at least it will be considered "effective" in terms of customer satisfaction (and therapists' ratings).

Unfortunately, therapists' ratings are biased, and customer satisfaction ratings evaluating treatment in child, family, and marital therapies have been discovered to be invalid as indicators of real change. This was one of the basic findings of the researchers at the Oregon Social Learning Center when they first started doing interventions. The parents reported that everything was now fine, even when the target children had not changed at all, as determined by observation or teacher reports. The parents simply wanted to say "thank you" to the therapists for trying, and they did so on the self-report measures of change (Patterson, 1982). So, in such research on change, we cannot rely on studies that limit assessment to self-report variables measuring therapeutic outcomes.

How general is this Oregon Social Learning Center result that would lead us to doubt self-report data alone as outcome data? Jacobson, Schmaling, and Holtzworth-Munroe (1987) conducted a two-year follow-up of the couples divided into two groups: "maintainers" who retained their therapeutic gains, and "relapsers" whose gains deteriorated. They wrote that "both sets of couples were unanimous in their positive feeling expressions about therapy: 80% of the maintainers and 100% of the relapsers expressed the belief that therapy had a positive impact on them, while only 6% of couples, across groups, insisted that therapy had not been useful" (p. 193). My conclusion is this: We cannot rely on "customer satisfaction" data to evaluate our interventions. We must insist on harder data that assess the outcome of our interventions.

GIVING SCIENCE A CHANCE

My hypothesis is that marital therapy is at a major impasse. Furthermore, I contend that it is at an impasse because it is not based on solid empirical knowledge of what is actually predictive of marital dissolution (what is "dysfunctional"), and what real couples do to keep their marriages happy and stable (what is "functional"). Here is a story that describes this one underlying principle.

When I was an assistant professor 25 years ago, I decided I wanted to help children without friends to make a friend. There was already a program designed by a famous behavior therapist, so I called him and asked him how he had designed his intervention program. He said that he and a few of his graduate students sat in his office and tried to remember how they made friends at age 4. Their program had kids going up to other kids and saying things like, "Hi! My name is Harold. What's your name? Isn't this a great day? I would like to play with you." Later, when I went to the library, I was surprised to find out that developmental psychologists didn't know how children made friends. So, I started making tapes of children making friends and talking to their best friends. I thought that I would find out how children actually made friends and talked to their friends, and that this would take me a year or so, and then I would get back to the intervention. We wound up studying children from age 3 up through the college years, and I had to design some observational coding systems, and it took me 13 years to find out how children make friends and how that changes developmentally and why (Gottman, 1983; Gottman & Parker, 1986). It turned out that the famous behavior therapist's conclusions about how young children make friends were *exactly* the way to get rejected if you were a preschool child. Young children do not start a play session with strangers by introducing themselves. Calling attention to yourself is guaranteed to get you rejected.

My point is that we cannot know how to design intervention programs for target populations in trouble by *imagining* what they need, or even imagining it according to some abstract theoretical position. We ought to give descriptive science a chance, and what I mean by that is that we have to do the hard work of description and prediction to find out how people who are doing well with particular problems manage to do the tasks competently. It's not a very hard concept. It is just giving science chance.

I am making an assumption in this approach that if we learn how couples normally go about the business of being married, staying married, and doing so happily, then we will discover a set of principles that could be used to help marriages that are ailing. This could be wrong. There might be a different set of principles for fixing ailing marriages. Just as orthopedics probably requires not only knowledge of how healthy bones work but also new principles of how to set bones that are broken, marital therapy may require some new principles.

However, it is my view that one set of principles is all we need. The research evidence does suggest that all marriages, happy or unhappy, seem to have to deal with the same "tasks" of being married. For example, it is well-known that the rank order correlation of problems by their severity across happy and unhappy couples is very high, in the nineties. Even when we consider the predictors of divorce, we do not find that these never occur in marriages that are stable and happy—they just occur less often. That is why we focus so heavily on repair mechanisms. Every couple in their daily life together messes up communication, and every marriage has a "dark side." It seems that what may matter most is *the ability to repair things when they go wrong.*

Nonetheless, the basic assumption of my approach, laid bare, is that what we need is a real theory of how marriages work and fail to work, and that theory ought to emerge from a study of what real couples do to accomplish the everyday "tasks" of being married. So far, we have done the reverse. We have decided that couples should communicate with one another the way therapists and clients communicate. We have not generated a theory of marriage by studying the various ways that people go about the business of being married. So all of the ideas I have to present to you come from this source, from this assumption about how therapeutic interventions ought to be designed.

DISPELLING MYTHS AND MISTAKES
IN MARITAL THERAPY

Caveat. Let me first say that my goal in dispelling these myths is not to insult anyone or to make myself look smart. Many of the people I refer to have made important contributions to our thinking in the area of marriage. I respect their contributions and try to build upon them. It is very useful to propose an idea that later turns out to be totally wrong. It is absolutely critical, however, in the interests of science, that the ideas we propose be capable of rejection—which means, they have to be testable.

For this reason, I will not say very much about ideas that have not been researched. It's not that I don't want to comment on these ideas; it's just that I can't really evaluate ideas that have not been subjected to research—and it has to be research that meets reasonable standards of measurement and experimental control. So, even if I wanted to say nice and complimentary things about some ideas, all I will be able to say is that, in my opinion, these are good ideas. I prefer to hold everyone, including myself, to these standards of scientific inquiry. In the intervention section of this book I will comment on some of the major orientations that have guided some of my thinking, and I will recommend a basic bookshelf on marital therapy for clinicians.

I want to emphasize that the search for what I will call "myths" is purely in the service of relentless pursuit of truth. I think that we need to take a hard look at what beliefs are embedded in the literature and carefully examine what, if anything, we can trust enough to "hang our hats on." What we identify as *dysfunctional* greatly influences what we recognize as the goals of therapeutic intervention.

In this field writers do a great service by clearly articulating hypotheses. You don't have to be right to make a significant contribution. You just have to be interesting. Sometimes a great service to knowledge is rendered by being totally wrong but clear. I kept careful track of my own hypotheses once and found I was wrong 60% of the time. It turns out that 40% isn't bad. But if I had not done the research, I would have believed I was right 100% of the time.

Active Listening Model

Perhaps the most influential theory of marital therapy is the "active listening model." This model forms the basis of most marital treatments (e.g., see Gottman, Coan, Carrére, & Swanson, 1998; Jacobson & Margolin, 1979). The hypothesis is that stable, happy marriages are characterized by active, empathic listening during conflict resolution, and that ailing marriages are characterized by the absence of this quality. That is, in order to have a happy, lasting marriage, partners need to be able to be nondefensive and empathic listeners, even when they feel they are being attacked by their spouse. In most marital therapies this assumption is translated into some form of the listener-speaker exercise. For example, let's say the wife starts as the speaker, wording her complaints as "I-statements." She complains she is hurt about the way her husband relates to their youngest child. She hates the way he ignores the boy and criticizes him. Then he is asked to paraphrase both the content and feelings of his wife's message and to verify that he has heard her accurately. Next he is asked to validate her feelings, to suspend judgment, and to respond nondefensively.

This hypothesis has formed a central core in marital therapies from all schools of thought. The behavioral school has referred to active listening as social skill training (e.g., see Jacobson & Margolin, 1979). The systems orientation has referred to active listening as a mechanism for introducing feedback in message systems of communication (e.g, see Gottman, Notarius, Gonso, & Markman, 1976). The psychoanalytic school has also included active listening as a way of increasing empathy, which is believed to facilitate developmental change and also help decrease narcissism (e.g., see Siegel, 1992, chapter 16).

Where does this "knowledge" that the active listening pattern is basic to a good marriage come from? When we teach couples this method, we are teaching them what Carl Rogers trained therapists to do: Provide unconditional acceptance and empathy. Rogers' approach inspired Bernard Guerney (Guerney, 1977; Guerney & Guerney, 1985) to develop empathy training for couples. Eventually, all the other marital therapies followed his lead. In fact, they expanded this suggestion in creating "communication skill training components." But what was the scientific justification for teaching these communication skills? How did they decide that "I-statements" are better that "you-statements"? How was *any* of it decided?

It may come as a surprise that even in psychotherapy research the original Truax therapist process variables of accurate empathy, warmth, and genuineness were never shown to relate consistently to therapeutic outcome. In fact, a great deal of doubt was raised in studies by Bergin and Garfield (e.g., Bergin & Jasper, 1969) in the late 1960s and early 1970s about this hypothesis. But even if these variables had been shown to be effective in individual therapy, it is an enormous leap to apply a therapy model to relationships that are symmetric, such as marriages. The therapist in Rogerian therapy does indeed empathize with the client, but the client is usually complaining about *someone else,* a third person. Once the client starts complaining about the *therapist,* it is called *resistance,* and the usual recommended intervention is no longer one of empathizing with the client.

Later I suggest that, in marriages, the proper place for empathy is when the partner is complaining about a *third person,* in the context of the stress-reducing conversation. Then empathy is a matter of colluding to trash a third party, for which there appears to be no more satisfying way of engendering solidarity and we-ness. It is extremely common in marital interactions, and it is very soothing. Wile (1988) stated the problem of "I-statements" quite effectively and pragmatically: "It is impossible to make 'I-statements' when you are in the 'hating-my-partner, wanting revenge, feeling-stung-and-needing-to-sting-back' state of mind. At such a moment you cannot remember what an 'I-statement' is, and frankly you do not care" (p. 2).

Wile's statement rings a gut-level bell, but we sought empirical data for it as well. The usual way to operationalize active listening sequences would be to look for a pattern in which one partner expresses negative affect and the other partner validates it. In our research paradigm we cast a wider net than the usual definition of active listening, examining all exchanges in which one partner expressed low- or high-intensity negative affect that was followed by either interest, affection, humor, or direct validation by the partner. In the stability analyses, all the statistics were nonsignificant: These sequences occurred very infrequently for all couples, approximately 4 seconds out of 900. In the satisfaction analyses, the statistics were again all nonsignificant. Hence, to summarize, these *active listening exchanges hardly ever occurred (4.4% of the time) and they predicted nothing.*

I was quite surprised by these results on the active listening model. I have even recommended this intervention (e.g., Gottman, 1994a, 1994b; Gottman, Markman, & Notarius, 1977; Gottman et al., 1976). To further investigate the variables, I conducted a series of qualitative analyses on the data from this study and on another longitudinal cohort we have been following for the past 13 years. I examined every videotape and transcript of every stable, happy couple in detail. It was not a big surprise to find that people were not paraphrasing their spouses very often, nor were they summarizing their partner's feelings (e.g., "sounds like this makes you pretty mad"), nor even summarizing the *content* of their spouse's statements ("you'd like it if we saved more money each month"). Furthermore, they almost never validated their spouse's feelings (e.g., "I can understand why this would make you upset"). In short, what I discovered was that couples were not doing much direct processing of emotion and not much empathizing after negative affect had been expressed. People said what they thought about an issue, they got angry or sad, but their partner's response was never anything like what we were training people to do in the listener-speaker exercise—not even close. When people feel attacked, they tend to respond negatively; usually, in stable happy marriages, they respond in kind, while in unstable and unhappy marriages, they escalate the negativity.

Given the data that do not support active listening, are we suggesting that couples stop being empathic with one another or that empathy is a bad thing? No, but it may be asking people to do something that is not natural, and that has too great a psychological cost, and it may be related to our major relapse problem in marital therapy.

Our data suggest that asking people to be accepting, nondefensive, active listeners toward their spouses when they feel they are being attacked may go against the natural grain of interaction, even in the best of marriages. Perhaps teaching people to be empathic when they are feeling attacked is like trying to teach couples a form of *emotional gymnastics,* when, in fact, they are feeling emotionally crippled and are even having trouble walking, so to speak. If, indeed, we are trying to teach emotional gymnastics to the emotionally lame, it is no wonder our therapies stop working when the therapist is no longer on the scene.

Of course, just because couples do not naturally do anything like active listening does not mean it isn't an effective intervention for distressed marriages. Is there any direct research on this question? The answer is yes. There is a superbly conducted study by the Munich group, Hahlweg, Schindler, Revenstorf, and Brengelmann (1984). They followed Guerney's method precisely, comparing his active listening with a behavioral treatment that combined behavior exchange plus problem-solving training. To their credit they also used observational methods, and they had follow-ups at 6 months and a year. They reported that, in the short-term:

- Active listening showed decreases in negative interaction but no increases in positive interaction (observational data).
- Behavioral intervention showed both decreases in negativity and increases in positivity (observational data).

In the long term, Hahlweg et al. wrote, couples in the behavioral group reported significant and stable decreases of quarreling behavior compared to couples in the active listening group, who returned to pretreatment levels. On their communication self-report scale couples in the behavioral group remained stable, whereas couples in the active listening group relapsed to pretreatment levels. In assessing the clinical significance (not just statistical significance) of results, the typical couple in the behavioral group scored within the "happy" ranges of marital quality, whereas the typical couple in the active listening group was within the "unhappy" range.

Ultimately this discussion of the issue about active listening need not be a polemic. Clearly people in marriages need to listen to one another and listen empathetically. The issue is probably more about *how* this needs to be accomplished. I suggest later that this listening needs to be based upon a fundamental shift in the marital friendship.

The Model of Anger as the Dangerous Emotion

A pervasive marital therapy model is based on the hypothesis that anger is destructive of marital relationships. For example, Hendrix (1988), in a section titled "The Destructive Power of Anger" in his best-selling book on marriage, wrote:

> Anger is destructive to a relationship, no matter what its form. When anger is expressed, the person on the receiving end of the attack feels brutalized, whether or not there has been any physical violence; the old brain does not distinguish between choice of weapons. Further, because of the strange workings of the unconscious, the person who unleashes the anger feels equally assaulted, because on a deep level the old brain perceives all action as inner-directed. (p. 147)

This view of anger was also expressed by Parrott and Parrott (1995), who, in a chapter titled "The Deadly Emotion of Anger," wrote:

> It would be tough to find another emotion that has caused married couples more difficulty than anger. Why do we get angry at the person we love the most? Why do we allow ourselves to get angry when we know in advance that we will need to apologize? Why do we raise our voices when it does no good? (p. 78)

This negative view of anger is quite pervasive in most theories of marital therapies. In Greenberg and Johnson's (1988) emotionally focused marital therapy, one of the central tenets of the therapy is reframing anger in terms of what they claim are the underlying, "more vulnerable" emotions. Since they write from an attachment theory perspective, they suggest that these emotions involve fear and insecurity. This point of view is echoed and emphasized by Jacobson and Christensen (1996) as well as by Lewis's (1997) marital therapy. Where does this attitude toward anger come from?

I suspect it is a culturally biased view toward anger, probably not shared by cultures that place a higher value on emotional expression and discourse. Winkler and Doherty (1983) studied Jewish Israeli couples and compared them to Jewish American couples. The couples in the U.S. linked anger expression with marital unhappiness, while there was no such link for the Israeli couples. These researchers also found that the suppression of anger was related to physical violence in the U.S. couples. If these results are generally true, a more favorable attitude toward anger may reduce violence in marriages. This contrasts with the emphasis on anger control in violent marriages, an emphasis Jacobson and Gottman (1998) found to be misplaced.

In contrast to these views on anger Gottman and Krokoff (1989) reported that, although the expression of anger was associated with lower concurrent marital satisfaction, it was also associated with increases in marital satisfaction over time. In two longitudinal studies Gottman (1994a, 1994b) reported that anger in marital interaction did not predict divorce, whereas *contempt* and *defensiveness* did so reliably. This finding was recently replicated in a longitudinal study of newlyweds (Gottman et al., 1998). (Discriminating the differential effects of negative emotions is discussed in Chapter 2.)

I will return to this issue about anger as a dangerous emotion later (Chapter 6).

The Quid Pro Quo Error

Lederer and Jackson's (1968) *Mirages of Marriage* was a bold and daring book, in which they spelled out what is dysfunctional about ailing marriages and how therapists ought to go about fixing them. Their book was an important contribution to the study of marriage. There were lots of ideas in this book about romanticism, trust, and so on. Among the many ideas, Lederer and Jackson said that the sine qua non of marriage was the quid pro quo: that in good marriages there was a reciprocal exchange of positive behaviors, and that in bad marriages we were witnessing, for various reasons (like romanticism), the breakdown of these agreements, these contracts. This point of view was consistent with an economically based behavior exchange theory recommended 10 years earlier in social psychology by Thibaut and Kelly (1969). The Lederer and Jackson book had an enormous impact. In marital behavior therapy alone it led to the method of "contingency contracting" (Azrin, Naster, & Jones, 1973).

Anyway, it turned out that this quid pro quo idea was totally wrong. Not only aren't happy marriages characterized by the quid pro quo, but it actually characterizes *unhappy* marriages! Unhappy couples are the ones who keep tabs on positives given and received, whereas happy couples are positive unconditionally. Yet the erroneous and untested quid pro quo assumption not only spawned a new marital therapy but also continued as a major ingredient of marital therapy even after it was disproved by Murstein and his associates (Murstein, Cerreto, & MacDonald, 1977).

I think it is really amazing that contingency contracting continued to be used after Murstein et al.'s discovery. Imagine if, in trying to battle AIDS, I recommended a biochemical treatment process that was associated with patients' deteriorating from the disease instead of those who were winning it. Would you think I was crazy? Immoral? Of course. Not so, in social science.

Nothing ever seems to die in the areas of psychological treatment. In fact, no one is ever even willing to say that the Emperor has no clothes on—that a therapy method seems to be ineffective. It's not that the people who write the books we read aren't smart or well-intentioned. It's just that very smart people working on very tough problems can often be wrong. Interesting ideas are capable of disconfirmation. Often, more is learned by *dis*confirming an interesting hypothesis than from any other outcome of a study.

Noncontingent Positivity

The issue of the supposed value of reciprocating positive behavior led to a great debate in the behavioral literature. As a result, behavior exchange interventions have changed or evolved over time (since the early 1970s), in part due to experience with Stuart's (1980) "love days" and the use of the Weiss Spouse Observation Checklist (Weiss, 1975). The modification was introduced by Stuart and led to questioning the philosophy of "give to get" that formed the basis of behavior exchange intervention within the domain of couples' conflict. Eventually, the intervention became one of attempting to create overall greater positivity, kindness, and love in people's everyday interactions (not just conflict). Furthermore, the interventions became noncontingent. Therapists were training people to be nicer to their spouses, regardless of what they got back.

Perception wound up playing an important role in this equation of behavior exchange. Therapists had clients discuss whether they noticed the positivity or failed to see it. This is a fascinating modification of behavior exchange, and it led to an interest in modifying cognitions. In fact, Robinson and Price (1980) discovered that unhappily married couples underestimate the amount of positivity (compared to what objective observers detected in the couples' homes) by a factor of 50%! So the behavior exchange procedure eventually involved trying to change perception as well as behavior.

I will discuss this later, but let me say now that I believe that this evolution of the behavior exchange approach is responsible for a great deal of the effectiveness in both Jacobson's combined treatment and Snyder and Wills' insight-oriented condition. Later I will discuss these two key studies, which are the only studies in the marital therapy field to have produced lasting change more than two years post-treatment.

Unfortunately, Robinson and Price reported that only happily married couples were happier after attending to their positive interactions. So, increasing a couple's awareness of positivity may not be a very effective intervention with distressed couples. Why would this be the case? Later we will see that the answer probably has to do with the nature of the *attributional processes,* in which negative attributions become nondisconfirmable hypotheses: People who make negative attributions about their spouse discard counter-examples. The research of Donald Baucom (Baucom & Epstein, 1990) has informed us about the difficulty of trying directly to alter these negative cognitions. Instead, I will suggest that a theory that describes the processes through which these attributions arise can suggest how they may be altered.

The Harmony Model

Many writers in the area of marital and family therapy have suggested that all interventions are about equally effective, and that no "school" of therapy has produced better results than any other school. So, does it matter what our rationale and orientation are? I will try to demonstrate to you that it is critical. Let's continue looking at the assumptions that typically underlie the design of today's marital interventions.

A man I admire a lot, Harold Raush (Raush, Barry, Hertl, & Swain, 1974), who published the first study of couples experiencing the transition to parenthood, decided that he had three types of couples in his study. One type argued and bickered a lot, even about very trivial things (like how to load glasses in the dishwasher); another avoided conflict entirely and had little psychological insight; a third group he called "harmonious." He decided that the bickerers were dysfunctional and that they had to have what he called "symbolic conflict" and hidden agendas. No one could be so passionate about such trivia! The avoiders, he decided, were also dysfunctional, with "brittle" defenses. So, the two hypotheses suggested by Harold Raush were that:

- Conflict avoidance is dysfunctional.
- Bickering about trivial issues is dysfunctional and indicative of underlying symbolic conflict.

In my longitudinal research both hypotheses turned out to be wrong. Both conflict-avoiding and volatile, passionate couples can have stable, happy marriages. In fact, I discovered that the bickering, passionate couples were the only ones to still have a romantic marriage after 35 years (Gottman, 1994a, 1994b).

A Potpourri of Conflicting Hypotheses and Potential Truths

Superb examples of the confusion and resulting lack of efficacy in both marital therapy and research are the conflicting views on the benefits versus the disadvantages of *dominance* in marital relationships. There is actually research evidence to support both of the following hypotheses, so which one is actually true?

- A dominance structure is dysfunctional.
- The lack of dominance structure is dysfunctional.

The data on power and dominance in marriages are very confusing, because it is difficult to operationalize and measure the power implicit in the concept of dominance. Power may vary depending on what aspect of a marriage one studies, such as who wins in decisions, who gets greatest access to resources, and in which specific areas of the relationship. A complete review of these hypotheses would take us too far afield. Broderick's (1993) book on family process discusses power in terms of the "regulation of vertical space," which is an intriguing idea. Gottman (1979) defined dominance as an asymmetry in predictability in interactive behavior. This means that if one can predict the wife's subsequent behavior from her husband's immediate past better than the converse (predicting the husband's behavior from his wife's), then the husband is dominant. Statistical tests exist to make this determination. In an egalitarian marriage there is no such asymmetry. Gottman found that in distressed marriages there was greater predictability of one spouse's behavior from the other's than in nondistressed marriages. On low-conflict tasks both distressed and nondistressed couples showed an egalitarian dominance pattern. However, on high-conflict tasks the husband was dominant only in distressed marriages. My research has shown that sharing power, in terms of what I call "acceptance of influence" (particularly the husband's acceptance of his wife's influence), is critically important for the stability of marriages, even among newlyweds, and also critically important in understanding spouse abuse.

Another hypothesis:

- A "female-demand/male-withdraw" pattern (also called "female-pursuer/male-distancer" pattern) is dysfunctional.

The best work on this hypothesis has been done by Andy Christensen and his students (Christensen, 1987, 1988, 1990; Christensen & Heavey, 1990; Cohen & Christensen, 1980; Heavey, Layne, & Christensen, 1993). The pattern is not consistently descriptive of distressed marriages for two reasons. First, the demand-withdraw pattern is actually characteristic of *all* marriages. We have found this pattern even in our study of happy, long-term, stable marriages. Second, Christensen and his associates have discovered that the pattern can be changed greatly when the issue under discussion is the *husband's* issue. However, even if this pattern is generally true of all marriages, Christensen and his associates have shown that the pattern does indeed become exacerbated when the marriage is ailing. So the female-demand/male-withdraw pattern turns out to be one of the more reliable findings in the area of marriage. It is, however, important to understand the *etiology* of the pattern, because otherwise women get blamed for starting the conflicts in marriages. (We'll talk about that in Chapter 2.)

Here is an early behavioral view, to my knowledge advocated primarily by Neil Jacobson:

- Changing one another's behavior is essential to a happy marriage.

To the early behavioral marital therapists this almost seemed like a tautology. It is interesting that this hypothesis was never empirically established by behavioral marital therapists, and even more interesting that now Jacobson and Christensen (1996) claim that the goal of marital therapy ought to be first to get people to accept one another and *not* try to change behavior. The truth, as Jacobson and Christensen suggest, must lie somewhere between the two positions in an interesting dialectic.

This popular hypothesis has formed the cornerstone of nearly all marital therapies:

- Poor problem-solving skills are dysfunctional.

However, my research suggests that this hypothesis, in its simplest form, is also essentially wrong, and that the role of problem-solving has been greatly exaggerated in marital therapy. In fact, even in the best marriages, while some minor fraction of marital problems does get solved, over time most marital problems do *not* get solved at all; instead, they become what we call "perpetual" issues. What turns out to be important is the *affect* that surrounds the way people talk about (but do not really solve) these perpetual marital problems. They either establish a "dialogue" with these problems, or they go into a state of "gridlock." Later I will discuss that *what matters is the affect with which people don't solve their perpetual problems.*

Another influential hypothesis:

- Mind-reading is dysfunctional.

Mind-reading is attributing thoughts and feelings or motives to the other person. Instead of asking what one's partner is feeling, people mind-read and assume they know what their partner is thinking and feeling—and this is dysfunctional (for example, a statement like "You always get tense at my mother's house"). Watzlawick's great rationalist's hope (Watzlawick, Beavin, & Jackson, 1967) was that people's relationships would be fine if only they communicated clearly. For this reason concepts like "feedback" mechanisms were so appealing. The assumption was that if people could give one another feedback, then communication would become clearer and pathology would just vanish. This was a very good idea. Unfortunately, it just wasn't usually true.

In ailing marriages people generally communicate very clearly, but what they communicate is mostly negative. I believe this hypothesis came from the fact that the early systems therapists worked primarily with very disturbed families. Recall that family therapy was initially proposed as the cause and the cure for individual psychopathology. It is only recently that its goals have changed to improving family relationships. Probably the only consistent finding to emerge from studies of interactions in families with severe psychopathology was that the communication in these families was unclear, confusing, and hard to follow (for a review, see Jacob, 1987). Hence, it was natural to suggest that if one could provide feedback loops that could clarify messages (and discrepancies in their component parts), a cure could be achieved. Unfortunately, in distressed marriages the communication is often quite clear—and quite hostile. So improved clarity does little to help distressed couples.

People do, indeed, mind-read a lot in marriages (see Gottman, 1979). Instead of saying, "How do you feel at my mother's house?" the statement is made, "You hate going to my mother's house." That's because they usually already know. It isn't usually bad communication; it is real knowledge. Actually, whether mind-reading is dysfunctional or not depends entirely on the *affect* with which it is delivered. Mind-reading with positive affect acts as a "feeling probe"; it is the major way people in marriages generally ask about feelings. An example: "I've noticed that you always get tense at my mother's house." Nodding in agreement, the spouse answers, "Yes, I do. Maybe if the two of you didn't gang up on me, I'd be more relaxed." Mind-reading with negative affect has the same effect as a blaming statement. An example: "You always get tense at my mother's house." Bristling, the spouse retorts, "I don't *always* get tense there. Will you just shut up?" It turns out that spouses don't tend to ask questions about each other's feelings; they mind-read! They do not say, "How do you feel about my recent purchase?" Instead, they say "You think I'm a spendthrift." So mind-reading had a different meaning than Watzlawick thought it did. This knowledge can only be gained by doing basic descriptive research on marital interaction—a step many theorists tend to skip.

Here is a hypothesis about happy couples:

■ Engaging in meta-communication characterizes well-adjusted couples.

"Meta-communication" is any statement about the *process* of the communication. An example would be, "We are getting off the topic." In the original classic paper on the double-bind hypothesis of schizophrenia, early communication general systems theorists Bateson, Jackson, Haley, and Weakland (1956) targeted the confusing message of the mother of the schizophrenic patient who approaches him for a hug and then stiffens when he hugs her. He is damned if he does (hugs her) and damned if he doesn't (she feels rejected and lets him know it). There is the old Jewish joke of the mother who gives her son two ties for a gift. The next time she sees him he is wearing one of the ties. The mother says, "What's the matter? You didn't like the other tie?" Once again, this is an example of being damned if you do and damned if you don't.

What did the general systems theorists suggest the schizophrenic son *do* to escape this double bind? They suggested that he comment on the *process*. Indeed, commenting on the process became the main tool of the systems approach to therapy. The sine qua non of good communication became *meta-communication*—it surely ought to characterize the problem-focused conversations of well-adjusted couples, but not those of distressed couples. In my early work, in which I sequentially analyzed marital interactions, I discovered that this hypothesis was simply not true. Furthermore, we now know that meta-communication is part of *repair processes.* What is most salient is *how the meta-communication is responded to,* not whether it occurs or how it is delivered. Happily married couples have short chains of meta-communication followed by agreement, and they use these often as repair mechanisms, but unhappily married couples have long meta-communication chains in which the affect transfers and escalates. This is a pattern of cross meta-communication. The meta-communication doesn't work and it doesn't change anything. In distressed marriages one meta-communication tends to be countered with another meta-communication (Gottman, 1979). These repair processes occur naturally in marital interaction even in the most distressed marriages, and they occur more frequently the more distressed the couple. They are also likely to be occurring when the interaction is negative affectively, so that they are often made with some irritability or sadness. When they work, they may sound like this: "Will you shut up and let me finish?" followed by "All right, damn it, finish!" That's an effective repair, because it usually takes the couple out of the negative affect chain. However, a more polite meta-communication is more likely to be seen as collaborative rather than adversarial (Wile, personal communication, 1998).

Here is a fascinating hypothesis proposed by Lederer and Jackson (1968):

- High expectations for marriage cause divorce.

They suggested that people's unreasonably high and usually romantic expectations for marriage were destructive. If people had more reasonable expectations, they proposed, they wouldn't get so disappointed. Donald Baucom has systematically investigated this hypothesis (e.g., Baucom, Epstein, Rankin, & Burnett, 1996) and has found exactly the opposite to be true. People who have higher standards and higher expectations for their marriage (including romantic ones) have the best marriages, not the worst. Therapist Dan Wile (1992) anticipated these results and recommended that people hold on to romantic ideals rather than compromising them.

Another hypothesis that has been put forward:

- We are all the products of very poor parenting, and for this reason we have a lot of unfinished psychological business to attend to. We search for this healing by pairing with someone who has the potential to heal us.

This is a fascinating hypothesis. Unfortunately, the mate selection process is not so purposeful or deterministic. It appears to be a much more random process, with some "similarity filters" put in place to insure that people of similar social class meet one another.

Here is a hypothesis that was first countered in the 1930s by Nathan Ackerman (1966):

- Healthy marriage is not possible unless personality issues and wounds from family of origin are resolved.

Ackerman earned a lot of disapproval and rejection from practitioners of the predominant mode of therapy at that time—psychoanalysis—when he suggested that two neurotics could have a happy marriage. It was almost a heresy at the time he suggested it. He also contended that the expectation that childhood issues needed to be resolved before one could have a happy marriage was not helpful.

The modern version of this hypothesis can be found in object relations theory and, more popularly, in the writings of Harville Hendrix (1988). He contends that most marital conflict stems from childhood wounds resulting from bad parenting. A goal of Hendrix's treatment is to help the couple develop what he calls "X-ray vision" so that they can see the wound behind the hostility. The argument goes that, if the perceived hostility or insecurity could only be expressed as a "vulnerable affect," then the marital conflicts would dissipate. But it takes the therapist to convince the couple of that, and once treatment is terminated, hostility just seems like . . . hostility. Likewise, Greenberg and Johnson's (1988) emotion-focused therapy, based on attachment theory, claims that all marital hostility comes from insecure attachment, so they also train their clients to see the fear or vulnerability "behind" the anger.

In these approaches the therapy essentially softens any negative affect by providing a personality theory that "explains it away" as really something else, so that the receiver of the hostile message will not be so upset. I am concerned that the problem with *the therapy* softening the issues for the couple is that, once the therapist leaves the scene, it may be difficult for the couple to apply the concepts to the hostility that continues to surface. We have found in our research that *reciprocated negative affect in marriages it is quite natural*—anger is met with anger—and it is *not* dysfunctional. Nevertheless, we *do* need to teach couples soothing skills to modulate negative interchanges.

Let's think about whether we really need these personality concepts in our marital therapy. What is the evidence that the individual's personality actually is important in our understanding and predictability of marital outcomes? In Howard Markman's dissertation (1977), the prediction of marital happiness two and a half years after the period of engagement was a factor of the *perceived similarity* between partners, not actual personality traits. In an ailing marriage, lasting negative attributions are made about the spouse's negative personality traits—but the *traits themselves* are not predictive. There is some evidence that measures of neuroticism predict later marital dissatisfaction and even divorce, but the predictions are quite weak, with correlations of about .25, which is about the level of prediction of marital satisfaction itself. In addition, the measures of neuroticism are confounded with distress assessments, and the statistics also have the problem of common method variance with the assessment of marital satisfaction.

In fact, many complex variations of the personality hypothesis have been explored in the marital literature. Probably the best known one is the Winch (1958; see also Tharp, 1963, for a review of research) need complementarity theory, originally embraced but then abandoned by psychoanalytic therapists. The idea was that if one person has a need (say, the need to dominate), he or she will be happily married if he or she marries someone with the complementary need (the need to be dominated). Winch's theory was abandoned when it received no empirical support.

Furthermore, research has shown that personality traits do not discriminate distressed from nondistressed couples, because people's interactions with their spouses are not predictive of their interactions with other people. Birchler, Weiss, and Vincent (1975) studied the interactions of distressed and nondistressed couples with each other and with strangers while engaging in a conflict resolution task (the Inventory of Marital Conflict, a set of vignettes in which husband and wife get different stories and have to decide who is most at fault in each vignette, husband or wife). Distressed spouses were significantly more negative and less positive with one another than nondistressed spouses, but the interactions of a distressed spouse with a stranger was no different from that of a nondistressed spouse.

In a study I did with Alan Porterfield (Gottman & Porterfield, 1981) on sending and receiving the nonverbal component of messages, distressed husbands were poor receivers of their wives' nonverbal behaviors, but they were fine at receiving the nonverbal behaviors of married female strangers. This result was replicated by Noller (1980, 1984) with Australian couples. Based on interviews, we suggested that this inability to receive their wives' nonverbal messages was the result of their emotional withdrawal in their marriages, and that these men had not always been so withdrawn.

Although the evidence for the contribution of individual personality traits to the predictability of marriage is not compelling, the area of violence may be an exception. Here we found that *highly antisocial men were violent not only to their wives but also to coworkers, friends, family, and strangers.* Here—and only for this subgroup of men—the aggression seems trait-related. So, at extremes of personality and psychopathology we may find it useful to consider personality, but in general it adds very little.

So why do marital therapy theorists such as Hendrix and Greenberg and Johnson use these concepts? The answer, I think, is that it can be very appealing to therapists to do a lot of the work that the couple should be doing in learning how to de-escalate and soften their conflicts.

When a marriage is not going well, *then* people perceive their partner's personality as a problem. It is generally the *perception of personality differences* that is related to marital unhappiness, not *actual* personality differences. Rather, as issues arise and become implacable and painful to talk about, people try to explain them in terms of their partner's perceived personality inadequacies. In a sense, the apparent personality change is *an artifact of declining marital satisfaction,* not the cause of it.

I think marriage is like the music a jazz quartet makes when the musicians come together. The marital interaction is the music. As they interact, the two people create a third element, just like the music of the jazz quartet is a new entity, the fifth element produced by the four musicians. It is the *music* we must study. The temporal forms that spouses create and the way they feel about what they create when they are together are the essence of marriage. The "temporal forms" are like music; they are the repeated sequential patterns or themes of the marriage. They can be measured quantitatively (see Gottman, 1979). As the spouses interact, they improvise around these central marital themes. To understand the music of the quartet, it helps very little to describe the personalities of the players. Even the solo work of the musicians will often not predict how much a particular quartet is, or is not, "in the groove"—that is, making beautiful music together.

The other possibility may be that we have not studied personality very well, because the field has relied primarily on self-report measurement. Perhaps if personality were studied using a multi-method perspective, we might find that it would, indeed, make some contribution to our understanding of marriages. However, Terman's (Terman, Buttenweiser, Ferguson, Johnson, & Wilson, 1938) original hope that there would be some ideal or optimal personality structure for successful marriage does not seem likely to be borne out.

I am not claiming that the past is unimportant. Later in this book I will suggest that discovering the origins of marital patterns is very useful in diagnosis and prediction. In the intervention section I will discuss the importance of how resistance to change can reveal a person's internal working model about salient marital processes.

Marital conflict is shared by both happy and unhappy couples, and the rank order correlation of severity of problems is about .94 across these two groups. (The maximum value is 1.00, so this is extraordinarily high.) The result is very important. It means that, for example, all spouses argue about finances and sex. It essentially means that in all marriages there are developmental tasks that need to be accomplished. Conflict is endemic to marriages because people have different ideas about how to go about accomplishing these tasks. The presence of marital conflict does not imply that our parents have failed in raising us. Conflict goes with the territory of marriage.

This hypothesis is primarily the work of Jacobson and Margolin (1979):

- Marriages start off happy—newlyweds are highly important and reinforcing for one another—but this pattern erodes over time. "Reinforcement erosion" is the source of marital dysfunction and divorce.

The idea is that during courtship we find a large number of things our partner does that are wonderful, exciting, and rewarding. After a while, however, this positive glow fades and our partner loses the ability to charm and delight us. We know the old stories, jokes, and behaviors, and they no longer ignite excitement. Though this is a rather cynical hypothesis, there appears, at first glance, to be some support for this idea. For example, the first longitudinal study of 1,000 engaged couples by Burgess and Wallin (1953) reported that, over time, the marital satisfaction of couples declined. After 15 years the couples reported communicating less, being less in love, doing fewer things together, having less sex, and not being sure they would marry the same person if they had it all to do over again.

But many couples followed the opposite pattern, growing closer over time. In long-term happy couples, people become generally more mellow and accepting of one another as they stay married, rather than less; it seems to get better and better, so we can actually contend that there is a reinforcement *gain* that occurs over time. In marriages that do not work very well the positive things don't erode; they are just done less and less over time, as people turn away from one another.

In our research on older couples (in midlife or facing retirement) who had been married a long time, the modal pattern was quite the opposite of reinforcement erosion. They wanted to spend more time with their partner, and affection increased with the length of time married. (These data are biased, however, because we are studying a sample of couples whose marriages have survived.) Carstensen (Carstensen 1992, 1995; Carstensen & Turk, 1994) proposed a "selectivity theory" of aging. Typically, as people age they become more selective about with whom they prefer to spend time, and spouses rank high on the preferred list. The reinforcement value of these special, close relationships appears to *increase* with time, not decrease. That is part of the good news—as it endures, the modal relationship generally gets better. We conclude that not all the data are in on this cynical hypothesis, but it is not the universal rule.

What might have been different about those marriages that did "erode" and those that did not? An analysis of Burgess and Wallin's data by Dizard (1968) revealed that those couples who became disenchanted moved toward less power-sharing and toward a traditional division of labor, with less joint decision-making.

There is also no research evidence for a period of "blissed out" love early in relationships. As far back as researchers have investigated the early formation of relationships (see Bradbury, 1998), there seems to be no such period of "bliss" when everything works well and partners are highly reinforcing of one another. Rather, it seems that patterns are established very early in a relationship and then they only stabilize further.

Here is a hypothesis that has received some research support:

- Similarity between spouses is the basis of marital stability and happiness.

Newcomb and Bentler (1980) found that similarity was indeed a predictor of marital stability. Fowers and Olson (1986) base their "Prepare" program of premarital counseling on helping couples explore their similarities in 11 different areas of the marriage. There are also consistent findings that spouses who are similar to one another in interests (Huston & Houts, 1998) or who share similar religiously conservative values are less likely to be unhappy or to divorce (Kahn & London, 1991).

Nevertheless, similarity is, at best, a weak predictor of marital outcomes for two reasons. The first is that measuring the similar variables often taps the degree of community support that the couple receives. This is especially true when the sample population shares conservative religious values. Being part of a supportive community turns out to be somewhat helpful for couples in trying times and accounts for martial stability in cultures that still arrange marriages (countries like Kuwait, for example). Les and Leslie Parrot (1995) and Mike McManus (1995) are now trying to recreate these results in less cohesive communities by using couple mentor programs. Still, similarity of values and interests is not a strong predictor of marital stability. The divorce rate is only slightly lower among Catholics than non-Catholics, for example. In addition, the presence of a similarity does not tell us anything about *process*, about how partners relate to each other in their sharing of beliefs and interests. An example: I love to canoe. I don't know how many times I have seen spouses canoeing down a river screaming contemptuously at each other, "That's not how you do a J-stroke, you idiot!" Yes, they have this interest in common, but being critical and contemptuous toward one another while they share the interest will carry greater weight—in the negative direction. Similarity is a weak predictor because it does not tap the processes that matter in maintaining, or destroying, a marriage.

Still more reasonable hypotheses could be generated, such as nonequalitarian marriages are dysfunctional, and so on. The question is, are any of these contentions true? If not, then what *is* true? What should a marital therapist select as a goal? What should a therapist decide needs fixing in an ailing marriage? My fundamental point is that we benefit from solid empirical knowledge about what may be "dysfunctional" and "functional" in terms of predicting what happens to marriages. A marital therapy needs to be developed that has *a process mode that is based on empirical findings*. One way to think about developing a marital therapy is by asking what factors are predictive of whether couples stay married or get divorced. In the context of this question, let's consider another area dappled by the misleading hypotheses that pervade our field.

DISPELLING MYTHS ABOUT WHAT PREDICTS DIVORCE

Myth: Affairs Cause Most Divorces

The most common myth is that extramarital affairs cause divorce. There are some writers—for example, Pittman (1989)—who have strongly suggested that the root cause of divorce is extramarital affairs. It is indeed true that about 25% of all marital therapy cases report a revealed extramarital affair as the major presenting issue. So, we do have to know how to help these couples.

However, it is very difficult to obtain reliable data on extramarital affairs, in part because the issue is so explosive and deception and secrecy are part of the phenomenon. It is as difficult as attempting to do a quick survey on whether 17 year-old boys are virgins and asking the question when their friends are present. In one large and important study done on sex in the United States (Michael, Gagnon, Laumann, & Kolata, 1995), interviewers asked about extramarital affairs while the spouse was in the house. As you might expect, they reported a very low rate!

The most reliable information I know of comes from work published in 1992 by Lynn Gigy and Joan Kelly of the California Divorce Mediation Project. I believe that, within this careful context of helping both spouses reach a less rancorous solution to dissolving the marriage, it is reasonable to trust the honesty of people's self-reports of the causes for divorcing. The major reasons for divorcing given by close to 80% of all men and women were gradually growing apart and losing a sense of closeness, and not feeling loved and appreciated. Extramarital affairs were endorsed as a cause of the divorce by only 20–27% of all the couples. Severe and intense fighting was indicated by 40% of the couples—44% of females and 35% of males.

This omission of affairs as the reported cause of marital dissolution is not a recent phenomenon. In William Goode's 1948 study (1956), the major reasons mentioned for divorcing were non-support and neglect (also heavy drinking by the man). Probably associated with increasing divorce rates and the shift of women into the workplace, Kitson and Sussman (1982) reported that women's most frequent complaints had shifted from such specific negative behaviors to affective or emotional deficiencies in the marriage. Thurner, Fenn, Melichar, and Chiriboga (1983) also reported a decline in citing economic problems and alcoholism as reasons for divorce. Cleek and Pearson (1985) found that communication problems, basic unhappiness, and incompatibility were the reasons given. In a Danish sample (Koch-Nielsen & Gundlach, 1985) "growing apart" was the major reason given by both men and women.

Furthermore, many clinicians, including Pittman, who have worked with couples in attempting to repair the damage caused by an extramarital affair, have been quick to point out that "affairs involve sex, but sex is usually not the purpose of the affair" (Pittman & Wagers, 1995, p. 298). In fact, most clinicians who have written in this area report that affairs are usually about seeking friendship, support, understanding, and validation. In Jacobson and Christensen's (1996) terms, they are about getting the acceptance that is missing in the marriage.

Gigy and Kelly (1992) concluded that loss of feelings of closeness and rising feelings of emotional barrenness, boredom with the marriage, and serious differences in lifestyle were the prevalent reasons given for divorce. The majority of respondents in their mediation project reported high levels of conflict and/or tension in their marriages. Also, 65% of men and 64% of women reported sexual intimacy problems as an important factor in the breakdown of their relationships.

In summarizing these research projects, "feeling unloved" was the most commonly cited reason for wanting a divorce (67% of the women in the California study and 75% in the Danish study), and sensitivity to being belittled has apparently increased the past 15 years: 59% of both men and women in the Danish study cited this factor, and American men show an increase in citing it since the early 1970s, from 0% to 37% in Gigy and Kelly's study. We must conclude that most marriages end with a whimper, the result of people gradually drifting apart and not feeling liked, loved, and respected.

The slow slide toward divorce, in what I call the "Distance and Isolation Cascade," suggests that the final stage of loneliness makes people vulnerable to relationships outside the marriage. This means that the interactions of couples in treatment are often *not* characterized by intense fighting but by emotional distance and the absence of affect. We have found that this is especially the case for couples divorcing later in the course of the marriage, in midlife, at around 16 to 20 years. It is not easy working with couples who are already at this stage of emotional disengagement. Intervening with this type of couple is one of the major clinical problems we will consider.

Myth: Monogamy Is for Women

Let us also lay to rest the spurious sociobiological theories that men do not need monogamy, that men need to philander and women do not, and that monogamous marriage is a "female thing." This view has been promulgated in part by

Helen Fisher (1992) in her book *The Anatomy of Love*. It represents a point of view that I believe has done a lot of damage. This is the general view that men need to philander and that women just have to get used to this fact. The argument is that this behavior is basically biological, part of male evolutionary heritage.

Actually, there is a fair amount of data to show that men benefit more from being married than women do! In a classic longitudinal study of longevity by Berkman and Syme (1979), being married predicted longevity for men but not for women (friendships were more important for women). In a famous analysis of this concept, Jesse Bernard (1982) also made this point, that marriages are more protective of men's health than women's. I think that the argument is overstated and that the evidence supports the idea that a high-quality marriage is beneficial for *both* men and women. But for many men, whose social support systems tend to be inferior to women's, marriage may provide the only close and supportive relationship they have. So it is not the case that monogamy is just for women. Furthermore, historically it is men who have tried to enforce exclusive rights to their wives!

Scientific analysis shows that the early data on gender differences in the frequency of extramarital affairs have been confounded by *opportunity*. Lawson (1988) found that, as women have entered the workplace in massive numbers, the number of extramarital affairs of young women has exceeded those of men (for a review, see Brown, 1991). According to Lawson, affairs now occur sooner in the marriage than in the past. Two-thirds of the women and half of the men who were having affairs were in their first five years of marriage. Twenty years ago the comparable figure was 20%. The summary finding is that "social background does not significantly influence a person's tendency to have an affair. Affairs, however, are significantly associated with dissatisfaction with marital intercourse, and with personal readiness!" (Lawson, 1988, p. 6).

Myth: Gender Differences Cause Divorce

This notion has become quite popular with the publication of John Gray's (1989) "Mars–Venus" books. However, a moment's reflection will show the logical fallacy in some of his writing.

Gender difference cannot explain divorce, because there is a male and a female in both couples divorcing and in those couples who may stay married—and all the males are "from Mars" and all the females are "from Venus." End of case. If gender differences are going to predict divorce, there has to be an *interaction* of gender differences with something (like marital conflict) that does the job of prediction.

There are, indeed, some reliable gender differences that do, in fact, only manifest themselves when there is intense marital conflict and the "vigilance system" of males is activated. These gender differences, in interaction with intense marital conflict, are differences in *attributional processes, physiological reactivity,* and *physiological recovery*. Later I propose why and how these differences are part of the evolutionary heritage of our species.

"HOME AWAY FROM HOME": CREATING A MARITAL LABORATORY

My research on marriage is based, in part, on a long (now 23-year) collaboration with my best friend, Robert W. Levenson, who is a psychology professor at the University of California, Berkeley. When Bob and I began doing our research on divorce prediction in 1975, there were nearly 2,000 published studies on divorce, only six of which were longitudinal prospective studies based on self-report measurements of personality. These six studies fared very poorly at prediction: The correlations were all around .25 or so. This means that the researchers could account for very little variance in their predictions. Also, the results were not very interesting theoretically, as far as I was concerned. For example, Newcomb and Bentler (1980) found that clothes-conscious women were less likely to divorce, while there was no such correlation for men. Imagine, as a humorous aside, a therapy based on these two results. The therapist would discuss Martha's wardrobe with her but tell George that it didn't matter in his case. There were also some weak results in the Kelly and Conley (1987) study that neuroticism predicted divorce. These results are hard to interpret for methodological reasons, and they are hard to use to design marital interventions. The methodological problems are that it is unclear in the Kelly and Conley study if neuroticism or marital unhappiness is being measured. Since the couple's friends filled out the self-report personality inventory in that study, they may have used items that purportedly assess such characteristics as depression to describe their friend's marital unhappiness, or its effects.

Bob and I brought a multi-method approach to the measurement of marital processes as they became manifest in three domains:

1. *Interactive behavior:* coding partners' behavior and emotion as they interacted in various contexts;

2. *Perception:* ascertaining individual perceptions of self and other through questionnaires, video recall procedures, attributional methods, and interviews;

3. *Physiology:* measuring autonomic, endocrine, and immune system responses.

We found that we could use all three domains to predict the longitudinal course of a marriage.

I built an apartment laboratory at the University of Washington where couples lived for 24-hour periods (the cameras turned on at 9 A.M. and off at 9 P.M.). We asked only that they do what they would normally do on a Sunday at home. We videotaped each couple's behavior during the camera-on slot. We observed couples talking about how their day went after they had been apart for a least eight hours; we observed them talking about, and trying to resolve, areas of continuing disagreement; and we observed them talking about enjoyable topics. We also recorded their physiological responses: When they sat down in our "fixed lab," we were able to obtain data on respiration, electrocardiogram, blood velocity to the ear and the finger of the nondominant hand, skin conductance, and gross motor movement via a "jiggle-ometer" attached to the base of their chairs. We used Holter monitors from SpaceLabs (who conducted the physiological measurements of NASA astronauts) and their beat-to-beat computer program for analyzing the couple's electrocardiograms. We also assayed urinary stress hormones, and, in collaboration with an immunologist, Dr. Hans Ochs, we took blood samples for standard immunological assays.

Later we played the videotapes for the couples and asked them to tell us, using a rating dial, what they were feeling and thinking. The rating dial is a dial we ask people to turn to reflect their own feelings. It goes through an arc of 180° and is labeled from "extremely positive" to "extremely negative." We also asked them to guess what their partners were thinking and feeling. This step was prompted by Bob Levenson and Anna Ruef's (1992) research that had discovered that those people who physiologically relived their own physiology were terrible guessers of the feelings of another, while those who relived the other's physiology were much better. People presumably relive their partner's physiology by mirroring the partner's emotional reactions. We measure how closely the physiology of the two people parallels one another. Those people whose physiology, while they were watching the videotape, more closely resembled their partners' during the interaction had rating dial data (when asked to predict how their partner felt during the interaction) that closely matched their partner's. If their physiology (while watching the tape) matched their own physiology, they were bad at guessing how their partner felt during the interaction. This was a physiological way of defining empathy.

We also sometimes replayed interviews of specific moments (selected on some salient dimension, such as their ratings, their behavior, or their physiology). The interview of specific moments asked people how they perceived the moment. They viewed the moment, and then we asked them questions about how they were feeling, how they thought their partner was feeling, and what their goals were during that moment. They also filled out a questionnaire about that moment. From these we learned that there were two basic categories of negative reactions: an "innocent victim" type of perception, associated with whining and defensiveness; and a "righteous indignation" perception, associated with contempt.

We developed interviews to ascertain spouses' perceptions of the history of their marriage, their parents' marriages, their philosophies of being married, and their levels of comfort or discomfort with the basic emotions. We also developed an interview for the purpose of eliciting the rituals, roles, life dreams, goals, symbols and myths that guide their search for meaning.

We coded spouses' behavior from the videotapes using objective coding systems with trained observers who describe facial expressions, voice tone, gestures, body positions and movements, the distance between them, and so on.

And then we followed the couples for many years. We have now studied newlyweds, couples in the first seven years of marriage, violent marriages (with Neil Jacobson), and long-term couples in their forties and in their sixties. We have followed couples becoming parents and interacting with their babies, their preschoolers, and their teenagers. We have followed kids from ages 4 to 15, and are now following 650 couples in five different longitudinal studies. These studies are part of the database upon which this book is based.

The database of my research includes 7 longitudinal studies with a total of 677 couples (see Table 1.1). The longest we have followed couples is 15 years. The studies range across the life course, from the newlywed stage through the transitions to retirement. In the past 5 years, in addition to these studies, we have been conducting intervention research in which we study the effects of brief interventions on marital interaction. These brief interventions will include 8 experiments with approximately 500 couples. In the past two years we have been conducting weekend couples workshops with over 900 couples to date. In these intervention studies couples are followed for 2 years.

In my book *What Predicts Divorce?*, I employed Studies 2 and 3 to ask, "What is dysfunctional in marriages?" This research was also reported for the general public in the book *Why Marriages Succeed or Fail*. Study 2 is our longest longitudinal study (15 years).

Study 3 was a 10-year study of couples with a preschool child. In addition to focusing on the marital relationship, this study also investigated parent-child interaction and children's social-emotional development. The books *Meta-Emotion* (Gottman, Katz, & Hooven, 1996) and *The Heart of Parenting* (Gottman & DeClaire, 1996) came from this study. Study 4 is a replication of study 3, and we are still analyzing the data from it.

Table 1.1   Guide to Gottman and Colleagues' Longitudinal Studies

Begun in Year	Number of Couples	Sample	Comments and Sample References
1. 1980	30	young couples	Levenson & Gottman (1983, 1985)
2. 1983	79	varied from newlyweds to old age	Gottman (1994a,b)
3. 1986	56	couples with a preschool child (Midwest sample)	Gottman, Katz, & Hooven (1996)
4. 1989	63	same as 1986 study (Seattle sample)	None
5. 1989	130	newlyweds (Seattle sample)	Gottman et al. (1998)
6. 1989	156	middle-aged and couples in sixties (San Francisco Bay Area)	Levenson, Carstensen, & Gottman (1994)
7. 1989	160	four groups: highly abusive, moderately abusive, distressed nonviolent, happily married nonviolent	Jacobson & Gottman (1998)

In Study 5 I ask basic questions about what is dysfunctional when newlywed marriages head for divorce and what is functional in those early years of marriage. The first of our reports of this work is the paper by Gottman et al. (1998). In this newlywed study we had a group of 130 newlywed couples who were representative of the major ethnic and racial groups in Seattle, whom we studied in the first few months of their marriage in cohorts of approximately 40 couples each. Then we formed three criterion groups based on how their marriages turned out 3 to 6 years later. There were 17 divorced couples, and we picked 20 happily married, stable couples and 20 miserably married (very unhappy) stable couples as comparison groups. Could we use specific models of marital successs to predict which criterion group a couple would eventually be in? Let's look at the models we tested.

In the analyses we conducted, we sought to make two types of predictions: (1) a *marital stability prediction,* in which we combined the two stable groups (happy and unhappy) and attempted to predict divorce or stability from their time-1 marital interaction (taken within the first six months of marriage) using various process models; and (2) *a marital happiness prediction,* in which, controlling for stability, we tried to predict a couple's time-2 marital happiness or unhappiness (from their time-1 marital interaction taken within the first six months of marriage) using various process models. These models were based on the observational data. We tested models of whether anger was a dangerous emotion in marriage (as some have argued, e.g., Hendrix, 1988), or whether what I have called "The Four Horsemen of the Apocalypse" predicted divorce. We examined whether reciprocating negative emotions in kind (anger by one spouse is met with anger by the partner, for example) predicted divorce. We examined whether accepting influence and sharing power predicted marital stability. We studied the active listening mode. We looked at how the conflict discussion started, the role of positive affect, de-escalation, balance of positive and negative affect, and the role of physiological soothing.

We continued to study these newlyweds as some made the transition to parenthood (50 couples so far). We studied them in their 6th month of pregnancy and built a laboratory to study their interactions with their 3-month-old baby. (This laboratory duplicated that of Elizabeth Fivaz-Depeursinge of Lausanne, Switzerland.) We are finding that marital conflict transfers to the baby and makes it difficult for the baby to self-soothe, to restore physiological calm after being upset or overstimulated. These children are now approximately 4 years old. Approximately 70% of the parents experienced a precipitous drop in marital satisfaction in the baby's first year of life. We are now able to answer the question of what predicts if a couple will wind up in this 70% group or in the group whose marital satisfaction was maintained. This transition to parenthood study will form the basis for a new preventive intervention for expectant couples that will supplement birth preparation training.

The intervention studies I am conducting are still in their early stages; in fact, we are seeking funding for some of them at the time of this writing. The studies will converge on the active ingredients of the intervention by combining the marriage experiment approach (in which we change only one or a small number or variables) with randomized clinical trials. They are also part of the marriage clinic we are building in Seattle. This clinic combines research (basic and applied) with training and service delivery. Ten percent of the service delivery hours of treatment are devoted to an ongoing research study evaluating the treatment. The clinic also contains a marriage research laboratory.

We were quite delighted that in this longitudinal work we were actually able to predict divorce and stability with a very high degree of accuracy. Since we have now found these results in three longitudinal studies, I am fairly confident that they are reliable and accurate.

Some have asked how intrusive our research methods are and how natural the couples' behavior is in the laboratory apartment. We have systematically studied this issue by comparing our data to that obtained when spouses interact at home without an observer present (using either audio or videotapes that they make). The answer is that the behavior of people in our labs is different from their behavior at home, and the difference is that all spouses are much nicer to each other and more polite in the lab. Therefore, in the lab we *underestimate* the real differences between happy and unhappy couples. Given our ability to predict what will happen to the marriage longitudinally, this is not a serious problem. How natural are the couples? In general, it appears that after about 45 minutes in our lab, couples forget the cameras and other recording devices. This oblivion is fostered in part by the physical arrangements in the lab (cameras placed above eye level) and the fact that we form a very good rapport with our couples, and in part because the spouse is such a strong stimulus for eliciting well-ingrained, repeated behavior and thought patterns.

There used to be a skit on "Saturday Night Live" in which male and female anchorpersons sit at a raised dais. They are talking about an upcoming event as if it were a sporting event, but all we see on the set is a kitchen table, chairs, and a coffee pot. In comes a sleepy lady in a bathrobe, who pours herself a cup of coffee and sits down. Then in comes her husband, also in bathrobe; he pours his cup of coffee, sits down, and then opens up a newspaper. The commentators go wild. One says, "Did you see that, Bob? He totally shut her out. That was a masterful move. Worth at least ten points. Let's check with the judges. Yes, it was a 10." "Yes, that was amazing, Jane," says the commentator, "Let's see how she counters." And so it went throughout the breakfast.

This skit was hilarious to me because essentially it showed what we actually do with our data. We code marital interactions, using our observational codes. Then we weight them, giving positive points and negative points. Our weights are guided by the research on what discriminates happy from unhappy couples. We cumulate the amount of positive minus negative points each person earned at his or her turn at speech. We create something like a "Dow-Jones industrial average" of marital conversation, which I will describe in Chapter 2.

Repair and the Core Triad of Balance

 In this chapter I introduce the ideas of balance and repair in marriages. I discuss balance in the context of three domains: interactive behavior, perception, and physiology. With this basis, I go on to answer the central question of this chapter: "What is 'dysfunctional' when a marriage is ailing?"

BALANCE IN MARRIAGE

Modifying an Unfortunate Heritage

The original family general systems theorists were inspired by a book written by von Bertalanffy (1968) called *General System Theory.* In this book von Bertalanffy argued that all systems—biological, organizational, or interactive—were the same and followed some general principles. He had little idea what these principles might be, but he supposed that there would be some mathematical relationship between the parts of the system—a relationship that governed the system's dynamics. He suggested that every system acts to maintain its homeostatic balance, or stable steady state. Like a thermostat, the stability of a system would be maintained by feedback mechanisms that brought the system back to its steady state if it were perturbed.

This meant to von Bertalanffy that in a marriage it would be possible to write down equations that told us precisely how change in each person over time was affected by the other person. This led to the idea of "circular causality": that each person's behavior is affected by the other. Instead of labeling one person as pathological, each person's pathology could be viewed as a reaction to the other's. In families this point of view called attention to *patterns of interactive behavior,* rather than to the personalities of individual people.

Von Bertalanffy did not know how to write down these equations, nor did the family general systems theorists, so this dream never became a scientific reality. Eventually the idea of actually creating a mathematical model for families was abandoned. All that remained were von Bertalanffy's metaphors.

Unfortunately, as Wile (1992) pointed out, these metaphors have put therapists into an adversarial position with families. Wile wrote:

> Practitioners from all major schools of systems theory start with the assumption that they must find some way of dealing with family homeostasis—that is, the tendency of families to maintain their pathological patterns and resist the therapist's constructive efforts. The major disadvantage of the concept of homeostasis is its assumption of an adversary relationship between therapist and family. Individual family members are viewed as active proponents of the family system, willing victims of this system, or both. Since the aim of systems oriented therapy is to challenge the family system, a task that requires disrupting the family's homeostatic balance, these therapists often see their goals as directly opposed to those of the family (p. 28). . . . [there is] the tendency of some to see family members as being duplicitous and manipulative, as using "ploys" (Jackson, 1959) or Eric Berne type games to get what they want. The systems approach thus appears to lead to a picture of the conjoint therapist struggling gallantly against great odds—against concerted family efforts to maintain homeostatic balance, against family forces sabotaging all attempts to change the family system, and against subtle maneuvers and deceits employed by family members. (p. 29)

Wile goes on to point out that this adversarial position has led to particular approaches to family therapy:

> Thus Ackerman (1966) deliberately charms, ridicules, and bullies family members; Haley (1963b) and Watzlawick, Weakland, and Fisch (1974) strategically manipulate them with paradoxical instructions; Jackson and Weakland (1961) tactically place them in therapeutic double binds; Haley (1977) systematically browbeats certain partners who fail to do the tasks he assigns them; Minuchin and his colleagues (1967) "frontally silence" overbearing wives to "rock the system" and show their passive husbands how to stand up to them; Speck (1965) openly engages in "power struggles" with families; Satir (Haley and Hoffman, 1967) forcefully structures the therapeutic session and undercuts all attempts to challenge her control; and Zuk (1968) intentionally sides with one family member against another, challenges the whole family, and does so in inconsistent patterns in order to shake them up, keep them guessing, and "tip the balance in favor of more productive relating." . . . It is perhaps surprising, considering the dramatic nature of these methods, that they have been incorporated into the couples and family therapy traditions with so little discussion and debate. . . . An entrant into the field is often taught this general adversary orientation as if it were the only possible way of doing family and couples therapy. (p. 29)

I believe that these adversarial consequences are an unfortunate result of not actually doing the scientific work of writing real equations. This has led to our having inherited an incorrect view of what homeostasis is in family systems. Let me explain what I mean.

Five years ago I began a project with the world-famous mathematician and biologist James Murray to model marital interaction with the kinds of equations von Bertalanffy envisioned, except that they turned out to be nonlinear. These equations reveal that homeostasis in couples is a dynamic process in which the couple has its own mechanisms of self-correction and repair when the interaction becomes too destructive. Also, there are *two,* not one, homeostatic steady stages for each couple, one positive and one negative. The therapist and the couple have the same goal, which is strengthening the attractive power of the positive homeostatic steady state and weakening the attractive power of the negative homeostatic steady state. The mechanism that makes this happen is making repair more effective. This view of repair provided by the mathematical modeling has an interesting result. It puts the therapist on the side of the mechanisms of repair that are natural in marital interaction, rather than in an adversarial position regarding pathological processes. This simple change entails a major philosphical shift about homeostasis. It ends the adversarial position of therapist against family.

In our research we also gathered data from three domains of human experience: behavior, perception, and physiology. These three domains are not independent; rather, they are intricately linked in a relationship I call the "core triad of balance." The idea is that every marriage establishes a steady state, and the "system" of the relationship is repeatedly drawn to this stable steady state. Also, each marital system is capable of repair when this is needed.

To review the classic concept of homeostasis, or "stable steady state," in biological and behavioral systems, consider body weight. By controlling metabolism, the body will act to maintain a particular weight so that the person will either temporarily stop eating or get very hungry and begin eating, regardless of his or her weight. This principle holds true even if the person is anorexic or grossly overweight. When we try to change our weight away from that stable steady-state weight, the body will act to maintain the status quo, a constant internal milieu, a stable homeostasis, even when this stable steady state is not a healthful one. Recently, we heard in the news about a young man who weighed 1,000 pounds when he died and whose body had to be lifted out of his apartment with a crane. Many people (Dick Gregory, for example) had worked with this man on diets, and he lost a lot of weight at one time, only to gain it back again. When his weight fell, he got very hungry. This was his body's attempt to maintain what was ultimately a very dysfunctional stable steady state for him.

Steady States, Influenced and Uninfluenced

In marriages, we look at the balance (or weight, to extend our analogy) of positivity and negativity in the couple's interactions. Our theory assumes that every relationship is a system that develops its own balance or stable steady states, with respect to the ratio of positivity and negativity in behavior, perception, and physiology. These stable steady states are a way of quantifying the old idea of homeostasis in general systems theory.

In the theory I developed with James Murray, my student Regina Rushe, and his students Julian Cook, Jane White, and Rebecca Tyson, there are two kinds of stable steady states in human relationships: uninfluenced stable steady states and influenced stable steady states (Cook et al., 1995). The uninfluenced steady state is what each person brings to the interaction before being influenced by the partner. This is determined both by the history of the relationship and the person's temperament. The influenced steady state is how an individual is affected by the partner in the process of interacting.

In our model we defined a parameter we call "emotional inertia," which assesses how much continuity or rigidity there is once someone is experiencing a particular affective state. We thought that emotional inertia would be harmful to a marriage, based on the research that showed a greater reciprocity of negative emotions in unhappy couples. We also ascribed threshold parameters to the influence functions that tell us when, say, a particular husband would start noticing and reacting to his wife's negativity or positivity. How positive did she have to get to elicit a response out of him? How negative?

What are the influence functions? There is one influence function for the husband's influence on the wife, and another for the wife's influence on the husband. They tell us, on average, how the husband (and wife) affect the spouse's next behavior. For each value of positivity to negativity, we plot an average influence. In Figure 2.1 we see one form an influence function can take. Look at the positive side of the horizontal axis of Figure 2.1. The husband has no effect on his wife until he passes a threshold, C; then he has a constant effect of magnitude A.

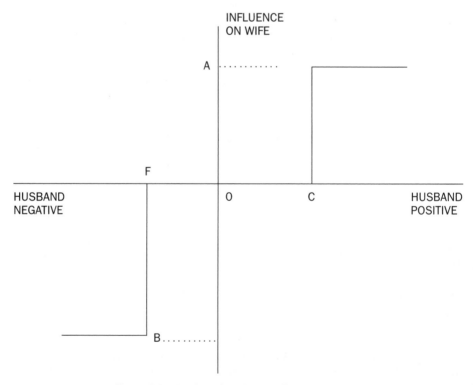

Figure 2.1   Husband's influence function on wife

Now look at the negative side of the horizontal axis. Again, until the husband passes a threshold of negativity, F, he has no effect. Then, when he becomes more negative than F, he has a negative effect on his wife's next behavior of magnitude B. At zero, we assume he has no influence on her.

Our hypothesis was that people bring to every marital interaction a set of *uninfluenced stable steady states* in behavior, thought, and physiology. This is their average level of positivity and negativity when they are not being influenced by their partner. These "uninfluenced" stable steady states depend on the individuals' temperaments, their personal histories, and the history of the relationship. We discovered that the *uninfluenced* stable steady states of the couples headed for divorce were far more negative that those of stable couples. This means that, in couples headed for martial meltdown, what each partner brings to the interaction is already quite negative. Then the spouses proceed to interact, and this interaction has characteristic influence functions through which a husband affects his wife, and she in turn affects him, creating *influenced stable steady states* in behavior, perception, and physiology. The interaction can move each individual's uninfluenced stable steady state in either a more negative or more positive direction. The marital system drives the uninfluenced stable steady states of partners in predictable ways to create the influenced stable steady states in behavior, perception, and physiology.

For relationships to work well, these stable steady states must reflect a very large balance of positivity versus negativity in perception and behavior; in the physiological domain, there must be a state of calm and well-being versus a state of mobilization for flight/fight, subjective upset, vigilance, or danger. We discovered that the positive/negative ratio in interactive behavior during conflict resolution is at least 5 to 1 in stable, happy marriages. In marriages headed for divorce the positive/negative ratio is only .8 to 1, so that there are 1.25 as many negatives as positives. We estimate both influenced and uninfluenced stable steady states using a mathematical modeling procedure we developed.

In Figure 2.2 we see a two-dimensional graph representing "phase space." The axes are *husband positive* to *husband negative*, and *wife positive* to *wife negative*. We have discovered two things that separate stable couples from those who eventually divorce: (1) The uninfluenced stable steady states of the partners in the stable couples are more positive than those of the couples who will eventually divorce; and (2) in the stable couples partners influence one another in a more positive direction, while the partners who will eventually divorce influence one another in a more negative direction. Later we will learn an intervention (the Dreams-Within-Conflict intervention) that temporarily enables emotionally disengaged spouses headed for divorce to interact so that their influence patterns are more like those of stable couples.

I really fell in love with all this math because it gave us a new theoretical language for talking about marriages. We could talk about what people brought to each interaction at the very start ("start-up"), how they influenced themselves ("inertia"), how they influenced one another, and what their thresholds were. People are drawn to their steady states, very much as gravitational forces hold us to the earth.

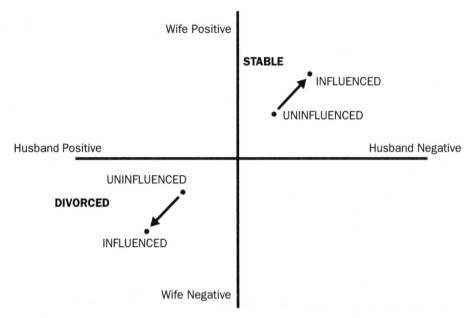

Figure 2.2   Phase space. In the lower left quadrant we see the pattern for couples headed for divorce: The influenced steady state (which is negative) becomes more negative than the uninfluenced. In the upper right quadrant we see the pattern for couples headed for stability: The influenced steady state (which is positive) becomes more positive than the uninfluenced.

Repair

The portion of the mathematical model that makes it potentially self-correcting is an additional *repair* term. In all marriages people display the behaviors that are predictive of marital dissolution. They occur significantly less in stable, happy marriages than in marriages headed for divorce. However, the reason for this reduced frequency was that repair attempts were made, and they were effective. Repair makes homeostasis an active pattern. Families who are ailing not only show patterns that are dysfunctional, but also display mechanisms of health, and the therapist can become allied with these mechanisms in treatment.

Catastrophes

We could also use the math model to better formulate how "catastrophes" occur in marriages. A mathematical "catastrophe" occurs when a parameter changes gradually until it crosses a critical threshold when there is a sudden, *qualitative* change. This is the mathematical equivalent of "the straw that broke the camel's back." The math gave us a means of quantifying gradual mutual influence and sudden change in relationships.

The math is the answer to the general systems theory dream of identifying equations that govern how a particular system will behave. Using nonlinear equations, we can simulate some very complex marital situations with very few parameters. In our work this mathematical language has facilitated a real breakthrough: It makes it clear exactly how the elements of the core triad of balance (interactive behavior, perception, and physiology) affect one another and how, in each domain, the spouses create "attractors" that keep their marital system on a particular trajectory, for better or for worse. The theory of nonlinear dynamics explains our ability to predict. It also suggests experiments for making changes, which we are currently undertaking (Gottman, Swanson, Murray, Tyson, & Swanson, in press).

THE CORE TRIAD OF BALANCE: INTERACTIVE BEHAVIOR

Negative Affect Reciprocity

In the following sections we will begin discussing the interactive behavior part of the core triad of balance. Later we will move on to perception and physiology.

In my laboratory, we always use many observational systems. No one system captures interaction in all its complexity. We primarily use a system called the "Specific Affect Coding System." All observers are trained to recognize facial features involved in emotion [following Ekman & Friesen's (1978) Facial Action Coding System]. They also code the voice, gestures, and the content of what people are saying. They code such emotions and behaviors as sadness, fear, anger, disgust, contempt, belligerence, domination, defensiveness, stonewalling (listener withdrawal), interest, affection, humor, listener tracking, joy, surprise (positive or negative), and neutrality. This "coding" is done with the assistance of the computer, so that the classification of each person's actions is synchronized to the video time code, perfectly aligned with the physiological data. Two observers code independently, so that when a couple leave my laboratory two observers have coded the entire interaction for both people. This makes it possible to compute the reliability of observers over and above chance levels of agreement.

The best and most consistent correlate of marital satisfaction and dissatisfaction across research laboratories, both in the United States and in other countries, has turned out to be a construct researchers have called "negative affect reciprocity." This term refers to the increased probability that a person's emotions will be negative (anger, belligerence, sadness, contempt, and so on) right after his or her partner has exhibited negativity. This means that my negativity is *more predictable* after my partner has been negative than it ordinarily would be.

For example, say I am negative toward my wife 25% of the time. Negative affect reciprocity would mean that when she behaves negatively toward me, I am *more* negative right after, say, 35% of the time. There has been an increase in the ability to predict my negativity over and above my usual relatively high level of negativity. Negative affect reciprocity has been the most consistent discriminator between happily and unhappily married couples. It is far better a measurement even than the amount of negative affect. This discrimination has been replicated in labs worldwide (for a review of this research, see Gottman, 1994a, 1994b).

In many books about marital therapy and in many advice books for couples, conflict is proposed as the royal road to intimacy. But what is the real role of conflict in creating and preserving intimacy in a marriage? Is there also a role for other kinds of interactions? Should they be positive ones or mostly neutral ones? To find empirically-based answers to these questions, I created a coding system called the Rapid Couples Interaction Scoring System (RCISS). First, I reviewed the research literature and extracted all the positive and negative codes used in all the studies that had significantly discriminated happy from unhappy couples. For example, "put downs" in the Marital Interaction Coding System (MICS; Weiss & Summers, 1983) were effective in discriminating, so they became a part of the new RCISS coding system. I organized the codes into listener-speaker codes and positive-negative codes. Then I organized the speaker codes into whether they involved the presentation of the problem, a response to this presentation, or emotional maintenance (reinforcing the status quo).

"Dow-Jones" Ratios

I began by looking at only one summary variable from this coding system: *the ratio of positive to negative exchanges during interactions involving conflict resolution.* This variable is like the "Dow-Jones industrial average" of a marital conflict discussion: a sum of all the positive things during one person's turn at speech minus all the negative things. Then we plotted the pattern of these interactions on graphs. We divided couples into two groups: one where the husbands' and wives' curves went generally up, indicating more positive than negative interaction; and all others. We call the positive group "low risk" and the other "high risk" (see Figure 2.3).

In Figure 2.3 we see a graph of the total cumulated points husband and wife earn in a conversation. Negative points are earned by behaviors such as defensiveness and criticism. Positive points are earned by behaviors such as agreement. The graph on the top goes through local ups and downs but its general trend is up for both husband and wife. The graph on the bottom, on the other hand, has a general drift toward the negative. We call a conversation "low risk" when people generally have more positivity than negativity (the trend is up for the cumulative total score). We call a conversation "high risk" when the trend is level or negative for at least one spouse.

We discovered that this one variable (positive/negative), obtained from the couple's interaction, was able to predict marital outcomes quite well, as Figure 2.4 shows. High-risk couples were lower in marital satisfaction at time-1 (graph a), and lower in marital satisfaction four years later (graph b) than low-risk couples. The high-risk couples had more persistent thoughts of separation and divorce (graph c) than low-risk couples. High-risk couples were more likely to separate (graph d) and divorce (graph e) than low-risk couples. Since time-2 is four years after time-1, we can say that the simple "Dow-Jones" type curve of a marital discussion did an excellent job predicting what would become of the marriage. This prediction was the start of our attempt to understand what factors, qualities, and characteristics are related to the longitudinal course of marriages.

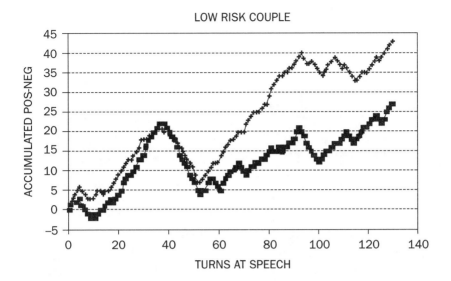

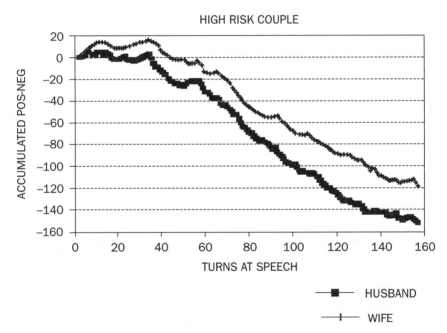

Figure 2.3   Examples of cumulative speaker point graphs for a low-risk couple (showing a trend in which positive exceeds negative), and for a high-risk couple (in which positive does not generally exceed negative)

More recently I created a way of weighting the codes in my Specific Affect Coding System (SPAFF) to create very similar types of Dow-Jones graphs. The advantages of the new system are: First, it is faster, since we no longer need a verbatim transcript of the conversation; second, we add up the points over uniform

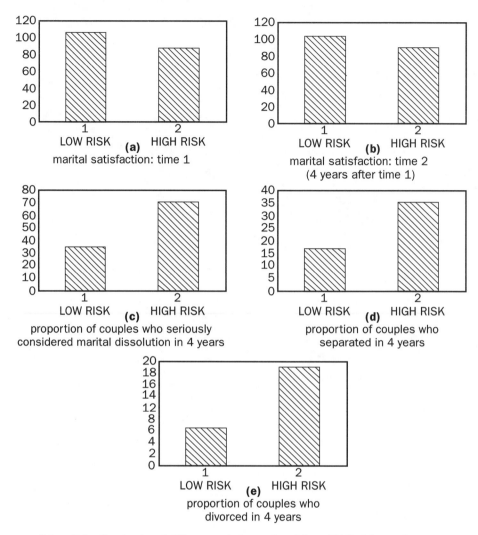

Figure 2.4 Bar graphs of differences between low-risk and high-risk couples over a 4-year period

six-second intervals, so we get a uniform number of 150 data points for each spouse in 15 minutes; and third, we can code any conversation (not just conflict) with the SPAFF. With both systems, we get the same kind of Dow-Jones graph. The basic result of these predictions is that *the ratio of negativity to positivity predicts marital outcome.*

One implication of this *ratio* finding is that *marital therapy should not declare war on negative affect,* for it serves many positive functions in marriages. It culls out what does not work and renews courtship via a dance of closeness and distance. The whole range of emotions is our heritage, not just cheerfulness and joy. There are everyday occurrences that make us a little sad, or disappointed, that worry us and scare us. Fear is a part of human experience. So is anger. It is as necessary to respond to one's spouse's "dark side" as it is to respond to his or her excitement and interest. We need the negativity. Just imagine a marriage with no negativity at all—it would be a nightmare, reminiscent of *The Stepford Wives*. Stable and happy marriages provide a very rich climate of positivity compared to negativity, but *they are not without negativity,* not at all.

Start-up: A Little Goes a Long Way

Another question to be considered when looking at interactions over time is, How important is the way the conflict *starts*? How much of the data from a 15-minute interaction do you need to make a prediction? In our research only 4% of the graphs ever reversed directions, that is, looked like a check mark. For the other 96% only *the first minute of data* was necessary for the prediction of divorce or stability. My friend and colleague, Dr. Sybil Carrére, recently did a similar analysis to determine whether we needed all 15 minutes of our data to predict what would happen to a couple. She proceeded to lop off the last three minutes of data and try the prediction. She continued this way, and the prediction was still not seriously compromised even with only *the first three minutes* left for prediction. In short, start-up, the way a topic of disagreement is broached, is critically important in predicting marital outcomes.

Harsh start-up (escalating from neutral to negative affect) *by the wife* was associated with marital instability and divorce. Women (especially in ailing marriages, but actually in all marriages) are consistently more likely to criticize than are men. Men, on the other hand, are consistently more likely to stonewall or withdraw emotionally than women. As I noted earlier, this has been called the demand-withdraw pattern by Christensen and his associates. It is also called the pursuer-distancer pattern, in which one person, the pursuer, keeps bringing up the issue in the marriage, and the other person, the withdrawer, tries to minimize or avoid discussing the issue.

Not All Negatives Are Alike: The Four Horsemen of the Apocalypse

After examining the finding that we could predict the fate of marriages with our simple Dow-Jones-like average of a marital conversation, we realized that we were weighing all negatives as if they were equally negative. But is this really true? *Are all negatives equally corrosive?* Or is it the case that our prediction of what will happen to the marriage would improve if some negatives were differentially weighted in our Dow-Jones-like average? The answer was: Not all negatives are equally corrosive. Four behaviors, which I call "The Four Horsemen of the Apocalypse," are most corrosive: *criticism, defensiveness, contempt,* and *stonewalling* (see Figure 2.5). Examples that bring these Four Horsemen to life are probably the best way to get a sense of these additional prediction parameters.

The First Horseman—Criticism

Criticism is any statement that implies that there is something globally wrong with one's partner, something that is probably a lasting aspect of the partner's

NOT ALL NEGATIVES ARE EQUALLY CORROSIVE

1. CRITICISM

2. DEFENSIVENESS

3. CONTEMPT

4. STONEWALLING

Figure 2.5   The Four Horsemen of the Apocalypse

character. Any statement that begins with "you always" or "you never" will be a criticism rather than a complaint. Criticism quite naturally elicits defensiveness. We can see this in the following transcript when the husband (H) says "But I . . . " in response to his wife's (W) assertion that having guns in the house points to a major flaw in his personality.

> W: I feel like it could have a lot to do with how violent you are. You worry me so . . . and that's another thing that bothers me about having guns in the house. You've really got a violent temper.
> H: But I . . .

He defends himself, trying to show that he really is an okay guy, that it is not really his problem, that he does lots of good stuff in this marriage, that he feels like an innocent victim. The clincher is "You've really got a violent temper." She has instantly transformed her point, the complaint about not wanting guns in the house, into a criticism. Her statement has gone from specific to global and from situational to personal.

The difference between a complaint and criticism is very important. If I complain, I might say, "I'm upset that all through dinner you talked only about yourself and you didn't ask me anything about my day. That hurts my feelings." That's a complaint. It's okay. It does not predict anything negative in marital outcomes. But I can easily add blame to make this criticism. With each complaint I can add, "How can you treat me this way?" "Don't you care about my feelings?" Or I can make it very personal. "What kind of self-centered person are you?" Or, one of my favorites, "What is wrong with you?" or "Why would you do a thing like that?" There are a whole set of "why questions" that really aren't questions at all. Haim Ginott (1965) pointed out that adults ask children these questions all the time, and they are actually insults. Examples are: "Why are you so slow?" "Why are you so clumsy?" "Why are you so inconsiderate?" "Why are you so insensitive?" "Why do you insist on treating me so bad?"

Or I can use the word *always* or *never;* each is very effective in transforming a complaint into a criticism. We are all very creative in our varieties of criticism. In the old days, behavior therapists thought that the bad part about criticism was that it was not specific but global, and so they taught people how to state their criticisms in terms of specific negative behaviors they wanted to see less of and specific positive behaviors that they wished to see more of. The basic idea was: If you are specific, it won't be a criticism. However, this simple formula doesn't really work. An example: Jim comes home and sees that his wife is banging doors and slamming down the dishes on the table. He says, "What's wrong, honey?" Sheila then proceeds to take out an overhead projector and puts up this overhead titled, "What's Wrong with Jim?"

A long list of saved-up, very specific complaints will create the effect of a global rejection of the partner's personality. Why would someone store up these complaints and not discuss issues as they arise? Usually, the motives are positive, such as not wanting to make a mountain out of a molehill, not wanting to seem

What's Wrong With Jim

1. JIM DOESN'T LISTEN.
2. JIM DOESN'T SHOW HIS FEELINGS.
3. JIM IS NOT A GOOD FATHER.
4. JIM DOESN'T HELP AROUND THE HOUSE.
5. JIM DOESN'T RECYCLE.
6. JIM IS LOUSY IN BED.
7. JIM RUNS AWAY WHEN THE FEELINGS GET HOT.
8. JIM ISN'T A GOOD PLANNER.
9. JIM DOESN'T PAY BILLS ON TIME.
10. JIM NEGLECTS HIS FRIENDS.
11. JIM DOESN'T CALL HIS MOTHER VERY OFTEN.
12. JIM FLIRTS WITH OTHER WOMEN AT PARTIES.
13. JIM RUSHES ME WHEN I'M TRYING TO GET READY.
14. JIM LEAVES HIS DIRTY CLOTHES ALL AROUND.
15. JIM BREAKS DISHES WHEN HE WASHES THEM. I THINK HE DOES THIS ON PURPOSE.
16. JIM DRINKS TO EXCESS.
17. JIM YELLS AT OTHER DRIVERS AND IT SCARES THE KIDS.
18. JIM IS A COUCH POTATO.
19. JIM GOES GROCERY SHOPPING AND THEN FORGETS THE LIST, SO HE DOESN'T GET THE ESSENTIALS LIKE TOILET PAPER.
20. JIM OFTEN FORGETS TO FLUSH.
21. JIM DOESN'T ASK ME ABOUT MY DAY, HE JUST TALKS ABOUT HIS DAY.
22. JIM DOESN'T SHARE HIS INNERMOST FEELINGS WITH ME.
23. JIM GETS ROWDY AT PARTIES.
24. JIM DOESN'T CLEAN UP AFTER A PARTY.
25. JIM IS TOO LENIENT WITH THE KIDS.
26. JIM IS SOMETIMES TOO STRICT WITH THE KIDS.
27. WHEN JIM PAINTS, HE LEAVES SPOTS UNDONE.
28. JIM'S ATTITUDE TOWARD WOMEN IS SEXIST.
29. JIM FORGETS TO FEED THE CAT.
30. WHEN JIM DOES FEED THE CAT, HE DOESN'T WASH THE FORK OFF BUT LEAVES IT TO GET CRUSTY AND YUCKY IN THE SINK, SO I HAVE TO CLEAN THE DISGUSTING THING.
31. THERE'S RARELY FOREPLAY BEFORE SEX.
32. WHEN HE TALKS, HE BRAGS. I COULD LAUGH, HE'S SUCH A FOOL.

Figure 2.6 What's wrong with Jim. Many specific complaints that are criticisms.

so negative and complain all the time, not really feeling entitled to one's complaints, and so on. But whatever the motives, the effect is to transform complaint into criticism (see Figure 2.7).

In the film *The Accidental Tourist*, the estranged married couple get together again and the wife says, "The trouble with you is . . . ." The husband blows up at this point, deeply hurt, experiencing the statement as a deep criticism and realizing that their attempts at reconciliation are hopeless. The trouble with "the trouble with you" is that it is perceived as an assault on the partner's personality. When one's personality is under attack, the only thing to do is to dig in, entrench, and defend the bones of who you are.

The form of the criticism can be is as troubling as the content. So there are lots of ways, not just one way, of moving from complaint to criticism. There is no single rule for avoiding this, like only using "I-statements." Our research shows that women are more likely to use criticism than are men. Furthermore, this use of criticism creates a harsher rather than softer start-up of the problem discussion. Harsher starts are correlated with storing up grievances and suppressing negative emotions. This suppression, in turn, heightens physiological arousal (Gross & Levenson, 1993; Notarius & Johnson, 1982; Notarius & Levenson, 1979; Notarius, Wemple, Ingraham, Burns, & Kollar, 1982). *Caveat:* When we discuss the etiology of the Four Horsemen, we will see that it is a fallacy to blame women for harsh start-ups. It is only a part of a cycle that includes angry and unresponsive husbands.

The Second Horseman—Defensiveness

Defensiveness is any attempt to defend oneself from a perceived attack. Here is a common example that involves volleying a complaint with a counter-complaint. The wife is just getting done with explaining what upsets her when her husband drinks a lot of alcohol at parties.

> W: And you get so aggressive after a few drinks, that's the part I don't like, that's the part I fear.
> H: How about when *you* explode into a tantrum?

There are many ways to be defensive. In their amusing book, *How to Avoid Love and Marriage* (1983), Greenburg and O'Malley talk about "retroactive deserv-

---

COMPLAINT:

"I'm upset that you talked about yourself all through dinner and you didn't ask me anything about my day. That hurts my feelings."

CRITICISM:

"You talked about yourself all through dinner and didn't ask me anything about my day. How can you treat me this way? What kind of self-centered person are you?"

Figure 2.7 The difference between complaint and criticism.

ing" as a method for ruining marriages. In retroactive deserving, you never admit that you are wrong, and you blame your partner for not somehow preventing the mistake you made, which was, therefore, your partner's fault. If you forgot to do something important (like ordering tickets to the concert), it is *your* partner's fault for not reminding you.

Defensiveness is a general stance of warding off a perceived attack. In marital interaction it takes the common form of the innocent victim posture, with accompanying *whining*. The message is: "What are you picking on me for? I didn't do anything wrong. What about all the good things I do? I never get any appreciation. Poor me. I'm *innocent*."

Unfortunately, defensiveness usually includes denying responsibility for the problem, and this fuels the flames of marital conflict because it says the other person is the culprit, the guilty party. It is not *both* of you who have the problem, but the mean bully you unfortunately happen to be married to. In the example we see a common form of defensiveness, counter-complaining, or counterattacking when attacked. Deflect, divert, attack, and defend. The wife finishes posing her side of an issue that concerns her and the husband responds with, "How about when *you* explode into a tantrum?" He attacks and adds a dash of contempt at the same time (using words like *explode* and *tantrum*, which imply that she is an out-of-control child).

The Third Horseman—Contempt

Contempt is any statement or nonverbal behavior that puts oneself on a higher plane than one's partner. In the following excerpt the husband imitates his wife in a lightly mocking tone of voice, responding to her complaint about his driving too fast and too recklessly by mocking the way she sits in the car with her feet up on the dashboard emitting high-pitched, fearful complaints.

> H: The problem is, I don't want you to put your feet up on the dashboard, and then, you know, put your feet through the windows, then [*imitating someone with an exaggerated, high-pitched voice*] "God, we're gonna die" or "You're going to kill us," because no, I'm not going to kill us.

In this example contempt takes the form of mockery: "God, we're gonna die." It almost seems like an attempt at humor or teasing, but only one person is laughing. Mockery is a very powerful form of contempt (especially when it is delivered in public), but people can inflict sufficient harm using garden-variety contempt. My favorite one is correcting someone's grammar when he or she is angry with you. An example: "It's not, 'I could care less,' it's 'I *couldn't* care less.' At least get that right!"

There is also a universal facial expression of contempt. In Paul Ekman and Wallace Friesen's (1978) coding system, the dimpler muscle, or "AU14," is the "action unit" of the facial muscle (called the buccinator) that mediates the expression. Ekman was actually looking for a facial expression that was not universal across cultures when he started studying contempt, but he found a universal expression instead. The dimpler muscle pulls the lip corners to the side and creates a dimple in the cheek, but the dimple isn't cute. The AU14 is often accompanied by an eye roll and an upward glance, as if imploring the Lord for help.

This contemptuous facial expression is powerfully corrosive. When we turned off the sound on our videotapes and just counted facial expressions of contempt, we found, to our astonishment, that a certain number of contemptuous facial expressions by husbands was predictive of their wives' infectious illnesses over the next four years (Gottman, 1994a). The prediction didn't work the other way around: We could not predict illness in husbands unless we included a loneliness factor. *Lonely* husbands who were married to *contemptuous* wives got physically ill more often than other husbands.

The Fourth Horseman—Stonewalling

Stonewalling occurs when the listener withdraws from the interaction. At home, when the spouses are not wired up as they are in our lab, stonewalling would probably involve one spouse leaving. The listener typically gives the speaker all kinds of cues that he or she is tracking by mirroring or responding via eye contact, head nodding, facial movements (such as raising and lowering the brows to show concern, worry, expectation, or delight), and brief vocalizations and grunts (the words *yeah* or *uh-huh* are called "assents" in the Marital Interaction Coding System; Weiss & Summers, 1983), and so on. There is a marvelous dance of nonverbal behavior between speaker and listener that, in effect, regulates turn-taking in conversation and shows the speaker that the listener is "there." Speakers do such things as look away from the listener as they begin talking, while listeners maintain a steadier gaze until they switch roles.

Stonewallers don't do any of this. Instead, they use brief monitoring glances, look away and down, maintain a stiff neck, vocalize hardly at all—in effect, convey the presence of an impassive stone wall. The monitoring glances appear to be more on the order of checking out the ogre. Is the ogre still there, or has the ogre magically vanished in accordance with their prayers? They will use "control facial expressions" (expressions designed to *conceal* facial indicators of emotion) like tightening the chin and jaw.

Men are consistently more likely to stonewall than women. Eighty-five percent of our stonewallers were men (Gottman, 1994a,b). As you might imagine, when women stonewall, it is quite predictive of divorce! This is also true of male stonewalling and the reciprocation of stonewalling. Women are more likely than men to criticize. Interestingly, when we computed a demand-withdraw index for couples based on the wife criticizing more than the husband and the husband stonewalling more than the wife, this index significantly predicted *both* earlier and later divorcing. The likelihood of both criticism and stonewalling was, in turn, predicted by the total positive affect experienced by both husband and wife during the preceding events of the day. In other words, the negative behaviors have an etiology in nonconflict interaction. Here is an example of a husband's stonewalling in response to his wife's tentative complaint.

W: But there you're focusing on me again.
H: Yeah.
W: Well?

H: I always seem to do that, don't I? [*Husband now looks away and stonewalls, and there is a pause.*]

W: [*Wife gets very nervous, and her heart rate rises.*] Yeah. I'm not attacking you either. I think, for the most part, we get along pretty damn good [*she laughs, but he does not*], but . . .

On the videotape the husband abruptly has "left" the interaction, looking down, not responding. It is as if he were gone. Most wives find this "away" behavior quite aversive, but few ever comment on it directly. Instead, they tend to make efforts to repair the interaction, as they become more physiologically aroused.

In this example, after the husband stonewalled, the wife's heart rate spiked dramatically as a prelude to her trying to repair things by minimizing the problem (saying that they had a pretty good relationship most of the time and trying unsuccessfully to get them both to laugh). Usually, men stonewall after their own physiology has become highly aroused. It is a withdrawal in the service of self-soothing. Unfortunately, male stonewalling is very upsetting for women, increasing their physiological arousal and intensifying their pursuit of the issue. It doesn't work as a strategy for men if their goal is to reduce the intensity of the conflict. Since women so rarely stonewall, it is quite dramatic when they do and a very bad prognosis for the marriage.

The Relationship among the Four Horsemen

Figure 2.5 illustrates the fact that the four horsemen generally come in a sequence, with criticism starting it all off. It is important to note that our best single predictor of divorce is contempt. It is not the case that in happy, stable marriages criticism, defensiveness, and stonewalling never occur. They just occur less often, and they tend to be effectively repaired when they occur. So everyone "messes up" in marriages, but not all repair attempts are successful.

Contempt, however, was in a category of its own. The amount of contempt in stable, happy marriages is essentially zero. I recently attended a conference on marital therapy in which a presenter demonstrated a version of the active listening method. In the demonstration, she ignored the husband's contempt toward his wife, instead empathizing with his feelings of disappointment and loneliness and urging the wife to be empathic when she was being insulted and called names by her husband. I found this horrifying. I recommend that therapists label contempt as psychological abuse and unacceptable. I call it the sulfuric acid of love.

The fact that the other three horsemen were not zero in happy, stable marriages has profound implications for intervention. It means that what we must focus on is *repair*. Indeed, the reason that criticism, defensiveness, and stonewalling occur significantly less often in happy, stable marriages is the result of effective repair. Effective repair leads to interest, affection, humor, and lowered tension occurring more often even when the interaction becomes negative.

No Horsemen in Sight: Emotional Disengagement

Many times marriages do not have the Four Horsemen of the Apocalypse galloping through their living rooms, and the marital interaction is not characterized by high levels of negativity. When interviewed, the spouses may talk about how they have adjusted to things and that "everything is really okay." Still, the marriage can be highly problematic, because the couple may be in the advanced stages of the Distance and Isolation Cascade but be resolutely determined to adapt to this state of their relationship.

This absence of negativity in marriages can be confusing for therapists, and they can wind up accepting the spouses' portrayal that everything is fine, even when they have come for marital therapy. The problem in these cases is the emotional disengagement itself. What is very clear in these marital interactions is *the absence of positive affect*. Such couples appear not to make any emotional connection, and there is almost no humor, affection, or even active interest in one another. There is an underlying tension and suppressed sadness. In these marriages we see a complex pattern of characteristics:

- There is an absence of affect; the marriage appears to be emotionally dead. There is no joy, affection, or humor, nor is there the engagement of anger and conflict, except on rare occasions.
- Partners are like passing ships in the night, leading parallel lives.
- They do not appear to experience each other as friends.
- There is a lot of unacknowledged tension (facial, vocal, and somatic).
- They keep saying everything is okay. They appear to feel as if they should not really complain, that there is something wrong with them for not being happier.
- There may be a high level of physiological arousal in one or both people during the conflict discussion.
- There is little attempt on the part of either person to soothe the other.

Trying to *induce* positive affect with these couples will fail, though it may incite them to become overtly hostile with one another. In Part III we will examine an intervention that facilitates partners' reconnection to what they *don't* like about their relationship.

Repair Attempts

As noted earlier, the critical portion of the mathematical model that makes it self-correcting is repair. Everybody does three of the Four Horsemen. It is not the case that in happy, stable marriages people are not critical, are not defensive, and do not stonewall. (However, I did find that contempt was essentially zero in happy, stable marriages, but the other three horsemen occurred with some frequency.) These behaviors occurred significantly less in stable, happy marriages than in marriages headed for divorce. The reason for this reduced frequency was that repair attempts were made, and they were effective.

What is repair? It can be almost anything, but it is generally the spouses acting as their own therapist. They comment on the communication itself, or they support and soothe one another, or they express appreciations to soften their complaints.

Negative affect continues when the couple have few effective mechanisms for getting out of the negativity, for repairing the interaction by making it less negative. Even in the most distressed of marriages, however, you will see repair *attempts*—in fact, rapid ones—at the rate of about one every three minutes. Indeed, the more distressed the marriage, the higher the rate of repair attempts and the higher the rate of their failure.

Nancy Dreyfus (1992) first called my attention to repair attempts in her book, *Talk to Me Like I Am Someone You Love.* She inspired our research into this important process of attempting to change the affect during marital conflict resolution. We started studying repair attempts systematically to develop an observational means of detecting them and to figure out why they worked sometimes and failed other times. This research led us to decipher *how nonconflict resolution in marital interactions is related to conflict resolution.* As clinicians, we must first notice repair attempts and then teach the couple to see them when they occur. What determines the success of these repair attempts? We have found that, surprisingly, the answer does not lie in how couples resolve conflict.

In the following transcript a married couple in their first few months of marriage are engaged in a distressful interaction (they eventually divorced). Unfortunately, the whining, eye rolling, and increasing sarcasm—in short, *defensiveness* and *contempt*—that creep into this interaction are far better captured on the videotaped version. Nevertheless, the gist is apparent from the words alone. Of note is the husband's repair attempt. After a pause, he finally says, "Problem is neither one of us is paying attention to what's important to the other." He is using meta-communication, commenting on the process of their communication in a manner that does not affix blame: Both of them are viewed as being responsible for the problem. And it is said in a neutral tone. In short, the statement (and his delivery of it) contains all the components that *ought* to make it an effective repair attempt. But it is a total failure.

The husband claimed that his wife never told him about an upcoming picnic nor that his father was coming to visit. Notice the defensiveness and contempt in both individuals' conversation.

W: I told you, Sunday . . .

H: No, you didn't.

W: Yes, I did. I told you that we were going to the picnic at 6:30, the picnic's at 6:30.

H: You told me once, about Wednesday.

W: No, I didn't.

H: You said I didn't have to go if I didn't want to.

W: No, I told you that I didn't *care* if you went or not, but that's . . . I mean, you never said one way or the other that, no, you didn't want to go or, yes, you did want to go.

H: Right. And then I forgot about it. And when I saw your face change, I said, "What's wrong?" and you wouldn't tell me, so how am I supposed to remember?

W: I told you many times that the picnic was this afternoon. I even told you when I did the laundry, when I was cleaning clothes for you to wear to the picnic.

H: That was Wednesday. You did a load of clothes on Wednesday.

Here we can see defensiveness in action. Each of them felt blamed for the misunderstanding, and each of them wanted to be the one "in the right."

W: I did three loads of laundry on Sunday.

H: No, that's not what you said. You said that Wednesday.

W: No, I told you that Sunday, when you were still in bed and I was doing laundry—I asked, "What do you want to wear to the picnic?" "Oh, shorts and a tee-shirt," you said. So that's what I did. I did your shorts, I did your tee-shirts, I did your underwear for this picnic on Sunday.

H: That was pretty brilliant to ask me when I'm in bed, half asleep.

W: It was 2:00 in the afternoon.

H: So?

W: So!

H: You knew I was half asleep.

W: You shouldn't be half asleep in the afternoon!

They were smiling during this last segment in a sincere but vain attempt to soften and de-escalate their dispute. The smiling could be seen as a kind of repair attempt in itself. There was a pause and then the husband picked up where they left off. The interaction resumed a tedious rhythm of accusation and defense. After a few intense minutes, there was a very long pause and then the husband made another repair attempt, delivered sweetly, with no negative affect.

H: Well, I guess the problem is, I'm not remembering things that are important to you for me to remember, and you're not remembering things that are important for me to remember.

This was an excellent example of a repair attempt, but, alas, it did not work. The wife responded with defensiveness and accusation and the husband picked up the dispute, once again drawn back into the fray.

In our research it became very important to me to understand why the clumsiest or most negative repair attempts would work in some marriages while the smoothest ones didn't work in other marriages. It was a total mystery. We will return to this issue of what determines the success of repair attempts later. For now, I will simply summarize our finding. A repair attempt's success, as far as we could ascertain, *cannot* be determined by the method of its delivery or its antecedents. In fact, it is not possible to predict its success from any parameters within the interaction. This finding is fairly damning of a pure social skill model approach to marital therapy, for such an approach would say that the profile of the repair attempt—the parameters of its timing, content, and delivery—should determine whether or not it works. But we can't find these parameters.

To dramatize the importance of this finding, consider the idea that the only successful outcome we need in marital therapy is for the couple to be able to *suc-*

cessfully repair their interactions when they encounter negativity. Wouldn't that be enough to accomplish? In some senses, it is enough. Maybe their marriage isn't great yet, but the therapist has put them on a very different trajectory if their natural repair attempts now are more successful. Thus, it becomes very important to understand why repair attempts fail.

One of my honors students, Michael Lorber, analyzed a tape of an interaction between spouses. The husband is a chemist who cannot know when he will be able to leave work because his experiments have a timing that is sometimes not predictable. His wife complains that the kids get very hungry. The husband suggests feeding them a snack, and his wife gives him a look and says, "What do you think I've been doing all along?" Realizing that he has inadvertently insulted her intelligence, he then delivers a very stupid grin as a sort of apology—and it works. His wife laughs. This film clip shows dramatically that the success of the repair is just not predictable from within the conflict interaction. Later we will see why this is so. For now, we will explore an important refinement of one of our predictors of divorce.

The Four Horsemen alone allow us to predict divorce with 85% accuracy. Why isn't the prediction nearly perfect? The answer lies in the effectiveness of repair. We recently discovered the importance of the effectiveness of repair attempts and a less negative threshold at which they take effect. The *threshold parameters* tell us how negative things have to get before repair attempts start being made by each spouse. The *effectiveness parameters* tells us how effective repair is once it is made. In a study of 130 newlywed couples, we found that even when the Four Horsemen were above the median, if repair was effective, then 83% of these couples wound up in stable and happy marriages. Hence, the effectiveness of repair made all the difference for these very negative couples. This meant that we could predict the ultimate fate of 97.5% of the couples just by using the variables of the Four Horsemen and repair effectiveness.

In the next chapter, I suggest that enabling couples to repair their own interaction is the central goal of marital therapy, and that we should terminate marital therapy not when the marriage is a great marriage, but when the couple is capable of repair without us. Because of this objective, understanding what predicts effective repair becomes crucially important.

The Influence Factor in Marital Outcomes

As noted earlier in this chapter, the factor of "negative affect reciprocity" increases the probability that a person's emotions will be negative (anger, belligerence, sadness, contempt, and so on) right after his or her partner has exhibited negativity.

Negative affect reciprocity can result in an escalation of the negativity from ordinary negative affects (like anger, fear, and sadness) to the Four Horsemen to violence, each escalation being more predictive of divorce. Negative affect reciprocity can occur in three possible combinations: (1) reciprocating low-intensity negative affect in kind (e.g., anger is met with anger); (2) reciprocating high-intensity negative affect in kind (e.g., contempt is met with contempt); and (3) escalating from low to high intensity affect (e.g., anger is met with contempt).

In the research on negative affect reciprocity (for a review, see Gottman, 1994a,b), researchers hypothesized that the pattern of *reciprocation of negativity in kind* would be related to marital unhappiness. In our research we were able to test which of three different possibilities would be most predictive of divorce. We found (Gottman et al., 1998) that it was the *escalation of negativity by husbands* that predicted divorce, which turned out to be an index of the husbands' refusal to accept influence from their wives.

I thought that this result was quite amazing. It meant that even in the best of marriages spouses reciprocated negativity in kind (both low intensity, like anger being met with anger, and high intensity, like defensiveness being met with defensiveness). Therefore, a pattern that many marital researchers had thought to be a symptom of dysfunctional marriage was not at all a symptom. Apparently it was nothing at all to worry about! How were we to understand this result?

The answer came from a study of violent marriages that Neil Jacobson and I had been conducting for the past nine years (Jacobson & Gottman, 1998). Watching videotapes of violent men interacting with their wives on a conflict-resolution task reminded me of baseball players at automatic pitching machines, batting back every pitch; these men refused to be influenced by *anything* their wives had to say. Even reasonable statements or small complaints were rejected with a highly escalated degree of defensiveness, belligerence, or contempt.

This observation led me to formulate the hypothesis that *marriages will work to the extent that men accept influence from, share power with, women.* Next I applied this hypothesis to a longitudinal study of 130 nonviolent newlywed couples and found that, amazingly, those in which the men who did not accept influence from their wives wound up divorced. The prediction rate was very good, 80% accuracy, and it did not work the other way around: Most of the women accepted influence from their husbands, and the acceptance predicted nothing.

The Escalation of Negativity as the Husband Rejecting Wife's Influence

In the following transcript we see an example of a violent husband rejecting any attempt his wife makes to influence him. She has raised the issue of her husband trying to get along better with her mother, to which he responds:

> H: So, what do you want anyway? You want me to just be agreeable all the damn time, do what you want, do what your mother wants?

Inadvertently, this husband has hit the nail on the head. Accepting influence means exactly that, finding in one's partner's complaint something one can be agreeable with. Unfortunately, this wife says no. Instead, she just asks her husband to give it a chance, which is an attempt at softening her request, to no avail.

> W: No. You bitch because she doesn't give you a chance. You're not giving *her* a chance.
>
> H: I gave her two and a half years. Invited her to our house, let her spend the night, let her husband crawl in bed with me, let him get drunk in

my living room, let her crawl up on the top bunk with Teddy. What the hell do you want me to do? Hand her the house keys too, and the car keys, and my check?

This last statement is a good example of our belligerence code. It is an escalation of anger to its provocative form that states the problem in extremes and challenges her. He is letting her know that she cannot push him at all. She promptly becomes intimidated.

W: No.
H: What the hell else is there for me to do? I gave her one hell of a good chance. I never got invitations to her house. I never spent the night at her house with her permission. She never asked me any questions like I asked her. I was curious about who she was, what she did. She never asked me one goddamn question. And you never gave a shit. It didn't seem to matter to you, as long as Mommy could come over and take the kids whenever she wanted to, do whatever she wanted with the kids.

This mockery has escalated the belligerence into contempt.

W: You let your sister do it [what she wants with the kids].
H: No, I don't.
W: You let your sister favor Amanda over Teddy.
H: How in the hell am I supposed to do something about that?

This interaction makes it very clear (especially in videotaped form) that there is absolutely nothing this wife can say that the husband will agree with in any way; he swiftly and forcefully bats back every complaint, refusing to accept her influence. Every request this fearful wife makes is made with great trepidation; it is obvious she expects him to tromp all over it. In the transcript the husband says, "So what do you want? You want me to just be agreeable?" Although the wife says "No," this is exactly what we *do* want. This transcript demonstrates a distorted influence pattern. The violent marriage is a one-way power struggle gone wild.

Husband Accepting Wife's Influence

In this next excerpt we see a husband easily accept his wife's influence when she simply and clearly tells him what she would like to see changed in their lives:

W: I want you to work at home one day a week.
H: Right by me. Right now, I have enough stuff to do I could easy work at home.
W: I know.

This transaction took only a few seconds. It was easy. It shows that one doesn't have to be a mental health worker to accept influence from one's partner. The husband found a way to be agreeable with what he evaluated as a reasonable request from his wife. In marriages that work well, both people (particularly men) appear to be actively searching for common ground. It is not the case that they are being compliant and going along with the partner just for the sake of keeping the peace. They are actively delineating areas in which they agree and also delineating areas in which they disagree for compromise later on.

Here's another example, taken from the interaction of a newlywed couple in which the wife wants the husband to get more involved with their church. She starts with a de-escalated request.

> W: I'm asking you to keep an open mind to the possibility of participating more in church activities. I don't like you going just because of me. I don't want you to feel like a hypocrite. I guess part of me wants you to look at it as one option of what we need . . .
> H: Yeah.
> W: . . . rather than rule it out.
> H: No, I haven't ruled it out.

Here the wife initially softens her request. She is very clear about what she wants, but has made her request by reassuring her husband that she will not ask him to do anything that will make him feel like a hypocrite. But she wants him to keep an open mind. He then accepts her influence, saying that he has not ruled out being more active in the church. Later she voices some of her own reservations about taking religious things too literally, saying she doesn't know if she believes . . .

> W: . . . the garden of Eden, the snake, and everything else.
> H: Well, no, I can't believe that either.

Raising her own doubts makes it easier for her husband to express his reservations. But then she adds:

> W: I want a little more involvement from you than just Easter, Christmas, and Mother's Day—maybe not every Sunday, but I don't want our kid saying to me "Well, Mom, how come you go all the time but Dad never goes?"
> H: [joking] "Because, Junior, Dad is an agnostic." [Both laugh heartily.]

They have used humor to soften their area of disagreement. He then quickly adds:

> H: That's what I've been thinking lately. Our son should have a solid ground to build on later in life. I do want him to know that this is not the only thing . . .
> W: I have no problem with that.

So they are establishing their common ground, finding a way to *honor both viewpoints*. This is an enormous strength. Later the wife adds that she wants her husband to find some way of being genuinely involved with the church. He laughs and says that she doesn't want him to be involved "just to make my wife happy," and they both laugh again. They both discuss how corrupt many clerics are in American life and both do what we call a "we against others" in trashing corrupt clerics like Jimmy Swaggart. In this joining they are forming solidarity again and soothing one another. She also assures her husband that she is not asking for an enormous involvement:

W: I'm not asking you to get as involved as Laura's husband.
H: Mmm-hmm.

The husband says that it would be helpful to him if he could find some part of the belief system to agree with. She acknowledges that would indeed help. This frees him to talk about how extremely disappointed he was in their minister during his mother's funeral, when the minister said things that showed that he didn't know her at all. But this upsets her a bit.

H: It's like Mom's service.
W: Well, the guy didn't know her and that was kind of weird.
H: Yeah, I thought that was just total crap! Half the time I felt like giggling because it was such BS.
W: That would not have been a good thing.

By expressing her own doubts, they again find shared humor. Then the wife says that one thing she can say for the church is that it helped their neighbor's teenage daughter avoid trouble by joining the church's youth group. He agrees with her, and this is one program that he feels he can heartily participate in. The wife agrees, and they now feel that there is some basis for a compromise. Note that in this conversation softening and soothing were repeatedly offered, primarily by the wife, and the husband consistently accepted influence from her and genuinely tried to find some way of honoring her request without compromising the core of his own basic position.

To summarize the discussion so far, factors that predict divorce in the area of marital interactive behavior are:

- Low or negative "Dow-Jones" ratio of positivity to negativity,
- Harsh start-up,
- The presence of the Four Horsemen (criticism, defensiveness, contempt, and stonewalling),
- The failure of repair attempts,
- The husband's escalation via his unwillingness to accept influence from his wife,
- Pervasive emotional disengagement.

Interestingly, we discovered that negative affect reciprocity *in kind* (anger is met with anger, for example) appears to be characteristic of all marriages (the exception was stonewalling, which was characteristic only of unstable marriages). What did predict divorce was the wife's negative start-up, escalating to low-intensity negative affect, and then the husband's escalation, batting back any attempts she makes to influence him with her negative affect. In stable marriages, on the contrary, the husband de-escalates whatever low-intensity negative affect the wife expresses, but wives do not, and no one does so when the negativity escalates, even in happy marriages. This suggests that, for the most part, there is not much of a "brake" in most marriages once negativity begins.

The Regulation of Conflict, Not Its Resolution: Dialogue with Perpetual Problems

I contend that the current emphasis in marital therapy on problem-solving is greatly misplaced. We have now studied the stability of marital interactions over a four-year period and discovered remarkable stability in these interaction patterns, particularly in affect. In looking at the videotapes of most of the cases, it was as if the couple had changed clothes and hairstyle, while continuing to talk about the same or analogous issues in precisely the same ways. One thing I had never looked at was the *content* of the interaction. In classifying the discussions of these couples' major areas of continuing disagreement, we found that 69% of the time they were talking about a "perpetual problem" that they had had in their marriage for many, many years. These were problems that usually had to do with differences in personality or needs that were fundamental to their core definition of self. Only 31% of the discussions involved situationally specific problem-solving.

We discovered that, instead of *solving* these perpetual problems, what seems to be important is whether or not a couple can establish a *dialogue* with their perpetual problems. If they cannot establish such a dialogue, the conflict becomes *gridlocked,* and gridlocked conflict eventually leads to emotional disengagement. Hence, I think that *the goal of most of the therapy around problem-solving ought to be to help the couple move from a gridlocked conflict with a perpetual problem to a dialogue with the perpetual problem.* These are issues they continue to talk about, occasionally making some progress, or at least making the situation better for a short time, but then, after a while, the problem reemerges. In each case the marital discussion is an attempt to establish a dialogue with the problem, which, admittedly, will never go away or ever be fully resolved. The problem is like a chronic physical condition that one needs to adapt to, since it can never be cured. The dialogue is the adaptation to this persistent, perpetual problem.

When the problem is perpetual but gridlocked, the spouses have become entrenched in their positions, refusing to engage in any give and take (accept influence); they both feel hurt and there is vilification of one another. There is very little positive affect in these discussions, and some of the Four Horsemen are present. An example is one couple for whom the gridlocked issue was that he wanted to spend less time with her and more time with his buddies. She objected that what he does is go to bars every Saturday night with his buddies, usually topless bars, get drunk, and flirt with women. She felt very hurt and rejected by his wanting to do this. He viewed her objections as completely unacceptable. She was rejecting his personality, infringing on his freedom, and making him reject his loyal (if somewhat immature) friends.

Our findings suggest that people, including therapists, need to change their expectations about solving fundamental problems in an intimate relationship. We encourage couples to think of these relationship problems as inevitable, much the way we learn to deal with chronic physical ailments as we get older. The chronic back pain, the trick knee or tennis elbow or irritable bowel do not go away, but we learn to have a dialogue with these problems. We keep trying to make things a little better all the time, but we learn to live with these problems and manage our world so as to minimize them. We avoid doing things that provoke them. We learn how to see them coming early. We learn what to do when they occur, what medications to take, and so on. We develop a relationship, or a dialogue, with them. So it is in all relationships.

This is very much like something Dan Wile wrote in a book called *After the Fight*. He wrote that "choosing a partner is choosing a set of problems" (p. 12). He said that problems would be a part of any relationship, and that a particular person would have some set of problems no matter who that person married. Paul married Alice; Alice gets loud at parties and Paul, who is shy, hates that. But if Paul had married Susan, he and Susan would have gotten into a fight before they even got to the party. That's because Paul is always late and Susan hates to be kept waiting. She would feel taken for granted, which she is very sensitive about. Paul would see her complaining about this as her attempt to dominate him, which he is very sensitive about. If Paul had married Gail, they wouldn't have even gone to the party because they would still be upset about an argument they had the day before about Paul's not helping with the housework. To Gail when Paul does not help she feels abandoned, which she is sensitive about, and to Paul Gail's complaining is an attempt at domination, which he is sensitive about. The same is true about Alice. If she had married Steve, she would have the opposite problem, because Steve gets drunk at parties and she would get so angry at his drinking that they would get into a fight about it. If she had married Lou, she and Lou would have enjoyed the party but then when they got home the trouble would begin when Lou wanted sex, because he always wants sex when he wants to feel closer, but sex is something Alice only wants when she already feels close. Wile wrote: ". . . there is value, when choosing a long-term partner, in realizing that you will inevitably be choosing a particular set of unsolvable problems that you'll be grappling with for the next ten, twenty, or fifty years" (p. 13).

The goal of that part of our intervention that deals with problem-solving is not to try to get couples to resolve their problems, but to move the gridlocked perpetual problems to perpetual problems with which the couple has a dialogue. Only less than a third of their problems will have real solutions, and we teach the elements of effective problem-solving based on what we have learned about effective problem-solving on those issues that have a solution.

This is not so far-fetched. After all, does any one of us have a relationship, with siblings or friends, for instance, that is perfect? Probably not. Yet, after having a friend over for an evening we are unlikely to say anything like, "I was expecting far more intimacy and community tonight. This friendship is over!" Instead we have learned to accept our friends as they are, grateful for what they do offer us and accepting of their limitations.

There is a Woody Allen film in which he is searching for the perfect woman. He finds the perfect woman's body, but her brain is very limited, and he finds the perfect woman's brain, but the body is unattractive to him. So he gets a famous neurosurgeon to perform a delicate operation in which the brains are switched. He now has one woman with the perfect body and the perfect brain, and a second woman with an imperfect body and an imperfect brain. Then he proceeds to fall in love with the second woman!

What we have discovered in our research is that what is important is not solving the perpetual problem, but, rather, the affect that surrounds the discussion of the perpetual problem. Is there any positive affect at all during the conflict discussion? Or have the Four Horsemen taken over? Are partners gridlocked on this perpetual problem?

The Positive Affect Models

An aspect of marital interaction that has received scant attention is the role of positive affect (such as humor, affection, and interest) in predicting the eventual outcome of marriages. An exception is Birchler et al. (1975), who used a self-report diary measure of "pleases" and "displeases" (a precursor of the Spouse Observation Checklist, a version of the Marital Interaction Coding System) to code general conversation while the researchers were supposedly setting up the equipment and preparing for the Inventory of Marital Conflict discussion (Olson & Ryder, 1970).

In the summary-MICS code wording, the code called "positive" included: agreement, approval, humor, assent, laughter, positive physical contact, and smiling. Distressed couples produced an average of 1.49 positives per minute, while nondistressed couples produced an average of 1.93 positives per minute, a significant difference. In the home environment, distressed partners recorded significantly fewer pleasing and significantly greater displeasing events than was the case for nondistressed partners. The ratio of 29 pleases to 66 displeases also discriminated the nondistressed from the distressed (4 pleases to 30 displeases).

In our newlywed study we used an observational coding system that was able to provide considerably more detail than the system Birchler, Weiss, and Vincent had used. Using this system we discovered a remarkable thing: The number of seconds of positive affect (interest, humor, affection, and engaged listening) during timed interactions in the first few months of their marriage turned out to be a great predictor of whether the couple would eventually (six years later) be in one of three groups: divorced, together and miserable, or together and happy.

I was puzzled by the finding that the whole difference between the three groups of newlywed couples was, in each case, about *30 seconds of positive affect*. That is, in the first few months of marriage, out of 900 seconds of a conflict discussion, couples who eventually wound up happy and stable had 30 seconds more positive affect (interest, affection, humor, etc.) than couples who wound up unhappy and stable, and unhappy stable couples had 30 seconds more positive affect than couples who wound up divorced.

What was going on? Can 30 seconds make a huge difference in the ultimate fate of a couple? Thirty seconds of positivity a day amounts to about 100 positive words a day; multiplied by 365 days a year, this comes to 36,500 words—

enough to fill a book of poetry. Is the positivity systematic and functional, like a gardener planting a garden? Or is it like Johnny Appleseed, scattering his bounty at will?

The answer turned out to be (Gottman et al., 1998) that in marriages that work (wind up stable and happy)—and *only* in these marriages—positive affect was used with great precision in the service of de-escalating marital conflict and moving the overall affect from negative to a less negative (even a neutral) state. The de-escalation was also related to physiological soothing, usually self-soothing, but occasionally the wife soothing her husband with humor.

This result was important for designing interventions. You cannot tell a distressed couple to be more positive affectively. They just cannot do it on a consistent basis. People have tried to do this very thing. Behavior therapists suggested it in the use of "love days." However, distressed couples can do this only for a short time, and even then they do not notice most of their spouse's positivity. Now that we know that the positive affect is in the service of *de-escalating the conflict*, and that it is strongly related to *self-soothing*, we can try to alter these processes. Indeed, we find that when we do that, positive affect seems to increase naturally.

The Etiology of Dysfunction

Dysfunctional interactive patterns of behavior observed in the context of conflict resolution have their "origins"—in a bidirectional sense—in everyday *non*conflict marital interactions. Furthermore, patterns like that of demand-withdraw, in which females start up the conflict, have their etiology in male emotional withdrawal and anger in nonconflict contexts. These results suggest the hypothesis that, for meaningful and lasting change, marital therapy cannot focus only on the context of conflict resolution.

Still missing in the process of designing interventions based on empiricism is an answer to the question of *etiology:* That is, how do people get into dysfunctional patterns in the first place? It is well-known that women typically start most conflict discussions (Ball, Cowan, & Cowan, 1995; Oggins, Veroff, & Leber, 1993). It is also well-known that in distressed marriages there is a female-demand/male–withdraw pattern (Christensen, 1987, 1988, 1990; Christensen & Heavey, 1990; Cohen & Christensen, 1980). Even though this pattern characterizes all marriages, it becomes exacerbated when marriages are ailing. This gender pattern could be taken as blaming women for marital distress, unless it, too, has an etiology.

We designed a study that was uniquely able to address the etiology question. Bob Levenson and I asked couples to meet at the end of a day in our laboratory after being apart for at least eight hours. The first thing we asked them to do in the lab was to talk about how their day went. Then we asked them to engage in a second conversation in which they were to discuss an area of continuing disagreement in their marriage. The question Bob and I asked was, "Were negative patterns of interaction on the conflict conversation predictable from the events-of-the-day conversation?"

All major marital therapies focus on the conflict resolution and problem-solving context. The clinical assessment of marriages has become synonymous with the assessment of conflict resolution, and therapies have become oriented toward teaching couples more effective means for resolving their core conflicts. However, it could be the case that patterns of emotional behavior during everyday nonconflict situations, such as discussing the events of the day, could determine the significant predictors of divorce during conflict resolution. If this were the case, it might make sense for therapists to also explore modifying couples' affective interaction during less emotionally heated interaction situations, such as conversations about events of the day.

We compared the two conversations (nonconflict and conflict topics) and measured the amounts of positive and negative emotionality for husband and wife separately and then the total amounts per conversation. Positive affect was defined as the sum of expressions of humor, affection, interest, and joy. Negative affect was defined as the sum of expressions of anger, contempt/disgust, whining, sadness, and fear/tension. Neutral affect was excluded from these computations. Indeed, we found that the *husband's* affect in talking about the events of the day was critical in predicting the wife's affect during the same conversation, and even important in predicting the extent to which the couple showed the demand-withdraw pattern. It makes perfect sense that women would be more critical in trying to resolve conflicts when there are some basic things going wrong emotionally in the couple's everyday nonconflict interactions. This research showed that the answer to the question of etiology confirmed the view of marriage as a system, and it made the husband's role critical in predicting whether marriages function or dysfunction in the long term.

We also found that there was enormous consistency in the affect across the two conversations. Using my Specific Affect Coding System, the amount of positive and negative affect was computed for both conversations. For both husbands and wives, the correlation between positive and negative affect in the two conversations was significant and high. The highest correlation was obtained for overall amount of emotional behavior, with lower correlation for specific affects. The specific husband affects that were most consistent were humor, affection, interest, joy, anger, contempt/disgust, whining, and fear, but not sadness; the specific wife affects that were consistent were humor, anger, contempt/disgust, whining, and fear, but not affection, joy, or sadness.

It was also possible to develop regression models across the two conversations predicting the ratio of positive to negative affect on the conflict conversation from the same ratios for both spouses on the events-of-the-day conversations. This ratio during conflict was very useful in predicting divorce. Stable couples had a ratio of about five times as much positive as negative affect, while the comparable ratio for couples headed for divorce was .8. We found that, for both the husband and wife ratios of positive to negative affect in conflict, we could predict quite powerfully from the events-of-the-day ratio of positive to negative affect, accounting for between 25% and 50% of the variance.

We also examined the potential "etiology" of wives' negative affect during conflict interactions. The specific hypothesis we tested was whether the husband's *events-of-the-day* negative affect would predict the wife's *conflict* negative affect.

A partial correlation was clearly the appropriate test here: We found that the partial correlation of the husband's negative affect during the events-of-the-day conversation and the wife's negative affect during the conflict conversation was statistically significant. Even controlling for the predictability between the wife's negative affect in the conflict conversation from her immediately prior negative affect in the events-of-the-day conversation, the contribution of the husband's negative affect during the events-of-the-day conversation was significant. The following correlations (not controlling for wives' events-of-the-day levels) were significant predictors obtained from husband's *specific* negative affects in the events-of-the-day conversation and the wife's total negative affect in the conflict conversation: the husband's anger, the husband's disgust/contempt, and the husband's fear/tension.

We also found evidence that during the conflict discussion, the wife used more criticism than the husband, and the husband stonewalled more than the wife. This much was consistent with the Christensen demand-withdraw pattern. A variable was then created called "demand-withdraw." It was very interesting that this variable predicted the dichotomous variables of *both* early and late divorcing. So this is further evidence that the demand-withdraw pattern is indeed a dysfunctional one.

Thus, we found evidence for a wife-demand/husband-withdraw pattern during conflict resolution, and this pattern was predictive of both early and later divorcing. However, the results also suggest that there is a nonconflict etiology to these patterns. In particular, both the wife-demand/husband-withdraw pattern and the hypothesis that wives start marital conflict discussions and are more critical than husbands may be due to the husband's role in creating or maintaining this pattern. The women who did not begin conflict resolution discussions as negatively were those who were paired with men who were less angry and whiny during their nonconflict interactions. There was less wife-demand/husband-withdraw during conflict when there was more positive affect by both husbands and wives during the events-of-the-day conversation. *These patterns may be less a function of gender differences during conflict than a residual of how well the spouses connect affectively when conflict is not the topic of conversation.* This notion has lead to the development of a new component of marital therapy presented in Part III.

Our findings suggest that there are *setting conditions* for dysfunctional marital conflict resolution patterns, and that simply changing the way a couple resolves conflict will not be effective in creating lasting change. The all-too-common assumption among both troubled couples and therapists, that if the couple could just solve their problems they would be happy, is incorrect. If they could magically solve their problems, they would have nothing, only a void. Many distressed couples come together only in conflict. In nonconflict contexts they either do not know how, or choose not, to engage emotionally. The marital friendship has either deteriorated greatly, been neglected, or was never there in the first place. I believe that to obtain clinically significant and lasting change in the marriage, this aspect of the couple's world together must be a part of the marital therapy.

Violent Marriages

It is instructive to talk about violent marriages for two reasons. The first is that these marriages evidence an exaggeration of processes that are present in all marriages, particularly the processes of *influence/power* and *resistance to change.* These marriages display extreme one-way patterns of exerting power. My research with Neil Jacobson revealed that anger and its management are not the issue in violent marriages, but that the exertion of power is. The violent male will not accept influence from his wife, even when she makes very reasonable requests.

Second, in our clinical practices we must always assess for violence. It's at such a high base rate in the United States that we have to assume it could be present in any couple who comes for treatment. There are two ways to do this. First, use the Conflict Tactics Scale and the Waltz-Rushe-Gottman Emotional Abuse Questionairre in Appendix A. Second, interview the husband and wife separately. There is no way around this one. Women in violent couples have a lot of fear and shame. One statistic, which has been minimized or avoided, is: In 71% of all violent fights, the woman engages in the first physically violent act (for a review of this amazing fact, see Dutton, 1988, 1995a,b). This is a very politicized area. Women tend to reciprocate violence and it cannot be attributed merely to self-defense. We need to realize that the helpless battered woman's syndrome Lenore Walker (1984) described is not typical at all. Also, there is the "Bonnie and Clyde" type of marriage where *both* people tend to be antisocial. Despite this statistic, it is only men who use violence to systematically terrorize, control, and subdue their wives. Battering is not simply the use of violence, but its use in the service of control, intimidation, and domination.

Neil Jacobson and I identified two categories of violent men (Jacobson & Gottman, 1998) initially discriminated by differing physiological patterns: From the baseline to the start of the conflict discussion, type-1 husbands showed decreased heart rates, and type-2 showed increased heart rates. This basic distinction turned out to be associated with many others: Type-1 men were more likely to use a knife or a gun when threatening their wives, while type-2 men used their fists. Type-1 men were also violent with friends, coworkers, and family, while the type-2 men were not. Type-1 started the marital discussion by being immediately belligerent, defensive, contemptuous, and intimidating, while type-2 showed more of a "slow burn" or buildup of these patterns. The men who *looked like* they were going to burst an artery (type-1) had the calmer physiology.

When we examined the type of control and intimidation practiced by the two kinds of men, they were also very different. The type-1 men encouraged their wives to be independent; what drove them crazy were reasonable attempts by their wives to control their actions. Type-2 men tended to isolate their wives socially, act very jealous, and control their wives by using a domineering pattern we call "gaslighting." This pattern comes from the film *Gaslight,* in which Charles Boyer tries to convince his bride, Ingrid Bergman, that she is crazy. This type of mind control is very common among type-2 men. By the way, violent men hardly ever stonewall. They are fully engaged in vigilant and controlling behavior.

After two years we checked on the status of the marriages of the two types of men. The divorce/separation rate was 38% for the type-2 men and 0% for the type-1. Women were not divorcing the type-1 husbands. Recently, we had two successful divorces in this group; *successful* here means no homicides.

In all these cases the male refuses to accept influence from the wife, even when reasonable requests are made. Note that this is not an issue of anger management but of avoiding the loss of control. There is also the issue of what could be called the male "honor culture," in which some men see it as a loss of face to accept influence from a woman. Furthermore, it seems that the type-2 male is responding to a fear of abandonment, whereas the type-1 male is responding to a fear of being controlled. These two fears engender very different patterns of intimidation and abuse.

Type-2 Violent Male and His Wife

This case involves a type-2 man who is very jealous and possessive and has tremendous fears of abandonment. He attempts to isolate his wife and control her every move. He is not usually violent outside the marriage. He operates on a "slow burn" pattern in which his physiological arousal escalates as he increases his expressions of contempt, defensiveness, and belligerence. His style of controlling his wife is particularly insidious. He attempts to redefine reality for her, so that she will come to rely on him for knowing how *she* feels.

> W: I could never have imagined in my wildest dreams this scenario, that this would be the end of my marriage, to be sitting here, like this, all wired up [*chokes up, crying*]. Pretty sad, huh?
>
> H: Yeah, it is. So, you go ahead.
>
> W: Communication?
>
> H: Uh-huh.
>
> W: Well, like I said before, it's the hardest part of marriage, and I think that's the key with any marriage is people have to be able to talk without escalating, without you, either person . . .
>
> H: . . . okay, okay . . .
>
> W: . . . attacking for the least little . . .

That's as much as this husband can tolerate before taking over the reins of control. He now steps in.

> H: Okay. Hold it. We *do* do that and we did that last night. We did talk calmly up to a certain point, okay? And then it started escalating. Why? We took different stands. You said, "This is the way I believe," and I said, "This is the way I believe." And at that point, like I said, like we've always said, it has to be cut there. Okay? People can't . . . obviously can't get along, don't belong with each other. Okay? If people oppose each other on basic philosophies on how to relate to another person, as we do, then of course it's going to escalate and get violent if we force each other to do that. How do you feel about what I just said?

Notice that this was a very long statement, kind of like a lecture. He concludes that if people disagree and take different basic stands, things have got to get violent, and he wants her to agree with this. Notice that she says something very general about respect.

> W: I really feel that you can both . . . there should be a certain amount of respect where, you know, if you can't communicate and just be open with somebody . . . it's not that we're just opposing . . .

He cannot even let her have this general point about the importance of respect. Next he uses the gaslighting tactic of "lowballing," which is designed to make her statement about respect sound preposterous.

> H: We do. That's what we did, okay? And, no, you don't have to respect somebody. If you believe in molesting children, I don't respect that. I don't respect your viewpoints. I don't respect the things you say and try to defend. That's my right. Okay?
>
> W: But it's not like we're talking about . . . each time we try to talk, we're not talking about really major crimes that we've done. We're talking about interpersonal relationships . . .

He cannot let her have even this much influence on him by acknowledging her point that respect is important in a marriage.

> H: They're major to me. They're primary to me.
>
> W: I'm saying that . . . to compare it to something that bad . . . I mean, I know it's bad but it's not like . . . we should at least be able to discuss . . .
>
> H: We don't have to get into the levels of how bad it is. The point I was making is that if you think a certain way that goes against everything I believe in, that's the point. Nobody respects somebody. . . . You wouldn't respect me if I believed in molesting children, okay?
>
> W: But what if it's a matter of, just that I would handle a situation differently than you and you feel that I'm wrong. But who's to judge? What I'm saying is, why do you judge . . .

She then brings up the argument they had the preceding night about her not noticing that there was something wrong with the car. Notice the patronizing way he begins:

> H: Okay, but another problem is that . . . what is another problem about that that upset me?
>
> W: Well, that's the first thing I said and you got mad and called me stupid.
>
> H: But *why* would I get mad? *Why* would I call you stupid? *Why* would I get mad?
>
> W: Because I didn't notice anything different, or because . . .
>
> H: That's one part of it, but I can deal with that. It wouldn't cause me much anger. What other things would cause me to react like that and become angry?

W: Well, you obviously felt that I wasn't being sensitive to you.

H: Right.

This was the right answer, obviously an oft-rehearsed one on her part.

W: You called me stupid for my answer.

H: Yes, I did call you that, but the point is, I gave you the chance for empathy and for caring. It wasn't there, okay? At that point, then I get angry for all the reasons since mentioned, because it was a stupid thing for you to do, and that starts to make me angry at that point because you're thumbing your nose at me. "I couldn't care less about it, don't ask me about these things, I don't want to hear about it." Your attitude. Your lack of empathy. I've told you, this is the truth. My God. That's all I ask for. You could walk all over me, you could use me in any kind of way you wanted. I've told you this before. That's all, that's all you have to do. That's all you have to do.

She then tries to explain how she reacts when she is called stupid.

W: When somebody calls me stupid, that pretty much kills a lot of stuff right there. I think that would kill a lot of stuff in you, you know?

H: Yes, I would agree.

W: If I had answered back to you like that . . .

H: Not necessarily. If somebody calls me stupid and I've *done* something stupid, I care about that. I want to know, am I stupid? Have I done something stupid? The fact of the matter is, if that was me in your situation, I'd go, "God, that is stupid, isn't it? Ha, ha, ha, what a dummy. You must think I'm a dummy."

He is telling her that her feelings about being insulted are crazy and that *he* would think about learning to become better if he were called stupid. In this way he is challenging her very perceptions of reality and her right to have feelings in reaction to his insults.

In this excerpt we see the type-2 male gaslighting the female. He starts off being sad about this "joke" of his marriage ending with him "all wired up," referring to our physiological monitoring equipment. But notice that when the wife brings up how important respect is, the gaslighting starts. He says, "You don't have to respect somebody." He begins attacking her notions of what is real. He says in effect, "There's no reality with you. You change things." But then he tells her that he was upset about their conversation last night because she was not empathic toward him. She says that it is hard for her to be empathic when he calls her stupid. Then when she protests that she cannot be sensitive to him if she is being insulted, he disagrees with even this perception of reality. He says, "If somebody calls me stupid . . . I want to know, am I stupid?"

Type-1 Violent Male and His Wife

This couple met just after they had both been released from prison. He was in prison for second-degree murder and she for child abuse. They decided to live together immediately, and were soon married. Both have a history of abuse in their backgrounds. He enjoyed scaring our research assistant. When asked what his occupation was, he said, "I'm a burglar and me and my friend, who does the burglary with me, are usually armed."

In this example we see his immediate use of belligerence, contempt, and intimidation. This is very typical of an "in your face" style of intimidation. He accuses his wife of having a bad attitude, and does it in a threatening manner, after she has expressed a desire for better communication between them:

H: Would I be wrong in thinking you have an attitude?

When she says no, he does a very strange nonverbal act that he repeats throughout this interaction: moving his head very rapidly toward her and then suddenly inhaling and smiling. It is as if he is feigning an attack, and then saying, "just kidding."

W: Okay. Why *don't* we communicate?
H: Because you only hear what you want. And you change everything I say. [*sudden glare*] Don't interrupt me. [*pause*] Okay?

This sudden "don't interrupt me" was said in a very threatening manner. Most people watching this part of the videotape find even this brief threat quite terrifying.

W: Wasn't going to.
H: Same old, same old. For four years I've been telling you that you only hear what you want, and if it ain't what you want to hear, you twist it around to make it what you want.
W: But why do I do that?
H: I have no idea. I'm not you.

He then withdrew from the conversation. After a pause the wife began.

W: What about all the times when I ask you, "Is this what I heard, is this what it means?" And all I ever get out of you is, "If that's what you heard, I guess that's what it means." And then you turn around and tell me I'm wrong.
H: Because when I tell you, "No, that is not what I mean, this is what I mean," you can't accept it.
W: Yes, I can, but you never tell me. You just tell me, "If that's what you hear, then I guess that's what I said."
H: As usual, you're right, I'm wrong.
W: No. I'm not saying I'm right. I'm not saying I'm wrong. I'm not saying you're right, I'm not saying you're wrong. If you don't tell me whether what I'm hearing is what you're saying, I don't know. If you tell me that what I heard is what you said, then what am I supposed to think?
H: Think whatever you want. It's what you're going to do anyway.
W: No.
H: Yes.

W: No. When you explain things to me, Michael, that no, that's not . . . yes, sometimes I go off in left field and then I stop and think, *yeah, you're right and I was wrong,* and I come and tell you that, and then you start, no, no.

There is an enormous amount of tension in this very confusing dialogue. After a long pause, the husband begins again.

H: Well, let's try this for a little communication here. Uh, this morning we had to talk. I remember hearing one person say what they had to say about what they thought about, what they were trying to do. I didn't hear anything out of you.

W: Yesterday you said, "Let's go in the room and talk." We spent 45 minutes in there, and you said maybe five minutes worth of conversation. It's the same thing. And yes, I gave you input. You asked me this morning what I thought about whether you should go for this interview tomorrow, whether you should stick with the job you've got . . .

H: Whoa whoa, let's stop right there. I'm talking about *yesterday* when we had our little fucking argument . . .

W: Yeah.

H: And I walked out to go to work. I told you to think about three fucking things, right?

W: You told me think about things that might help.

H: Uh-huh.

W: You told me to think about separating and you told me to think about seeing a lawyer and I told you I had, and you told me I hadn't, so, hey, I guess, you know? I guess I don't know what I thought.

H: Somehow you missed my point.

W: Well, explain.

H: The point is that I'd like to know what the hell you came up with. You insisted on knowing what I came up with this morning.

W: What did I come up with? I told you that this morning.

Here is an unusual moment in the interaction of a wife with her type-1 abuser. She has become confrontive. This is a very dangerous transaction.

H: Whoa, where was I?

W: You were sitting in front of me. Obviously, you weren't listening.

Once again she has dared to confront him, and he then becomes very threatening, raising his voice and glaring at her.

H: Obviously you're full of shit.

W: No.

H: Yes.

She keeps trying to be reasonable, daring more and more in the interaction to confront him with their communication problem, hoping to get him to accept some responsibility for it. He periodically flares up and escalates the negativity, and then acts as if, with great restraint he is controlling his aggression and quieting down. This pattern of flaring up and self-restraint is very effective at stifling her expressions of anger and is very typical of type-1 men.

Summary on Interactive Behavior

In marriages headed for divorce, look for the following patterns of interactive behavior that characterize "dysfunctional" relating between partners:

- During the discussion of an area of continuing disagreement, there is more negativity than positivity. In marriages that will wind up stable, the ratio of positivity to negativity during conflict resolution is about 5 to 1; the balance of positivity to negativity is overwhelmingly in favor of positivity, even during the conflict discussion.
- Four negative behaviors, the Four Horsemen of the Apocalypse, are most corrosive: criticism, defensiveness, contempt, and stonewalling. Emotional disengagement, the presence of underlying tension and sadness, and the absence of positive affect are also predictive of divorce.
- The conflict on "perpetual issues" in the marriage is "gridlocked" or characterized by emotional disengagement rather than dialogue.
- Repair attempts fail.
- There is harsh start-up of conflict discussions (usually by the wife, but the etiology of this harshness is in a nonresponsive husband during nonconflict conversations).
- There is repeated refusal by the husband to accept influence from his wife.
- There is an absence of de-escalation attempts.
- There is little positive affect (interest, affection, humor) expressed.

In the next section we will discuss perception, the second element in the core triad of balance.

THE CORE TRIAD OF BALANCE: PERCEPTION

How spouses in both happy and unhappy marriages perceive and interpret positive and negative actions of one another is revealing and instructive. In a happy marriage, if one spouse does something negative, the other tends to evaluate the negativity as fleeting and situational. For example, the thought might be something like, *Oh well, he is in a bad mood. He has been under a lot of stress lately and needs more sleep.* The negativity is viewed as unstable (highly alterable, fluctuating), and the cause is viewed as situational (external). On the other hand, in an unhappy marriage, the same behavior is likely to be interpreted as stable (enduring, unchanging) and internal to the partner. The accompanying thought might be something like, *He is inconsiderate and selfish. That's the way he is. That's why he did that.*

In a happy marriage, if the spouse does something positive, the behavior is likely to be interpreted as stable and internal to the partner. The accompanying thought might be something like, *He is a considerate and loving person. That's the way he is. That's why he did that.* On the other hand, in an unhappy marriage, the same positive behavior is likely to be seen as fleeting and situational. The accompanying thought might be something like, *Oh well, he's being nice because he's been successful this week at work. It won't last and it doesn't mean much.* So the positivity is viewed as unstable, and the cause is viewed as situational (external and fleeting).

Putting perception together with interactive behavior was pioneered by an amazingly innovative paper by Notarius, Benson, Sloane, Vanzetti, and Hornyak (1989). We have followed their lead.

The Subtext

In the Woody Allen film *Annie Hall,* a man and a woman who have just met are talking and subtitles appear on the screen to tell the viewer what they are *actually* thinking and feeling at the time. Woody Allen makes some very intellectual comment about photography when he sees her photographs and the subtitle is "I wonder what she looks like without clothes on." That's the idea of the subtext. It is what people are actually thinking and feeling at the time.

Psychologists dating back to Osgood and colleagues have learned that this subtext is actually quite basic. Most of the variance in people's experiences of social interaction is in the *evaluation* component (Osgood, Suci, & Tannenbaum, 1957), and it is fairly either/or: They report *either* feeling fine or feeling bad (threatened or angry). There is evidence that people only start processing information in a complex manner if something very negative and unexpected occurs. Then they have to stop and figure things out.

In our lab, couples view their videotapes and rate their interactions. There is a portable screen placed between the spouses so that they cannot affect one another during the rating. In an innovation of this video recall procedure designed by Bob Levenson, spouses view the videotape a second time and attempt to guess how their spouse would have rated it. Levenson and Ruef (1992) discovered that people who are accurate raters of others' emotions relive those people's physiological responses while they are rating them.

The rating dial is then synchronized to the video time code of the interaction and to their physiological responses as they view the tape. An interaction is quantified as $+1$ if the person is in a state of well-being and -1 if he or she is in a state of disquiet that moves toward distress. Let's see how our rating system works in an actual conversation, in which the wife's issue is jealousy (P = perception).

> H: Well, the issue is your jealousy.
> W: Which has gotten a lot better lately.
> [P = +1. Nonverbally she reflects a sense of well-being.]
> H: Yes, it has. Since I made a commitment to my family, it has gotten better. Now if you saw me driving in my car with a woman during the day, you wouldn't get jealous probably.

W: Why? Is there a woman in your car?
[P = −1. She sounds a bit alarmed, but not very much.]

At this point in the conversation the wife is calm and relaxed. Her rating dial perception fits her low level of physiological arousal.

H: No [*laughs*].
W: Good [*smiles*].
[P = +1. She is relieved.]
H: Actually, Laura Neville and I are going to ride together to a workshop.
W: A workshop? What about?
[P = +1. She is asking for information in a neutral manner.]
H: Commercial real estate. It's business.
W: Oh. No, I wouldn't be jealous of that because I know it's purely professional.
[P = +1. She is quite calm.]
H: You know, it does bother me though, just for a hypothetical, that, say, I wanted to see Jeannie again, just say for lunch, you know.
W: No, that's . . . Jeannie is a different story. You were lovers.

Here she is still rating the interaction as somewhat positive, but we can hear (on the tape) some alarm in her voice. She is starting to drift to an in-between zone where there is a higher probability that she may shift to a rating of −1.

H: But that was way before I met you. And you know that I have made a commitment to our family. It is just not an issue. It's like seeing an old chum.
W: It doesn't matter. That's a very different kind of relationship. She simply has no place in our lives. It's not like a chum. She's a woman.
[P = +1. She accepts this as a hypothetical discussion and is relaxed talking about it, giving her views.]
H: See, that's where I think you're wrong. She's a person that I once liked a lot and it's a shame to lose touch with her. As a friend. As an acquaintance.
W: Why should she come into our lives, into our home? Why should my children know her?

Now her rating dial is definitely negative (P = −1), and there is a clear alarm in her voice. Her heart rate has now exceeded 100 beats a minute, and she is headed for what we call "diffuse physiological arousal" (DPA). Her face looks quite distressed.

H: She's very interesting, you know. You both went to the same college. You'd have a lot in common.
W: Wait a minute! Do you want to see her? Is that what you are saying?
[Now P = −1. She looks and sounds fearful. Her heart rate is now well over 100 beats a minute.]
H: Yes, I would. Why not? I'd like to find out how she's doing, talk to her again. Yes.

W: Then I think we have a serious problem. We need counseling.
[P = −1. She has clearly left the region of well-being and may be on the
   verge of a flooded reaction.]
H: Well, maybe we do.

Attributions: Relationship-Enhancing or Distress-Maintaining

As more and more interactions contain a subtext of alarm, people's perceptions undergo a gradual and subtle shift so that eventually the subtext is perceived as involving far more than just this particular interaction. It becomes more global. This "fundamental attribution error," whereby each spouse sees the marital problems as residing in a defective character trait of the partner, becomes the most common presenting complaint in marital therapy. Each partner brings to the therapist the defective spouse and says, in effect, "Fix this person and I will be happy. I will show you in our session today the character flaw in my partner that is ruining our marriage. Then you will see what I have had to live with and feel the same tremendous sympathy for me that I feel."

Holtzworth-Monroe and Jacobson (1985) used indirect questions to investigate when couples "naturally" search for causes of events and what they conclude when they locate these causes. They found evidence for the hypothesis that distressed couples engage in more attributional activity than nondistressed couples, and that attributional thoughts primarily surrounded negative impact events. Nondistressed couples engaged in "relationship-enhancing" attributions that minimize the impact of negative behaviors of the partner and maximize the impact of positive ones; distressed couples engaged in "distress-maintaining" attributions that maximize the impact of the partner's negativity and minimize the impact of his or her positivity. Moreover, *distressed husbands generated more distress-maintaining attributions than nondistressed husbands, but the two groups of wives did not differ. The researchers suggested that males may not normally engage in much attributional activity, but that they outstrip women once relationship conflict develops.*

In an experimental study by Holtzworth-Munroe et al. (1989), distressed and nondistressed couples were randomly assigned instructions to "act positive" or to "act negative." They found that distressed couples were likely to attribute their partner's negative behavior to internal factors, whereas nondistressed couples were likely to attribute their partner's positive behavior to internal factors. These attributional patterns, once established, make change less likely to occur. Behaviors that should disconfirm the attributional sets tend to get ignored, while behaviors that confirm the attributions receive attention.

Attributional processes may tap the way couples think in general about the marital interaction as it unfolds in time. Berley and Jacobson (1984) noted that Watzlawick et al. (1967) were talking about attributional processes when they discussed the "punctuation fallacy," i.e., each spouse views himself or herself as the victim of the partner's behavior, which is seen as the causal stimulus. Attributions and general thought patterns about negative behaviors thus may be theoretically useful in providing a link between the immediate patterns of activity seen in behavioral interaction and physiological response, on the one hand, and more long-lasting and global patterns that span longer time periods, on the other. Indeed, these more stable aspects of the marriage are better predictors of long-term outcomes such as divorce than the factors ascertained from behavioral observation.

The dimensions of negative attributions that have been studied include *locus* (whether they are directed at partner, self, relationship, or outside events), *stability* (e.g., enduring, because they are due to partner's trait, or fluctuating, because they are situationally determined), *range* (the number of areas of the marriage affected), *intentionality* (whether the attributions are selfishly or unselfishly motivated), *controllability* (whether the partner has control of making the attributions), *volition* (whether the attributional act is a conscious choice or not), and *responsibility* (e.g., how much blame is attached to the attribution). Fincham, Bradbury, and Scott (1990) reviewed experimental evidence for these dimensions and concluded that, by and large, they have been well established by research. For attributions about negative events, all of the studies reviewed supported significant differences between happily and unhappily married couples on the two dimensions of range and intentionality. In my view it is the reliability of the significance of attributional processes that leads to the strong correlations among self-report measurements of the quality of a marriage.

Narratives Engraved in Stone

In our Oral History Interview (see Appendix C) we ask couples to describe how they met and to talk about the various periods in their relationship; we also ask them about how they view their parents' marriages and their philosophy of marriage, mining their long-lasting perceptions of their relationship and the stories they tell to reflect those perceptions When marital relationships are distressed, the subtext and negative attributions become reified in the stories or *narratives* couples tell themselves. This reification process is tapped in our laboratory by our Oral History Interview. The subtext provides an entry into the *immediate* perception of the interaction. When these subtextual thoughts become habitual, altered conceptions of the marriage and the partner coalesce and attributions slowly change. When they are apart, partners (particularly husbands) rehearse distress-maintaining attributions. Slowly the narratives—and with them the metaphors, symbols, and myths—about the marriage change. The story of the honeymoon will be cast in the minds of one or both partners. For example, a husband may say to himself, "I should have seen these signs earlier. There was something weird that happened on our honeymoon. We ran into this male friend of hers and she didn't introduce me. I thought nothing of it at the time, but then after the honeymoon she was distant and tense."

The Distance and Isolation Cascade

This process of changing perceptions and creating engraved narratives happens in the context of what we call the Distance and Isolation Cascade (see Figure 2.8), which is characterized by *flooding, seeing problems as severe, thinking it is best to work out problems alone, adapting to parallel lives, and, finally, loneliness.*

DISTANCE AND ISOLATION CASCADE

FLOODING

PROBLEMS SEEN AS SEVERE

BEST TO WORK PROBLEMS OUT ALONE

PARALLEL LIVES

LONELINESS

Figure 2.8   The Distance and Isolation Cascade describes how the immediate perceptions of negativity are transformed to create negative and lasting narratives of a relationship's decay.

Later, in the throes of divorce, an "account" of why the marriage fell apart is created by each ex-partner, and, needless to say, the two accounts may not match (Weiss, 1980).

The first element in the cascade is *flooding*. In Ekman's (1984) concept of flooding, one emotion or a set of emotions becomes so averse and so prominent that it takes over the emotional world of the person. In essence, a person becomes shell-shocked by the way his or her partner is expressing negative emotions and reactions. Flooded partners might say that they feel "overwhelmed" by the onslaught, that it "comes out of nowhere," that they "would do anything to stop it." They become hypervigilant for cues that this negativity might be in the offing. The perceptual disorganization caused by flooding renders them vulnerable to "hair-trigger" reactivity, further intensifying their conviction that they will get nowhere by talking things over with their spouse. This is a major step in turning away from the marriage and creating parallel lives by arranging household schedules so that they don't intersect very much anymore. Partners eat together less and spend less "down" time together; they work more and socialize (if at all) separately. Loneliness is the inevitable outcome. This is particularly true for men, whose social support systems outside the marriage are usually minimal. Loneliness increases one's vulnerability to relationships outside the marriage, and probably affects what Thibaut and Kelly (1969) called "CL-ALT," the comparison level for alternative relationships. When the marriage is a happy one, other potential relationships don't look too good, or they seem unduly risky and costly. If the marriage is ailing, other relationships start looking *good.*

The Marital "Poop Detector"

There is another important dimension of perception that we have recently discovered through our mathematical modeling of marital interactions. We found that, in our "influence functions," the threshold for negativity is set lower for newlywed couples whose marriages develop as stable and happy. This is the point in the influence function when negativity starts to have an effect on one's partner's next actions. This was only true for husbands, which means that it is really a "wife effect." In marriages that wind up happy and stable, newlywed wives notice lower levels of negativity. I call this effect the marital "poop detector": These wives have a negative response to lower levels of negativity from their husbands. In other marriages wives adapt to and try to accept this negativity, setting their threshold for response at a much higher (more negative) level. It's as if they are saying to themselves, "Just ignore this negativity. Don't respond to it unless it gets much worse." Our research shows that this kind of adaptation to negativity is dysfunctional (Gottman, Swanson, Murray, Tyson, & Swanson, in press).

This finding might explain two mysteries. The first is the fact that people delay a very long time in getting help for an ailing marriage (Buongiorno & Notarius, 1992). Our own finding suggests that people delay getting help because they have systematically raised their negativity thresholds, thereby making it seem as if help is not needed. Our finding also suggests that wives in ailing marriages play a key role in fostering the delaying process by *adapting* to their husbands' negativity. In marriages that work, wives don't make these adaptations. Our interviews with couples suggest that wives who do not adapt to negativity bring up the issue about which they are unhappy fairly quickly, within days of things becoming negative. This is an example of longer-term repair. The advice in Ephesians, "Don't let the sun set on your wrath," is usually taken to mean, "Don't go to bed angry. Always kiss and make up." So the key to avoiding decay in marriages is probably to help couples reset their marital poop detector to lower levels of negativity and teach them ways to do repair on a continuing basis.

The finding about the threshold for negativity also suggests the hypothesis that partners in marital therapy relapse after initial therapeutic gains because the therapy has temporarily affected the levels of positivity and negativity in the marriage, but *it has not reset the negativity threshold.* We suggest that this should be one of the goals of any marital therapy: resetting the marital poop detector so that couples can make repairs as needed.

THE CORE TRIAD OF BALANCE: PHYSIOLOGY

Diffuse Physiological Arousal and Marital Prediction

Physiology can also help us predict what will happen to a marriage. In the body, as well as in interactive behavior and perception, there is a balance between positivity and negativity that is mediated by the two branches of the autonomic nervous system: the sympathetic and the parasympathetic. While it is a bit of an oversimplification, the sympathetic branch is primarily responsible for activating the body to respond to emergency situations, while the parasympathetic branch is responsible for restoring calm in the body.

The most important predictive concept is that of *diffuse physiological arousal* (DPA), which is the body's general alarm mechanism, inherited from our hominid ancestors, who developed it through evolutionary means. This is a *diffuse* physiological arousal because many systems are simultaneously activated to mobilize the body, so that we can cope effectively with emergencies and situations perceived to be dangerous. The general alarm mechanism is mediated by the sympathetic branch of the autonomic nervous system, which signals the adrenal medulla to secrete the catecholamines (dopamine, norepinephrine, and epinephrine), and activates the *hypothalamic-pituitary-adrenocortical axis* to produce cortisol (see Gunnar, Connors, Isensee, & Wall, 1988; Kagan, Reznick, & Snidman, 1988).

The accelerating functions of the sympathetic nervous system are typically measured by heart rate reactivity or stress-related endocrine responses. When danger is perceived, a series of alterations is immediately initiated, starting with the inhibition of the vagus nerve, which rapidly releases the parasympathetic "brake" on the heart so that the heart speeds up. When the heart speeds up to beyond 100 beats per minute (bpm), its "intrinsic" pacemaker rhythm, the body starts secreting epinephrine, which is made by the inner part (medulla) of the adrenal glands that sit on top of the kidneys. Now the heart increases its contractility as well as its rate, and blood flow to the gut and kidneys is shut down. The peripheral arteries constrict and blood is drawn in from the periphery to the trunk to minimize the potential damage to the body from hemorrhage. The kidneys activate the renin-angiotensin system, which increases blood pressure and attempts to conserve fluid volume, again in the event of hemorrhage. The limbic system (particularly the amygdala, hypothalamus, cigulate gyrus, hippocampus, and prefrontal lobes) has been activated (see Fuster, 1989; LeDoux, 1997). The liver converts glycogen into glucose and sends this fuel into the bloodstream. Blood flow to the brain is maintained. Fight or flight reactions become more likely as the cortex is engaged to evaluate the stimulus conditions, so that the associative cortex can mount a plan for coordinated action. The attentional system becomes a vigilance system, detecting only cues of danger, and at this point is severely limited in its ability to process other information.

These are the processes that are catalyzed when we narrowly avert a car accident, for example. Perhaps it is surprising to learn that all these extreme physiological alterations also can *and do* happen during marital conflict. When this is the case—that is, when marital conflict gives rise to DPA—the psychological consequences are quite negative. In the short run couples experience a reduced ability to process information, for it is harder to attend to what the other is saying. Even in the best marriages it is hard to listen during DPA-laden circumstances. There is less access to new learning and greater access to habitual behaviors and cognitions. That is why fight/flight responses become more accessible and creative problem-solving goes out the window.

Among couples whose marriages eventually ended in divorce, husbands in our lab had heart rates 17 bpm higher than husbands in stable marriages (even in our "close eyes and relax" condition), and wives in doomed marriages had faster flowing blood, with greater evidence of the general alarm reaction. Malarkey, Kiecolt-Glaser, Pearl, and Glaser (1994) took blood from 40 newlywed couples as they discussed an area of conflict. Couples were divided into two groups based on the amount of the time they exhibited the Four Horsemen. The couples spent 24 hours in a clinical care center of a hospital for this study; using in-dwelling catheters, a nurse behind a screen periodically took very small samples of their blood as they talked. The blood was later assayed for epinephrine and other stress-related hormones. To assess recovery, a blood sample was also taken a half-hour after the conversation. They found that negative marital interaction codes (on the Marital Interaction Coding System—MICS) were related to a greater secretion of epinephrine and other stress-related hormones in these newlywed couples. Also, there was far less recovery from these stress-related hormones a half-hour later. Figure 2.9 illustrates these dramatic results.

This graph of the two groups of couples (high and low negativity ratings) shows the couples' average epinephrine secretion by time. At time-1, immediately prior to the conflict conversation, there are no significant differences between groups. By time-2, early in the conversation, the high-negative group is secreting more epinephrine than the low-negative group. The high-negative group shows an increasing slope over time. The time-by-group interaction was statistically significant. Time-4 is a recovery period a half-hour after the interaction ended. There are still significant differences between groups at this time point, showing far longer recovery for the high-negative group.

Marital conflict appears to be ideally suited for generating this kind of diffuse physiological activation. Later I will review what appears to be the minimum psychological state necessary to accomplish this feat, when I discuss the Henry-Stephens model.

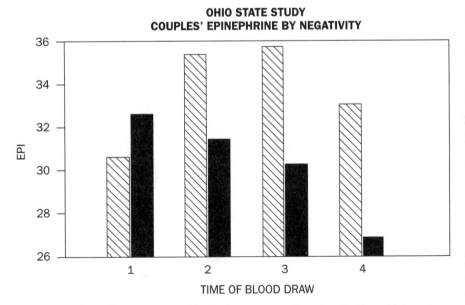

OHIO STATE STUDY
COUPLES' EPINEPHRINE BY NEGATIVITY

TIME OF BLOOD DRAW

Figure 2.9 Epinephrine in the blood of two groups of newlyweds, those high on the Four Horsemen (striped) and those low (solid).

Vagal Tone and Emotional Regulation

The *parasympathetic* branch (and its major nerve, the vagus, located on the brain stem) innervates all the same organs affected by the sympathetic nervous system but "antagonistically," to slow things down, restore calm, and refocus attention. It also innervates the thymus gland, which matures the immune system's t-cells. Research by Steve Porges and his colleagues (1994) at the University of Maryland on the parasympathetic nervous system revealed a strong association between high vagal tone and good attentional abilities, and there is evidence that these processes are related to emotional regulation abilities. Evidence for this contention has come from various sources (e.g., Fox, 1989; Fox & Field, 1989).

Mirsky (Mirsky, 1996; Mirsky et al., 1991) presented an empirically-based model identifying the elements of attention, which he and his colleagues tested with factor analysis. There were three major factors: (1) a factor for focusing attention and acting, (2) a factor related to shifting attention, and (3) a factor related to sustaining attention. In general, while high vagal tone is important in *focusing* attention, the ability to suppress vagal tone is important for engagement with more complex social or cognitive tasks. Vagal tone is suppressed during states that require highly focused or sustained attention, mental effort, focusing on relevant information, and organizational responses to stress. This is true independent of context; that is, we may assess this construct in either cognitive or social tasks (Huffman, Bryan, Pederson, & Porges, 1992). Research on the sympathetic nervous system indicates that endocrine secretion of catecholamines and cardiovascular reactivity are related to attention, behavior, and resiliency by directing the allocation of these attentional resources.

Perhaps even more fundamental to emotional regulation are *attentional processes* (both the ability to *sustain* and to *shift* attention). Attentional fluctuations appear to be lead indicators of a wide range of psychopathologies driven by aggression, depression, and anxiety. Attention is the first thing to go when powerful destructive forces, such as chronic marital stress, are operating in the environment.

Porges (1994) reviewed evidence that suggests that *baseline vagal tone* is related to the capacity to react and to self-regulate. Porges' research in the early 1970s (Porges, 1972, 1973; Porges, Arnold, & Forbes, 1973) demonstrated a link between heart rate reactivity and spontaneous base-level heart rate variability. Initially, he demonstrated that, among college students, baseline heart rate *variability* was related to heart rate reactivity and reaction time (higher variability was related to faster reaction times). This research was then extended to measuring newborn infants' heart rate variability and their reaction to simple visual and auditory stimuli (Porter, Porges, & Marshall, 1988). They found that newborns with greater heart rate variability had shorter latency responses, and only the infants with high heart rate variability responded to the stimuli as the illumination was lowered. Because heart rate variability is related to many factors other than the functioning of the vagus nerve (respiratory, blood pressure changes, thermoregulatory influences), Porges and his colleagues developed a more precise measure of vagal functioning by using only that portion of heart rate variability that is related to respiration (known as respiratory sinus arrhythmia). It is well known that heart rate increases when we inhale and decreases when we exhale. This pattern induces a rhythmic respiratory component into heart rate variability, which can be extracted statistically with methods known as time-series analysis (e.g., Gottman, 1981; Williams & Gottman, 1981).

Porter et al. (1988) showed that baseline vagal tone is related to the ability to react as well as to regulatory processes. During circumcision, infants with a higher vagal tone showed larger heart rate accelerations and lower fundamental cry frequencies. Behavioral levels of reactivity and irritability on the Brazelton Neonatal Behavioral Assessment Scale (Brazelton & Nugent, 1995) were also associated with higher basal vagal tone. DiPietro and Porges (1991) found that vagal tone was related to reactivity to gavage (forced) feeding. Fox (1989) reported that infants who had higher basal vagal tone were more likely to cry during mild arm restraint than infants lower in vagal tone. The babies with higher vagal tone were responsive, not calm and placid, babies. These infants are probably more adept at getting caretakers to notice them and respond to their needs. As these infants become preschoolers, their higher vagal tone is related to less whining in stressful situations and greater ability to inhibit inappropriate behavior.

This relationship between basal vagal tone and reactivity is usually associated with greater self-regulatory abilities as well. Infants with higher vagal tone are more likely to look longer at novel stimuli (Linnemeyer & Porges, 1986), are less distractible (Richards, 1985, 1987), and habituate to novel stimuli more rapidly than infants with a lower vagal tone (Stifter & Fox, 1990). Hofheimer and Lawson (1988) found that high basal vagal tone in premature infants was significantly correlated with the percentage of focused attention they exhibited while with the mother; the associated higher reactivity may predispose these infants to receive greater caretaking responses and to elicit more face-to-face positive interaction from the mother as well. Huffman, Bryan, Pederson, and Porges (1988) found that less soothing was required and distress was more easily relieved in infants with higher vagal tone. Fox (1989, 1994; Fox & Field, 1989; Stifter & Fox, 1990; Stifter, Fox, & Porges, 1989) also found that the same infants who, at 5 months, had higher basal vagal tone and were more reactive to mild arm restraint were, by 14 months, better at self-soothing, higher in exploring a potentially scary novel stimulus, and more likely to approach a stranger.

Another dimension of vagal tone that needs to be considered briefly is its *ability to be suppressed*. In general, vagal tone is suppressed during states that require focused or sustained attention, mental effort, and organized responses to stress. Thus, the ability to perform a transitory suppression of vagal tone in response to environmental, and particularly emotional, demands is another important physiological index of self-regulatory abilities.

Once again we see the important role of *balance*. In our bodies there is a balance maintained by these two branches of our autonomic nervous system: the sympathetic branch, which prepares the body to react to emergencies and maintain vigilance against danger, and the parasympathetic branch and its main nerve, the vagus, which restores calm. When we reviewed the domain of marital interaction (one part of the core triad of balance), we noticed interaction patterns, such as those when the Four Horsemen were evident, that involved activation for either fighting or fleeing. There were also interaction patterns like softened start-up, accepting repair, de-escalation, and accepting influence that were related to softening and making the marriage a port in a storm. When we reviewed the domain of perception, we found a balance of positive and negative perceptions. When the marriage became an ailing marriage, this balance began to shift. The shift began with the subtext, in the form of temporary perceptions of danger and the absence of well-being; gradually these perceptions led to attributions that became more resistant to change, and eventually they became engraved in stone as the couple recast the narratives of their relationship history.

In helping couples we can intervene in any of these systems—behavior, perception, physiology—to help restore balance. The distressed marriage is chronically activated toward the negative rather that the positive, in behavior, in perception, and in physiological activation. In each domain, for the negative set of actions there are antidotes in the positive. We just need to have a theory that tells us how to engage these positives in a practical, meaningful, and effective fashion.

A misconception that needs clearing up is the idea that strong emotions lead to the state of diffuse physiological arousal. Though DPA does not seem to occur by increasing the intensity of any one emotion, it is very harmful to one's ability to process information, and that strongly affects the marriage and the immune system. What, then, creates DPA in people's bodies? The best available model, in my view, is the Henry-Stephens model.

DPA and Emotion Blends: The Henry-Stephens Model

To the best of our knowledge, DPA does *not* arise simply in response to strong emotion, such as intense anger. Paul Ekman (personal communication, 1996) claims that specific emotions continue to have specific autonomic "signatures" (for example, the hands get hot in anger and cold in fear) as the intensity of the emotion increases. Greater intensity of a *specific* emotion does not result in DPA. Instead, DPA arises in response to *blends of strong emotion*.

I think future research will show that these blends involve those emotions that activate the two axes identified by the Henry-Stephens stress model (Henry & Stephens, 1977). This model proposes that the two avenues of physiological activation (the sympathetic nervous system and the brain) each mediate different psychological states: Active coping, anger, and hostility give rise to *sympathetic*-adrenal activation and catecholamine secretion; helplessness, passive coping, depression, and pessimism give rise to *cortical* processes (the hypothalamic-pituitary-adrenocortical axis), leading to the secretion of cortisol. As I reviewed earlier, Malarkey, Kiecolt-Glaser, Pearl, and Glaser (1994) have shown that marital conflict among newlyweds can activate both axes. So it is probable that DPA results from feeling hostile and simultaneously feeling helpless about being able to change anything. Henry and Stephens believe that chronic activation of *both* stress-mediating systems results in physical illness.

Chronic DPA and Immunosuppression

Indeed, there is a great deal of evidence to suggest that chronic physiological arousal leads to suppression of immune functioning. Classic research (Berkman & Breslow, 1983; Berkman & Syme, 1979; Orbuch, House, Mero, & Webster, 1996; Verbrugge, 1985, 1989) has shown that the best predictors of physical health and longevity involve the presence and the quality of close relationships, particularly marriages and friendships. We now have some ideas about what mechanisms may mediate the powerful effects on health of marital disruption. Recent evidence has suggested that the quality of the marital relationship is correlated with parallel in vitro measures of immune functioning. Kiecolt-Glaser et al. (1987, 1988) found that *lower marital quality* was related to a *suppressed immune system* and, in turn, to poorer cellular immunity. Using dose response curves with two mitogens (these stimulate the immune system but are harmless), called PHA and ConA, they found a significant difference in the proliferation of T and B cells between low and high marital quality subgroups for all concentrations of PHA and for the higher concentrations of ConA.

The *dissolution* of marital relationships is known to be a more powerful stressor than marital unhappiness and it is also related to greater suppression in immune functioning. In the Kiecolt-Glaser et al. study, recently separated or divorced women had reduced immune response compared to married women. This reduced response was indicated by significantly higher Ebstein-Barr virus (EBV VCA) titers, significantly lower numbers of natural killer (NK) cells that control tumor growth, and lower numbers of T-lymphocytes than in the married women. There were also differences in the blastogenesis data between the two groups for PHA and the higher doses of ConA. Furthermore, although the two groups differed on self-report psychological variables, they did not differ markedly on other variables assessing sleep, nutrition, and weight. Couples undergoing separation with partners who differed in the emotional conflict surrounding the separation could also be discriminated using the in vitro immune measures. Separated or divorced women who were still high in attachment to their husbands had lower lymphocyte proliferation to ConA and PHA than similar women who were less attached. Attachment was assessed by self-reports of preoccupation and disbelief about the separation or divorce.

In our longitudinal study of newlyweds we collaborated with an immunologist at the University of Washington, Dr. Hans Ochs. We collected blood from 50 couples who stayed in the apartment lab for 24 hours and then used their blood to derive standard measures of immune functioning, including natural killer cells, antibody, and T and B cell counts, and the response of these lymphocytes to various mitogens and pathogens, such as the herpes virus. We found that our Oral History Interview variables, in which we coded people's narratives about their marriage and its history, were strongly related to the immune system variables. One variable we code is simply the amount of room people have in their brain for the relationship, a dimension we call "cognitive room." People with a lot of cognitive room recall a lot of detail about various parts of the relationship, how they met, what their first impressions of one another were, and so on. This dimension is related to what I call "Love Maps," by which I mean actively making maps of one's partner's psychological world. People who make these maps can tell you the name of their partner's friends, what their partners worry about, what their partner's current stresses are, and their partner's hopes, aspirations, and life dreams. Another variable we code from this interview is the strength of what we call the "Fondness and Admiration System." This taps into affection and respect in the marriage. Both cognitive room and fondness and admiration are dimensions we have found to be critical in predicting the future of a marriage and both dimensions were strongly related to immune system functioning, even in these young and healthy people (Carrére, Gottman, & Ochs, 1996).

A New View of Strong Emotions in Marital Therapy

It is likely that a great deal of learning involving strong emotions is *state-dependent* in nature. This means that in order to have access to, say, learning about anger, people need to *be in the state of anger*. Gordon Bower (1981) originally suggested that the memory of any learning that takes place in a particular emotional state would be more accessible in that state. He initially found evidence for this contention, but the effect was not replicated (Bower, 1986, personal communication). My hypothesis is that only information specifically organized around a particular emotion and in relation to coping *via* that emotion is more accessible when that emotional state is activated.

This is a very new way of thinking about emotion. The old view, primarily promulgated by Murray Bowen in the marital and family field, was that a person could not think while in an emotional state. The therapist first needed to calm down the couple before they could be rational enough to understand a therapeutic interpretation. Bowen's view of the therapist playing the role of family soother and facilitator of rational thought is understandable, given that he worked with very disturbed families. However, I believe that his view of emotion and the therapist's role in soothing are not generally useful for marital therapy.

The new view is that the time to work with anger, sadness, fear, hurt, disappointment, or contempt is *when people are in those emotional states*. The therapist obviously needs to be comfortable with strong emotions and willing to facilitate their expression in the therapeutic setting. Child psychologists Haim Ginott (1965) and Fritz Redl (1965) made this same point in working with children when they independently contended that the most efficacious moments for working with children's fear, anger, or sadness is when they are actually having the emotion. This perspective constituted a revolution in child treatment at that time. I discuss our research in this area using "emotion coaching" in the book and accompanying film, *The Heart of Parenting* (Gottman & DeClaire, 1996).

When blends of strong emotions are activated, particularly those involving both stress-mediating systems in the Henry-Stephens model, the couple will likely be in a state of DPA. In the therapeutic setting both spouses need to learn how to *self-soothe* and to *soothe one another* to reduce states of DPA. This will also help reverse the conditioning that has been taking place at home as a result of chronic flooding and the Distance and Isolation Cascade that invariably follows.

Taking breaks and creating a *withdrawal ritual,* a time away from the discussion, is an essential aspect of soothing for physiological reasons. Because of the slow decay of the sympathetic neurotransmitters (such as norepinephrine and epinephrine after their release into the bloodstream), an effective break must be at least 20 minutes long. It cannot involve rehearsing distress-maintaining thoughts like "I don't have to take this," or "I'm going to get even," but it should include a specific time to get back together again. Later, I will review research that shows that men are particularly vulnerable to rehearsing distress-maintaining thoughts and staying vigilant for danger.

The parasympathetic nervous system mediates the soothing so crucial to successful intimacy. Spouses need to learn how to help restore calm in self and partner following stressful interactions or any source of stressful response. In this way, the marriage becomes a port in a storm instead of the source of flooding. In this way therapy can begin to reverse the "escape conditioning" that inevitably occurs in continued marital conflict. Escape conditioning is the second most powerful form of conditioning (the *most* powerful is conditioned taste aversion). In the classic animal experiment the rat is exposed to a signal light and then given an electric shock that produces sustained pain, until the rat inadvertently presses a lever that raises an escape door, and the rat escapes. This learned escape response of lever-pressing is very resistant to extinction, as is the bodily reaction to the signal light and the subsequent hypervigilance for the onset of the light. This is a useful metaphor for what happens when a marriage is ailing due to intense negative affect. The equivalent of the signal light are all the cues related to the spouse's mood. The equivalent of the electric shock is DPA. The equivalent of escape is the Distance and Isolation Cascade.

Marital therapy needs to reverse this escape conditioning process. It needs to change all of the things that have happened in partners' *bodies* as a result of escape conditioning. It needs to depotentiate the hypervigilant "patrol" for danger as well. In short, people need to be able to soothe self and partner at the very level of physiology. *They* need to learn to do this, not have the therapist do it *for* them. The antidote for flooding and the Distance and Isolation Cascade is *soothing.* It is a sad thing, but in most marital therapies it is the therapist who does the soothing for the couple. "All right," the therapist says, in effect, "let's calm down now and think about that last interaction." The therapist plays the role of emotion regulator, de-escalator, and physiological soother.

Is it any wonder, then, that after the therapy is terminated, processes of escalation take over, DPA sets in, and all the learning of therapy goes out the window? The spouses do not have access to what they learned anymore, because the therapy never occurred in a state of DPA and they never learned to *soothe one another.* They never learned how to make their marriage a port in a storm, instead of just one other storm in their already stressed lives. To use the therapeutic learning they acquire in any form of marital therapy, they first have to learn how to reduce their own states of DPA.

A working knowledge of physiology is usually not in the armamentarium of the marital therapist, but I think that it should be. I also think it is crucially related to our relapse problem in marital therapy. Just as there is an optimal heart rate for aerobic exercise, there is also an optimal level of heart rate for marital interaction, and it should be well below 100 bpm. Larry Rowell's (1986) work on the response of the cardiovascular system (over 100 bpm) to physical stress shows that the body starts secreting epinephrine and revving up for a DPA. This means the sympathetic (fight or flight) nervous system responses become more likely.

No fancy equipment is necessary for assessing DPA. The therapist just needs to teach the couple how to take their heart rates, something most people who exercise regularly already know how to do. I recommend that the critical cutoff be set at about 95 bpm for normal healthy adults ages 20 to 55.

Critical Gender Differences in Physiology

Sex differences cannot explain why some marriages end in divorce and others do not. In fact, there are very few sex differences in happy marriages. Yet, when a marriage is ailing, some very key sex differences emerge.

The evidence we have from our lab suggests that after an unpleasant marital conflict, men are much more likely to have distress-maintaining thoughts than are women. We have discovered that these thoughts fall into two categories: those with themes of *righteous indignation* and *innocent victimhood*. The men stay aroused and vigilant. Women, on the other hand, are more likely to rehearse relationship-enhancing thoughts to calm themselves.

Here is the critical gender difference: In the face of perceived danger men are more likely than women to stay vigilant. There is convincing evidence from anthropologist Leakey (1994) that this gender-specific factor is part of our evolutionary heritage. It seems quite likely that we Homo sapiens evolved from those hominids in whom there was gender specialization of a particular type. The males hunted cooperatively in large groups over large spaces; of evolutionary value was the ability of the males to maintain vigilance and work efficiently together in teams. The females worked together in small groups and small spaces, gathering food, grooming one another, and sharing the care of babies (milk letdown was essential for survival). This means we evolved from female ancestors who had a greater capacity for self-soothing via this oxytocin-based response of nursing. The males, on the other hand, had to be able to respond quickly and aggressively, staying vigilant to potential danger. The males had to learn to suppress emotion in the service of this continued vigilance.

A very simple but brilliant experiment by McCarter and Levenson (1996) shows the modern-day reality of these gender-specific differences. It is well known that between the ages of 20 and 50 men are twice as likely as women to die from cardiovascular disease. The researchers hypothesized that any stimulus that suddenly evokes this male response to danger and vigilance would produce a greater adrenergic response to stress in men than in women. As their stimulus they used an acoustic startle, which is a sudden and unexpectedly loud sound (like a gunshot). They hypothesized that men (1) would have a larger cardio-vascular response to the startle, (2) would show more anger, contempt, and disgust, and (3) would take longer to recover from the cardiovascular arousal than women. Essentially, all of these hypotheses received support. Interestingly, they found no gender differences for anger but large gender differences for contempt and disgust, which tap into the most corrosive of the Four Horsemen.

This experiment clearly demonstrates the gender differences that explain why men and women respond so differently in marital conflict situations that arouse the danger and vigilance system of the male, the situations that lead to flooding. For this reason the male's ability to self-soothe is critical if marriages are to survive.

Zillmann (1979) has studied male-female differences in anger-provoking situations, finding a similar result. When men and women who have become angry (their blood pressure increases) are then asked to calm down, the women can do so and the men can't. Only when men are given a chance to retaliate can they then calm down. When women are compelled to retaliate, their blood pressure goes up.

These gender differences are nobody's fault; they are simply part of what we have inherited as a species. They do not matter very much in conflict situations unless contempt and disgust are evoked. But in marriages where conflict is serious and chronic, the differences become highly salient. So those marriages that have learned to "soothe the savage male"—and this means both male self-soothing and the wife soothing the husband—are way ahead of the game in terms of marital stability and happiness.

This perspective does not mean that women's physiological activation in distressed marriages cannot exceed men's in some spheres, or that women's physiological arousal is to be ignored. Nothing could be farther from the point. In the important area of immune suppression, women's responses exceed men's, presumably because women do not withdraw from an ailing marriage the way men do. There is evidence that, in some contexts, women are less aware of bodily physiological signals than are men, and they take their cues about affect from the social environment more than men do. They keep trying to work on a doomed, contempt-ridden relationship far longer than men do, often to their physical detriment As noted, the research evidence (Gottman & Levenson, 1988) suggests that in a relationship climate of negative affect, such as pervades unhappy marriages, men withdraw emotionally while women do not (the "female-demand/male-withdraw" pattern identified by Christensen and Heavey [1990]).

Gottman (1994a,b) reported that men are emotionally flooded by lower levels of negative affective behavior than is the case for women. To further evaluate this finding, in our newlywed study variables related to either partner's *positive affect* and *de-escalation of conflict* were used as events in interrupted time-series analyses of heart rate data collected synchronously with the video time code. The extent to which soothing of either spouse took place in relation to these positive affective events was then assessed and used as a predictor of marital outcome.

Our hypothesis (Gottman & Levenson, 1988) would be supported only if the only predictors of marital outcomes involved *physiological soothing of the male*.

We computed the proportion of time that there was a statistically significant reduction in heart rate (its level or slope) following either husband or wife doing one of the following: (1) humor, (2) affection, (3) showing active interest, (4) nonverbal responses that show that the listener is tracking the speaker, or (5) de-escalating the conflict. These positive events could potentially significantly soothe the heart rate either of the person doing the positive action or of the partner, or both. For the newlywed study we next assessed whether or not this probability of soothing (self-soothing or soothing one's partner) would predict whether the couple six years later would be in one of the three groups: divorced, married but unhappy, or married and happy. We found that the husband's soothing of himself (by using de-escalation, affection, interest, or listener tracking) and the wife's use of humor to soothe her husband predicted a positive outcome for the marriage.

Clearly, the final story is not yet in on the complex and interactive ways that marital conflict, peripheral autonomic physiology, cardiovascular reactivity, the endocrine system, the immune system, and illness are associated in similar and different ways for men and women. Nevertheless, our empirical research offers evidence of several basic characteristics of happy, stable marriages that point to a "gentleness model" of marital therapy, which would facilitate soothing in all three domains of behavior, perception, and physiology. To reiterate these all-important characteristics: softened start-up of conflict discussion by the wife; husband's ability to accept influence from wife and de-escalate low intensity negative affect; wife's use of humor to effectively soothe husband; husband's use of positive affect and de-escalation to effectively soothe himself.

SUMMARY

In this chapter I reviewed evidence that there is a "core triad" of balance in marriages. This means that we can evaluate the extent to which the marriage has established a balance of positivity and negativity in interactive behavior, perception, and physiology. Using this core triad of balance model, we asked the following question: What is "dysfunctional" when a marriage is ailing or headed for dissolution? The answer to this question determines, in large measure, the goals of marital therapy. In general, I reviewed evidence for the idea that, when compared with marriages headed for stability and happiness, marriages that are headed for divorce or unhappy stability are characterized by greater negativity than positivity in interactive behavior and perception and by chronic levels of diffuse physiological activation and the inability to self-soothe or be soothed by one's partner. Marriages that are working well are characterized by a specific form of gentleness and kindness toward one another that involves starting a discussion of a marital issue in a softened way and accepting influence from one another.

Table 2.1 What Is Dysfunctional in Ailing Marriages

In the domain of interactive behavior:
- ☐ more negativity than positivity
- ☐ the Four Horsemen of the Apocalypse
- ☐ emotional disengagement
- ☐ gridlock versus dialogue with perpetual issues
- ☐ harsh start-up of conflict discussion
- ☐ the failure of men to accept influence from their wives
- ☐ the failure of repair attempts

In the domain of perception:
- ☐ negative perception in the subtext
- ☐ failing to see the positivity that is there
- ☐ negative attributions about one's partner's personality
- ☐ recasting the historical narratives of the marriage in negative terms
- ☐ the Distance and Isolation Cascade

In the domain of physiology:
- ☐ chronic diffuse physiological arousal
- ☐ an inability to physiologically self-soothe
- ☐ an inability to soothe one's partner
- ☐ chronic immunosuppression

The dysfunctional elements in each domain of the core triad of balance that have been replicated in the research literature are summarized in Table 2.1.

The Sound Marital House: A Theory of Marriage

🐛 *In this chapter I review research addressing the question of what is going well when a marriage is stable and satisfying to both spouses. I take a look at three types of stable, happy couples, and examine the role of perpetual problems in stable marriages, including a transcript of two spouses who are masters at dialoguing with perpetual problems. Finally, I introduce the Sound Marital House theory, which gives clues about how to intervene in distressed marriages.*

I used to think it was enough to describe what is dysfunctional when a marriage is ailing, but then I discovered that there is new and valuable information to be obtained in answering the question of what is going right—that is, what is *functional* when a marriage is working well. Marriages that are working involve a variety of very positive factors that need to be built into any marital therapy program design to help couples create a satisfying relationship.

As noted in Chapter 1, most marital therapies are based on only one model of marriage: the validation or active listening model. There are actually two other models of successful marriages that are quite different from this one model. I've mentioned Harold Raush's longitudinal study of the transition to parenthood, starting with newlywed couples, which suggested three types of couples—arguers, avoiders, and those who were "harmonious"—and two hypotheses: (1) Conflict avoidance is dysfunctional; (2) a high level of conflict about trivial issues is dysfunctional and indicative of symbolic conflict. In fact, I found that Raush's different types were really just different ways to have a stable and happy marriage and that both of his hypotheses were wrong!

THREE TYPES OF STABLE, HAPPY COUPLES

There are three types of stable, happy couples, not just one. These three types—volatile, validating, and conflict-avoiding—have very different attributes yet are similar in that they all have a 5 to 1 ratio of positive-to-negative exchanges. This ratio suggests that there is something like an "emotional bank account" that is operating to make these marriages very rich climates of positivity, yet very *different* rich climates. The volatile couple do it with a great deal of affect, the validating couple with intermediate amounts of affect, and the avoiding couple with very little affect at all. The idea of looking at a marriage as if it involved an emotional bank account of positive and negative exchanges during conflict resolution was first suggested in a series of papers my students and I published in the 1970s (e.g., Gottman, Notarius, Markman et al., 1976; Gottman et al., 1977). In those early studies we built an experimental apparatus we called "the talk table." The talk table required only one person to speak at a time and for each spouse to use a 5-point scale to rate the "intent" of messages sent and the "impact" of messages received. Using the talk table we were able to operationalize many of the concepts of behavior exchange theory proposed by the brilliant social psychology theorists Thibaut and Kelly (1959). The talk table has since been replaced by Markman's "communication box," and by the "rating dial" that Levenson and I employ. This concept of an emotional bank account has recently been used by Covey, Merrill, and Merrill (1995) in a book on families.

The Critical Distinctions: Influence Attempts and Emotional Expressiveness

In our mathematical modeling of the marital interaction, what we call the "influence functions" of these three types of couples (Cook et al., 1995) showed that they used three distinct styles of trying to resolve conflict. We have also found that these couples have meta-emotional differences as well. However, *one style is not superior to another.* (I used to think that these three styles would have very serious implications for raising children, but I was wrong. I thought that a conflict-avoiding style would be bad for kids because they would never see a role model of how to resolve conflict by mutual persuasion. I also thought that a volatile style might make kids anxious that their parents might divorce and that there would be too much conflict. But, as far as we can tell, all three styles are equally likely to foster great parenting.)

Volatile couples begin influence attempts right away and remain at a high level throughout the interaction. They are clearly the most emotionally expressive of the three. Positive affect (humor, affection, interest, teasing) as well as negativity are freely expressed. They have a philosophy about being open and expressive with one another. These are strong, passionate individuals. They begin a marital discussion with immediate attempts at persuasion, which is also a sign of attentive listening. For them the argument itself is a sign of caring and involvement. They show high levels of disagreement as well as affection and humor. They love to tease one another and enjoy the "we against them" stance. Men who prefer volatile marriages are as likely as women to bring up issues. They don't stonewall. These couples stay romantic (and jealous) for many, many years, and there is a continual renewal of courtship. This is partly because they place a high value on openness and honesty and they often have to re-court one another after hurting each other's feelings. This is the union of two people who like to see strength in one another and are very supportive of mutual independence.

Validating couples peak in their influence attempts in the middle third of the interaction; the level declines in the first agenda-building phase of the conversation and again later in the negotiation phase, and is highest in the middle arguing phase. They believe in emotional expressiveness, but in moderation, at the right times, and only on really central issues. There is a great emphasis on we-ness and companionship in this marriage. It is a chum-ship.

Conflict-avoiders never throw down the gauntlet. They are never going to say something like, "Okay, I see your point of view. Now let me tell you why you are wrong and I am right. Let me convince you." Instead, they "agree to disagree." They minimize the importance of the problem; they gossip; they talk about the strengths in the marriage; they reiterate their shared belief systems; they reaffirm their commitment to one another; and then they end the conversation on some note of solidarity or philosophical optimism. Interestingly, at times the avoiders are more willing to explore their emotions and perceptions of the issue because the goal is *acceptance* and agreeing to disagree, not compromise, persuasion, or problem-solving. They can be emotionally expressive, but it is generally low-key and tempered.

Let us look at case examples to see how these three types of couples differ in their communication patterns.

The Volatile Couple: A Case Example

In our laboratory we ask spouses to identify the major areas of continuing disagreement in their marriage. Then they discuss these areas for 15 minutes (after either a 2-minute or a 5-minute pre-conversation silence, during which we obtain physiological baseline data). They are alone during the 15-minute conversation. There are no interruptions, and there is no therapist present. In this case the issue to be discussed is a "perpetual" one concerning the husband's contempt toward his wife's parents. Although she objectively agrees with his criticisms of her parents, his attitude still hurts her. He starts off teasing her about what he was thinking about during the 5-minute quiet time before the marital conversation. He says he wasn't thinking about them but about his opening statements "in court" (he is a lawyer).

> H: Okay, Elizabeth, this quiet time is helpful for me because Lou said I should do a 2- or 3-minute opening in this thing, so it gives me time think about it. We've got a lot to think about.

Notice how active the husband is in bringing up the issue. As noted above, this activity and involvement are more typical of husbands in volatile marriages; these husbands rarely stonewall.

W: Right.

H: Well, it's good. I think I know which problem area in our marriage I want to discuss.

W: I'm glad.

H: I am surprised that you get so upset about the way I related to your parents last Christmas vacation.

He is trying to minimize this issue and his wife realizes it, and so she confronts him directly.

W: I still don't think that you realize how often I think about the tension between you and my parents and how despairing I feel over it. It's much deeper in me than you realize.

H: I'm sure that's true. It's not important to me. It really isn't. So I don't think about it.

W: Just from an objective standpoint . . . just, you know, daughter versus parents versus brother versus sister—the whole circle of it should interest you at least.

H: Well, I've certainly always been willing to talk about it with you when you wanted to. Have I ever turned you down when you wanted to discuss it? And I realize that's not what you're looking for, but that's true, isn't it?

W: To an extent.

H: To what extent have I *not*? I know that I don't bring it up, and I know that I won't inquire. And that's wrong. I mean, that's back to that dichotomy: Is a lie not telling the truth? I mean, I can't justify or really say that I've shown interest merely because I've discussed it with you when you've wanted to.

W: Well, I don't think that it goes away every time there's a period that we don't talk about.

H: No, I can't say I think that, and I think I'm more aware that it is more on *your* mind.

This husband is still telling his wife that, for him, this is not a big issue and he is not going to get very distressed about it—it's not *his* issue. But she intensifies her confrontation of him.

W: Doesn't that spur you to . . . I mean, I'm your *wife*. Aren't you interested in things that bother me?

H: I think if I saw that it was negatively affecting you, I'd be more interested. But I don't see that, and I'm certainly not aware of that. I don't see any changes in your day-to-day life or in the way you are with me, or with Tina.

W: So when I tell you it's a real problem and it's deeper than you think, it still is not enough for you? I mean, it has to get to a point where it starts to affect my life before you will attempt to help me with it?

H: I don't see that my position is unreasonable. I mean, if I battle over something I'm concerned about inside . . .

He is telling her that for him to believe that this is a big issue for her, he needs to *see* some real negativity! He is telling her she has to be far more confronting if he is going to react. This is the volatile philosophy at its heart. His wife tells him that she doesn't really like this approach. She doesn't want to fight about this issue.

W: . . . it seems to always turn into a fight and I'm a little gun shy.
H: I don't know if it's turned into a fight over the last five or six months. Has it?
W: No, it hasn't, but that's not a very long time.
H: That's true, that's true.

Again, she confronts him and doesn't let him minimize the problem or dump it onto her shoulders.

W: So, how are we going to deal with this in the future?
H: Let's see, it seems to me that your parents' house is midway between our house and my parents' house. I don't know, maybe if I leave you off at the corner. How would that be?

Notice how teasing humor is a central part of the volatile style of dealing with conflict.

H: I don't know. I've always had a feeling of ambivalence about your parents: It bothers me that they don't interact with you or us, or Tina more. But at the same time, I don't have any desire for them to be more involved. I think you feel the same way. Now that they've moved closer, though, maybe they will surprise me and/or you.
W: Well, my dad is retired.
H: That's right, I mean, maybe they will be more willing to get in the car and come down.

The couple continue to try to deal with the differing feelings they each have about this issue, and they are trying to accept their differences in a way that doesn't keep hurting her. She is trying to accept his personality and the fact that it will always fail to mesh with her parents' lifestyle. They are successfully establishing a dialogue with this chronic problem that will never go away in their marriage. They communicate in a direct and vigorous way—no fluff, no "beating around the bush." In general, when we use our observational data, volatile couples express the most emotion of any couples. These are passionate marriages, the only marriages we have studied in which people stay romantic after 35 years. These marriages also have a ratio of 5 to 1 positive to negative affect. Hence, there is a lot of direct disagreement, anger, hurt, and so on, communicated in these discussions, but a huge amount of humor, affection, and enormous interest communicated as well.

The Validating Couple: A Case Example

The discussion is one in which she wants him to spend more money toward their entertainment. He disagrees, and then she suggests that they use money from his stocks. Notice how carefully she starts the discussion. She begins by softening the issue before disagreeing.

W: Do you want to start it or should I?

H: You tell me what you think, and I'll start screaming when it hurts.

W: My point of view has gotten closer to yours over the years we've been married, but your idea of saving and investing in the future and thinking about children when they come along, and saving our money for the house we're going to need and the care we're going to need and the clothes and the kids and all that stuff—I think there's some value to it, but . . .

H: Thanks for proving my point.

W: You know, I'm still young and I want to have some fun in life. You've gotten better, so it's not as big of an issue as it used to be. But, still, coming from the family that I come from, and the situation that I'm used to, going from that to the situation that I'm in is still quite an adjustment, even after three years. And it's gone from . . . not from frivolousness but from . . . I don't know. If I wanted, like I said, a new dress, I could go out and get it. Or if I wanted to splurge or go out to dinner because I felt like it, I would. You and I have to think about . . . you know, it cuts out a lot of the fun . . . it cuts out some of the spontaneity of life.

H: Oh, yeah.

W: When we *do* go out, I worry about how much money we're spending, or if we should be saving that money for something else. My feeling is, if it's good for the moment, then we have a good time, and the money is well spent. If it's an investment in our relationship, which I think going out to dinner and doing things spontaneously is, then it's money well spent.

H: As long as we've earned the money, I fully agree. That's where the conflict is.

W: Uh-huh. Well, we don't earn enough.

H: Well, that's our problem.

W: And there's nothing we can do about it.

H: But that's accepted though, so that's . . .

They agree on the main problem that they don't earn enough money, but she will not let it sit there. She goes on to raise the issue of his stocks.

W: We could get real personal here about your stocks, but I don't know if you want me to say that or not.

H: Well, I want to know the way you feel about them.

W: Um, that a portion could be used for our entertainment or our fun.

He disagrees with her idea and argues hard that such a strategy would burn up the money in no time. He has to defend this investment against her "frivolity." She tells him that she has become very frugal lately and that his attitude is harmful to their marriage. At first he disagrees, but then he becomes convinced that she has a point. He asks her how much money she is talking about, and she says no more than 10% of his stocks. He says that he can live with that amount. She adds that they should make it a priority to put the money back in the investments as they get extra money. He says that isn't necessary. She is delighted but then feels a little guilty, wondering if he is just giving in but doesn't *really* agree with her. No, he says sincerely, I am meeting you halfway. They have solved a problem and successfully persuaded one another.

The Conflict-Avoiding Couple: A Case Example

This couple is discussing a sexual problem: He wants to have sex more often than she does. You would never know that they are discussing a sexual problem from the content of the conversation. We know it from doing the set-up interview, the play-by-play interview. Our play-by-play interview was developed in the early 1970s as a method for making the conflict discussion grounded and not abstract. We ask the couple to identify a recent discussion they have had of a problem issue. For example, the issue may be "communication." But as we interview them about the issue, it turns out that when it last arose they were getting ready to go to a dinner party and this is roughly what happened. She feels he rushes her when she is getting ready. He is very concerned about being on time and frustrated that she keeps making them late. She wants him to compliment her spontaneously (just because he wants to) on how pretty she looks. Instead, by the time she is ready he is furious. On the way to the party in the car they start arguing about this. He gets so mad that he gets out of the car and walks to the party in the snow. She drives to the party, and he arrives an hour late. They actually have a good time at the party and make love when they get home. With the play-by-play interview the conflict discussion is much more specific, direct, and powerful.

This obscurity in this case is fairly typical of most couples attempting to openly talk about sex. It is quite typical of conflict-avoiding marriages for a sexual problem to exist without ever getting resolved. In one study we conducted, 30% of the major problems among conflict-avoiders were sexual (mostly mismatches in desired frequency of intercourse).

At the outset of the following excerpt, we see what I call a "we against others" strategy. The wife is trying to minimize the importance of the problem by using social comparison (their friends, Peg and Dave) and by getting her husband to admit that the problem has gotten a lot better lately.

> W: To reiterate a conversation I had with Peg about her attitude . . . it probably didn't move. Her statement was that just because Dave is a man and she's a woman, she's not going to drop everything she wants to do just to satisfy his needs. Um, and if *I* had that attitude . . .
>
> H: Yeah, that kind of attitude would disturb me. Peg shouldn't really be thinking about it like that, like it's disturbing her . . .
>
> W: Well, in contrast to that, do you think that we have . . . I don't know . . . do you feel better about ours? Maybe stop and think back three years ago, right? Right after we first got married.
>
> H: Yeah.

W: Or two and a half years ago when you really started considering the problem.

H: Started what?

W: Started considering the problem?

H: Yeah.

The husband is a bit confused about whether they are talking about their issue or Peg's.

W: And think about how you felt about it then and maybe how you feel about it now? I mean, have *we* come to some sort of agreement or something?

H: Oh, I think better than *they* have. I don't know if I fully understand what Peg was saying. She just wants no part of it, is basically the way you said it.

W: No part of what?

H: Of pleasing him at all.

W: No, no, it was more like, just because he has needs at 2:00 in the afternoon or 6:00 in the evening, if she's busy, she's busy. She doesn't want to be bothered, and just because she's Dave's wife, he doesn't need to think that she can just constantly take care of him. I think we need to get into a discussion about *ourselves,* though, as opposed to a discussion of them. Stop and think about your feelings two and a half, three years ago, and how we dealt with the problem and how we felt. I mean, think. It was much more of a problem then in my eyes than it is now.

H: I think we're more secure together now than where we were then. I don't know, I would say we haven't dealt with the actual problem any differently since then, I don't believe. I don't know if we've really changed.

W: Do you feel any differently about it though? I don't think . . . I don't . . .

H: How do you feel?

Notice that he is being very careful here. He is not going to stick his neck out and maybe tell her that things are really not good for him. First, he asks her what *she* feels.

W: Well, I know how I feel, and I know I can verbalize my feelings, but I'm afraid you're not going to say anything then. Two and a half to three years ago, I viewed the problem as something that was going to ruin our marriage . . . could ruin our marriage.

H: Yeah, well we discussed that part of it.

W: And we were real worried . . . *I* was real worried about us not making it.

H: Yeah.

Now she again tries to confirm that the problem really has improved, and he agrees.

W: And, um, I don't really worry about that anymore.

H: Yeah, I never considered it a threat to our marriage. I know you did, but I never did.

W: Okay. And maybe feeling more secure now is why I don't . . .

H: Yeah, I think that's it. I think we're both more secure, but I never did consider it a threat.

Minimizing the problem is their strategy for dealing with any conflict. That is the secret in understanding the conflict-avoiding marriage.

W: I consider it almost not a real problem anymore, as just part of us. That's kind of the way we function now.

H: That's just accepting.

Raush was wrong in his contention that conflict-avoiding couples lack psychological insight. In some ways, they are the most validating and naturally empathic. Why? It helps to understand the interior of an issue from your partner's perspective if your goal is going to be to accept your partner's position and not try to change it. One conflict-avoiding husband said it very well: "I'm also reluctant to argue. It strikes me as wrong to expose disagreement or to seek it. The whole point is to converge."

Mismatches, the Real Problem

The *mismatches*—mixing types in a couple—may explain why is it that some people get divorced who have a lot of everything else going for them, but they just don't have what feels like a "right" or a "natural" or "deep and meaningful" connection in the marriage. They may even be able to manage many of the practical aspects of being married and appear to be an ideal couple. Yet they experience their marriage as hollow, as "just not working." The passion is either "off" or simply not there. Appearances to the contrary, they are unsuited for one another. Often these feelings of an ill fit are due to a fundamental mismatch in typology. Some researchers, like Mary Ann Fitzpatrick (1988), have asserted that successful mixed types are possible. Indeed, I have seen mismatched partners work out a marital arrangement that creates an in-between type. I do believe that people can make these adjustments, and in therapy I help people with the process of working out this middle ground. It's just not easy.

There will always be predictable costs to making such a fundamental adjustment, because it guarantees that they will have "perpetual problems," about which they have to be able to establish ongoing dialogue. These perpetual problems are very basic ones that arise from differences in what feels to people like the right amount of self-disclosure and openness, the right amount of fighting, the right amount of arguing and "really" discussing issues deeply, the right amount of passion—the right amount of "real connection" in the marriage. In one common mismatch pattern the wife is very emotional and somewhat unstable, and the husband is unemotional and rock solid. She is drawn to his stability and he to her life, passion, and verve. After they marry, however, she finds herself wanting him to be more open and expressive, less rational all the time, less hidden. He finds himself wanting her to be less volatile, more dependable, like himself. Table 3.1 provides an overview of three mismatched combinations.

Sometimes these mismatches lead to gridlocked perpetual problems that cause a great deal of pain and feelings of rejection, and they invariably lead to the basic demand-withdraw pattern that appears to be characteristic of all marriages—and, to some degree, to be an epiphenomenon of these mismatches.

PERPETUAL PROBLEMS IN STABLE MARRIAGES

As I noted in Chapter 2, our research has revealed that an overwhelming majority (69%) of couples experience perpetual problems—issues with no resolution that the couple has been dealing with for many years. Whatever the specific context of a perpetual problem, it will also include: (1) basic difference in partners' personalities, and (2) basic differences in needs that are central to their concepts of who they are as people. For most perpetual conflicts in marriages, what matters is not the resolution of the conflict, because it will generally never get resolved, but the affect around which the conflict is *not* resolved.

A Master Couple: Establishing Dialogue with a Perpetual Problem

In the following transcript you will meet the masters of a long-term stable *and* happy marriage. These African-American spouses discuss two longstanding issues in their marriage, two of their perpetual issues: (1) the fact that he doesn't talk very much, and she wants him to talk more, and (2) financial differences. These issues are never going to change fundamentally in this marriage. In fact, both of them basically accept that there will always be differences between them, and they essentially accept one another as they are. Still, they stay current, doggedly pursuing these two issues and appearing to make some headway. Actually, all they are

Table 3.1 Mismatches and the Demand-Withdraw Pattern

Influence Function Mismatches	Results
1. Validator with Avoider	The validator is constantly pursuing the avoider and feeling shut out emotionally. The avoider starts feeling flooded.
2. Validator with Volatile	The validator starts feeling not listened to and flooded, like he or she is doing combat duty all the time. The volatile feels that the validator is cold and unemotional, distant and disengaged. There seems to be no passion in the marriage.
3. Avoider with Volatile	This is the worst of the pursuer-distancer combinations. The avoider quickly feels that he or she has married an out-of-control crazy person. The volatile believes that he or she has married a cold fish and feels unloved, rejected, and unappreciated.

doing is showing us that they are capable of having a dialogue, and it is the ability to exchange viewpoints that keeps them from getting gridlocked.

Clinicians at my workshops have told me that one of the things they like best is getting to see what healthy, stable, happy marriages—with all their "abnormalities"—look like. They rarely get to see healthy functioning in their work. This couple, who are typical of our long-term couples, are real masters of how to be married, of how to use positive affect to de-escalate conflict. Another function of positive affect, namely, physiological soothing, is also amply demonstrated. While this couple pursues the two issues of her wanting him to increase his self-disclosure and the clash of their two philosophies about paying the bills without enough money, the husband frequently yawns. This yawning (usually a sign of physiological quiescence) is probably a sign that they are keeping their arousal levels low. Throughout the transcript, notice the wide array of strategies used to de-escalate the conflict, such as expressing appreciation, softening the complaint, responding nondefensively, backing down, and using humor. It is the *two of them* who do this together. (In another marriage, a husband might have found the wife's humor irritating, but this husband is totally delighted by his wife.)

The two important points to note are: (1) What these middle-aged spouses do to respectfully influence one another is exactly what newlyweds who wind up stable and happy do; and (2) this process moves them toward some semblance of problem-solving. They are going to try, once again, to make this perpetual problem a little better. Notice he still describes her on the phone as "yappity yappity," a teasing reference to their personality differences, and she teases him for "not opening his lips" and telling her "his inner feelings." This movement toward some problem-solving is a relatively rare event in marital interactions.

What this master couple has effectively accomplished is to actualize the marital paradox that in order to change, it is necessary to feel that you do not have to change. In Jacobson and Christensen's (1996) terms, they have successfully communicated to one another that they like and accept each other. Now that that issue is out of the way ("I accept you as you are"), they communicate, "Now will you *please* change?" This is the great marital paradox, that people can only change if they don't have to.

> W: You be waiting for the little light to come on. Okay, now. Back to the communication problem. Okay, what do you feel like? What do you feel about that? Tell me? Tell me your inner feelings. [*laughter*]

Notice the use of humor in this softened start-up; they are both laughing.

> H: Like I said, a lot of times I don't know. I've always been quiet.
> W: Is it just because you don't have nothing to talk about, or is it because you don't want to talk about it? Or is it because I'm not saying anything at the moment?
> H: I don't know. A lot of times I don't know.

They both define the issue, minimizing it at the same time. She playfully puts herself down when she says that it could be because she isn't saying much at the time. But she is going to get down to the issue, and she is going to be relentless in her pursuit of this perpetual problem.

W: I mean, what's the sense in going out . . . okay, example.

H: Uh-huh.

W: When we went to Lake Bariessa. I mean, I can understand that you couldn't find your way around and everything, that was fine. That's understandable. But it still doesn't hurt to open your lips, you know? So, um, you know, say something . . . like I have to start a conversation . . .

The feeling around the "open your lips" line is one of humor. They are both laughing hard about this characterization of him. They are both playful and affectionate. This brief interchange dramatizes the finding that couples will not solve their perpetual problems, but what is important is *the amount of positive affect around which they don't solve the problem.*

H: I was kind of burned out that day, I was thinking about . . .

W: Well, it was *you* who suggested we go to Lake Bariessa.

H: I was trying to take you out somewhere, then I was trying to figure out my money in the bank and I end up coming up short . . .

W: You did that all driving out to Lake Bariessa?

H: Yeah. Yeah. And I was trying to figure out my balance in my bank account and how I was going to do that and all that stuff. You know, to have the gas money for the week.

W: So, you didn't want to burden me.

H: No, I didn't want to tell you that.

W: Okay, I'm glad you didn't because I really didn't want to hear it.

Here she is joking with him. First she tells him that she wants him to tell her what is on his mind, and now she says, in essence, keep it to yourself if it's about money. She is joking because she knows that this relates to another one of their perpetual problems, their differences in how they deal with money.

H: That's why I didn't tell you.

W: Not at that particular moment, no.

H: That's why I took you down there. I figure we'd go over there and check it out.

Now she returns to her central topic.

W: But it was like, when we got there . . . okay, you didn't want to talk. So when we got there, after we got off the truck and everything, we got set up, you know . . . and you ate your sandwich. You ate your little bologna sandwich. [*both laughing*]

H: Yeah. I was starving. [*laughing*]

W: I know you were. And then it was like . . . after that you just . . . you still didn't want to talk, you know, so Dominique and me started playing tennis.

She is telling him how patient she was that day waiting for him to tell her what he was brooding about.

H: It was almost time to go then [*pause*] and I had to drive back.
W: I know, you was like, "come on, let's go," and I said, "No, let's wait. We're sitting here enjoying it. We didn't come up here and pay this money just to do nothing."
H: I didn't want to come and check it out.
W: Yeah. I thought it was such a nice drive. It was *so* relaxing. [*Her voice is very soft and affectionate.*]
H: I didn't know it was going to be that far.
W: And I really appreciate that [*again, her voice is soft and affectionate*].

Notice this expression of appreciation. You do not have to be an emotional gymnast or a mental heath worker to do this. It is low-cost, psychologically. Here we are seeing positive affects in the service of de-escalating the conflict. Their heart rates remain quite low.

H: Thank you very much [*his voice is soft and affectionate*].
W: You're welcome [*soft and affectionate*]. But, I don't know, it's like we'd be coming home from, oh, Momma's or coming from the hospital. I can understand why you wouldn't want to say nothing coming from the hospital, but it's all the time. And when we're coming from the hospital or something like that, I don't mind you talking about the bills, but like I said, we're not going to worry about the bills. We'll pay what we can pay. Don't worry about it.
H: Yeah, but you don't seem to understand. Every time I tell you, this is how much we owe, that's when the trouble starts. [*There is irritation in his voice.*]

He is letting her know that he is angry about this difference between them on finances. But this is pure anger, free of contempt, and anger alone need not be destructive.

W: What? We don't worry about the bills? [*laughter*]
H: Yeah. This is what I'm steadily trying to impound on you.
W: Yeah, but we can only pay what we can pay, so why worry about . . .
H: Cause that's how I am. [*smiles*]
W: You shouldn't do that. [*smiles*]

In this interchange they both recognize and accept the difference between them in a playful way.

H: Well, I can't help it. I'm always trying to be preventive.
W: Okay, Preventive [*laughs*].

Amazing moment! On the spot she has made up a playful nickname for him—"Preventive"—and they both laugh about it. Again this communicates acceptance in the context of wanting change. This is a masterful performance, like a high-wire act. They make it look so easy.

H: I can't help it. I have learned from my mistakes [*tension and irritability enter his voice and face*].

> W: We need to come up with a solution [*affectionately*].
> H: Okay [*affectionately*].
> W: On that.
> H: Okay. Once I know that's in the bag, I'll be all right [*affectionately*].
> W: Like I said, what you should do . . .

But he wants to revisit this issue again. This is much of what Les Greenberg and Susan Johnson (1988) noted in their book, *Emotionally Focused Marital Therapy*. Couples often need to cycle through a small affective resolution twice.

> H: [*teasing*] Have you ever heard of people worried about bills, worried about bills? Have you ever heard of such people . . .
> W: I've heard of those people. I'm one of those people.
> H: And I'm one of those people.
> W: I'm one of those people.
> H: Whether you know it or not.

Here they are saying that they are both similar on this issue that divides them. An amazing attempt at resolution.

> W: But the thing of it is, you know, I just pay what I can pay and the next person will have to wait. You can't give everybody money at the same time, especially when you don't have that money to give.
> H: That's true.
> W: Okay, but what we should do . . .
> H: But that's what burns me about you. We don't have that money to give, but you can go to Circuit City and buy a tent [*irritated*].
> W: [*laughing*] That's right.

There is delight in her voice and face. She is saying that she likes herself the way she is. She has no intention of being as tight-fisted with money as he is. She is telling him that buying that tent on sale is the thing to do if you can do it. So she is being playful with one of their perpetual issues. Then she gets serious.

> W: But the thing of it is, okay, what should we do about this situation, since the bills bother you? What should we do?
> H: What do you think we should do? Pay the bills [*he is irritated*].
> W: That's simple [*tense laughter*]. No, we should, like, have a little plan.

There is a long pause, after which he discloses his major source of worry. This makes it possible for them to move things slightly forward on this perpetual issue of the finances—as well as on the perpetual issue of him not disclosing his worries. This is a very gentle, but also very dramatic, moment.

> H: The only thing I can do with that is have life insurance for me and you. I paid the kids'. Now I can't pay ours.
> W: Well, that's why I told you, you know, about the extra money that I have left over to go to Circuit City. You know, I'll pay that. I'll be willing to pay that. But you've got to let me know, honey, you've got to speak up.

H: I have been letting you know about the last month or so.

W: About the insurance?

H: Uh-huh.

W: So you haven't paid the insurance in a month and a half?

H: I paid the kids', but haven't been able to pay ours.

W: You see, you don't say anything, so I been thinking that everything is okay.

She gets back to her issue again. If she doesn't know what he's thinking, then they can't solve the problem, and she lets him know that before she moves in with her solution.

H: Yeah, I gathered that [*laughter*].

W: [*laughter*] Honestly. But what we should do is, like, when we get our paychecks . . . *before* we get our paychecks, like at the beginning of that week . . .

H: You see, I already know where my check is going before I get it. PG & E, the house note, and what else? Gas money and a little food.

W: What we need to do is sit down and work out how much that insurance is and how we're going to pay it.

H: Yeah.

W: You told me that you have to pay it every three months?

H: Right.

W: We need to figure out how we can pay that before it's due. Like, maybe I can take out so much of my money, you know, and put it to the side. We'll get through. I mean, the same thing with the phone bill.

H: But without knowing this, how am I to know? Yeah, the phone bill. I've been trying to keep that down.

W: Yeah, I took that over.

H: But you haven't been trying to keep it down.

W: How come I haven't?

H: Huh! Yappity, yappity, yappity.

Now here he is teasing her in a good-natured way about the personality differences between them. He thinks she talks excessively. She thinks he is too quiet.

W: I cut back last month, so this month's bill shouldn't be that much.

H: Huh.

W: Honestly. I haven't been making that many calls. And then like the Visa. Now I've been paying that.

H: Uh-huh.

W: Then, like I say, the extra money I've been taking to buy me stuff . . .

H: And I told you that this first year at the house is going to be kind of rough because we're still paying for your car.

W: I know.

H: At least to the end of the year, we both know that.

W: To the end of the year and it will be over. But then, like I say, what we should do . . . you just tell me. We sit down this week or this weekend. Do you have plans for this weekend?

H: Do I have plans?

W: That I don't know about?

H: Oh, it's just me, I'm just calling to let you know I'll be home late.

W: Okay, so plans, no plans, we'll sit down and we'll kind of come up with a plan for how we're going to pay that insurance, okay?

H: Uh-huh.

W: And, like I say, if it boils down to . . . since you done told me this now . . . it boils down to that, I'll just take so much out of my check.

H: That's what I had planned to do, but it didn't quite work that way.

W: Well, we'll try to figure it out, we'll try it. We'll both of us try to take something out. Whatever we can come up with on the side after we get through paying everything else. We won't worry about it. We'll come up with what we can come up with.

H: Yeah, that's easy to say.

W: But when it gets towards the end to pay for it . . .

H: Something will be there.

W: Yeah, we'll have at least something in the kitty to help pay instead of trying to come up with the money all at once.

H: Right. That's what I'd like.

W: All right. Work with me, baby [*there's joy in her voice*]. Okay, so that's what we'll do. And as far as this communication problem, now maybe you'll start talking more on the way home.

They are feeling good about making some headway on a major perpetual problem of theirs.

H: On the way home?

W: Uh-huh.

H: Yeah.

W: Away from home, whatever.

He is even ready to bring up another financial issue that has been bothering him.

H: Yeah. Well, you see, I thought I'd have some extra money to buy some more wrenches, but I ain't got no money to do that.

W: What do you need wrenches for? You didn't tell me that.

H: I need that big wrench I was looking for that time I went to Fremont.

W: So, you've got to buy another big wrench.

H: I could get one from the flea market now, instead of getting a brand-new one—you get the same quality and they last just as long, you know?

W: Well, how soon do you gotta have these?

H: I just need them, you know. Instead of asking everybody else, "Hey, can I use your wrench?"

W: What can I do, let's see. We worked that one okay. Hmmmm.

H: What?

W: We can get . . . well, no, we can't run that bill back up. We can work that out, yeah.

H: We can work that out.

W: Like I say, once we get through paying for that car, things will really ease up for us.

H: It sure will for you.

W: So it sounds like to me . . .

H: What?

W: Your main problem is this bill. We'll work on it.

H: Yup, those iddy biddy bills.

W: It's those iddy biddy bills that eat you up.

H: Like if I take some money out of my paycheck, it goes toward those house repairs . . .

W: Now see . . .

H: Let me finish, let me finish this. Then I have to go get stuff for the house with that money and I wished that money was going somewhere else. That's why I was harping on that.

W: See, now you're sitting up here talking about this. And like that day at the park. We could have talked about that. It was a nice relaxing moment to discuss these things.

H: I don't know what happened then. Maybe that was my intent, I don't know, but when I got there, I don't know, I was blowed out.

W: Totally turned around, huh?

H: Un-huh.

W: Oh, well, we'll work on these things. But like I say, you've got to tell me. If you sit down and talk with me like this—do you mean to tell me I have to wire you up? [*laughter*]

She raises her issue again, using her sense of humor to do it. He laughs. They are both feeling good about the interaction concerning these two perpetual problems. They are doing so well that they tackle another perpetual problem, getting time for themselves away from the kids. And this is all in the same 15-minute period.

H: Think about it. When do we have a chance to sit down?

W: On weekends.

H: I don't think so.

W: I have to wire you up like this to get a conversation out of you like this going? I'm going to go out and buy me this kind of equipment. We'll work on it. Okay?

H: I don't think we have enough time on the weekends to sit down.

W: Why we don't?

H: Dominique jumping around, we be trying to do this and do that.

W: See, that's why I said we need to take a day for ourselves. Momma would keep Dominique for a day. We take a day for ourselves. We've got to start focusing on ourselves more.

H: Hmm-hmmm.

W: Haven't I been telling you that?

H: Oh, yeah.

W: Okay. Momma can keep Dominique every now and then. It doesn't have to be on a continual basis, just every now and then so we can do something for ourselves, even if it ain't nothing more than taking in a movie.

H: Yeah.

W: Or go have dinner. When was the last time we had dinner in a restaurant?

H: I can't remember.

W: Right. I've really been thinking about this. We need to focus on ourselves more.

H: We're always having dinner with Dominique. She's like, "Come on, Daddy."

W: Okay. Don't be a wise-cracker.

H: "Come on, Daddy" [*mimicking his daughter lightheartedly*]. She be telling me what to do!

W: [*laughter*] I noticed that.

H: "You come on in here, Daddy, and go to bed."

W: Uh-huh. My mom wouldn't mind keeping her every now and then. You know, maybe once a month. One day set aside for us to do something together. I can think of a lot of things.

H: I can too.

W: But what?

H: Like I told you before, the first thing is we don't have no baby-sitter.

W: Well, I just told you what we can do.

H: Yeah.

W: It don't have to be done on a continual basis. Just one time out of the month. Maybe once every three months, once every three months. As long as we take one day for ourselves to do something together.

H: That would be nice.

W: I think so, too.

H: Go to a movie. How you do it? First you go have dinner, then you go to a movie. [*laughter*]

W: Or if you go to a movie early enough, you can go have dinner afterwards. [*laughter*]

H: Right.

W: Right.

H: It works either way, huh?

W: Yes.

This couple is exceptional in their ability to deal with major perpetual issues through humor and affection and other positive affects that keep their physiology calm. They make it look easy, just like any high-wire act makes it look easy. They are "athletes" at marriage, and that is one reason we did this study with long-term marriages. There is a marital magic in what they do. *The only function of my research is to make this marital magic of the marriage masters clear so that therapists can teach it to other couples.* The intervention has as its goal teaching couples the techniques of these masters. The research also seeks to discover the limits of this approach.

THE SOUND MARITAL HOUSE

The two necessary "staples" of marriages that work (whatever their typology) are (1) an overall level of positive affect, and (2) an ability to reduce negative affect during conflict resolution. These two empirical facts give us the basics of marital therapy: To create lasting change in troubled marriages, interventions need to enhance the overall level of positive affect in both nonconflict and conflict contexts, and teach couples how to reduce negative affect during conflict by accepting one another's influence.

Our research on newlywed couples led us to identify the "particulars" of these two key staples and culminated in my concept of the Sound Marital House (Figure 3.1).

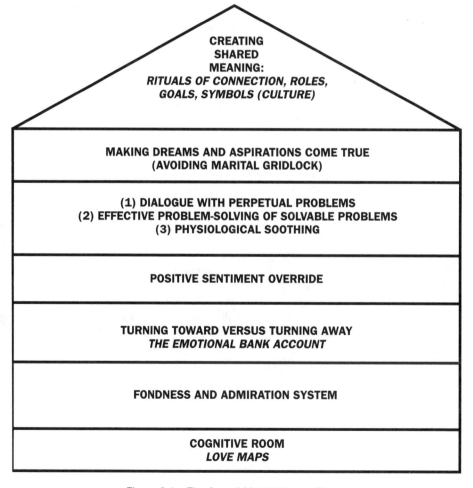

Figure 3.1 The Sound Marital House Theory

The essential elements of the theory are:

- The foundation is composed of marital friendship and its ability to create three levels of positive affect in nonconflict contexts. We have identified these three components of the marital friendship: (1) cognitive room (which leads to our "Love Maps" intervention), (2) the Fondness and Admiration System, and (3) turning toward versus turning away (the emotional bank account).

- These components of friendship lead to the next level of Positive Sentiment Override if they are working well, or to Negative Sentiment Override if they are not. Sentiment override determines the success of repair attempts during conflict discussions.

- Conflict and its regulation (not resolution) form the next level. There are three parts to this level: (1) establishing dialogue, not gridlock, with perpetual problems, (2) solving solvable problems with some basic skills, and (3) physiological soothing (which is mostly self-soothing).

- The final level has to do with creating a shared meaning system, which consists of (1) meshing individual life dreams, and (2) meshing rituals of connection, goals, roles, myths, narratives, and metaphors. This level then feeds back to deepen and strengthen the foundation of marital friendship.

The Foundation of Marital Friendship: Creating Positive Affect in Nonconflict Contexts

We have found that friendship and the positive affect that naturally flows from it are major accomplishments achieved by couples in happy, stable marriages. Unfortunately, it is difficult to create positive affect in a distressed marriage that has lost it. The admonition to be positive or the setting-up of behavioral exchanges is usually doomed (Vincent, Friedman, Nugent, & Messerly, 1979). We have discovered that it is usually not very difficult to rebuild the friendship in the marriage in a short time, but getting it to *last* is more difficult. This first level of the Sound Marital House involves an atmosphere of positive affect in nonconflict contexts, and we have successfully developed a "technology" for recreating this part of the marriage.

It is well-known that over half of all divorces occur in the first seven years of marriage. A cascade toward divorce often follows the birth of the first child. In our longitudinal research on newlyweds, 70% of all couples (mainly wives) experience a precipitous drop in marital satisfaction. We attempted to discover what factors in the first few months of marriage would predict whether a couple would wind up in the 70% group. We found these predictors using our Oral History Interview (see Appendix C). Each of these factors either adds to or subtracts from the strength of the marital friendship foundation:

- The amount of *cognitive room* partners allocate to one another (especially husbands);
- The frequency of spontaneous expressions of *fondness and admiration;*

- The frequency of spontaneous expressions of *disappointment and negativity;*
- The degree of *we-ness* in their conversations;
- The degree of *couple efficacy* with which partners address their problems;
- The degree to which couples describe their lives as *chaotic* and *out of control;*
- The degree to which their differences relate to *gender issues;*
- The "size" of their *emotional bank account,* evidenced by the frequency of "turning toward" versus "turning away" from one another in nonconflict interactions.

Creating Positive Sentiment Override

The first three levels of the Sound Martial House provide the materials for the next level: what Weiss (1980) termed "positive sentiment override" (PSO). Weiss suggested that reactions during marital exchanges could be determined by a global dimension of affection or disaffection rather than by the immediately preceding valence of the stimulus. We extended Weiss's ideas to suggest that Positive Sentiment Overrride (PSO) and Negative Sentiment Override (NSO) have their basis in everyday, mundane, nonconflict interactions. These overrides are measured experimentally by the use of "insider-outsider coding discrepancies," as follows: In PSO a spouse says something with negative affect (as judged by observers), and it is received as a neutral message, perhaps *in italics*—signaling that the receiver recognizes this is an important issue to the spouse. In NSO a neutral message (as judged by observers) is received as if it were negative. I suspected that if partners had enough "emotional money in the bank," they would demonstrate PSO. To put it another way: Sufficient positive affect in nonconflict interactions makes PSO possible.

In our laboratory M. Hawkins recently discovered that the critical variable in PSO was the wife's perception of her husband's anger. In marriages that were destined to become happy and stable, the wife noticed and responded to the anger but did not evaluate it as negative. In marriages headed for unhappiness or divorce, the wife's rating of her husband's anger was negative. It is important to note that this was a categorical, not a small, difference. Another way of stating these findings was that the emotionally intelligent wife recognizes the husband's anger as important information but does not take it as a personal attack.

Regulating Conflict

Positive Sentiment Overrride, in turn, is the basis of successful repair attempts that de-escalate negative affect during conflict discussions and provide physiological soothing—creating the next "floor" of the marital house. Repair has two parameters: a threshold of negativity at which repair kicks in for both husband and wife, and the effectiveness of the repair for both husband and wife. What is fascinating is that, even for newlywed marriages that initially scored high on the Four Horsemen, when repair was effective, 83.3% of these couples wound up stable and happy 8 years later. Many of these ideas on the importance of mutual understanding needing to precede problem-solving were presaged by Notarius and Markman (1993; see especially pp. 217, 219).

As noted, we have found that it is the *regulation* of most conflicts—and not their resolution—that is predictive of longitudinal outcomes in marriages. (These are also the processes operative in couples in their forties and sixties.) Happy couples know how to negotiate the terrain of both resolvable and unresolvable (perpetual) problems. Facilitating *both* types of problem areas will be discussed in Part III.

Creating Shared Meaning

Each family creates a unique culture—a unique compilation of meaning—complete with its own symbols, metaphors, and narratives. The degree to which a marriage enables both partners to feel that their life dreams are supported can make or break it.

I am often asked how these principles from my research on marriage vary across cultural, ethnic, and racial groups. This is a limited use of the idea of culture. In most issues with couples, we are actually dealing with what things *mean* to individuals in the marriage—and meaning is a cultural issue, even in regard to very basic things. For example, family dinnertimes can mean very different things to partners. Barbara Fiese (1997) has studied the narratives that people have about dinnertime in their married family and in the family of origin. She has shown that how people actually behave during these times is quite consistent with these narratives. This is but one example of how we are always encountering the symbolic meaning of everyday things in marriages. Money is another example. Money is almost never just about money—it is about freedom, power, independence, love, security, competence, achievement, and so on. What does a "home" mean? What does "love" mean? What rituals and roles do partners associate with illness, and what do these mean to each of them? I knew one couple in which the husband believed that is was very important to be nurturing and solicitous when a person was sick, whereas the wife believed that this was a time to be left alone. How they each acted around times of illness was a critical part of their conflict.

In many senses spouses are constantly creating a "culture" in their marriage by creating a shared meaning system. Their values, ideals, and philosophy of life are manifested in the way they think of, and the meaning they ascribe to, even the most mundane activities in the marriage.

In exploring shared meanings (or their absence) with couples, we examine four areas:

- *Rituals:* This includes a broad range of shared activities, from daily routines such as dinnertimes and running errands to annual events such as religious holidays and family vacations.
- *Roles:* Wife, husband, son, daughter, doctor, homemaker, student, dancer, etc.

- *Goals:* These tangible markers involve both short- and long-term aspirations: from working out four times a week, to owing a home, to getting an advanced degree or a raise in salary, to becoming a grandparent.

- *Symbols:* These involve the intangible existential ponderings around the fundamental question, What is the *meaning* of . . . home, family, love, trust, autonomy, dependence, ad infinitum.

I have encountered an elitism in some therapists who (often unconsciously) believe that a college education or some advanced degree is necessary in order for people to live an examined life. Nothing could be further from the truth. Even young children begin asking questions about death, become aware of the possibility of their own death, and start wondering about what it all means. Conversations among friends of all ages and all walks of life are filled with efforts to understand and create some meaning out of the everyday routines. In her classic book on blue-collar marriage, Mirra Komoravsky (1962) talked about an interview with a couple who had just made the last payment on their home. This was an especially significant event for them because, they explained, they were the "runts" of their families, who thought it amusing that the two "dummies" had found one another. This family rejection was clearly a painful part of both of their childhoods. But, they said proudly, their children were doing well, in contrast to those of their brothers and sisters, and their marriage was the only one still intact. The two runts had banded together and done very well, indeed. This is a dramatic example of how a couple can develop a strong friendship based on a common shared meaning system. *Everyone* is an existential philosopher. It is the creation of this *shared* meaning that is at the heart of the creative resolution of marital conflict. In helping a couple to explore what shared meanings they can create—and have already created—with one another, the therapist is tapping into a natural system that is a very important ingredient in the couple's friendship.

The formation of a marriage and a family involves the active creation of a new culture that has never existed before. Even if the two people come from the same racial, ethnic, and geographic background, their families of origin will be very different, and so their union will inevitably involve the creation of a new world of meaning. The levels of the Sound Marital House are interconnected by the narratives, dreams, and metaphors that give meaning to marriage and cycle back to the foundation, which is the marital friendship (Figure 3.1). We have discovered that affectlessness and emotional disengagement in marriages occurs when partners have dealt inadequately with this level, which leaves them with no margin of emotional "overdraw" to fall back on during times of conflict.

Potential Contributions of the Sound Marital House Theory

How does my theory of the Sound Marital House alter current thinking about marital therapy? It suggests a number of principles:

1. Marital therapy should *not* be based solely on how couples resolve conflict.

2. The effective resolution of conflict is based on the middle level of the Sound Marital House, which is composed of everyday martial interactions that produce either Positive or Negative Sentiment Override.
3. When conflicts have a solution, the conflict resolution skills that most therapies target (active listening) are the wrong targets. This theory proposes alternative ones.
4. Most marital conflict is about "perpetual" problems that never get resolved; what matters most is the affect around which the problems doesn't get resolved. Either the spouses establish a dialogue with the perpetual problem and communicate acceptance to one another, or the conflict becomes gridlocked.
5. The resolution of conflict, especially when it's gridlocked, must involve an exploration of the symbolic meaning of partners' positions on the gridlocked issues. This part of the marriage—the metaphors, symbols, narratives, and dreams—cycles back to the foundation, fueling either intimacy or estrangement.

In Part II we will see how the pieces of the Sound Marital House can be used to begin establishing a therapeutic contract.

Part **II**

ASSESSMENT

Chapter **4**

The Assessment of Marriage

 In this chapter I introduce the 7 assessment questions I use when a couple comes in for therapy. I review the best methods for answering these 7 questions via questionnaires, interviews, behavioral observation, and physiological measurement.

This chapter provides an overview of methods for assessing a particular marriage, toward the goal of selecting a specific method of intervention that is suitable. The assessment, which includes studying the strengths of the marriage as well as the current challenges, also serves as a tool for developing a beginning therapeutic contract.

Communicating the assessment plan is very important in building the couple's expectations about what is going to happen and why. Partners entering marital therapy are often in a great deal of pain, sometimes even quite desperate. In some cases there are differential levels of commitment to the marriage and dissimilar expectations for the therapy. One person may want out of the marriage and the other want to stay together. Most commonly, the spouses come in with the belief that, if they only could solve their problem issues, they would be happy. This is not so, as the theory of the Sound Marital House suggests. But within the couple system are two stories to be told. Usually spouses are desperate to tell them and to begin to understand the sources of their pain. They need a sounding board for their pain, and they are often looking for understanding and hope.

Assessment is not an intellectual but a very emotional exercise for the couple, whose core issues and interactive processes are being observed and evaluated. For most people, the idea that *process is everything* is entirely new. They are mostly thinking that one person is right and the other wrong on each issue, and they typically view therapy as fixing the major disorders *in the partner*, with perhaps some minor adjustments on their own part. They usually both have this view (the "fundamental attribution error").

113

Assessment is, by itself, a very powerful experience for couples and is no different from intervention to them. It is different only *for you, the therapist,* because it guides the development of the treatment plan for the couple and perhaps for the partners as individual clients. The assessment phase can be referenced during the course of treatment to better understand some aspect of a couple's dynamics. The assessment methods I describe in this chapter provide an intellectual framework to structure this very emotional and crucial phase of therapy, in which the beginnings of a therapeutic alliance based on caring, affection, and respect are forged.

WHAT I WANT TO KNOW WHEN A COUPLE COMES IN FOR TREATMENT

I use the Sound Marital House theory as my guide for assessing a marriage. I am looking for (1) strengths in the marriage as well as (2) areas that need improvement. Those are my only two final summary categories. In my wrap-up of the assessment I tell the spouses what I see as areas of strength in their marriage, and what I see as the areas that need improvement.

My *minimal* assessment takes three sessions—a conjoint session that lasts an hour and a half, and two individual sessions, one with each spouse, each a half-hour long. In the more complete assessment package I have put together here and in the appendices, I have included far more than this minimal assessment, to provide a library of what I think are the best clinical assessment tools currently available. I am investigating 7 different questions, all related to the Sound Marital House:

- Overall, where is each in the marriage?
- What is the nature of their marital friendship?
- What is the nature of their sentiment override? Is it positive or negative?
- What is the nature of their physiologies and capacities for soothing (self and partner)?
- What is the nature of their conflict and its regulation?
- In what ways are they able to honor one another's life dreams and create shared meaning?
- What potential sources of resistance exist?

I recommend that you use the Clinician's Checklist in Table 4.1 as a way of guiding and summarizing your assessment.

Conjoint Session

For the conjoint session couples arrive having filled out the following forms that have been mailed to them: The **Locke-Wallace Marital Adjustment Test,** the **Weiss-Cerreto Marital Status Inventory,** which assesses divorce potential, and the

Table 4.1 Clinician's Checklist for Marital Assessment

Check the items you see at issue, and then add specific notes at the end.

Overall, where are they each in the marriage?

☐ Marital satisfaction (Locke-Wallace)

☐ Divorce potential (Weiss-Cerreto)

☐ Each person's commitment to the marriage

☐ Their hopes and expectations for the marriage (including potentially getting out of the marriage)

☐ Their hopes, expectations, and theory of the therapy

☐ Their big cost/benefit analysis of the marriage. Discrepancies between spouses?

☐ Pattern of emotional abuse? Therapist to confront this.

Marital Therapy Contraindicated?

☐ An ongoing extramarital affair (secret or revealed)?

☐ Ongoing physical abuse?

☐ Other? Betrayals?

The Marital Friendship

☐ In Gottman 17-Areas is there:
    ☐ Emotional engagement or disengagement?
    ☐ Lifestyle needs similar or different?
    ☐ Passion and romance in the marriage?
    ☐ Sexual satisfaction and intimacy?
    ☐ Fun?
    ☐ Spiritual connection?
    ☐ Loneliness?
    ☐ Parallel lives?
    ☐ Other salient areas? (e.g., finances)

☐ Positive affect (interest, excitement, affection, humor, validation, amusement, pleasure, joy)?

☐ The Fondness and Admiration System?

☐ Physical affection?

☐ We-ness versus me-ness?

☐ Cognitive room (Love Maps)?

☐ How do they talk to each other in a nonconflict context?

☐ What do they see as the strengths of this marriage?

☐ Feeling one's personality is accepted?

☐ Feeling fundamentally criticized and disliked?

☐ How do they move through time together?

☐ In events-of-the-day discussion or stress-reducing conversation, is there requited interest, excitement, humor, affection?

☐ Map out a typical week day.

☐ Map out a typical weekend day.

☐ Map out a typical vacation.

☐ Map out a typical getaway.

☐ How do they renew themselves and each other when they are fatigued and highly stressed?

☐ What is the nature of their daily rituals of leave-taking in the morning, reunion, eating together, and what do these rituals *mean* to them?

☐ Meta-emotion discrepancy?

Table 4.1 Clinician's Checklist for Marital Assessment (*continued*)

Sentiment Overrides

☐ Existence of negative sentiment override
☐ Existence of positive sentiment override
☐ The frequency and success of repair attempts during conflict discussions
☐ How humor and anger are responded to
☐ How they perceive one another's anger and humor; Innocent victim or a righteous indignation perception of this moment
☐ Flooded by the way their partner complains
☐ Diffuse physiological arousal
☐ Ability to self-soothe
☐ Ability to soothe partner

Regulating Conflict

For problems that can be solved (not perpetual):

☐ Softened or harsh start-up
☐ Accepting influence
☐ De-escalation
☐ Repair
☐ Compromise
☐ Positive affect

For perpetual problems:

☐ Dialogue
☐ Gridlock
☐ The Four Horsemen (criticism, defensiveness, contempt, and stonewalling)
☐ Positive affect
☐ Emotional disengagement

Meshing Life Dreams and Creating Shared Meaning

☐ Their own life goals, their missions, their dreams: Are these known?
☐ Are they honored? How so?
☐ Fear of accepting influence?
☐ Have they been able to create shared meaning in
    ☐ Rituals
    ☐ Goals
    ☐ Roles
    ☐ Symbols
☐ Overall progress toward being able to create shared meaning system

Potential Resistances

☐ Differential levels of commitment to the marriage
☐ Different hopes and expectations for therapy
☐ Betrayals, current or past
☐ Psychopathology. Specify:
    ☐ Past trauma
    ☐ Disorders of individuation
☐ Conflict in values
☐ Issues of friends
☐ Issues of community

Gottman 17-Areas Scale.* I begin with their narratives and move into a combined Oral History and Meta-Emotion Interview (see Appendix C), which I can
now do in about a half-hour. Then I use the Gottman 17-Areas Scale to have
them identify two issues, one on which they are gridlocked, and another smaller,
solvable problem. That takes about 10 minutes. I then ask them to talk to one
another for 6 minutes about each problem, trying to come to a resolution. During
these two interactions I do not intervene; I stay silent. I may ask them to also pick
an area they enjoy talking about (see **Krokoff-Gottman Enjoyable Conversation
Scale**) and to talk about this area for 6 minutes. For the next approximately 20
minutes I end the session by doing part of the Meanings Interview (see Appendix
C). I want to know what their marriage has meant to each of them, and also what
their disappointments have been. I also ask them to tell me how they see their
marriage and what their hopes and expectations are for marital therapy. Then I
state the ground rules for the individual sessions and schedule them.

I suggest that you discuss the ground rules of seeing them individually, which
is that there are no secrets, that everything that gets said is potentially public
information, at your discretion to reveal. Be careful with the ground rules of these
individual interviews. I make sure each spouse knows that there will be no
secrets. Otherwise I could find myself in a pickle, like when one spouse says, "I'm
having an affair, but don't tell my spouse." I explain that the session after the
individual sessions will be conjoint again, and that in that session we will discuss
the therapeutic contract, what their goals are, and what plan seems best. Coping
with issues of secret affairs and other betrayals that are revealed to the therapist
but not the spouse are complex. It would be glib to suggest that there are firm
guidelines for dealing with all of these issues.

Individual Sessions

I supplement the conjoint session with two individual interviews, seeing husband
and wife separately. In the individual session I get information on the following:
Do the spouses have different commitments to the therapy process? Are there differential hopes and expectations? If so, this could explain paradoxical reactions
to therapeutic progress later. In these individual interviews I assess:

- each person's commitment to the marriage;
- their hopes and expectations for the marriage (including potentially getting out of the marriage);
- their hopes, expectations, and theory of the therapy;
- their overall cost/benefit analysis of the marriage: How do they evaluate
  the benefits and costs of staying in and working on making this marriage
  better versus getting out?

Another reason for doing individual interviews is to assess the presence or
absence of violence, the existence of an ongoing affair, spouses' personal goals,

*These questionnaires, along with the others mentioned in this chapter, are included in Appendices A
and B. Inclusion in the appendices is indicated by the first mention of the scale appearing in **boldface**.

and possible individual psychopathology. The assessment of violence is very important today. Current estimates are that physical violence has occurred in 35–50% of all couples in the U.S. I am not as concerned with the occasional eruption of physical violence as with detecting a pattern of psychological or physical abuse that is designed to control and intimidate the partner. The **Conflict Tactics Scales (CTS)** (Straus, 1979) is the scale used most widely to detect physical aggression in marriage, although it has many limitations. For example, it assesses the act of aggression but not the intensity of the act or the damage created by it. "Shoving" can be shoving someone down a flight of stairs or a less aggressive shove. Nonetheless, for reasons of comparability and standardization, most researchers use the CTS.

We developed the **Waltz-Rushe-Gottman Emotional Abuse Questionnaire (EAQ)** to assess the less tangible signs of abuse: social isolation, degradation, sexual coercion, and destruction of property. Interestingly, we have found that many violent couples present with high marital satisfaction scores, but this appears to be an artifact of shame; interviews with the wife alone reveal a great deal of marital unhappiness, despite Locke-Wallace scores to the contrary.

Glass and Wright (1997) suggest that the incidence of extramarital affairs may range between 25 and 50%; 25% will present with this issue, and another 30% may reveal an affair during the course of the treatment. This issue is quite complex to deal with and may create complex issues for many individual assessments. An unknown affair that is over may be revealed and the therapist will have to decide how to cope with this information. An unknown existing affair may come to light at the start of the assessment or later in treatment. Guidelines for both assessment and treatment are described by Glass and Wright (1997).

The Sound Marital House Questionnaires (Appendix B)

I have recently designed and validated a comprehensive set of 15 self-report questionnaires that assess each important process in the Sound Marital House theory. This was research done with my student Kim Ryan. These questionnaires are not a substitute for the Oral History, Meta-emotion, or Meanings interviews, or for actually observing marital interaction. But they do offer a detailed snapshot of the couple's perception of each level of the Sound Marital House. Their responses are strongly related to how spouses score on the Locke-Wallace marital satisfaction scale, the Weiss-Cerreto divorce proneness scale, and the SCL-90 psychopathology checklist. I suggest that the packet of questionnaires in Appendix B, along with the Gottman 17-Areas Scale, be given to each spouse to take home prior to or after the first conjoint session. Make sure that they understand that they are to fill out the questionnaires individually and that they are not to discuss how they filled them out with one another. Privacy is important in this process. This will help to guarantee, at least to some degree, that their responses will be honest. Explain that you will share their responses, but in an overall summary fashion, as you move to a summary of the assessment.

The Sound Marital House questionnaires include:

- **Love Maps:** a 20-item questionnaire.
- **Fondness and Admiration System:** a 20-item questionnaire.

- **Turning Toward or Away:** a 20-item questionnaire.

- **Negative Perspective:** a 20-item questionnaire that assesses negative sentiment override.

- **The Gottman 17-Areas Scale:** You will notice that each of the 17 areas has six specific true-false items for a quantitative score and a question about whether each area is a source of perpetual problems. In this way the clinician can assess specific areas of gridlock. I have found the brief write-in commentary very informative. This questionnaire can also be used as a basis for forming the initial therapeutic contract.

- **Start-up:** a 20-item questionnaire that assesses the perception of harsh start-up by one's partner.

- **Accepting Influence:** a 20-item questionnaire that assesses the extent to which both people perceive that they accept influence from their partner.

- **Repair Attempts:** a 20-item questionnaire that assesses their perception of the success of repair attempts.

- **Compromise:** a 20-item questionnaire that assesses their perception of their ability to compromise.

- **Gridlock:** a 20-item questionnaire that assesses each person's perception of whether gridlocked conflict exists in the marriage.

- **The Four Horsemen:** a 33-item questionnaire that assesses their perception of whether or not criticism, defensiveness, contempt, and/or stonewalling characterizes their interactions.

- **Flooding:** a 15-item questionnaire that assesses the degree to which each person feels flooded when arguing with the other.

- **Emotional Disengagement and Loneliness:** a 20-item questionnaire that assesses the degree to which each feels disengaged from the partner and lonely in the marriage.

- **Innocent Victim and Righteous Indignation Scale:** a 22-item questionnaire that assesses the degree to which each sees him/herself as innocent during arguments.

- **Shared Meanings Questionnaire:** a questionnaire divided into sections that elicit shared meaning in family rituals, roles, goals, values, and symbols.

ADDRESSING THE SEVEN QUESTIONS

Overall, Where Is Each in the Marriage?

People often tell you things on questionnaires that they do not tell you in any other way. The fact that these questionnaires have standard scores and cutoffs is very important, but the couples, of course, do not know this when they fill them out. Yet the cutoffs are very reliable indicators of the state of the marriage. That is part of your interpretation. I have selected a small set of questionnaires from the vast array that is available.

The measurement of marital satisfaction, also sometimes called "marital quality," has a long and venerable history. The tradition began with the first published study of marriage in 1938 by Terman et al. Terman was the psychologist who began the famous longitudinal study of intellectually gifted children and was involved with the development of intelligence tests. Terman hoped to find a kind of general marriage aptitude, like an IQ, but he was not successful. After many different ways of operationalizing marital satisfaction and marital "adjustment," sociologists eventually decided in the 1950s that all these scales were very highly correlated. In 1959 Locke and Wallace developed a short form measure of marital satisfaction, which became fairly standardized. Then in the early 1970s, Spanier developed another measure, which he called the "Dyadic Adjustment Scale" (DAS), literally taking almost all of Locke and Wallace's items and replacing *marriage* with *relationship*. His supposed test of "validity" of his "new" measure has been its high correlations (in the .90s) with the Locke-Wallace measure.

The Locke-Wallace was standardized so that, like the IQ test, it has a mean of 100 and a standard deviation of 15. Distress is usually defined as at least one spouse with a score of marital satisfaction that is less than 85. However, it is really a continuum, and people with a marital satisfaction of just under 100 have also been described in the literature as distressed.

There is a variation across the life span, with newlyweds (approximately the first four years) generally 15 to 20 points higher than this mean of 100. For about 70% of all couples martial satisfaction, particularly the wife's, declines precipitously after the first baby is born. Marital satisfaction is a significant but weak predictor of divorce, because low marital satisfaction is only the start of a cascade of processes that occurs as a precursor of divorce.

Periodically, someone develops another scale to tap some other dimension of marriage, but it is hard to find a scale that is not correlated with marital satisfaction. In general, this is true because of two "halo effects." Unhappy couples will agree to almost anything negative about their spouses, as if they say, of the negative items, "Oh, I never thought of that one, but it is also true." Happy couples agree to almost anything positive.

The Weiss-Cerreto Marital Status Inventory (MSI) is an effective tool for measuring the extent to which a person ponders the dissolution of the marriage or has already taken action toward getting a divorce—a very useful piece of information to have in an initial assessment. Total scores are the most useful, but individual items can also be revealing, particularly as probes in an individual interview. We have also used this scale in our longitudinal follow-ups. Weiss says that if the total score exceeds 4, the marriage is in serious trouble (personal communication, 1996). In our research the MSI was significantly related to low marital satisfaction scores and high levels of "husband physical illness." It was predicted by the husband's loneliness and the number of "wife disgust facial expressions" during the conflict resolution discussion, indicating that both the husband and the wife experienced their problems as severe and were feeling emotionally flooded by the way their partner expressed negativity.

I always use these two scales in combination—the Locke-Wallace scale to assess marital satisfaction and the Weiss-Cerreto scale to assess divorce potential.

In particular, I look at how partners have answered the Locke-Wallace items of (1) If they had it to do over again, would they marry the same person, not marry at all, or marry a different person? and (2) To what extent do they confide in their partner? It is important to remember, however, that clients are very likely to be *unaware that they are in these states. For example, if you ask people who score about 4 on the Weiss-Cerreto how they feel about staying married, they usually say they are quite committed. Nevertheless, these scores are a guide for me.*

I use the Gottman 17-Areas Questionnaire to explore specific sub-areas in the couple's relationship. This scale also helps me to work toward a therapeutic contract; it can be administered as an exercise by having three copies of it handy. First, each person fills out the scale and is asked to think about which areas he or she would like to work on in therapy. Then the couple does this task together, by consensus.

What Is the Nature of Their Marital Friendship?

As noted, in my first conjoint session in roughly 30 minutes I do a combined Oral History and Meta-Emotion Interview (see Appendix C). I don't use all the questions with each couple. Only the information I need to score the couple on the friendship dimensions of the Sound Marital House (Love Maps, Fondness and Admiration Systems, turning toward or away).

The Meta-Emotion Interview asks people about the history of their relationship regarding the primary emotions—anger, sadness, fear, love, and pride—and about their philosophy of emotion. Because discrepancies in the spouses' philosophies about the expression of emotions are so extremely predictive of divorce (with only one variable, the meta-emotion discrepancy predicted divorce with 80% accuracy; see Gottman et al., 1996), I always look for similarities or profound differences people have in their experiences with specific emotions and the implications of these experiences for the marriage.

During this combined Oral History and Meta-Emotion Interview I look for affection and positive affect between them (How are they sitting? How do they look at one another? Do they finish each other's sentences? Are they touching or holding each other?). I am looking closely at:

- Is there cognitive room (Love Maps)?
- Is there an obvious or covert Fondness and Admiration System?
- Is there positive affect (interest, excitement, affection, humor, validation, amusement, pleasure, joy)?
- Do I see we-ness, rather than me-ness, and is this an issue?
- Is there turning toward versus away in their everyday lives?

In my observations of how spouses discuss areas of continuing disagreement in the marriage (both on problems that can be solved and on perpetual problems) and any assessments I make of how they talk to each other in a nonconflict context (like reunion at the end of the day), I look for emotional connection, or what I call "requited emotions": reciprocated interest, excitement, humor, affection, and validation or support. I look for an active engaged listener, who gives cues that he or she is tracking the speaker emotionally or, on the other hand, a disengaged or disinterested listener (stonewaller). I am looking for signs either of emotional life or deadness and disengagement. During these interviews I look for aspects of the marriage and marital history where the spouses brighten toward one another. This is then an area of strength in the marriage. For example, a husband and wife I recently interviewed were sitting very far apart and hardly looked at one another. However, when they discussed the birth of their son, they brightened, looked at one another, touched each other, finished one another's sentences, and became affectionate. This was clearly an area of their friendship that could be built upon in therapy.

I want to know how they think of one another when they are not together, to see if there is an active Fondness and Admiration System in place. I want to know how they move through time together, whether they typically have events-of-the-day discussions or stress-reducing conversations. The Gottman Turning Toward or Away Questionnaire (see Appendix B) is sometimes useful for this assessment. I ask them to map out a typical weekday, and a typical weekend day, a vacation, a getaway. I am interested in how they renew themselves and each other when they are fatigued and highly stressed. I want to know their daily rituals of leave-taking in the morning, reunion, eating together, and what these rituals mean to them.

An important part of what I am always on the lookout for here is meta-emotion discrepancy. I look to see if one person is basically emotion-dismissing while the other is emotion-coaching, if one person thinks being emotionally expressive is healthy and important, but the partner thinks it is inappropriate, out of control, throwing gasoline on an open fire, and so on. I use the **Gottman Marital Style Questionnaire** (Appendix A) to assess mismatch in preferred type or style of marriage. These ideas are discussed more fully in my books *Meta-Emotion* and *The Heart of Parenting*.

In using the Gottman 17-Areas Scale, especially as a conjoint exercise in which each spouse fills out the scale individually and then they discuss it together, I am particularly interested in evaluating the following areas:

- Degree of emotional engagement
- Lifestyle needs being similar or different
- Degree of passion, romance, and intimacy in the marriage
- Degree of sexual satisfaction
- Presence or absence of simple fun
- Presence or absence of a shared spiritual connection
- Any potential target area of conflict
- Areas that are going well in the marriage and reflect their strengths

On any of these 17 areas in their lives, I want to know how accepted they feel as people, or how criticized, rejected, and basically disliked they feel. I want to know how the spouses are handling the daily stresses and hassles of life and whether they feel like their partner is their friend and ally or if they feel alone and lonely. The Gottman Emotional Disengagement and Loneliness Questionnaire (Appendix B) is helpful here.

In recent research, Kim Ryan and I found that couples' answers to my questionnaires that assess the first three levels of the Sound Marital House are strongly related to the quality of their sex life and to the degree of romance and passion in the marriage as reported by both (relating to about 70% and 65% of the variance, respectively). Measures of how the couple perceived their handling of conflict were related much more weakly to the quality of their sex life and to the degree of romance and passion in the marriage. Of course, we have to be careful about drawing conclusions from these findings because of the problem of common method variance (all measures are questionnaires), but they are interesting, and they are in accordance with the hierarchy suggested by the Sound Marital House theory.

What Is the Nature of Their Sentiment Override?

Negative sentiment override makes people discount neutral or positive statements and interpret them instead as hostile, personal attacks. Positive sentiment override means that people see negative statements as if they were just neutral ones, though emphasized to underscore the importance of the information. Interestingly, people who engage in positive sentiment override also find their partner's humor really funny and are physiologically calmed by it. In our data men's responses are particularly important here, so I especially look for guys not getting defensive when their wives are angry and enjoying their wives' sense of humor and wit.

Sentiment overrides can be assessed with the questionnaire I specifically designed for that purpose (Negative Perspective). But generally you can see this in a couple's interaction in the first conjoint session. My basic image of negative sentiment override is that of a person with a "chip on the shoulder"— someone who is hypervigilant for slights and attacks. The listener with positive sentiment override, on the other hand, seems to have a filter that strains out the personal element from, say, complaining and irritability, allowing the listener to extract the information in the message without much defensiveness. I also look for:

- The frequency and success of repair attempts during conflict discussions.

- Whether they feel flooded by the way their partner complains (use the Flooding Questionnaire).

- How humor and anger are responded to. (Even in the assessment phase I sometimes use video replay to see how they perceive one another's anger and humor. I actually replay specific moments on their videotape and have them fill out the Innocent Victim/Righteous Indignation Scale after viewing the moment to judge their perception of it. This can be quite a powerful event.)

What Is the Nature of Physiologies and Capacities for Soothing (Self and Partner)?

I also look for physiological responses and find that asking the spouses to take their heart rates is easy and adequate. They place two fingers just over the carotid artery (under the jaw line below the right ear), count how many beats occur in 15 seconds, and then multiply by 4. Rowell's (1986) data on the cardiovascular system's response to physical stress shows that at around 100 beats a minute the body begins secreting epinephrine and diffuse physiological arousal (DPA) can begin, depending on the context. I use a cutoff of 95 beats a minute. In my office I have two inexpensive table-top pulse oximeters (one for husband and one for wife) that display the heart rate and oxygen consumption; they can be set to any heart rate to produce a biofeedback alarm. We measure:

- *Baseline physiology.* Since there are so many individual differences in "resting" physiology, it is important to obtain each individual's baseline. We use two, an "eyes closed and relax" baseline, and a pre-conversation 2-minute baseline.

- *Physiology during conflict interaction (or right after).* At any time you can ask spouses to stop their interaction and take their heart rate. Also ask them what they were thinking and feeling. Use your clinical intuition, and look for a series of cues before intervening in this way. It doesn't matter if you are wrong and the heart rate is low. You are still sensitizing them to the fact that processes going on in their bodies are going to affect their perceptions and interactions. They will start to get the idea that they themselves ought to monitor to see if they are in a state of DPA and, if so, to think about taking a break.

- *Recovery.* I assess the percent recovery toward baseline heart rate 10 minutes after their discussion of a conflict issue.

If the heart rate of either spouse is elevated, the issue they are discussing is probably one that has become gridlocked. However, if there is no evidence of physiological arousal, I consider this a strength of the marriage.

Even in the first conjoint interview I introduce the concepts of diffuse physiological arousal and flooding. I tell them that therapy makes extensive use of creating "a port in a storm" in the marriage that minimizes the spillover of stress from the outside world into the relationship. Just having spouses take their heart rates once gets the message across that a lot of dysfunctional marital processes are nobody's fault, but just the effects of fight-or-flight behaviors once people become flooded. I tell them that one of the most powerful things we have found that people can do for their resolution of conflict is to *take breaks.*

Following is a list of cues that tend to accompany heightened physiological responses. These cues are by no means foolproof, but if you see a number of them happening together, it may be a good time to ask people to take their heart rates. Here is my list:

- Long eye closures or eyelid flutters (person has gone inside and may be censoring). (This is Paul Ekman's suggestion.)

- Increases in any of the Four Horsemen: criticism, defensiveness, contempt, stonewalling.

- Arms akimbo position (arms folded across chest).

- Hips swiveled away from partner. (This is Elizabeth Fivaz-Depeursinge's suggestion.)

- No positive affect.

- Controlled facial expressions (chin boss tightens, lip or inside cheek biting, hands to face).

- Anger: Lips are pressed together or upper lip has tightened.

- Sadness or distress: The inner corners of the brows are drawn up and together and medial brow furrows are created. (This is called Darwin's grief muscle.)

- Fear brow: The brows go straight across.

- Auto-involvements (like playing with hair) or involvement with a prop (for example, a pencil), or other "away" behaviors that say "I am not here."

- A movement from a chest to a head register in fundamental frequency; the voice gets higher.

- Any indication of held or shallow breathing. (Sighs are usually indicative of sadness; whining tends to mean that the person is feeling like an innocent victim.)

- "Non-ah" speech disturbances like not finishing sentences, repetitions, slips of the tongue, omissions, stuttering. "Ah" disturbances are people's attempts to hold onto the floor.

These are just cues to use to sensitize you to the possibility that either partner may be in a state of physiological arousal. They can be helpful in building with the couple a ritual for withdrawing from the intense conflict and engaging in self-soothing.

Physiological Recovery

As noted, I take people's heart rates 10 minutes after the conflict conversation and assess the percent return from the end of the conversation to the baseline. Most people whose heart rates go over 100 beats a minute will have only recovered about 15% toward baseline in 10 minutes. Overall fitness and resilience affect marital interactions and, I think, the couple's "carrying capacity" or tolerance for negativity in their interactions. In my laboratory we use the Queens Step-Up Test, which is appropriate to use with people who exercise and are fairly fit. Have partners step up and down a block of wood about 16 inches high to a metronome for 5 minutes. This increases their heart rates rapidly to about 120 beats a minute. Then we measure the percent recovery to the baseline in 5 minutes. One hypothesis I have is that people who are more physically fit may adapt to negativity in marriage more readily, which is not necessarily a good thing. This still has the status of a hypothesis.

What Is the Nature of Their Conflict and Its Regulation?

Recall that I am going to observe the couple's interaction on two kinds of conflict: one concerning an issue that can be solved, and one with a perpetual issue. I have questionnaires to ferret out these two topics: the Perpetual Issues Questionnaire (Table 8.1), the **Gottman Areas of Change Checklist** (Appendix A), and the Solvable Problems Checklist (Table 8.2). Sometimes I need all three, but not usually. However, I need to point out that the seeming severity or triviality of the issue is not a useful guide to whether it is solvable or perpetual and gridlocked; people can reach gridlock on even the most seemingly trivial issue. It is often necessary to carefully explain these two kinds of conflict. At times I will use Krokoff-Gottman's Enjoyable Conversation Scale to find a topic they enjoy talking about (e.g., a grandchild) and then ask them to discuss that topic for another 6 minutes.

Following the identification of these two issues, I set up the conflict discussion by preceding it with the play-by-play interview (see Hooven, Rushe, & Gottman, 1996). This keeps the conversation grounded for all kinds of couples. Solution-focused therapy questions are helpful here; they involve asking questions about the conditions that may be operating when the problem is better. Often there is a natural variability on any issue—spouses hold fluctuating views—and facilitating the expression of this variability can be helpful in determining the couple's strengths and the range of factors that affects the problem for better or worse.

In discussion of problems that can be solved (not perpetual), I look for:

- Softened or harsh start-up
- Rejecting influence (usually escalating a mild complaint of the partner to one of the Four Horsemen)
- Accepting influence (de-escalation)
- Repair attempts and their effectiveness, or not
- Compromise versus stubborn "digging in" and gridlock
- Active searching for common ground by either partner, to some degree.

For perpetual problems, I look for the stages of what happens when conflict on perpetual problems becomes gridlocked. I want to understand something about the history of the problem and what stage of gridlock they are in—a "hot stage," in which the problem generates a lot of pain, or a more dangerous stage of emotional disengagement. I want to understand the internal conflicts generated within each person by the partner's position, and what the positions *mean symbolically*. The meanings are usually very close to core concepts each person has about the self, which is why they are so threatening. These are the major signs I look for:

- The Four Horsemen
- Vilification
- Partners seeing one another as enemies
- Feeling unaccepted and criticized

- Entrenched positions with polarization
- Fear of accepting influence
- The pattern of emotional disengagement. Not all the patterns of disengagement need to be there, but I look for a "dead" or dying marriage in which partners inadvertently arrange their lives in parallel and become increasingly lonely. Look for:
  - Tension, particularly facial
  - Almost no positive affect
  - Underlying sadness or fear
  - Partners telling each other that everything is okay, which may translate into feeling un-entitled to one's complaints
  - Loneliness
  - Internal conflict
  - Physiological arousal, though this is not a necessary indicator.

In What Ways Are They Able to Honor One Another's Life Dreams and Create Shared Meaning?

I am looking for ways in which people have denied themselves and remained undeveloped as individuals, confused, uncertain, empty, directionless. We have found that women, in particular, seem to feel that they are not entitled to dreams that are not about relationships.

In this interview we start by asking the couple about family rituals, roles, goals, and symbolic meanings in their lives. We go to their home or we ask them to bring in their photo albums, if they have them, with photos not only of their own family but also from their two childhoods. This interview also elicits concepts that are now placed by some writers broadly within the realm of "spirituality." These will involve the exploration of common ground as well as differences between them.

There are many ways of "honoring" one another's life dreams. A spouse can provide support and tolerance or actually share in these dreams more fully. Or the spouses may be gridlocked because they can't honor one another's dreams on any level. This is all important information.

The Shared Meanings Questionnaire (Appendix B) is designed to answer this question. Also see Appendix C for detailed questions for the Meanings Interview.

What Potential Sources of Resistance Exist?

I look for signs indicating where the couple is located on the cascade toward divorce. I can usually tell this from the interviews, but if I need additional information I use the **Distance and Isolation Cascade Questionnaires** (Appendix A). I also assess the following:

- Differential levels of commitment to the marriage and different hopes and expectations for therapy.
- Betrayals, current or past (this includes marital violence, emotional abuse, and extra-marital affairs, and other betrayals).
- Psychopathology, including suicide potential, depression, eating disorders, drug and alcohol abuse, and personality disorders (particularly antisocial, borderline, or narcissistic personality disorder). I use the following standardized assessment tools: the symptom checklist SCL-90, the MMPI-II, the Beck Depression Inventory (Beck, Steer, Ball, & Ranier, 1996), and the Millon MCMI-III (Millon & Davis, 1997). I use the symptom checklist SCL-90 most often. Always assess whether a referral for psychotropic medication is in order.
- Past trauma, either within this relationship or in other parts of people's past, particularly post-traumatic stress disorder (PTSD), or sexual or physical abuse history.
- Disorders of individuation, in which one or both persons have not developed themselves as individuals separate from the relationship.
- Conflict in values with respect to relationships and their importance. Often this involves imbalance between work and family.

THE ASSESSMENT OF PHYSICAL HEALTH

Physical health and marital quality are two-way feedback systems. Don't ignore physical health. A variety of self-report measures can be used to reliably assess physical health. For a long time we have used the venerable Cornell Medical Index, and I like this scale, but some newer measures are available. Marital quality has long been known to be related to physical health, and there is now evidence that it is related to immune system functioning.

WHEN IS MARITAL THERAPY CONTRAINDICATED?

I think it is a good idea for each clinician to identify his or her own criteria of when marital therapy is contraindicated. My criteria are:

- Ongoing extramarital affair (secret or revealed)
- Ongoing physical abuse

In my view marital therapy can proceed if the relationship is emotionally abusive, but I think there is an important thing that every clinician should do when first encountering emotional abuse: *Do not ignore it.* Do not simply empathize with the disappointment, fear, or rage behind the abuse. I tell the couple about the Monty Python Argument Clinic, which immediately distinguishes between abuse and argument. I tell them that contempt is the best predictor of divorce, and that while the other three Horsemen occur in good marriages and can be repaired, contempt is essentially zero in marriages that work well. I tell them that contempt is sulfuric acid for love, that it has to be banned from close relationships, and that I will stop them whenever it occurs in my presence and have them rephrase it in terms of their underlying feelings. To not intervene is to collude with the abuse.

You might think that another context in which marital therapy is contraindicated is when there is an active alcoholic pattern. However, McCrady's work (McCrady, Stout, Noel, Abrams, & Nelson, 1991) and O'Farrell's work (O'Farrell & Rotunda, 1997) show that marital therapy is actually the treatment of choice in this case. McCrady treated 45 alcoholics and their spouses in one of three conditions, one of which was alcohol-focused spouse involvement plus behavioral marital therapy (reciprocity enhancement and problem-solving skills training). The percent of separations in this group was 11.1%, compared to 36.5% and 28.6% in the two groups that had no marital therapy. The authors of this study also noted that the separations in the marital therapy group were quite short.

One might also initially expect that marital therapy would not be the treatment of choice for psychopathology. However, there is reason for optimism (and for further development of marital interventions) for marital therapy affecting a wide range of psychopathologies. Marital therapy alone has been shown to produce significant effects on reducing a wide class of general psychopathologies (Cookerly, 1974), in the treatment of depression (O'Leary & Turkewitz, 1978), in enhancing drug effects with depression (Friedman, Tucker, Schwartz, & Tomilson, 1995), and in moderating the effects of unemployment on depression (Price, 1992). Spouse-aided intervention significantly enhances individual treatment for persisting psychiatric disorders (Hafner, Badenoch, Fisher, & Swift, 1983). This is not to say that individual therapy in these cases is not needed. However, if there is also an individual therapy component, it is absolutely critical to coordinate the individual component with the marital.

CASE EXAMPLE OF ASSESSMENT CONCEPTS: MURPHY AND ROSE

This assessment was done as part of an informational television show. The couple was in therapy with California therapist Lois Abrams. The husband was a pediatrician who ran an intensive care unit for babies. Everybody at the hospital called him "Dr. Murph," and he was beloved among his staff. He was a reserved man who was also capable of great warmth, humor, and charm. He was a workaholic, doing everything himself, rarely delegating much to other staff. He slept in the hospital an average of 20 nights a month. He didn't know the names of his children's friends. When he was asked for the name of his family's dog, he did not know it (they'd had the dog for three years). When asked where the back door to the house was, he actually turned to his wife, "Rose," and asked, "Where's the back door of the house?" When we asked him why he did not know where his own back door was, he replied, "I just go in and out of the front door."

A turning point occurred for Rose in the marriage a little over a year ago. He was working Christmas day, and she decided to pack a picnic and bring the kids to the hospital. As they were eating the picnic in the waiting room, he told Rose that he resented what she had done. "Why do you do these things?" he had said, "It is really embarrassing. None of the other doctors' wives does this." As he became angry with her, the phone rang; it was a nurse he worked with, and he suddenly became polite and sweet. When he finished his conversation, he turned back to his family with what she described as a mask of anger. She had had it. She picked up the picnic, packed up the kids, and went home. After that incident, she decided that she would do things for herself.

The couple had a live-in nanny, and Rose began to do things at night alone. She started to do the things she had always wanted to do and was not necessarily available to her husband on those rare times when he came home from the hospital. She studied karate and earned a black belt, took dancing classes, and then she began acting in a local theater. Eventually, she was "discovered" by a film director, and she began acting professionally. She was no longer waiting for Murphy to come home; she was no longer at his beck and call. This lasted a year, during which time Murphy became very lonely and quite resentful. Our video recall questionnaires revealed Murphy's righteous indignation, and the Four Horsemen were evident everywhere.

I have edited the conflict conversation of this couple into those moments that illustrate specific components of their marital discord. In the first clip the husband talks about what he missed when Rose was "gone" for a year. He expresses his feelings while his wife stonewalls.

> Murphy: I need emotional support. I find I have to have it. Obviously, I wouldn't ask for a divorce if I wasn't pretty serious about it. I have to have it and I don't get it anyplace else. I have to have you talk to me and I have to have you touch me.

Rose's stonewalling was quite dramatic, since women rarely use this modality. But she followed her stonewalling response with a repair attempt to bring them closer emotionally, which failed.

> Rose: I didn't know you needed those things.

This was a chance for him to accept her repair attempt and to say something appreciative like, "Yes, I really needed you, and I *still* need you. You have no idea how much I miss the great emotional support you used to provide." Instead, he acted injured, the wounded party who is duly self-righteous.

> Murphy: If I didn't, I wouldn't have asked for a divorce! If I was that cold about the whole thing or that self-sufficient, I would have taken care of the kids and said, "Go ahead and do what you will, I'll keep the family together, I'll let Rose go her way and everything would be okay." But I need it badly. I need it badly enough that I would deal with my family, deal with everything. So, I do need it.

This statement objictified his need instead of personalizing it, which is what Rose was looking for. In part, because of this statement, she responded defensively.

Rose: But I thought I was giving it to you before and you didn't want it. You didn't place a high enough price on it that you would cherish it and not let anything get in the way of that.

Here he could have said, "But I do cherish it, more than I ever realized." Instead, he again responded defensively by demeaning the emotional support she had given him in all the years prior to the past one. In fact, he suggested that it wasn't support at all but a demand, that she had not allowed him to be real, that he had to be cheerful all the time.

Murphy: What I was feeling was *demand*. I don't think you were giving me support, I think you were demanding things. I'd come home and you'd hug me and say, "Hi," and be real bubbly. If I didn't respond in a similar way, if I was morose or depressed, you'd get angry. It was like a test. If I came home and wasn't cheerful, I flunked. So instead of support, it was just the opposite. You were giving me these challenges. You'd call me on the phone just to gauge my emotional reaction.

This criticism hits Rose at the very heart of why she "left." She was afraid that he didn't value what she was providing, and here he is telling her that she is right, he didn't value it. She responds with a facial expression of contempt.

The couple also reveal a meta-emotional mismatch. Notice in the next segment that the husband says he thinks he should be "more open," which he thinks his wife wants, but then he uses insulting terms to describe people who are open, describing them as "inappropriate," "emotionally labile," and "uncontrolled." These are really his internal metaphors about being emotionally expressive.

Murphy: I know I should be more open, and there are times when people can be more open. When I go to a baseball game, I yell and shout. I don't do that naturally. That's something I could learn to do, because it's not connected with work, it's not a time which is appropriate to be in control. I have trouble adjusting to that because I don't know of any time when it's *in*appropriate to be controlled. That has never happened to me. There's been no time in my life where it's been inappropriate, where it was appropriate to be emotionally out of control or emotionally labile, or anything.

Despite this apparent put-down of emotionality, his wife, amazingly does not get defensive. She tells him that it is more important for him to find his own balance between expressiveness and control. She refers to an injury she sustained to her arm in karate class (her wrist is bandaged at the time of this taping), which made her slow down.

Rose: But I think the problem is the balance. And I learned that because I went off on the other end of the spectrum. I was also very controlled; then when I became completely open, completely carefree, it didn't matter anymore. Now I know what the other opposite end is, so I found a balance. And you think it's my arm, but it's not my arm. I

> found a balance. You need to find a balance, too, and I can't tell you
> where it is or how to do it. You have to do it yourself.
> Murphy: No, I couldn't do it myself. If I did it myself, there wouldn't be
> any balance, because I'd just be myself— which is controlled.

Now there is a second repair attempt by the wife.

> Rose: Well, but now we're here. Don't look back. Learn from it. I'm going
> to learn from it.

She is suggesting that they start all over again. He responded well to this at first.

> Murphy: Some of us learn more slowly than others.

He said this in a softer way, with the charm he is capable of. This was clearly a
strength this man had, something that could be built upon. But then suddenly, as
if a dark cloud had descended over his face, he scowled.

> Murphy: But don't expect me to change into a different person and
> become . . .

His wife interrupted him with another persistent repair attempt.

> Rose: I don't want you to change . . .
> Murphy: . . . and become all that emotional about everything, because it
> won't happen. Even if it happened a little bit, it wouldn't happen that
> way all the time. I know it.

The wife then apologized for any hardships he experienced when she was off
"doing her own thing" for a year.

> Rose: I'm sorry to put you through that, I was going through a crisis. I was
> very scared, and that's how I was reacting to being scared.

This is a great opportunity for him to respond to her statement that she accepts
him as he is and her apology. Instead, he takes the "high moral ground" and criticizes her, which is ultimately contemptuous.

> Murphy: So, what do you think you should do for our children and me?
> How do you see yourself?

He has put the children between himself and his wife, as if he and the children
were the injured parties. Undaunted, she ignores his contempt and keeps up her
optimism.

> Rose: Well, I think the children will be a lot happier now, if we get this
> resolved and get back on track again. Maybe it will be even better than
> before.

He finally catches her constructive mood.

> Murphy: If we're back on track, how would it be?

One of the really fascinating things about this case is that the you see all the
Four Horsemen of the Apocalypse here, but their therapist, Lois Abrams, suc-

ceeded in turning this marriage around, and to her great credit she had done a two-year follow-up with this couple, and they are fine. Murphy totally changed his workaholic life. He trained a resident to take up much of the work he had single-handedly been doing at the hospital, and he started eating dinner every night with his wife and children, and he also started going on dates with his wife, especially to her folk dancing classes.

One of the reasons this marriage was salvageable was their mutual fondness and admiration, even if it was just a glowing ember. This couple sat close to each other during the interview, very comfortable with physical intimacy. When they talked about their first date, Murphy revealed that he decided, on the spot, to have a least a five-year plan to woo Rose. Murphy said that he was very aware of how nervous Rose was, especially given the fact that she was sheltered by her Armenian parents and had very little experience dating.

> Murphy: I think she was very nervous, and I had some background about why she was nervous, some cultural things that she was trying to live with. And because of this I knew this was gong to take a long, long time. So, I wasn't nervous at all. I figured this was stage one of a five-year marathon, so I wasn't all that excited about it. We were just having a bunch of talks so it wasn't a big deal for me, and I probably didn't realize what a big deal it was for her.

His wife responded strongly to this statement about what he was thinking on their very first date.

> Rose: You mean you had a five-year plan already on the first date?
> Murphy: Maybe that's exaggerating, but I knew it would take more than one lunch.
> Rose: Wow.
> Gottman: Yeah, but that's amazing that you really . . . I mean, you mostly hear about guys going, okay, what can I get from this date, you know? But here you're taking this attitude of, "It's really going to take a while to get to know her, and she's worth it."

Murphy said that she was the most vivacious, interesting, and beautiful woman he had ever met. Rose was moved by this, and when I asked, she said she had no idea that he had felt this way about her at the time. I suspected that he rarely complimented her or expressed his admiration for her openly. Nonetheless, there it was, a very alive Fondness and Admiration System, but unexpressed. When Rose asked Murphy how he could tell that she was so nervous on their first date, he said that when he asked her if she wanted any wine, she'd said no, that she didn't drink, so he ordered a glass of wine for himself—and when it arrived, Rose grabbed it and drank the whole glass in a single swallow. They both laughed about this.

THE CASE OF GEORGE AND EMMA

This case illustrates assessment of a basically strong marriage in which an issue has arisen. I used the Oral History, Meta-Emotion, and play-by-play interviews, as well as an analysis of the conflict interaction. In this case there was a simple, direct, and effective intervention. The case begins with the Oral History Interview.

Gottman: You ready? I guess we'll just start by telling me how you met. You want to go first?

Emma: I would love to go first. I first saw George from afar on June the 19, 1994. I didn't see him again until August 4. I was coordinating a meeting for a youth retreat, which I do every year and was on the committee. When I walked in the room and I saw him, I said "Oh, there's that man again." And we just shook hands and that was it. A month later we went on our first date.

Gottman: Well, what do you mean "that was it"?

Emma: We just shook hands. There was no interaction, no communication.

Gottman: Was there electricity?

Emma: The only thing I thought was "there's that man again." That's all I thought.

Gottman [to George]: Do you have any impressions of that moment?

George: Yes. The pastor asked me if I'd come to this meeting. I am retired and I try to keep busy. I was willing, and the next thing I know, I was on a committee, and I was working with her. At first there seemed to be a little friction there . . .

Emma: [nodding her head]

George: You know how couples are. They aren't obvious. It looked like everything I was saying was contradictive.

Emma: He was probably one of the most obnoxious men that I had ever met!

Gottman and George: [laughter]

Emma: He really, really wore on my nerves, but I always wanted him to be at the meetings. I always hoped, when we planned a meeting, that he'd be there.

Gottman: Obnoxious but interesting, huh?

Emma: Very interesting, because no one had ever treated me like that before. I have always been given the highest respect from men, all of my life, but I found him really annoying. He was so contradictory. He would counteract everything I said to plan the retreat with something else.

George: From that point on we started working with one another, and we *had* to communicate. I found myself talking to her more and more then, and I was contemplating asking her out.

Gottman: Do you remember when it switched from business to personal?

Emma: I remember very clearly. The retreat had ended, and we didn't have to meet anymore. I wanted to have a debriefing meeting. One more meeting. One Saturday after the debriefing meeting he called me, and we talked for a long time. At the end of the conversation I thought "I really enjoy talking with him." Something shifted right then. It was

prior to Labor Day weekend and I asked him, "If you could do anything on Labor Day, what would it be?" He said, "I want to be with
you," so we went to Pike Place Market. We spent the whole day there
and that was great.

Gottman: Wow.

Emma: No holding hands. Nothing. But we sat there at the little table by
the wharf and he told me that he loved me.

Gottman: Whoa, wow, that was fast.

Emma: It was very fast.

George: Oh, yes, very responsive. I had never done anything like that
before, and the feeling was there, and like I told her, she asked a question and I had been wanting to say it. It was on my mind from the conversations we had and in talking to her, she'd said, "If there was
anything in the world that you wanted to do, what would it be?" If
you could do anything . . .

Gottman: Yeah.

George: If you had the option to travel, whatever, what would it be, and I
said, "Be with you."

Gottman: Just like that.

Emma: Mmm-hmm.

George: Just like that, automatically. It came out. Spontaneous, no hesita-
tion, no nothing.

Gottman: Did you surprise yourself?

George: In a sense, yes. But then, in a sense, no, because it was my feelings,
it was from my heart. I didn't actually think about what I said—it was
my feelings that gave the response.

Gottman: So this had never happened before.

George: It had never happened like that before.

Gottman: And neither to you [*turning toward Emma*].

Emma: No, as a matter of fact I honestly thought, having just moved to
Tacoma from Mississippi, he would say, "I want to go back home, I
want to go fishing on the bayou." I was expecting that answer, so this
took me totally by surprise.

Gottman: You were shocked.

Emma: And I almost hung the phone up. I just didn't, didn't . . .

Gottman: This was on the phone?

Emma: This was on the phone. Oh, in the Market when he told me he
loved me, we were at the table. I did not respond at all to that.

Gottman: I see. So the "I want to be with you"—that was on the telephone.

George: Um-hmm.

Emma: That was on the telephone.

Gottman: And that led to the Pike Place Market.

Emma: And we spent the entire day together.

Gottman: What was that like?

Emma: It was nice. It was very light. I call it a very "thin" existence
because it wasn't muddied by any plans for a relationship. It was just

nice and light. We walked and just chatted. But the night and the evening when he brought me home . . .

Gottman: So you had dinner there, and . . .

Emma: Nothing. We didn't eat or anything, and he apologized because he forgot.

George: I was in the conversation so much that I forgot. I hadn't even asked her if she wanted to eat something.

Gottman: You had forgotten to eat.

George: And I apologized.

Emma: He did apologize to me.

Gottman: And did you forget you were hungry?

Emma: Well, I don't eat a lot anyway. But when we did get home, on my front porch, this was very Victorian. I was opening the door to go in, he said to me, "I have something to tell you." I said, "What?" and he said, "You're going to be my wife." And I cried and I cried and I cried. Buckets and buckets of tears. I cried and I said, "Are you the one?" and he said "Yes."

Gottman: God. What a date!

Emma: I know.

Gottman: That's the first date, right?

Emma: The first one. And that was a total shift. Yes, that was the first date, and I knew then that he was the one I had been waiting for.

Gottman: [All sigh.] Passionate, romantic.

Emma: It was very quick, but it was real. It was so real that I knew that he wasn't some fly-by-night person. He did say also, "You're in love with me but you don't know it." I didn't respond to that either.

Gottman: Why do you think you cried?

Emma: I cried because it was a kind of a verification in my heart that he was the one, and the tears were just expressing what words couldn't.

Gottman: Wow. He was right then.

Emma: Oh, yes. He was right. That was real powerful. I had never experienced anything like that either.

Gottman: After a first date like that, I wouldn't know what to do! Want to go to a movie? Want to see Toy Story? [laughter]

Emma: Or something. It was the only date we had—we were engaged a month later. September 5th was our first date, and then a month later, October 5th, he bought me an engagement ring.

Gottman: You have all these dates down?

Emma: I do. I do.

Gottman: Do you usually do that?

Emma: Pretty much, pretty much. We planned a December wedding.

Gottman: You don't mess around, George.

Emma: That was really a whirlwind.

Gottman: Now, what happened during that month? Did you meet parents and . . .

Emma: No. I have some relatives in Tacoma whom he met. We became very close in a church circuit.

Gottman: You're in the same church?

George and Emma: Yes.

Gottman: And the retreat was part of it?

Emma: That's right.

Gottman: You became close in the context of the church.

Emma: Yes, and the only other outing that we went to was a Washington Fair at the end of September. I would bake breads for him early in the morning and he would bring me Starbuck's coffee every morning.

Gottman: This is really a Northwest romance.

Emma: It is. And every morning we'd sit in my living room and just eat and that was the most exciting part, not hotels and restaurants, but . . .

Gottman: . . . the Starbucks and the French bread.

Emma: Yeah. It was exciting—and I loved our courtship.

Gottman: It's kind of like you were married, that level of comfort.

Emma: Yeah. But after we were married—and then I'll back up—after we were married I wanted to court more! You do get down to the responsibilities of marriage.

Gottman: This was in December.

Emma: Actually, we had planned a December wedding, but in October he had some heart problems that put him in the hospital. I married him at his bedside in Veterans Hospital.

Now Emma shows that she was not just a woman whose only role was to be responsive. She took charge.

Gottman: Your first date was in Labor day and the wedding was in October.

Emma: Yeah, in the hospital.

Gottman: In intensive care?

Emma: In coronary care. He was to have a heart catheterization. And the reason I married him was that I didn't know the outcome of it—if he was going to have open heart surgery, and that was a possibility the next morning—so I got the marriage license and marched over to the hospital that night and said, "We're gonna get married."

Gottman: Were you scared?

Emma: I was terrified, but I knew that I wanted to care for him when he came out. I wanted him with me, *legally.* I didn't know what the outcome would be.

Gottman: You went through an enormous transformation.

Emma: I did. Even thinking about it now and verbalizing it, my heart is going like [*makes a thumping sound on her chest*].

Gottman: Well, take it easy, I don't want you in the coronary care unit!

Emma: No.

Gottman: But it really was an enormous change.

Emma: Tremendous, tremendous change for me.

Gottman: A real career woman, flying around, eating in the best hotels.

Emma: Yes. It was kind of a quiet time for me, but marriage itself brings its own responsibilities. That quickly dispersed into the reality of life.

Gottman: So what's your marriage like?

Emma: I want time with him. I want time. We never had a honeymoon. I want time.

The theme of her narrative now emerges. She longs for time and continued romance with her husband.

George: Well, I have an 11-year-old daughter, so I try to separate things. We do some things with her, and keep some time to ourselves. We need time to ourselves.

Gottman: She lives with you?

George: Yes.

Gottman: And what's her name?

George: Marlena. That summer we took a trip to California, but she was with us, so . . .

Gottman: That's not exactly romantic.

George: No, it's not what we wanted. In June my brother was getting married and he said, "Come out to Oakland for the wedding," and I thought what a fine time to take advantage of that. So just Emma and I went—the child stayed back, we didn't take her with us—and after the wedding we had time. I rented a car. We stayed in a hotel in San Francisco, and I thought that would be ideal.

Emma: I want more of that. I now know in my life for the first time what it's like to be in love with someone. And being in love, you crave, you want. There are things that have to be done, but I miss that lengthy courtship. I thought it would continue once we were married. And it really hasn't. We have just not had the time. So . . .

Gottman: So that's a potential issue—how to build more time together into your marriage.

George: Oh, yes, we have to work at it constantly. I'm also in school at night and dealing with the church functions.

Gottman: You're a student.

Both: Umm-hmm.

George: Theology. There always seems to be another church function—for instance, last night I had a class to teach, and then they asked me to preach on Sunday. That's one of the things—I realize I can't do everything. Almost every day of the week there's something to do, or to administrate! It may be choir rehearsal or some meeting. And then there's the community. I'm involved with the juvenile justice system. I formed an alliance with the Tacoma ministry and the juvenile justice system in the development of an adolescent diversion program. I'm involved with that and I got my wife involved, too, so we'll have some camaraderie.

Gottman: Right.

George: In a worthy cause.

Emma: [*looks like she wants to speak*]

Gottman: [*to Emma*] Were you consulted about this?

Emma: Er, no. It just happened. I'm a volunteer also, but that's not the togetherness I would want.

Again Emma returns to the theme of time together that is just for them.

Both: [*laughter*]

Emma: No, it really isn't. It isn't. But I'm amenable, I'm flexible, and I'm still waiting. Because if you demand the time, it's not the same. Spontaneity. So, we'll see what happens.

Gottman: Well, I hear that. I hope you hear it too, George. [*Everyone laughs.*]

George: Oh, yes. I try to do some things, catch her by surprise in something spontaneous. But it's kind of hard . . .

Emma: [*nodding in agreement*]

Spontaneity is somehow linked in this couple's collective mind with continued romance. I make a note of that in my mind and wonder if this is an issue for them and, if so, how it is played out.

George: I know I have to be sensitive to her needs and take more time out. But sometimes, even after we've spent time together, it's like she wants more.

Emma: Yes, that's true.

Gottman: I want to ask you some other things. What were your first impressions of one another?

Emma: This is the way I say it. We're of the same race, but we're not from the same culture. I'm from the Northwest; He's from the Deep South— different dialects, different food tastes, different everything, so we're trying to find a common ground that we can share. Even word usage, verbiage, those types of things differ tremendously.

Gottman: So you're working on merging your two cultures.

Here they are talking about creating a culture of their own that honors the background and values of both people. This is the area of creating shared meaning.

Emma: Yeah, yeah, and we're making great strides in that area. So I think that we're both becoming a little flexible and we're on this journey toward oneness and that's where I want to go.

Gottman: Well, tell me more about that and what it means.

Emma: What it means is that we're coming from two different worlds, and each day I think we should drop off something that can keep us on the same plane.

Gottman: I see.

Emma: And pick up things too, the more common things. Eventually there's a merging.

Gottman: And for you, George?

George: Our differences I find exciting—there's always a challenge. I think it adds flavor to our relationship, things she is used to are something totally different for me. It's exciting and I like that.

Gottman: Can you give me an example?

George: Different things that we say from the South that she may not have heard. It can be romantic, but in a different perspective. I like that. Certain things that I'll do that catch her totally off guard.

Emma: Some things I would have considered very disrespectful as a woman. But he's a man from the South and that's the way they react.

Gottman: Can you help me here with an example? I'm having trouble.

Emma: I can think of a lot of examples, but I . . .

Gottman and Emma: [*nervous laughter*]

Emma: . . . don't know whether to mention them or not. Certain things are really Victorian . . . things you just don't say . . . except in certain ways that are personal and private.

Gottman: It's more intimate?

This theme of intimate sexual talk will emerge later in their interaction. For now I do not explore it.

Emma: Yes, and that's something that I had never ever been exposed to, so I initially took it as very much of an insult. So now I'm learning that's just his way.

Gottman: That's a sort of a continual theme—of George being very abrasive and yet very interesting, fascinating.

Emma: I compare him to a plow horse [*taking his hand*]. Is that right?

George: Umm-hmm.

Emma: A plow horse. And I feel more regal. That's the way I view myself. For example, that whole month that we were engaged, I had a splinter stuck in my foot. I was limping at church and he came over with this huge first aid kit, drags out my foot, puts it on his lap and just goes to cleaning it. I felt like a farm animal!

Gottman: [*laughs*]

Emma: And that's just not something that I am accustomed to. I am used to sterile gauze and all these things but he was tending to this, and I had never experienced that, so it was kind of . . .

Gottman: It kind of bowled you over.

Emma: It did, it really did. I can't say that there was real excitement there, but there was a tenderness. Out of all of that I saw a tenderness and a caring person, which maybe I wouldn't have seen.

Gottman: It was real.

Emma: Um-hmm. It's very real. Not the candlelight kind of guy but really caring. Candlelight means nothing if the caring is not there.

Gottman: So you see the candlelight inside of him.

Emma: Yeah, but see, my part is to introduce him to the candlelight existence! So there's that merging again, kind of give and take.

George: I traveled quite a bit and I know, being from the South, that I will always have these traits. But I have been in the North and you never can take the South out of me, but the other part I learned to respect and I know. She is used to that, so I always like to bring something new that she has not seen. Even with the Southern traditions and the things that may seem abrasive to her, in the Southern culture it's not abrasive, it's as romantic as the candlelight. It's a different way but it's from the heart.

Gottman: So would you say that it is characteristic of you to view the differences between you as resources?

Emma: Exactly.

George: Hum-hmmm.

Emma: I have said that I don't want to lose me, the me who I am, and I don't want him to lose who he is. I want us to remain individuals but at the same time [*makes gesture of her hands coming together*].

Gottman: So it's an interesting kind of merging.

George: We incorporate the both without her losing what she is, and without me losing what I am. I realize that we can't change each other, but we come to an agreement [*he moves his hands together*], a perspective and a respect.

Emma: Um-hmm.

George: And join as one, it's very important to do that . . . because then that bond is closer and it's not trying to change either one of us. To incorporate the two differences together and still have that Southern and that Northern, that Northwest.

Gottman: You know, I am getting the idea that you are both very philosophical people.

George: Oh yeah. We are.

Emma: Very much so. I was thinking as he was talking that we are very culturally diverse.

Gottman: You are, but you are both very philosophical, intellectual about this. [*Both are nodding.*]

Emma: I could see how it could stand in the way for someone else, but it's a glue for us.

Gottman: Yeah, it's your style.

Emma: Yeah.

Gottman: I want to ask you next what role religion plays in all of this, with you being a minister and the church having been the center of a lot of your work and time together. Does that play a role?

George: Oh, yes, very much.

Emma: It's the common ground that we both stand on. That is the adhesive that keeps this whole thing together. And regardless of the challenges we have incurred, which we really have, the times . . .

Gottman: . . . getting married in the intensive care unit . . .

Emma: Yes. But always there is a common ground that we both stand on.

Gottman: Tell me about it.

I want to understand how their shared religious beliefs are played out and manifested in their marriage. Knowledge of shared beliefs is not adequate for understanding how they are used in the marriage on a day-to-day basis.

Emma: The belief that we have is in the Word of God. We really believe, both of us believe. I think if we did not have that [*moves hands apart*], we would be just scattered. But I think that's the focal point [*moves hands together*] that keeps us together. Things do go awry but we still have that basis and that foundation we always refer back to, always.

Gottman: How does that work?

Emma: Through a lot of prayer. We pray together, we pray separately. We read and know the Word and we believe it. We believe the Word and so that's kind of our map of life.

Gottman: Like a road map.

Emma: You bet. And if we feel like we are derailed, it always brings us back on track [*hands moving together*].

I still want to understand how prayer is used in their marriage.

Gottman: I see. How does it do that? Let's say you're going through a tough time and fighting about something, had a misunderstanding, or your feelings got hurt, for instance. How would you actually use the Word of God in your interaction?

George: Any problem that we are having we can always refer back to the Bible, and the Word of God will explain to us that there will be trials and tribulations, regardless of what they are. And there are scenarios there, factual things that happened, and we can look back there and see the different characters and events, and it tells us how we're going to make it through. It will explain to us why and what will happen.

Gottman: I see. Does it seem more like a journey then?

George: [*Emma nodding*] It's a continuous journey understanding the Word of God for us. Every problem we have or are going to be confronted with, we already know. But facing them . . . once we get to the point that that's the focal point, that's when we go back to the Word of God to get our answer. If it's forgiveness . . .

Emma: Umm-hmm.

George: Or if you're sorry, it's hurt.

Emma: Umm-hmm.

George: Or understanding. All of it's there.

Emma: Umm-hmm.

George: And it's all there. And if you believe in the Word of God, and you look back at it, the answer is right there.

Now Emma explains how they actually use prayer as a way of dealing with potential conflict and defensiveness: They pray for guidance from God to be able to see their own responsibility in the issue, and they use the alone time to calm down.

Emma: I want to add to that though. There are two other factors that are very important for us. In the midst of a conflict we separate. We separate. He may go for a ride around the block or a walk, or something.

We separate for 30 minutes to get a different perspective on the whole picture. During that period we're praying, I'm praying. I'm thinking back over it to see "Is it really that bad?" But to stay in there for us would not work, because we need to have that time-out.

Gottman: Umm-hmm. Why wouldn't it work to stay together? Is it about your emotional makeup?

Emma: You hit the nail on the head.

Gottman: [*laughs*]

Emma: We're both very philosophical and we would get into philosophical debates. The dialogue would never end.

Gottman: [*laughs*]

Emma: It wouldn't, it really wouldn't.

Gottman: Okay, so you split up for half an hour and you . . .

Emma: . . . and then when we come back, we have a different perspective. There is a real quietness once we are back together and from that quietness we begin the dialogue. The communication is the second factor that has to take place. For us it would not take place without [*hands apart*] separating.

Gottman: I want to ask you something, Emma. Is it intimidating, given that religion is a real common ground here, being married to a minister?

Emma: No. Not at all.

Gottman: Because I would be intimidated—he, being the expert.

Emma: [*George is smirking.*] No, it's not. As a matter of fact, I embrace that very much. I'm glad that he is. Part of the prayers I prayed when I was single is that I would have a man who loved God very much, who was in the ministry, because that's where my whole being rests.

Gottman: I see. So you're right up there with him.

Emma: Right up there with him.

Gottman: Wow. What do you think [*to George*]?

George: Yes. One thing, being a minister doesn't change the fact that I am still human. Ministers have the same problems as everybody else. It's just that we have to keep our focus on the Word of God and keep focusing on communication. It's a strong point, you have to be able to communicate, and it's different for everyone. But for me, for both of us, it's that time-out period that's important. Argument is not going to solve anything when tempers, your emotions, are high. To separate for a few minutes or an hour or so is a cool-down period. It's a time to meditate and pray and you can look back and then you think, "There's a problem." So you ease, you calm yourself down. You say we need to communicate about it, let's be open, let's discuss it and resolve it.

Gottman: You don't get into this thing where you are able to say, Luke, chapter 4, verse 20.

George: No, no, no, no, no.

Emma: We never do that.

George: Never do that.

Emma: And I'm glad.

Gottman: It's really from the heart.

Both: Yes.

George: Be very careful with the Word of God. You don't want to use what He said and change it or turn it around . . .

Emma: . . . to be a weapon.

George: To be what you want it to be.

Gottman: Yeah.

George: That's a sin to do that. You can't do that, but you base it on what God has said, and you contemporize it for what you are dealing with today.

This is an enormous strength in this marriage.

Gottman: Well, that's an incredible strength, I can see. You're using it as a way of guiding your feelings.

Emma: It's a principle we use and not as a tool or a weapon—knowing it and applying it, but not the exact word.

I now turn to exploring how they each see their primary families.

Gottman: Now I want to ask you, how much of this has come from your parents? Is this something you came to on your own?

Emma: No, this was funneled down to me by both my parents. They weren't in the ministry as we know it today, but they had very high ideals, high morals. They were very emphatic at being the best of whatever you were. My mother said that whatever you are going to be, be the best at it. They funneled this down and I mentioned to someone the legacy that they both left to me, the enrichment of my life. We feel that they are both still living—through me, the kindness of my acts, through compassion.

Gottman: So you were pretty close to both of them.

Emma: Very close to them. And Mother taught by precept and example, not hounding and pounding into our heads with a stick. We watched her life. I was thinking about this the other day, how the most memorable character and hero in my life was Daddy, a 315-pound huge man. Just wonderful, and I tended to look for him in other men. I always say to my sister [*patting George's thigh*], he's a real man because he is kind of like Daddy. Not ruling with an iron fist but from here [*touches her heart*]. Yeah.

Gottman: What did he do for a living?

Emma: My father? He was a federal government employee. He worked on the railroads and was a postal clerk. Before that he was the basketball coach at the college I attended in San Antonio.

Gottman: So he wasn't a quiet guy.

Emma: No, he was not. We really were very fearful of him. Not a lot of dialogue there. Daddy did not talk to us a lot, but we watched his life. We listened to what he said when he did talk. We did not have a lot of dialogue. And I'm glad. I think association brings on dissimulation and

I would have probably disrespected him a little bit if I got to know him, the man, person to person.

Gottman: But George reminded you of him.

Emma: Yeah. I can't really pinpoint it, but the quality is there. The strength is there, it really is. He reminds me of an old-fashioned person who lives off the land. He always asks me why I didn't marry a white-collar person and I ask myself that too, but it was something inside here [*touches her heart*].

Gottman: It was something real.

Emma: It was very real and I knew that it would be solid and lasting. I needed something that was going to be lasting. Facades come and go: so do candlelights, I guess.

Gottman: What about you and your parents, George?

George: Country boy—my father was a carpenter. We lived in the city but we moved to the country when I was six. I lived with my grandmother and we always went to church on Sundays. You know that saying that it takes a community to raise a child? Well, I was brought up in that kind of atmosphere where my teachers, my neighbors all were there, so everywhere I went it was like the family was there, and so they kept you straight! My Christian background comes from my rearing as a child. Growing up, I never turned from that.

Gottman: Was your father a quiet guy also?

George: No. My father was a very outspoken man. He traveled and we got along. My mother was kind of quiet. I got that.

Gottman: You got that from your mother, you mean.

George: Yes, but I've come out of my shyness. My family, as a whole, is very close-knit. We were always told that you had to do something with your life; most of my relatives are educators.

Gottman: That must have been intimidating, being a shy boy and having such an outspoken dad.

George: No, I kind of liked it because he was different, and he was a fun person. Everyone liked him because he was fun. He made everybody laugh and talk, so he was a very likable man. He got a lot of respect, and I kind of took on that trait from him. I am a fun person. I enjoy good times. And from there, as far as education, I was one of the first ones to get into education. Being a minister requires a shirt and tie— now I am comfortable with it, but I used to hate it. I am blue-collar. I like working with my hands. My brothers were different. They liked shirts and ties and the office type thing. I was totally different. I like utilizing my hands.

Gottman: So that's a lot like your father.

George: Uh-huh. He asked me if I was going to be a carpenter. I tried that, but I couldn't hit a nail straight. I'd hit my fingers, so he said, "You need to do something else."

Gottman: [*laughs*]

George: I have always been fascinated by electricity so I became a journeyman, I went to school and studied and became a journeyman. And I enjoyed that, the travel and all the things. I made a good living at it.

I am interested in the calming down period they use and in how each views emotions in general. So I begin integrating parts of the Meta-Emotion Interview with the Oral History Interview.

Gottman: [to George] What about anger in your family? Was your father an angry guy?

George: No. Happy-go-lucky. In fact, I never heard him or my mother argue one time.

Gottman: Interesting.

George: I don't remember most of my family members ever arguing. There wasn't any violence or anything of that nature. Back there in the country I saw a lot with husbands and wives that was totally different. My family was unique in that they didn't believe in it, and I myself don't believe in it and I don't do it.

Gottman: You don't believe in anger.

George: No. It has to be controlled, you don't let it take control of you. You may get upset and you may get angry, but you know that there is a cool-down period when you get there because anger can cause you to lose control.

Gottman: It's destructive . . .

George: It's a destructive emotion.

Emma: I agree. I don't have a lot of experience with anger. While he was talking, I was thinking about my mother, who was the most peaceful woman that I have ever known. Both parents were very tranquil people. It was always nice to go to their home and visit with them after I had moved away. Just very light and nice and thin existence, so I am not familiar with a lot of anger. Because I don't have that experience with it, I have been able to decide how I want to handle it.

Gottman: The 30-minute breaks sound like it . . .

George: Um-hmm.

Emma: Yeah, that works really well. That just happened for us.

Gottman: Like a lot of things for you, they just happened.

George: You can see around you what anger can do. I don't go that way.

Gottman: So, would it be fair to say that you both protect one another from anger?

Both: Yes.

Emma: And we have our daughter and because she is just 11, we want to make sure she has an example that she can use as she gets older. In schools now it's no fun because kids see quite a bit of anger, so we want to provide her with an alternative.

Gottman: Well, what about sadness? What happens when one of you is sad?

Emma: Of all the emotions we can experience, that is the one that I experience very deeply and carry just on the cuff. It's right there. Hurt and sadness, those two. Anger, no. But sadness, yeah. I'm a crybaby.

Gottman: So what happens when you feel sad in your marriage?

Emma: When I feel sad in my marriage it's a retreat for me, and then I read to get a different view on why I am sad.

Gottman: You try to figure it out. Do you turn toward George with it?

Emma: Not really. And the reason for that is that I would like to, but I feel that he has his own sadness he may need to deal with at the same time, and when I need it I need it right then, and I don't want to approach him with it and have him not be able to provide that massaging of my ego. So I handle it and it dissolves within me.

Gottman: Is that the way you would like it to be?

Emma: I would like him to be able to key in on it without my having to tell him, and I don't think that sensitivity is there yet. I don't want to always say it. It's like asking for a hug.

Gottman: Yeah.

Emma: I want him to sense when I need it and give it to me, and I think that we'll get there.

Gottman: [to George] How do you relate to that?

George: Sometimes I know, sometimes I don't. She's a very sensitive person and I understand that. I respect that and I'll give her the attention and the affection—not enough—but I try to be careful with it so she does not become dependent on that, because when you're sensitive it's a tough world. Sometimes you have to toughen up and still be sensitive and respect that part.

Gottman: Right. I see.

Emma: [nodding]

George: I guess I don't do it enough, as much as she wants, but sometimes I give her a hug and we talk, and I have learned to listen rather than to try to answer it.

Gottman: You're pretty good at that, not really coming up with the answers.

George: Uh-huh. I have learned that there is not an answer all the time; sometimes it's just an ear to listen that's needed.

Gottman: It's an occupational hazard of the ministry—wanting to just come up with the answer. She also says that she doesn't want to burden you because you have your own sadness. Is that right?

George: In a sense. But I think that's normal.

Gottman: You think she's right about that?

George: In a sense. But again, that's something we are learning and we are going through. A marriage is a daily thing. It takes work. It's an ongoing process. And learning to be sensitive to each other's needs is not all going to happen overnight.

Gottman: So in your mind it's a balance between being sensitive and also toughening up.

George: Ah-ha, yes.

Emma: I have to agree with him, and the one thing I didn't say is that I am glad that he does not respond to me each time I need it. I know if he was cueing in on every one of my feelings, I would be very dependent on him. I thought about this and I would love it and I crave being just cuddled and nurtured, but you know what? That would make me a pathetic person.

Gottman: It's certainly not the way your father treated you.

Emma: Exactly, so I'm really glad he is not there for my every beck and call because I would be very dependent on him.

Here is a shared philosophy about the balance of connectedness and independence in the marriage.

Gottman: So you both share the philosophy that it's a balance between sensitivity and toughness.

Both: Yeah.

Emma: It's that journey, and I am dropping off some things. That's not to say that I will never need him to be sensitive to me, but each time he isn't it makes me stronger.

Gottman: Okay, great. Well, thank you, this has been really terrific. Is there anything I have missed?

Emma: I can't think of anything. [*turning toward George*] You are very philosophical.

George: [*laughs*]

Emma: Yeah, that's great.

George: I am intellectual, too.

Emma: I'm impressed.

This example of a combined Oral History and Meta-Emotion Interview reveals a strong friendship in which this couple has managed to create a sense of shared meaning and to keep romance and passion in the marriage. The conflict area is clearly that this couple is so active and committed in church activities and being good parents that they have little time alone together. Emma feels lonely. Now we begin exploring the dynamics of this issue.

George and Emma: Assessing Interaction, and a Taste of Intervention

Pre-Intervention Interaction: Play-By Play Interview

In this abbreviated play-by-play interview, done by Julia Babcock, time alone together is an issue Emma has rated 100. Here is a part of that discussion.

Babcock: Has time alone together been an issue for you in the relationship?

George: Well, in a sense I know it's a problem and it's something I am working toward. I have to constantly remind myself that I have to take time with her. There's a need she has on the female issue, and I have to be more sensitive to that. And that's something I am working on and that is a big issue. To try to improve that.

Babcock: [*to Emma*] And what do you see the issue as being?

Emma: I have been alone for a long, long time. I have not been in a relationship with anyone but myself, really. I traveled alone for years. And now that I am married I want the companionship of a husband and a man. And that to me is two different things, but he can be rolled into one. But that's not happening. To me that was the main thrust of being married—companionship and all that.

Babcock: Um-hmm.

Emma: Now I just want the company of a man.

Babcock: You're married. You don't have to do it alone.

Emma: Yeah, and I crave that time, I really do. I crave time alone with him.

Babcock: So how does that relate to recreation?

Emma: Because, as I said to him a couple of days ago, let's just get out of the car and go to McDonalds and laugh, just get out of the car laughing, and let's have a great time. Just anything miniscule, walking in the park. I'm not looking for cruises and things. I'm willing to take the rock bottom, you know, just the minimal. Time with him.

Babcock: Just time alone with him, without your daughter, or can she be involved too?

Emma: Oh, yeah, sure. That's fine. But I have been around kids so long, I just need this man.

Babcock: What's getting in the way of this happening?

Emma: I think if we treat this marriage as a business partnership and plug in some dates on our calendars, it could work, but I guess I don't want that. I don't want it to be etched in stone that every Friday, you now, let's go for a walk around the block—really spontaneous! Our life is too structured and I don't want a structured lifestyle with my husband. I want spontaneity.

Babcock: [*to George*] And you like that, too, you are spontaneous?

George: Oh, yes. I like the excitement and I like to see the expression on her face when we do something spontaneously. It's more enjoyable and exciting to her and it's something *different*. I like to do something different, something new. You keep from getting bored. You can do things on a routine, but I don't like to do things on a routine.

Their lives are so structured and so duty-bound that taking time for their own pleasure gets postponed continually. She is not balking about this, she accepts it. She just wants him alone some of the time. Babcock instructs them to try to resolve this issue.

Pre-Intervention Conflict Discussion

Emma: Guess what? Here I am alone with you.

George: Finally, huh?

Emma: [*excitedly*] Yes! That's great, that's great. See, it took all this to be alone with you for 15 minutes. Isn't that great?

George: It's not the first time; we do it at the house.

Surprisingly, George has responded by becoming defensive.

Emma: I know. But guess what, you can't get in your truck and leave!

Emma has mounted a criticism.

> George: No, I'm going to stay.
> Emma: But, you know, she asked a question and I don't have an answer. She said, why don't we spend any time together alone? And I don't really have an answer.
> George: But we do—though maybe not as much time as you want.
> Emma: But do you think the ministry really is a problem with me?
> George: No, just that I'm busy with things and you understand that.
> Emma: Um-hmm.
> George: I try to be more sensitive to your needs, and I try to compromise.
> Emma: But you know the ministry has been my whole life. That's like saying, she's angry at me because I'm black.

Emma is hurt; George tries a repair.

> George: No, I don't say it that way. There are several different things that we need and I can understand that if we go somewhere or do something. I know I need to do it more but . . .
> Emma: But . . .
> George: . . . either I'm involved in something or you're involved in something. We have to make do with the time that we *do* have.
> Emma: Remember when we used to go down to the beach? On Saturday mornings? That was nice.
> George: Um-hmm. It was warm then, too. It's cold now.

George is still defensive; Emma tries a repair, reminiscing.

> Emma: Don't you have a coat?
> George: Hmm.
> Emma: No, you remember sitting in the car? And drinking coffee and watching the sailboats?
> George: Yeah. I know that.
> Emma: Do you?
> George: But on Saturday mornings usually you like to sleep late.
> Emma: I do? But I'm up and dealing with the Afro Pageant now.
> George: Yeah, you're dealing with the Afro Pageant now so that takes away that.

Emma again attempts to repair this defensive mode that George is in. She becomes direct.

> Emma: Can I ask you a question? Do you want to spend time alone with me?
> George: I don't mind.
> Emma: But do you *want* to?
> George: I don't have no problems with that.
> Emma: Okay, I just wanted to clarify that, but do you know what? Fifteen minutes in here with you, that's great. That's great. I enjoy that very

much. See, I can watch you and you don't have your keys jingling in your hands and you have no meeting to go to. See how nice that is?

Emma accepts this less than enthusiastic response. She starts addressing his avoiding her gaze, a partial form of stonewalling. She repairs things by referring the issue to a common enemy: other people always interrupting their time alone together.

> George: Mm-hmm.
> Emma: But you look like you want to jump up and run out.
> George: [*laughs*] Cause I know that once we get back home, there are several things I've got to do.
> Emma: I know once we get back, you're gonna be gone. But I get 15 minutes with you. Isn't that great? See?
> George: You still have time. I mean, we sat down and talked the other day, didn't we?
> Emma: That was really, really nice. I talked real fast because I thought it was going to end so I had to get all my words out really, really quick. You know?
> George: See, when I'm just sitting around the house, the kids come back, the phone rings.
> Emma: That's what I put on there was 100, the kids. I know.
> George: Somebody come a knockin' on the door. I mean, it's not my fault [*laughs*].
> Emma: [*laughs*]
> George: I don't talk on the phone, you know that, and when I do, it's brief, it's brief. A few seconds and then that's it.

Now, although Emma likes the romance of surprises, she wants to end the *need* for surprise. She just wants more time alone with him.

> Emma: Okay, but do you think we should have an existence where we plug in the fourth Friday or the second Tuesday or the third Wednesday after the full moon that we go out?
> George: Figure that. But don't make it routine, because you're gonna get bored with that, saying, here we go with this again. You don't want it to be that way.
> Emma: No, I don't.
> George: You don't want it to be that way. Uh-huh, no.
> Emma: Well, you've given me some nice little surprises, but, after a year, I don't want to have to count them. I mean, I can count them now on my left hand, like the other night when you said, "Let's go to the movies," I thought you had given me a trip to Tahiti. That was great.
> George: That was spontaneous, that was nothing planned. You do that every week and that would get boring. That's like, "Honey let's go to bed," going up to the bed, you know, you're gonna do that anyway.
> Emma: [*laughs*]
> George: Good Lord, something different.

Now Emma makes another repair attempt, bringing in a known strength of the marriage.

> Emma: And speaking of the bed . . . [*pause*]
> George: [*freezes*]
> Emma: What did you? Did you put zero?
> George: Um-hmm.
> Emma: Did you? I did too.
> George: I ain't foolin' with that. Ain't going that way. We all right there.
> Emma: Yeah, that's great.
> George: We got no problems.

The repair done and effective, she returns to the issue.

> Emma: But maybe that's the only time alone I should expect, huh?
> George: I didn't say that.
> Emma: Okay. When can we go to Pike Place Market and celebrate our first and only date?
> George: We'll do it.
> Emma: After the pageant is over?
> George: Gonna have to be cause you, you, you . . .
> Emma: I know I can't do it now, and you know that I don't like going to the Market in the middle of the day or the evening, because I like it early in the morning, early in the morning.
> George: Well, that will have to be one Saturday morning.
> Emma: Okay. Okay. Is that a deal?
> George: Uh-huh. What I'll have to do is, I'll have to make arrangements for Marlena to get up there to rehearsal so we don't have to rush back.
> Emma: Uh-huh. Right. Okay. Can I look forward to that?
> George: I'll surprise you.

Emma now tries reminiscing, building on the positivity they feel.

> Emma: [*laughs*] But this time why don't you buy me lunch, because you didn't buy me any lunch the last time. And did you really have any money back then? You probably didn't have any money.
> George: Uh-huh. Yeah, I had money.
> Emma: That was just an oversight, that you didn't take me to lunch?
> George: Yeah. I forgot.
> Emma: Were you so in love with me that you forgot to eat?
> George: No. We had all that food at the house I had cooked.
> Emma: That's right, cause you got up early, didn't you?
> George: I was up early cookin' cause I didn't want to be doin' that all day. I was just lost in conversation and forgot the whole thing. I had gotten back, the whole day was over, I'd forgotten the whole thing and I said to myself, Lord, I took this woman out and I didn't even offer her something to eat. That's bad, boy!
> Emma: I know you . . .

George: I told my brother about it and he said, he said . . .

Emma: What did he say?

George: He said, "You know better, you know you could always have come over here and eaten."

Emma: That's because you were so in love. Remember what Mama said? That you were infatuated with me?

George: My mama thought I was out of my mind.

Now Emma brings up an important issue in their sex life. She turned off a source of sexual excitement that she didn't understand, but she thinks she wants to turn it on again. This is a very delicate matter.

Emma: Well, I did, too, as a matter of fact. I did, too. I never had anybody approach me like that before, and all of this trash talk since we have been married is a little bit kinky.

George: That's, that's . . .

Emma: I know that's your Southern way of being.

George: But I stopped.

Emma: I know, but I want it now. I'll take anything now. It doesn't matter.

George: Yeah. When I stopped, you see you wanted me to be myself, so that's a . . .

Emma: Remember the little pats and things? You don't pat anymore.

George: You didn't like it.

Emma: Well, I have never had that before. I've never have been talked to like that before. I mean, men have always highly respected me.

George: I don't do it out in public. If you do it in public then, and everybody sees it, that's something different. I understand that being disrespectful, but it's not in your own privacy.

Emma: But I want it now. Can you try it just one more time?

George: Yes, I can try, I mean I know how to do it—

Emma: You do?

George: That's if you want it.

Emma: I want it. If I can get on my knees and beg for it, I'll do it. Whatever comes natural to you from that Southern culture, just be that way, just do it.

George: [*chortles*]

Emma: Oh, you mean there's more?

George: If I told you everything all the time, if you knew everything, then what would be new?

Emma: Oh.

George: It wouldn't be new, it wouldn't be exciting. Always remember that. It would be like the song BB King sings—the thrill is gone.

Emma: Okay, so you want to keep things a little fresh and spontaneous, is that it?

George: Keep it new. You don't want it to be the same every day. That's boring.

This issue of spontaneity emerges as a requirement for romance in George's mind. But the result of this requirement is that, except for his occasional delight-ful surprises, they do very little alone together. This is a knot in the relationship. Emma introduces a topic shift.

Emma: But tell me this. Recreation—if it was up to you—what would you want to do? I know your answer isn't going to be "I want to be with you," but if it was anything you could do, what would it be? Now we can get a good answer.

George: Well, we keep the sports things.

Emma: Not necessarily sports.

George: What other type of recreation do you like?

Emma: Well, you know.

George: It's not the physical thing or things of that nature.

Emma: I know. But remember when you first got your truck, you said that we were going to go down to Ocean Shores and ride on the waves?

George: But you said that you didn't want to get in that truck.

Emma: Well, that truck needs some shocks, okay, but, you know . . .

George: You'll have fun. Just shake you up a little bit, but I'll get you a pil-low. [*Both laugh.*] I'll take you out there.

Emma: Would you? Is that a promise—when it's warm, you'll take me out there?

George: I'll take you when it's cold! You won't go to sleep.

Emma: Okay, baby, let me ask you this seriously. What's keeping us from spending time alone together? Really and truly, really and truly.

George: Oh, I don't know exactly. We do. You just want more?

Emma: Well, I think now that I am not looking for more as much as I am a higher quality of the time we have together. If we have time alone, that's great, but I think I am looking for a higher quality, like dialogue. I notice that most of the time when we are alone, most of the conversa-tion is about something else or someone else. We haven't taken the time to talk about our things, what we want in terms of recreation or time alone or plans, those things. And I just wonder, can we gear our conversation to the you-and-I nucleus, the us part? All those other things are a diversion. Wake up!

George: I hear you. I'm listening.

Emma: Most of our conversation is regarding something else or someone else. I want it to be on me and you occasionally. Maybe once a month, twice a month. What do you think of that?

George: Um-hmm. I thought we did, but it wasn't enough, huh?

Emma: Well, I'm not looking for quantity now. I'm looking for quality, because I know that quantity is a little unrealistic, so I am looking for quality. A few times to be alone, I'd like it to be enriched and fortified. Conversation. I know we don't have a long history but I was noticing that we have already started developing some fun things, some memo-rable things, that we share. Have you noticed that?

George: Um-hmm.

Emma: That's where history starts, that's where history begins.

George: I understand what you're talking about. It's just figuring out the times. Saturday mornings seem good.

Emma: We are so busy, so many people come by and take up so much time.

George: That's true.

Emma: Does that bother you?

George: No, that's normal. Especially with kids.

Emma: You know what the answer is?

George: What?

Emma: Getting away.

George: That's it.

I think that there is clearly a knot they have gotten into that needs to be untied. This knot is the requirement that George "provide" more romance for Emma. The knot is that romance equals spontaneity and surprise, with the paradoxical result that they spend less and less time alone together. To be romantic he believes he cannot schedule time alone together but has to keep surprising her or things will become too boring. The pressure of this makes him want to leave. We saw lots averted gazes and partial stonewalling from him in the previous conversation. There was a strange tension and defensiveness on his part.

Processing the Previous Interaction

Gottman: So, how do you think that went?

Emma: I think it went really well.

Gottman: It's rare for you guys to have 15 minutes.

George: Um-hmm.

Emma: I loved it. I loved it. I really did.

George: Um-hmm.

Emma: I said, "Guess what? We're alone." It was wonderful.

Gottman: This could be something you could do on a regular basis.

George: Oh, yeah.

Emma: Oh, sure. I loved it.

Gottman: Take the phone off the hook.

George: Oh, yeah, she laughs sometimes because I say, okay we have the time. And as soon as the phone rings I say it don't be for me, so don't say it's me, or somebody will come by, it's not for me.

Emma: One thing that was unique about these 15 minutes was that we talked about each other, and other times it's always about something else or someone else.

Gottman: Yeah, yeah. Now there was a relentless quality to you in this conversation. You were going to make him understand just how important this was to you. Right? Do you think you succeeded?

Emma: I think he was aware of it. I wanted to make sure he was. It was kind of a double check system. [*laughter*]

Gottman: Yeah, right. [*to George*] Did she get through to you?

George: Oh, yes, I was aware of it. It's a slow process, and I know that she wants more.

Gottman: Right.

George: I understand that.

Gottman: I was reading your body language and, to me, it looked like you wanted to leave.

George: [*hearty laugh*]

Gottman: You looked like a butterfly that had been pierced through. Did you feel that way?

George: In a sense.

Emma: Yes, I pointed it out.

George: She pointed it out to me because I am constantly busy, and . . .

Gottman: No, no, I mean in this conversation.

George: In this conversation?

Gottman: Yes, in this conversation I was reading your body language and it looked to me like you wanted to leave.

George: Well, in a sense, but then again in a sense not, because it's not a conversation we haven't had before.

Gottman: I see. You know all the themes.

George: I know this, and the conversation is not new. We were working on it.

Gottman: Yeah, but I think that there was something she wanted that she isn't getting from you.

George: She wanted a solid commitment.

Gottman: Yeah, right. That's what she wanted.

Emma: Uh-huh.

Gottman [*to Emma*]: That's what you wanted. He did understand.

Emma: Yeah, right.

George: [*laughs*]

Gottman: But you wanted not to give it.

George: [*laughs*] Well, no. In a way . . .

Gottman: You're caught in a kind of bind here.

George: You have to be spontaneous.

Gottman: That's it.

George: And, you see, if I make that commitment . . .

Gottman: It'd get boring.

George: It gets boring. So I can't give her that commitment, I have to make it spontaneous.

Gottman: It's almost like you've got to write yourself a note to be spontaneous. [*laughs*]

George: To be spontaneous. And I have to remind myself, and I like to catch her off guard, like she said with the movie the other night.

Gottman: The movie that was just like a trip to Tahiti.

George: The movie [*snaps fingers*], and I knew that she wasn't even expecting that.

Gottman: Right.
George: And I said, "Hey, what about let's go to a movie?"
Gottman: Right.
George: And I listened. And sometimes she may not think I am listening.
Gottman: [*to Emma*] So he's good at it when he wants to be.

The surprise time together is very effective *when* it happens. But Emma keeps wanting to make the point that it rarely happens. Also, she wants to tell George that she doesn't need this because it puts her on pins and needles, waiting expectantly for the surprise. This is my opportunity to help them untie this knot.

Emma: Well, I don't want to start viewing it as crumbs, though.
Gottman: No, no.
Emma: Or, "let me sprinkle her with this." I want there to be a joint enjoyment of the spontaneity.
Gottman: Joint.
Emma: The adverse effect of the spontaneity for me is never knowing when it will come. I am like a child waiting for Christmas and the 25th isn't on the calendar!
Gottman: Right. Maybe it doesn't have to be a surprise.
Emma: Um-hmm.
Gottman: Maybe if you drop that requirement . . .
Emma: Yeah.
George: Hmm, uh-huh.
Gottman: Then you can *plan* for it.
Emma: Yeah.
Gottman: My wife and I go out on a date every Saturday unless we have company or something comes up. But we do it as often as we can, and it still feels spontaneous.
Emma: One thing I realize is that I am not looking for the quantity of time now, but I am really looking for quality.
Gottman: Yeah. That's exactly what you said.
Emma: Earlier in the marriage I wanted an endless quantity of time.
Gottman: Well, you said that this 15 minutes was really unique in a way.
Emma: Yeah, yeah. See, that means a lot to me.
Gottman: And it wasn't his idea. It was kind of planned.
Emma: Yeah, uh-huh. It was planned. I am at a point now where I am making a transition from wanting spontaneity. I am still there but I am ready to start planning now.
Gottman [*to George*]: Do you hear that?
George: Uh-huh. We do plan certain things, we go to social events at the church . . .
Gottman: Yeah, but George, I am hearing something different. I am hearing that she wants you all to herself.
Emma: Yeah.
George: All to herself, and I understand, but the church things . . .
Emma: I do.

George: All to herself, I understand that.
Gottman: It's not that the church things aren't important.
George: But she just wants more . . .
Gottman: . . . time alone with you.
George: More time just with me. And I heard that. Just with me.

Now that this theme is clearly communicated, I return to the other theme, a time together with no interruptions, which means truly getting away, as they used to during the courtship.

Gottman: I'll tell you another theme I heard here, and I want to make sure it gets communicated, and that is three words, three magical words called "OUT OF TOWN." Right?
Emma: Um-hmm.
Gottman: Am I right?
Emma: You're absolutely right.
Gottman [to George]: Did you hear that?
George: Oh, yes.
Gottman: Okay, all right.
George: I know. And there are times that I try to plan, and I have plans to get away sometime, and I know that we need that time.
Gottman: Okay, well, I am going to take a risk here. I have nothing to lose!
George: Go ahead.
Emma: Okay.
Gottman: I want you guys to plan a weekend away from the church, away from kids, right now, one weekend. Make a definite commitment. I mean, there are places like Salish Lodge—my wife and I go there occasionally, there are bed-and-breakfast places that are not too far from Seattle.
Emma: Right, right.
George: Um-hmm.
Gottman: Forty-minute drive and you're there.
Emma: And you're there.
Gottman: And you're in the mountains, you're in the country, and you're a country boy.
George: Oh, yes. Matter of fact, I want to go—I was planning on going up to Canada.
Gottman: Okay, I'm gonna step out of the room. I want you guys to plan one.
Emma: Does that include dates as well?
Gottman: Well, my minimum is one weekend, out of town.
Emma: Okay.
George: Okay.

Post-Intervention Conversation

Notice in this next interaction there is a dramatic shift in George from being reactive and defensive, communicating great discomfort and wanting to leave, a somewhat passive stance, to a direct in-charge approach. He looks directly at Emma throughout, maintaining eye contact.

George: Okay, I say the first weekend is the weekend of Valentine's day.

Emma: Ooohh!

George: We will go to Canada, we'll go there for the Valentine's Day celebration.

Emma: Are we going alone or with somebody?

George: No, we are going alone and it's gonna be you and me.

Emma: Okay, okay. How do you think that it'll be? So the weekend of Valentine, that's like the 14th?

George: Somewhere around in there.

Emma: Okay. Do you feel that you will be a little nervous?

George: No.

Emma: What kinds of things do you see us doing?

George: We will go to a nice restaurant, we will go somewhere where there's a nice tour so we get to see the water.

Emma: Uh-huh, yes.

George: Vancouver is surrounded by water and we can get out and see, decide what we want to tour.

Emma: Okay.

George: Maybe go on up further and spend a night in a different area.

Emma: Okay. You're a man of your word, so I'm going to hold you to that.

George: Yes.

Emma: Are you going to look forward to it?

George: Oh, yes.

Emma: Me, too. I think that's going to be nice. And you know what else? I'm going to have a gift for you. I don't know if the 14th is on a Friday or on a Saturday.

George: I said weekend, so it's going to be the weekend of—sometime either around or before.

Emma: Okay, that'll be nice, George. I really appreciate that. Does that mean a Sunday or Friday and Saturday?

George: We can make it a Friday and Saturday or a Saturday and Sunday, whichever one you think.

Emma: Okay, cause if we go on a Saturday we'll just stay one night, but if we go on a Friday we'll stay two nights.

George: It'll be two nights, because we can go make it two nights. We can make it a weekend. That'll be two nights.

Emma: Well, that's gonna be nice. Are you excited about it?

George: Oh, yes. I kind of planned it already.

Emma: Oh, really?

George: Oh, yes.

Emma: What were you gonna tell me?

George: Just to do it.

Emma: Okay, so you want to do Canada.

George: Yes.

Emma: I haven't been up there in years.

George: I told you I had wanted to go back up there again. There are some places up there you haven't seen.

Emma: Up in Canada?

George: Yes, I have been all over Canada. Avoid it when it's cold! It depends on how you feel about driving—you have to drive to get somewhere we can really see the view.

Emma: I know.

George: Places you haven't been.

Emma: Okay, so you'll be my tour guide.

George: Mm-hmm.

Emma: Okay. Did you say that you've been there?

George: Oh, yes.

Emma: Okay. I feel like I'm courting you again.

George: Good, good.

Emma: See, it doesn't take much.

George: See, I haven't taken off and run [*laughs*].

Emma: I know, but you were about ready to.

George: [*laughs*] No, with me sitting for long periods of time, the numbness part sets in so I have to move around a bit.

Emma: Oh, is that it? [*lighthearted sarcasm*]

George: Yeah.

Emma: So that'll be really nice. I am looking forward to that. I think that will be interesting, so we can do that.

George: Mm-hmm.

Emma: I'll even wear a nice red dress, a low-cut short red dress. How's that?

George: That'll be fine. I like seeing you in red.

Emma: That's exciting. I'll make one especially for you. But you'll have to promise you'll look at me.

George: I look at you, I look at you still.

Emma: Do you?

George: I look when you don't think I be looking.

Emma: Ooohh. Do you? Thrill. I like that. Ooohh, sounds nice, sounds exciting.

This is new. They have begun being able to plan for romance.

Chapter 5 &

The Disasters and Masters of Marriage

 This chapter provides a review of the basic processes of the Sound Marital House theory. For each "level" of the "house" there is an example of a couple who handles the process disastrously and one who handles it masterfully. The goal of this chapter is to bring the processes of the Sound Marital House theory to life with real examples.

LOVE MAPS

Love Maps measure the amount of cognitive room partners have for the relationship—knowing one's partner's psychological world, and being known and feeling known as well.

Disasters

The husband hardly looks at his wife, even when he is speaking.

W: But you never ask me what's wrong.
H: [*long pause*] Maybe I know.
W: No, I don't think you do.
H: [*long pause*] Maybe I just like the quietness of it. I don't know.
W: I seriously think sometimes that as long as we've been married, you still don't know very much about me at all.
H: [*long pause*] You know, I think that's true about both of us maybe.

In this interaction neither of them makes any move to change this state of not knowing one another and not feeling known by one another.

Masters

The wife is 7 months pregnant and talking about what she wants for the baby—
to be raised Catholic—but her husband is an agnostic. The husband maintains
eye contact throughout.

> W: I guess it gives me hope, you know.
> H: [*nods head*] For him.
> W: For him. I want him to be able to believe in something—something
> that's always going to be there for him. I . . . uh . . . [*starts crying*] . . .
> think the Catholic Church would give our family a little more struc-
> ture. We have structure now, but I'd like to have a little more some-
> thing to believe in, a little more something to look forward to . . . not
> that we don't have anything to look for now, but, a little more, it is
> just [*crying now, drinks water*] . . . . I'm sorry.
> H: It's all right, it's all right. You're making total sense, really.

The husband encourages her to express her deepest feelings about her son and
her religious beliefs, which are very different from his. He conveys nonverbally
(and by finishing her sentence) that he wants to know what she thinks, and he
tells her that her views make sense to him (even though they differ considerably
from his own views).

FONDNESS AND ADMIRATION SYSTEM

The Fondness and Admiration System reflects the amount and accessibility of
respect and affection partners feel for, and are willing to express to, one another.

Disasters

The context is an Oral History Interview.

> Interviewer: How did the two of you meet, and what were your first
> impressions of one another?
> H: Anne, how did we meet?
> W: We met at that big Christmas party Harry's office gives every year for
> friends of the firm.
> H: Oh, yeah. I had a little too much to drink, I think.
> W: Even back then you couldn't control it.
> H: Don't get started.
> Interviewer: Do you recall what first struck you about Anne?
> H: No, not really. [*pause*] I must have been attracted to her.
> W: Can't you even remember?
> H: Yes, of course, I was definitely attracted to you.
> W: Too late, you blew it. What was I wearing?
> H: What is this, a test?
> W: Yes.
> H: The blue dress?

W: Which one?

H: The short one?

W: No, I was wearing a beige gown that Doris loaned me. I thought I looked pretty hot that night.

H: You did.

W: [*sarcastic*] Right, Romeo.

There are no spontaneous expressions of pride or admiration in one another, or affection in reminiscing. Instead, the interview slides straight toward negativity and disappointment.

Masters

The context is an Oral History Interview.

Interviewer: How did the two of you meet, and what were your first impressions of one another?

H: I'll never forget the night. It was a miserable night in Seattle and my friend Larry wanted to go to a dance being held at the Puyallup high school gymnasium. It was a depressing scene. It had started pouring rain so we were pretty soaked when we arrived. Larry looked like a wet duck. The place smelled like socks, the walls were a military green, and the band was awful. I thought, I'm tired, why do I always humor Larry? And then I saw her, standing there in a yellow dress, and she looked like a flower. Really, she did. So I waited for the band to play something slow and I thought, *I will ask her to dance*. I'm no dancer, believe me. And I couldn't. I was frozen to the spot, my heart was pounding, when she suddenly walked up to me and asked me to dance.

W: Well, I wasn't going to wait all night, and I could tell you were interested. And I was, too.

H: Was it that obvious from across the room?

W: It was. And then I also noticed your cute butt.

H: That's the thing about Martha, she has got guts. She had it then, she has it now. This year our son was having trouble reading. Turns out he's dyslexic. So Martha goes down to the school and makes sure that he gets a reading curriculum just tailored to what he needs. She has real guts when it counts.

W: Why thank you, William.

H: I'm glad you do, because I would be terrible in that situation. I get intimidated by teachers to this day. I feel like I am four years old at any teacher conference.

TURNING TOWARD VERSUS TURNING AWAY

Turning toward versus away reflects emotional connection versus distance in the marriage. Both couples sampled below are in the Gottman apartment laboratory.

Disasters

> W: [*reading the newspaper*] This is an interesting interview. Very rare one. Pol Pot said, "my conscience is clear." Remember who he was? The head of the Khmer Rouge, who killed all those people, probably a million. What conscience?
>
> H: [*He ignores her, and just keeps reading his own paper.*]

This was a simple bid for interest, and the partner ignored it. There was no apparent subsequent hostility, which is typical of failed bids. However, we find that the probability of people "re-bidding" after their partner turns away is nearly zero. So it does seem that this failure to connect has impact. We think that the impact is cumulative, that it gets registered in the "emotional bank account."

Masters

> W: [*reading newspaper*] Police issued an arrest warrant for the attempted murder charge after ensign left the county jail. $2,500 bond. I saw that—he was on the side of the freeway. Police going at him.
>
> H: [*also reading his own part of the newspaper*] Oh, yeah. On TV, right?
>
> W: Yeah.
>
> H: Saw it. It was videotaped, right?
>
> W: Right. Whenever I hear about that I keep thinking of that comedy line "Don't videotape me. Just help me." [*laughs*]
>
> H: [*laughs*]
>
> W: Put that stupid camera down [*laughs*].
>
> H: Yes [*laughs*].

The masters not only convey interest by following one another's bids for attention but are also responsive to bids for humor. Later on in this tape we see ready expressions of affection and support.

SENTIMENT OVERRIDE

Sentiment override can be either positive or negative. Negative sentiment override means that people have "a chip on their shoulder": They are hypervigilant, looking for slights or attacks by their partner. Positive sentiment override means that even negativity by the partner is interpreted as informative rather than as a personal attack.

Negative

The wife is describing her struggle to get their girls dressed in the morning. They want to dress themselves but they dawdle, which results in her yelling at them and then usually dressing them over their protests.

W: I have told them to do it for themselves, they want to do it themselves, they don't want me to dress them. But then they sit there, so finally I say, "It's too late, you wanted to do it yourselves but you didn't do it yourselves, so now I am going to do it for you."

H: I just think with more supervision and less last-minute panic, these things can get done and it doesn't get into a situation where you have to make them do something that they don't want to do. I think the whole situation would be improved if you just made sure that more things happen the way that you want them to happen and the way that they want them to happen and I don't know, I don't see the . . .

W: Well, honey, I say all the time that I need to work on it, but I don't see why you never say, "Okay, well, I'll try." *It's always my fault.*

This sense she has that she is constantly being criticized with no recognition of anything she does right is part of negative sentiment override. It may even be true that she is getting lectured by her husband here, but her hypersensitivity to being criticized is what negative sentiment override is.

Positive

What is remarkable here is that the husband helps his wife articulate what it is about him that irritates her. This shows a remarkable degree of positive sentiment in the marriage that is used to override the irritability and the complaint.

W: I mean, there's something about the way you make your statements that has always indicated to me more than just your statements. It indicates that you . . .

H: It indicates that I am intolerant toward certain things.

W: No, it indicates that you have spoken, that you have spoken.

H: That I have spoken. So it's not the words. I mean, do you think that I am an authoritarian?

W: Um-hmm.

H: Okay.

W: Yeah.

H: I guess I am a little bit authoritarian.

W: That's what I mean when I say, in a booming voice, "You have spoken." I mean, it's not your opinion that I have the problem with, although . . .

H: It's the finality with which I give it.

W: Yes, yes.

THE REGULATION OF CONFLICT: PERPETUAL PROBLEMS

Conflicts that are perpetual never get resolved. Rather, couples whose marriages are ailing do not adjust to them and become gridlocked. Couples whose marriages are going well adjust to the perpetual problems and regulate the amount of conflict so that there is actually some gentleness and positive affect even when they are in conflict.

Disasters

The issue is the husband's difficulty getting up in the morning, which makes the wife late because they both drive to work in the same car and work in the same factory. She is a morning person and he is a night owl (food for a perpetual issue). She has breakfast ready and tries to wake him cheerfully, but he is sluggish in the morning and doesn't want to talk to her. She takes this as a rejection. His laughter is provocative and her contempt is an index of gridlock on this perpetual issue.

> W: It's *not* funny. And it pisses me off every day.
> H: Well, I know that it does [*laughs*] and I shouldn't laugh about it, because I used to hate when I was late on account of someone else, you know. I know what it feels like.
> W: [*angry voice tinged with sarcasm*] Oh, do you know what it feels like?
> H: Yeah, I know what it feels like.
> W: [*angry*] Then why don't you have a little respect for me?
> H: Well, I will, I'll try, I'll try to get out of bed in the morning when the alarm goes off and when you wake me up. I'll . . .
> W: Well, I'm not waking you up anymore. I'll just set the alarm for you.
> H: Well, you can wake me up.
> W: No, I don't want to wake you up. You don't like to hear my voice. It's just like the tone of your mother's.
> H: Well, it does sound like that [*laughs*] . . .
> W: That makes me feel real great, too [*sarcastic*]. And you don't like to talk to me in the morning.
> H: [*smiling*] Maybe if you had a different tone, maybe. You sound like you're commanding. It's a command the way that you tell me to get up.
> W: What am I supposed to say? "Please get up, dear. Would you get up?"
> H: Well, if you asked me to . . .
> W: Get serious.

This wife feels fundamentally rejected and disrespected by her husband. He, in turn, feels that his natural ways of being sleepy and disconnected in the morning are unacceptable to his wife and keep hurting her feelings, whereas they were considered okay and even charming by others in his past. He is trying to get his wife to relax around the issue of punctuality and even to laugh, but instead his efforts are interpreted by her as rejecting.

Masters

The issue is the husband's chronic lateness.

> W: Anyway, I feel like it's dumping on you to discuss as our point of disagreement *your* being late.

H: No, that's one of my few weaknesses. I do have some weaknesses. But I don't disagree . . .

W: [*laughs*] There's not much to argue about.

H: Well, that's it. I agree that . . .

W: You very nicely agree that you shouldn't do it, but you do it anyway.

H: Well, I try not to. I try to improve.

W: You have been better.

H: I'm glad to hear that, because I *do* try. I do have a few other faults, too.

W: When I first started working with you at the store, your lateness drove me crazy, but now I've learned to just expect it and plan around it. Even Norris [his brother] plans around it.

H: Yeah. He isn't as tactful as you are.

W: No, but he knows . . .

H: He deliberately comes real late when he picks me up occasionally . . .

W: Oh, because he knows that you'll be late?

H: [*laughing*] Not just a little late. Real late.

W: [*laughs*]

H: [*smiling*] Bugs me. Makes me angry.

W: [*laughs heartily*]

H: There it is. I can be late but he can't.

W: I think you're just getting back at your mother for all those times she left you swinging on those swings!

H: You know, you may be right.

W: Yes, and I think you should grow up and not do that. I mean, I am not your mother.

H: I am not conscious of that, but as you say, the reality of those times when she'd forget about me for hours—um, boy, those were very turbulent times for me.

W: [*nods head*] See?

H: Yeah. God, I hated her for that.

W: [*smiling*] Yeah.

H: The message was very clear. [*pause*] The message was very clear. Boy, life's complex. [*long pause*] What about those shoes, anyhow?

W: These are not fancy shoes.

H: No, they're pretty shoes, too . . .

W: I just got them.

H: . . . they're nice.

Although the wife expresses her irritation about the husband's chronic lateness, she also shows understanding and psychological insight about it in a way that is moving for her husband. After a tough emotional piece he eases his tension by this delightful comment about her shoes. Change of topic, rather than being dysfunctional, is a typical and natural way for couples to ease tension.

THE REGULATION OF CONFLICT: SOLVABLE PROBLEMS

For problems that are situational and not perpetual, there are five patterns of interaction that distinguish the disasters from the masters. These are: (1) start-up (harsh or softened), (2) influence (rejecting or accepting), (3) repair and de-escalation (failed versus successful), (4) compromise, and (5) using positive affect to self-soothe and soothe one's partner.

Disasters

The couple is discussing their financial problems. The start-up is harsh. There are also problems in the friendship aspect of this marriage, and so, because neither of them provides enough support for the other's position, both feel put down and are in an adversarial conflict. He has just criticized her for spending too much on the house, and she has then raised the issue of the expense of his smoking habit. She is contemptuous. The financial problem is situational and solvable. They do not have differing philosophies or values about money.

> W: Okay, well then I am going to start smoking too, because I am under stress too [*sarcastic*]. I have three kids who are screaming and carrying on. But no, I control it and don't smoke. It's like, you make that an excuse for your smoking.
>
> H: [*Husband provides no head nods or facial activity while wife is talking. He maintains eye contact, but his posture is defensive, arms akimbo.*] Well, that's true.
>
> W: And you say that I don't give you positive reinforcement—but for what? If you cut down, it wasn't enough that it was noticeable—and if you stopped, it wasn't long enough for me to notice.
>
> H: Well, how observant are you toward those things, Margo?
>
> W: I know that last night you had a very stressful night because when I went into the bedroom, it smelled like cigarette smoke, and I know you smoked three or four cigarettes, and you hardly ever used to smoke in the bedroom.
>
> H: I make it a point to usually just smoke at work. Unless I am downstairs . . .
>
> W: Unless you are downstairs working . . .
>
> H: in the shop, but . . .
>
> W: and you smoke in the car.
>
> H: Yeah, I smoke driving somewhere . . .
>
> W: when we travel someplace.
>
> H: I would ask you to be more perceptive and be more positive because you don't even know that I quit. I mean you didn't even pick up on this. And if you don't even pick up when I *don't* smoke . . .
>
> W: How long did you quit? A day? [*laughs, mockingly*] Two days? [*laughs*]

H: [*not joining in the laughter*] No, it was two weeks.

W: And you quit cold turkey?

H: Uh-huh.

W: Or you just cut back to where you weren't smoking at home?

H: I quit cold turkey for a week and you didn't even notice it. So then I started smoking again, just at work. And then I remember thinking that next weekend, well I'm just gonna, and then I started smoking out in the garage, and now I pretty much just smoke out in the garage.

Masters

The spouses are discussing money. Notice the following points: the wife's softened start-up, how engaged the husband is, the wife's arguing strongly for her position, his stating his own position but accepting influence, and their mutual search for common ground. Notice also their use of agreement and appreciation, humor and laughter, as well as an open expression of anger. Finally, they compromise.

W: Your idea of saving cuts out a lot of the fun when we do go out, because all I worry about is, how much is it going to cost, how much are we spending, and that we should be saving that money for something else.

H: Yeah, I know my natural tendancy is to enjoy the moment and have a good time. Then we will have the memory [*smiling*].

H: Okay [*smiling*].

W: And the money is well worth spending. When we lived in Magnolia Heights, you said it was all being spent on living and now it's going into entertainment.

H: Yeah, right.

W: I agree with you there.

H: Okay.

W: It's easier for me to deal with it when it goes into our entertainment than it is for you.

H: And I'm concerned because I have seen too many people go through their money so fast.

W: [*anger*] See, I resent that. You are generalizing, you . . .

H: I'm saying . . .

W: making it as if I am the same thing.

H: I am saying, that [*chuckles*] . . .

W: I will do the same thing.

H: Well, we are going through a large figure every year now. We finally have gotten everything in control.

W: Ten years from now I will be glad we saved.

H: Okay.

W: But at times now it gets awfully frustrating.

H: But then it's hard for me to have to be . . .

W: to hold the reins . . .

H: to be the willful one, and hang on to my guns, feeling—hopefully—that I know what I am doing because it's served me very well in the past.

W: But don't you think there's a happy medium somewhere? Spend a little and save a little? Instead of . . .

H: I could have spent it all when I was young!

W: I know, Frank.

H: I could have spent it all in high school!

W: I know, but that's what I am saying: There's a happy medium. You could spend it all, or you could save it all. That's the way you look at it.

H: [*laughs*]

W: But there is somewhere in-between.

H: How much? Name me a percent.

W: Well, now we're going to disclose something we want kept private here.

H: No, no we won't. Just name me a percent. Name me a percent. That doesn't disclose a thing.

W: Okay, let's say we spent $100 a month on fun, on going places together.

H: Okay.

W: Okay? That's $1,200 a year.

H: Okay.

W: And we're going to be here another, say, two years. Right?

H: Right.

W: $1,200. What is that? About $3,000, say, that's an overestimate, okay?

H: Okay.

W: $3,000 is not even 10%.

H: Okay. I'll give you $100 a month. [*smiles*]

W: [*laughs*] This may be very advantageous. [*both laughing*]

HONORING DREAMS

Every marriage needs to honor the life dreams of the individuals in the partnership to the extent this is possible. Often in our work with distressed couples these hidden and disregarded dreams are revealed only in times of conflict.

Disasters

The spouses are ostensibly talking about disciplining the children. They have been unable to make progress on this issue for years. Behind each position are dreams that are not being expressed or honored. For her these issues involve her idea of what their relationship should be like, and how connected one should be with people, in a marriage and with the children. The wife is quite dismayed by her husband's shutting out of the children and her.

W: I think there's a different way we can get the kids to listen to me. I don't know how, but . . . [*sigh*] you know I have been cooped up all winter long, too.

H: Well, when you take them and put them in a room, and they start saying [*mocking with an exaggerated whiny voice*], "Mommy, can I come out, Mommy, can I come out?" ignore them, shut it out.

W: No, because they just come on out.

H: No, they don't.

W: Yeah, they do.

H: When they come on out, put 'em back in.

W: And is that good for me all the time? No.

H: Is that hard on you?

W: [*angry*] Yes, anymore, yes.

H: Just shut it out!

W: Easier said than done.

H: You can't do that.

W: *You.* See, that's the difference between me and you. I don't shut things out. You do. Even with me—you shut me out.

H: Why not?

W: Even simple things you shut out. Why *not*?

H: Yeah.

W: Because it's not good.

H: Why sweat the small stuff? It's the big stuff that's going to come back and bite you in the butt, and that big stuff is death. All these little small things, eh [*snorts*].

W: See, that's another thing. You think anything I say is small.

H: No, I didn't say that.

W: Yes, that's exactly what you just said.

H: I said some of it is, some of it is, yeah.

W: Well, no! Well, you insinuate that everything is, more or less, because you say [*mocking*], "Why not, don't let the small stuff come up and bite you in the butt, it's the big stuff that's gonna get you."

H: Well, I don't listen. When I'm not listening to you, I figure all you're talking about is small stuff.

Masters

This excerpt is a striking contrast with the previous segment. Here, the children are central in revealing the wife's dream about marriage and her family.

W: Kurt [her second husband] has a family tradition passed on from his father and, I think, from his father's father. The way to break any tension at a dinner table is to ask for the butter, which happens to be in a tub. The first time that Kurt met my children my son asked Kurt to pass the butter, Kurt said, "Sure." He picked it up and my son Chris reached his hand out and Kurt turned the butter sideways and crammed it onto his hand—and so there was butter in this tub sitting on my son's hand! And Chris looked over at me and he said, "Be on *my* best behavior, huh mom?" [*laughs*] And I looked at Kurt and he was just dying laughing, and I looked at Chris and he laughed and everything was okay. I mean, it had worked. It was unorthodox, but it worked. [*Both spouses are laughing.*]

Gottman: [*laughing*] Pretty high risk.

H: And it worked. We formed a bond. And it's always been good.

Gottman: So, is it still based on humor?

W: Oh, I think so.

H: A lot of it is.

W: Yeah, yeah.

H: When my son Troy came down to visit [for the first time], the same type of thing happened. We were all sitting around eating spaghetti, and Chris, her son, got down to the last part, not the last spaghetti noodle on his plate by far, but the last noodle in his mouth, and he slurped it in, and Stephanie, her daughter, said, "That is so rude."

W: "That is gross, Chris."

H: Chris looked at Troy and at me and it was just like somebody planned it and we just all took our faces and buried them in the spaghetti.

Gottman: [*laughs*]

W: They had spaghetti . . .

H: spaghetti everywhere . . .

W: all over everywhere, their faces, and it was just like the three boys were saying, "We are going to stick together." I said, "Stephanie, you and I just don't have a prayer."

H: Get rid of it.

W: I think the thing that impressed me the most with Kurt occurred when we had been married only three weeks. His boss came in to him and said, "Kurt, I want to restructure some things and I'm going to put you on the road. I want you to call on all the other warehouses and organize everything the way you have done here." And Kurt looked at him and said, "No, I don't think so." And the boss said, "What do you mean, 'You don't think so'?" And he said, "I've traveled in my job for the last several years, and now I am with somebody that I don't want to be gone from, and money just doesn't mean that much. You know, I quit." And he did. And here we were. We'd been in the marriage three weeks.

Gottman: God!

W: We had three teenage kids. We came home that evening. We really always included the children, especially because we had joined families, so we included them in any discussion and any decision that was major to the family. We sat them all down and said, "Hey, this is what's happened, so we're going to need to tighten up and figure out what we're going do, until he decides what to do and gets another job." And Troy said, "Well, Dad, why don't you open up a bike shop? You know all about it. You've been fixing old BMX bikes and there's no other place to do it." He said, "Put up or shut up." And if you haven't gathered by now, our son is a real strong . . . individual.

H: He is.

W: And he has a real strong insight into everything.

Gottman: Yeah. This kid is incredible.

W: So we did. We opened up a bike shop, we opened a BMX race track and put the boys to work. And that's what we did for the next four years.

Gottman: Wow.

W: To me, what that said was that the kids and I were first in his life. Not money, not the job. Not anything else.

CREATING SHARED MEANING

A marriage is a new culture, reflecting the partners' unique ways of making this journey through life meaningful. To the extent that the couple can create shared meaning, the friendship is greatly enhanced, as is their ability to deal with conflict.

Disasters

This couple is in their sixth month of pregnancy. They are being interviewed about their experience of pregnancy and their thoughts and expectations for the baby and about becoming parents.

W: Being pregnant has been nice, mostly.

H: It's been a little weird, if you ask me.

W: Yeah, weird having something alive inside you, but kind of nice too.

H: We have become totally focused on this event, we talk about nothing else.

W: I liked it when the baby started moving.

H: I liked that too.

W: It was amazing to think of it as being alive, a little life of its own.

H: It gets a little old, though, being asked to feel it kick all the time.

W: I think it's a little acrobat.

Interviewer: So this has been exciting but somewhat stressful too?

H: Not very stressful.

W: A little stressful for me.

H: I am excited about getting away on this upcoming ski trip.

Interviewer: Oh, the two of you are going skiing?

W: No, just Jim.

H: We used to go all the time, but now just I'm going.

W: Yeah, I wish I were, but I can't.

H: We always used to laugh at fat people and we stayed in shape, but now, well, I know Judy isn't really fat, but she is sort of shapeless.

W: He calls me the whale.

H: Just a joke.

This couple displays the early signs of not moving through the transition to parenthood together. They are not becoming a team, both invested in becoming parents. The husband continues to hold onto his separate interests and disparages his wife's appearance. It is difficult for her to become excited about becoming a mother with him. If they continue this way, she will change philosophically when she becomes a mother, but he will not, and he will begin to withdraw from their new family.

Masters

For this segment I have selected three short excerpts showing people in the moment of creating a shared sense of meaning.

The first couple is talking about the death of a friend whom they cared about a great deal. Their friend was handicapped and somewhat eccentric. They are both moved by the fact that she touched so many other lives, despite her limitations.

> W: Pat said to me on the phone today how much she—how very shocked she was to hear yesterday that Jenny had died. And she was saying how . . . I think she used the word "vivacious," she remembers Jenny as being very vivacious.
>
> H: Oh, what a good—what a wonderful word.
>
> W: Isn't that nice?
>
> H: Yeah. [*inhales*]
>
> W: Yeah.
>
> H: When I gave her the news I didn't know what her reaction was actually, cause she was very conventional in her reaction.
>
> W: Oh, on the phone she said she was very shocked.
>
> H: I told her, and it's hard to judge. I thought that maybe she was just pretending, you know, being nice, polite. That it didn't mean so much. But what a wonderful word. I, I see that I, I was quite wrong.
>
> W: It's really nice to hear how people remember her. You know. It's been . . . good.
>
> H: In a way it just makes—it just reminds me how much we all have lost.
>
> W: I know. But you know almost every day . . . uh . . . I run into somebody or talk to somebody or hear from somebody who still hasn't heard.
>
> H: Yeah. Well—I don't want to make it a burden for . . . people but, uhh, it's . . . a very sweet thing to see how much folks care.
>
> W: Uh huh.
>
> H: And how much she impressed them. I try to remember how much of an effect a person can have on others. Even a person who—well, some people frankly just wrote her off. I mean even the p-people who one might have expected more from, like my relatives.
>
> W: Uh huh.
>
> H: Umm . . . I don't—I'm not angry at them. But, but, even a person with so many strikes against them could really exist in the world and influence people and make people think of them as vivacious, and . . .
>
> W: Uh huh?
>
> H: lively, and—
>
> W: Yeah.
>
> H: Other people have used interesting words, too. Uh, I try to remember that. Uh, it's not easy, but when I see somebody else, able-bodied or not . . .
>
> W: [*sighs, inhales and exhales*]

The second couple shares their ability to be close to their grandchildren and the deep love they feel for them.

H: The light just came on, Molly. So, you wanna talk about Jude?

W: [*exhales*]

H: First? How about that she slides around on her piano bench and her teacher has to turn it sideways?

W: Well, the thing is, I really enjoy her company. And umm . . . we talk about dreams and—

H: You do?

W: Uh huh. She'll tell me about a dream that she had and I'll tell her about a dream I had. [*inhales*]

H: Oh.

W: And we really—it's hard to keep things from her. And she reads me like a book.

H: Huh?

W: Like, taking her to school today, she said, "Boy, you've got a lot on your mind."

H: [*chuckle*] Goll.

W: Uh—well, first of all, I said, I'm starting to get that muscle pull back again . . .

H: Uh huh?

W: from pulling weights, I think. She said, "Now you know what it feels like." Because, see, she's had those from—probably ballet. And I said, "I know, Jude, I know what it feels like and it's not comfortable." And then . . .

H: Huh?

W: . . . uh, what else? Something else. She said, "Boy, you got a lot on your mind." And I thought "Uh huh." And I said, "And I'm thinking about today—the appointment—and wondering what that's going to be like. And I'm nervous about it. I'm anxious."

H: She reads you like a book because you talk to her all the time.

W: Uh huh, we verbalize. That's why I know there's a big difference between men and women, boys and girls.

H: Yeah, well Justin and I are pretty much on the same wavelength, too. We kind of know what each other's thinking.

W: But you don't use the amount of words that we do.

H: No. I mean sometimes, you know, we'll just smile. And we know that, uhh—you know, like if there's some of the other Scouts or something around, I'll say something and they won't understand what I'm saying. It's kind a like a—

W: Well, it's probably an inside joke, isn't it?

H: Inside joke, yeah, that's it.

W: Uh huh.

H: And so we're close that way. And of course Jack, he's in-between some-where.

W: And when I get close to him, it is so fulfilling and satisfying because it's like you've really accomplished something. I did go talk to Mrs. Kennedy yesterday and told her of my concern.

H: Concern about what?

W: With the girls scratching [*our grandson Jack's*] neck.

H: Oh. [*chuckle*]

W: And she listened to me and then at the end she said, "Well, you know, I think they like him . . ."

H: Yeah.

W: ". . . and maybe this is their way of showing it."

H: Oh, sure.

W: I said, "Well this is an unacceptable way."

H: Yeah.

W: "If you like someone," I said, "you don't draw their blood." [*laughs*]

H: [*laughs*]

W: So we both laughed. And then we were parting and she was going down the hall and I said, "Well, he can have his moments, too." I was talking about—you know, I wanted to defend him and all this. And she said, "He can have his moments, too." And I said, "Oh, I know. But when you see that little head on the pillow at night when you're tucking him in . . ."

H: [*laugh*] jeez.

W: . . . it just melts your heart." And she just laughed.

H: Ohh, jeez.

The third couple expresses pride in their children. They share a feeling of pride and gratification in how their children behave on vacation: They were so kind to other younger children and made sure that the older children included them.

W: I was thinking both of long-ago things and of recent things, and how nice this whole last vacation has been. And what . . .

H: Uh huh.

W: . . . fun it was doing something together with the kids and the family.

H: It was wonderful.

W: And just watching . . . the way our kids interacted with all those . . .

H: Yeah, with those little kids. I found . . . new ways to be proud of our kids. I knew Ron was good with kids, but Leo was going out of his way to be nice to Evan, and then when we were at Billie's house and the other kids were there . . .

W: And Emma fit in with the other kids.

H: I saw that. Well, since he was the big kid, Leo said, "Emma is my friend."

W: He got Emma working in with the other kids.

H: Right away. He said, "This is my friend." You know, put her in, included her in the group. . . . I'm floored. It's wonderful.

Part **III**

INTERVENTION

C h a p t e r **6** 🖎

Assumptions and Intervention Overview

 This chapter provides a review of the six basic assumptions of my therapy. It also reviews the structure of the therapy, a suggested outline of each therapy session, the intervention overview, the menu model of the Marriage Clinic, and the major traditions I draw upon.

Before describing the operational side of therapeutic interventions, let me summarize the philosophical underpinnings of intervention at our Marriage Clinic, so that therapists reading this book can decide for themselves if they agree or disagree with these assumptions. I encourage you to take a critical look at the six assumptions that comprise the philosophy of my therapy. Everything in the therapy is designed to minimize the possibility of the couple's relapse after therapy. The intervention is designed to provide a library of resources the clinician can use.

MY ASSUMPTIONS

Assumption 1: The Therapy Is Primarily Dyadic

The goal of my marital therapy is to move the therapeutic focus from an initial triadic one to a dyadic exchange in which the therapist acts only as a coach to the partners. The point is for the spouses to learn how to intervene with each other. In the most pragmatic terms the goal is to empower *them*. It is important for them to make their next conversation "better," that is, less like those of couples who are on a trajectory toward divorce, and more like those of couples who are on a trajectory toward happy, stable marriages. Therapy can terminate when partners have developed the ability to make their interactions, both conflict and nonconflict, less divorce-prone. This cannot be accomplished when the therapist remains central to the couple's ability to interact in constructive ways. In the therapy, then, the spouses must interact with one another more than they talk to the therapist. The therapist's role is to provide the tools that *they* can use with one another and make their own.

Assumption 2: Couples Need to Be in Emotional States to Learn How to Cope with and Change Them

Much of the emotional learning in marital therapy may be state-dependent (Bower, 1981). This means that, unless we permit individuals to become as emotional in our offices as they do at home, they may not have access to the important learning we have offered once they leave the therapy session. Some therapists are themselves uncomfortable with strong emotions. They may even believe that the strong emotions mean that things are "out of control" or "blowing up," and that people cannot hear insights or change their behavior in these volatile states. On the contrary, it is only by permitting spouses to do what they normally do and then working with them in these emotional states that transfer of learning becomes possible.

Each emotion has been found to have its own "autonomic signature." This work was pioneered by Robert Levenson, in collaboration with Paul Ekman and Wallace Friesen (Ekman, Levenson, & Friesen, 1983; Levenson, Ekman, & Friesen, 1990; Levenson, 1992; Levenson, Carstensen, Friesen, & Ekman, 1991; Levenson, Ekman, Heider, & Friesen, 1992). Other scientists have also contributed to this view, including Richard Davidson, Nathan Fox, and Geri Dawson (Davidson, 1992, 1994a,b; Davidson & Fox, 1982; Davidson & Tomarken, 1989; Dawson, 1994; Dawson, Klinger, Panagiotides, Spieker, & Frey, 1992), who expanded this view to include differential brain activation for different kinds of emotion, and Joseph LeDoux (1993, 1997), who mapped the subcortical limbic activation in the amygdala during fear conditioning. This autonomic signature idea entails such phenomena as the hands getting hot in anger and cold in fear.

In this therapy it is important for the therapist to adopt the view that all emotions and all wishes are acceptable and need to be expressed and understood. As Haim Ginott was fond of saying, emotions do not vanish by being banished. Instead, they just do not get expressed *to you*. They are still there, and the clients are alone with them. Giving spouses "tools" to work with in changing their marital interaction patterns is strikingly different from calming them down, then providing the insight and the new tool, and then asking them to continue their interaction. Even if this procedure goes perfectly, they probably will have less access to the tool when they become emotional again.

There is a scene in the film *The Producers* that comically illustrates this idea that people can process information while in an emotional state. The actor Gene Wilder is running around shouting, "I'm hysterical! I'm hysterical!" and Zero Mostel throws some cold water in his face (a classic attempt to calm him down). Wilder then yells, "I'm hysterical *and* wet!" When people are in a particular emotional state, that state is itself an organizer of information that is processed and stored in relation to the emotional state. For example, what we learn about anger when we are actually angry will be most accessible when we are next angry, and that's when we need this information.

What about DPA? Spouses need to get into a state of diffuse physiological arousal during the session if they are to learn the tools of recognizing the state and being able to self-soothe, soothe the partner, or take a break. They are not going to be very good at problem-solving, creative thinking, or cooperation when they are in DPA. They may *think* they can undertake such tasks, but this is an error. That's all they need to learn about this state. It will do no good to give them these tools for dealing with DPA when they are calm, because when they get into DPA they won't have access to these tools. All they will have access to are the usual overlearned DPA behaviors of fight or flight, summarizing oneself without end, escalating the frustration, increasing DPA. Because our ability to process information is greatly reduced during DPA, it is important to keep the intervention short and simple; for example, say, "BREATHE!" They will have to overlearn the tools for dealing with DPA when they are in this state to counter the normal reactions to run or aggress. They will learn the four parts of self-soothing (discussed later in this book), as well as exercises for soothing the partner and taking effective breaks when feeling flooded.

Assumption 3. The Therapist Should Not Do the Soothing

Murray Bowen (1978) viewed the therapist's role as similar to that of a control rod in a nuclear reactor: to intervene and soothe the couple. In this view it is the therapist's role to do the soothing in the marital system. The danger in Bowen's view is that it makes the therapist irreplaceable, and it may maximize the couple's relapse potential once therapy terminates. As just noted in Assumption 2, the therapist ought to allow the spouses to get very upset, even entering states of DPA, and then have *them* learn how to self-soothe and even to soothe one another. This approach accomplishes a great deal by reversing the escape conditioning that flooding has created in the marriage and dissipates some of the pressure that contributes to the Distance and Isolation Cascade. Instead of the partner's presence and voice being associated just with flooding, they (and other cues) can become associated with calm.

Assumption 4. Interventions Should Seem Easy to Do

By this I mean that interventions should not be costly psychologically or appear foreign to people. The reaction to interventions should overwhelmingly be, "Oh, is that all there is to this? I can do that." I hope this is the reaction of therapists who learn this new marital therapy: "I can do this. This is easy." This assumption is important in considering some frequently used interventions. For example, I think that we have discovered that active listening is too hard for most people to do when they feel under attack. Our research shows that people in happy and stable marriages do not do this very often, and when they do, it predicts nothing about marital outcomes. I have seen the Dali Lama respond nondefensively to a hostile questioner. It was a saint-like act. But for most of us mortals it is too hard not to defend when we feel attacked. Therefore, my assumption is, do not teach communication skills that amount to "emotional gymnastics" for people who cannot yet even "walk" emotionally. We should strive to make each step in the therapy seem natural and not foreign to couples' normal styles.

In child development this technique of creating interventions that are very close to the child's ability level is called "scaffolding," from the work of the Russian psychologist Vygotsky (1962). This means that when parents give children instructions, they are aimed at their current developmental level, or at just the next level, one they can easily reach for and assimilate. In this way very skillful parents and teachers scaffold the learning process for children.

Assumption 5. Marital Therapy Should Be Primarily a Positive Affective Experience

Individual psychotherapy is often a very positive experience. The client is central, and the exploration of the client's past life is the core of the therapy. The client usually is genuinely accepted by the therapist, and the client's growth and development are the fundamental concerns of the therapy. The therapist is clearly the client's ally. This is not to say that individual therapy is not also a challenging experience in which the therapist, at times, must confront the client's defenses, deal with complex transference issues, and so on.

For some reason, in most marital therapies an opposite state of affairs exists. Clients don't have a good time. Most clients who go for marital therapy arrive for the first session firmly committed to the belief—which is unbeknownst to them at that point, a fundamental attribution error—that they are basically innocent of creating these marital problems and it is their partner whose character is basically flawed and in need of major change and overhaul. They are certain that, once they show this sensitive therapist what they have had to put up with, the therapist will immediately see this to be a fact. Both spouses usually think something like this.

But these clients may be in for a disappointment, for instead of an ally they may encounter a therapist whose method is to point out their dysfunctional thought and behavior patterns and present alternative ones involving more empathy and less defensiveness. And that's on the gentle end of the therapeutic continuum. Let me explain what I mean by this seemingly outrageous claim.

The early formulations of general systems theory were books written by very intellectual people like Gregory Bateson, Murray Bowen, Nathan Ackerman, Paul Watzlawick, Don Jackson, Virginia Satir, Jay Haley, and many others. For a terrific history of our field, see Broderick and Schrader (1991). I think that the dazzling analysis of human communication and its foibles by these theorists helped set up what I call the culture of nailing people. I do not mean that individual therapists intentionally do this, but that it is implicit in many of our theoretical positions. Let's examine this idea historically.

Bateson was inspired by the writings of the great mathematician David Hilbert, who attempted (and failed) to put mathematics on a foundation of logic by suggesting that there were different levels of analysis, one of which was the "meta" level. Bateson thought that interpersonal communication could also be analyzed in the same manner. Toward that goal he spent hours in the zoo filming the play of animals and he discovered that they use meta-communication that signals, in essence, "This is play, it's not real fighting." *The Pragmatics of Human Communication* (Watzlawick et al., 1967) suggested that people (1) do not check out communication but instead "mind-read," and (2) engage in the "punctuation fallacy" whereby their partner is seen as causing the problem and they are just reacting to his or her faulty way of communicating.

The concept of "games people play" in communication was another formulation that nailed both parties. In Albee's play *Who's Afraid of Virginia Woolf?*, George and Martha's pathology was analyzed and laid bare. The "games" they played were named and principles of communication were suggested. Watzlawick et al. conceptualized families as cybernetic systems with "inputs" and "outputs," "homeostasis," "rules," and "feedback." A whole series of dysfunctional interaction patterns was identified and named, like "kitchen-sinking." Suddenly a whole method of analysis was available for thinking of family interaction and for analyzing one's own pathological family. The new knowledge was heady and thrilling. It led to many insightful conversations late at night about one's own family pathology. It also shifted pathology from the individual to the interaction itself, which was a major paradigm shift.

Armed with these new methods of analyzing people's behavior, a whole new generation of therapy gurus suddenly emerged. They were people who were often flamboyant, dramatic, heroic, charismatic, and persuasive, and who created followings among student therapists. Somehow, all of this analysis led to a culture of nailing people, of pointing out their "games" to them, delighting in finding the one perfect, dramatic, and succinct interpretation that would lay bare the family's pathology and lead to the great epiphany that would create instantaneous change. The implication seemed to be that somehow the couple or family would be dazzled, amazed, humbled, contrite, and extremely grateful to the master therapist for the brilliant insight that would change their lives forever. But more often than not, the brilliant insight also meant getting nailed—having the headlights turned on one's pathology and then having to own up to it and accept responsibility for change.

The psychoanalytic approach to couples therapy is also unflattering to clients, who are viewed variously as dependent, narcissistic, sadistic, or immature—not to mention controlling, manipulative, dominating, and "seeking or obtaining significant regressive gratification" (Wile, 1981, p. 19). Wile shows how these interpretations can lead to accusational and moralistic interpretations that often discredit individuals' feelings in the present by attributing them to developmental defects. Wile instead emphasizes that the problem in most marriages is that people often feel unentitled to their complaints. For example, attributing a partner's sadness to a projection based on a childhood reaction to an unavailable mother ignores the possible reality that a spouse may actually be unavailable.

Marital therapy need not be a process of nailing people; there is really no need to confront clients about their dysfunctional behavior. The challenge is how to make marital conflict a positive experience. When a client in individual therapy reports a marital conflict, the therapist can totally take the client's side. This can be a very gratifying experience. However, the marital therapist, who has the task of creating an alliance with both spouses, needs to be seen as eminently fair. Hence, both people need to feel equally understood and equally "nailed." Data do, in fact, support the view that no one is usually to blame in marital dysfunction, but that it is a system in which the causes of the dysfunction are created by the dynamic interactions of partners. Unfortunately, in my view, this delicate balancing act of responding with total equality usually does not work. Whichever way you turn it, marital conflict is quite aversive, and people would usually prefer watching the most boring sporting event on television to coming to see the therapist.

So, how does one make facing marital conflict a positive experience? I think the answer is to help partners find a way to honor both of their life dreams, which underlie their most gridlocked conflicts. In my therapy the entire problem-solving process is recast as one of identifying and harmonizing people's basic life dreams. Much of the process of conflict resolution is an exploration in using the marital friendship to help make one another's life dreams come true. It can even have that self-indulgent quality that is so wonderfully attractive about individual therapy.

In fact, it can be *better* than individual therapy. Couples love the Oral History Interview. They often relish talking about how they met and telling the dramatic story of how they created a marriage and a family. They are more than willing to talk about how their own pasts have shaped their particular philosophies and attitudes. They enjoy discussing their personal searches for meaning and the added challenge of finding shared meaning together. Much of the conflict resolution process can have this same quality of a journey through the photo album of the mind. It can be a growth experience in which the travel is not lonely because one's partner is there as well.

Assumption 6. I Am Not Idealistic About Marriage and Its Potential

There are many marital therapists who have high expectations for what is possible in marriage. David Schnarch, for example, has high expectations of what good sex can do for a relationship, and Harville Hendrix believes that a marriage can be a therapeutic endeavor that heals the spouses' childhood wounds. These are lofty goals, and these therapists may be right in encouraging couples to aspire to these heights. I am not opposed to these views, but I personally take a different one. I am a "plumber," not an idealist or a theologian.

I have studied the range of marriages, both terrific and pathological, across the life course, and I have a great deal of respect for the good ones I have seen. The marriages I have studied that are stable and satisfying to the people in them are usually very good environments for the development of both people and for raising kids as well. I am only interested in helping people to have the kind of marriages I have seen when marriage is at its best—which I define as high marital satisfaction and stability. I don't rate or judge marriages based upon some theory of individual or group development (as in object relations theory) or some theoretically-based idea of competence (such as attachment theory, or Bowen's individuation theory). Unlike Lewis (1997), I have no predefined notion of marital competence.

This is a deliberate scientific choice. Once one has defined "competence" or "maturity," there is less left to discover, there are fewer surprises. I see it as my job as a researcher to systematically describe the magic between people. I celebrate the things I have seen that work and appreciate what I have observed.

I come from a working-class background and am essentially an "anti-elitist." My great-grandfather was a butcher from Kobersdorf, Austria. The only book I ever threw away—and I threw it high over the rooftops of Boston from an elevated train platform—was Abraham Maslow's book on self-actualization. Was I "deficiency motivated" or "being motivated"? Was I part of the elite or just one of the unwashed masses? I finally decided that the book was driving me crazy, first thinking I was part of this blessed elite of "self-actualizing people" and then damning myself as a hopeless neurotic, motivated by needs very low on the hierarchy, eating food and eliminating wastes. I finally decided that I detested these elitist psychological views.

My views on what works well in marriages are based solely on what "real people" do to have stable and satisfying marriages, whatever their socioeconomic, ethnic, and racial attributes. I like to think of myself as a kind of quantitative Studs Terkel.

I have often described my goal as fostering the "good enough marriage." I am likely to think a marriage is good enough if the two spouses choose to have coffee and pastries together on a Saturday afternoon and really enjoy the conversation, even if they don't heal one another's childhood wounds or don't always have wall-socket, mind-blowing, skyrocket sex—or even if they aren't very individuated and even appear to some to be "symbiotic." It works for them.

THE MODULAR APPROACH TO INTERVENTION

I have designed a modular library of interventions that therapists can use to design an individualized therapy. As newer intervention components are invented and tested, they can be accessed from my web site at www.Gottman.com. It is not possible to be organized and systematic when it comes to intervention. What you do first depends a lot on the pressing presenting problems and the narrative of the dilemma the couple walk in with, as well as their expectations for the therapy and their idea of the therapy process.

Not all the components in my modular approach are necessary in each case. Your assessment should indicate parts of the intervention that are relevant, as well as the order of the interventions. I have made this approach modular so that you can "cut and paste," selecting the components you think are necessary for each case and discarding the ones that don't appeal to you. I suggest that you view the interventions I present as tools available on your shelf. It is up to you to design a particular therapy for each couple. That is part of the challenge, both artistically and scientifically, and it is what makes practicing therapy so exciting and, at times, frustrating. I am a big believer that dogma has no place in our work, just dialogue, insight, and science.

Four Parts of the Intervention

Assuming that you can make the appropriate adjustments for each individual case, I will describe the interventions in an orderly and logical fashion:

- First, interventions related to *changing the setting conditions (the marital friendship) that cause dysfunctional marital conflict resolution.* In practice you will probably want to integrate changing the couple's conflict resolution methods with changing these setting conditions.

- Second, after discussing changing the setting conditions that cause the marital conflict, move toward interventions related to *functional problem-solving and the regulation of perpetual conflict.*

- Third, I will discuss how to *deal with resistance.*

- Finally, I will discuss the *prevention of relapse.*

In the chapters that follow I offer you a library of interventions to be used in session. All the materials you need for each intervention and exercise are in this book. To use this library of interventions, each related to specific processes of the Sound Marital House, I suggest a flexible and novel approach to treatment and to structuring each therapy session.

An Overall Sructure for Treatment

The very general structure I use in marital therapy is to:

- create initial, rapid, dramatic change, and then to
- follow this up with structured change.

Create Initial, Rapid, Dramatic Change

Usually couples come into therapy with a gridlocked conflict on one or more perpetual issues that is damaging the marriage and undermining the couple's confidence. They feel somewhat desperate. Usually one or both score below 85 on the Locke-Wallace marital satisfaction scale and one or both are at 4 or above on the Weiss-Cerreto scale of divorce potential. On their first interaction they are in one of two states: Either the Four Horsemen are present and repair is ineffective, or there is great emotional distance and isolation with lots of tension, underlying sadness, and an absence of any positive affect.

In a 3-hour session subsequent to the assessment, I use the Dreams-Within-Conflict intervention on a gridlocked issue. After their first interaction, my intervention takes about a half-hour; then they talk to each other again without my interruption. I will demonstrate how to do this intervention in Chapter 9.

It is important to underscore that my goal is *not* solving the issue or resolving the conflict! The conflict will probably always be there for the life of the marriage. *The goal is to help them move from gridlock to dialogue on the issue.* What is important here is the affect around which they *don't* solve the problem.

Accomplishing this goal is a two-step process. The first step involves revealing the dreams that underlie the conflict. For this to happen both people have to feel understood and supported by the therapist. The marriage has to feel safe enough for these tender dreams to emerge. This is most likely to work when the friendship in the marriage is in reasonable shape, even if it is somewhat underground. If the Fondness and Admiration System is there (even covertly), this process will be relatively fast. (This is especially the case if the husband can accept influence from his wife.)

People often do not know that their own dreams are related to their entrenched position on the gridlocked conflict. This is most commonly the case for women. We have found that women usually have been socialized to *not* honor any dream that isn't about relationships. Dreams related to being a good mother, wife, daughter, sister, helper, or friend are okay. Although they know that they are entitled to develop as autonomous individuals and that any dream is okay to pursue as long as it is consistent with their moral choices, they have been raised to *believe* that it is selfish and bad to do so. Hence, we find many women who have not individuated to the extent that many men typically have. They need help to honor and hold onto their dreams.

Encountering the potential blocks to the Dreams-Within-Conflict intervention is very productive and revealing. It leads the couple and the therapist to the "bare bones" of the gridlock, which then become the focus of the intervention.

The second step in this process is helping partners to "honor" one another's dreams. I use the word *honor* very deliberately here. As I use it, honoring occurs along a continuum reflecting the extent to which one spouse can support the partner's dreams. At one end this honoring may involve only interest, respect, and words of encouragement. At the other end there is a joining in the partner's dreams and teamwork. Some spouses yearn for autonomy in their pursuit of a dream, not a joining. That is fine. It can change over time. It is always about respect. The spouses have to arrive at this themselves. You can't do it for them any more than you can clear up their existential questions about God. Getting them to any level of honoring one another's dreams is your goal. They may not stay there, but my experience is that as they talk about this issue over time, they will find new ways of honoring one another's dreams. This process will take *years*. All you are doing is starting them on a new trajectory. They will do the work necessary to move along that path in a way that is consistent with their personalities.

This second step requires changing the marital influence patterns on their perpetual issues. This is not difficult to do for a short time, but it is hard to maintain these changes. That might become the focus of the remainder of the therapy.

In the majority of cases, change can be accomplished in about 3 to 4 hours. My student Jim Coan once called this intervention "change your marriage in a half-hour, for a half-hour." There is some truth in this. The issue becomes maintaining the changes. However, in doing the Dreams-Within-Conflict intervention I have discovered that couples are amazed at experiencing what their marriage could be, and the changes, temporary as they often are, give the couple hope and direction.

Even though the intervention is brief, the changes that are obtained are far from superficial. In many cases spouses begin a process that opens up the issue and opens each person to the other. Often there is the feeling with emotionally disengaged couples of pulling the cork out of a champagne bottle: Feelings that have been buried fizz suddenly to the surface. There is often hidden anger and sadness, which are sometimes observable in the pre-intervention conversation in brief nonverbal signs. What happens when people talk about what the issue means, rather than talking about the issue itself, is that they stop being so concealing. They emerge, respectful of their partner's dreams, but seeing the need to hold onto their own dreams as well. This may entail more conflict at first, so that things may seem worse after the intervention than before, because they are more emotional. But there is also more positive affect, more interest, engagement, compassion, and support.

The intervention is most difficult when emotional disengagement has begun and the couple are on the Distance and Isolation Cascade. It is easiest when the issue is still "hot" and the Four Horsemen are present. Beginning therapists I have worked with often expect the opposite to be true, and they are dismayed by the intense hostility. However, the most dismaying cases are really those where profound emotional disengagement has become the entrenched pattern.

Follow Up With Structured Change

My goal is not to admonish the couple not to fight. Our research shows that fighting is natural in all marriages. *My goal is to get the couple to be able to effectively repair negativity during their interaction about a conflictual issue without my help.*

This is a three-step process. The first step is for them to be able to process the argument after it has occurred, usually in session. In Wile's terms, this is getting them to move from an "attack-defend mode," in which the Four Horsemen are present, to an "admitting mode," where people are willing to accept some responsibility for the problem and admit mistakes they made in hurting one another's feelings. Video playback is quite powerful in bridging the transition between these two modes. The next step is to move from the "admitting mode" to Wile's "collaborative mode" wherein spouses have the conversation they have needed to have all along. Here they are able to express their feelings without much attack (criticism) or defensiveness. They may still get somewhat attacking and defensive at times in this mode, but the therapist assists them in effective repair. The third and final step is for the couple to be able to repair negativity *while* they are having the argument. This last step is all that happens in good marriages.

The couple first needs to understand the fight. How did they get into this muddle? What is the meaning of the issue to them? What are the sources of their gridlock on the issue? In Wile's terms, "What was the conversation they needed to have, but didn't?" I maintain a Greenberg-Johnson emotion focus in this overview of a fight and in their movement from adversarial to admitting mode and then to a collaborative mode. In the first transition they needn't actually do this so much as be able to do a post-mortem on the fight.

Moving to a collaborative mode is a greater challenge. It is easier to do after the fight than during it, partly due to the effects of DPA. For this reason soothing is very important in moving the couple to collaborative mode, as are the processes related to negative sentiment override (humor, affection, interest, etc.). For this step I use the Aftermath of a Marital Argument Questionnaire (Table 12.1) to guide the couple through this process.

A final step in this phase might be to help the spouses have a dialogue about their issue, particularly if it is a perpetual one that will have no real resolution. Ideally in this dialogue they are able to use how they feel about the issue as a way of indexing the first three levels of the Sound Marital House. For example, suppose a wife tends to get angry with her husband because she thinks he is paying too much attention to the children. After many aftermaths of these arguments she eventually learns that this issue is reminiscent of her conflicts with her sister for her parents' attention. The problem doesn't go away, but it becomes an index of her not asking for what she needs from her husband. She begins to have a dialogue with the issue.

After the rapid initial change, I then begin working on specific content areas in the marriage, using the Gottman 17-Areas Scale. This is the basis of the initial therapeutic contract. I am using the Sound Marital House theory as a blueprint to guide my focus.

Recommended Structure of a Marital Therapy Session

I use a general approach containing seven parts for structuring marital therapy sessions. This approach is offered as a broad outline, not a rigid format. My sessions are each 1½ hours long. This structure has come from our research on brief interventions designed to obtain only proximal change in marriage.

1. *Catch up.* Catch up on marital events, especially checking up on any assigned homework from the last session. The couple will be bringing in their major issues of the week, and the moments they generate in session usually form the basis of all the therapeutic work of the session. The interactive moments this generates dramatize the issues the couple currently have. I will often have them *talk to one another,* instead of reporting to me, so the interaction is not mainly triadic. Generally, there are one of two such issues, either *a failed marital argument* or a failure of the friendship, which is usually about a *failed bid* (for interest, affection, humor, support, sex, and so on). (Working on the aftermath of failed bids is discussed in Chapter 7, and the aftermath of a failed marital argument is discussed in Chapter 8.) In my office I have two physical spaces. One is for interaction—it is where I videotape the couple. Using the analogy of the sport of boxing, I call this space "the ring." The second space is where we process the interaction and view the videotape. I call this space "the cor-

ner." The goal of this separation is to be able to process an interaction without getting into it again and to move to an admitting mode.

2. *Pre-intervention marital interaction.* Next the spouses interact with one another for 6 to 10 minutes about whatever they are currently working on. The interaction could be the weekly catch-up topic. How did they see the past week? Or the first topic could be a perpetual or solvable issue, or some other aspect of the marriage *they* are working on (see the Gottman 17-areas Scale, Appendix A). The therapist does not speak during this discussion but thinks of an intervention, preferably one that will provide the spouses with one tool they can use in their next interaction.

I think of the model of a boxing coach, who, after the bell signals the end of a round, gives the boxer one very simple suggestion that can be used in the next round. The boxer can hear only simple and clear directions, because he has been getting hit on the head in the past round. I always videotape this interaction, as well as the post-intervention interaction. I have been surprised at the fact that in my workshops only about 2% of the marital therapists use videotape at all. Especially in these days when videotaping is so inexpensive and, with such high resolution, so powerful, it is a mystery to me why one would not have this tool as part of one's practice.

3. *Intervention.* Before suggesting the intervention, first ask *them* to suggest an intervention based on their understanding of how the discussion went in the last interaction. We find that people accept their own ideas before they accept ours, and this builds an emerging independence, thereby militating against relapse. In fact, I suggest that you consider terminating marital therapy when couples can consistently come up with their own intervention that works reasonably well. Don't have high standards for this.

Generally, however, it will be your analysis of the last conversation and your intervention that is taken and used as a tool in the next 6-minute interaction. To facilitate their suggesting an intervention, I often use video replay of their 6 minutes. Video replay is often emotionally powerful, and it is helpful in moving them away from an attack-defend mode. I may also use the Aftermath of Failed Bids Questionnaire (see Appendix D).

4. *The spouses make the intervention their own.* Before they begin the second conversation, have them discuss how they understand the intervention you just suggested, and whether or not the intervention is seen by each of them as ego-syntonic or foreign and phony. How can they make it natural and consistent with their own personalities? We have often been surprised during this step. People do not usually hear it the way we said it. Sometimes the way they hear it is better, which is exciting.

5. *Resistance?* Resistance to change is discussed fully in Chapter 12. Sometimes you will encounter resistance in the stage of the couple owning the intervention. For example, my friend Jean Goldsmith once told me of a case in which she suggested that the husband listen nondefensively to the wife. He became quite angry and told her that this marriage worked because they each had a gun pointed at the other's temple. She was ask-

ing him to lower his gun. What would happen, he told her, is that he would get his brains blown out. Goldsmith explored the origins of this attitude and found that it had to do with his father, who continually humiliated him when he was a child. In retaliation he became extremely facile with words and became a very cutting, sarcastic person.

Exploring the resistance may lead to a discovery of the client's "internal working model" (a concept prominent in attachment theory) of relationships that is affecting particular levels of the Sound Marital House. An apparent intervention failure may be a therapeutic success, for you and the spouses have learned why processes at that level of the Sound Marital House are systematically distorted in this marriage and not working properly. When you encounter it, resistance becomes the focus of the therapy. What is its history? What is its story? What is the meaning of the internal working model underlying the resistance? Here we can begin to explore past injuries and their healing—the ways that this person suffered and survived, healed the self, and insured that this injury would never recur—and the implications of these crucial processes for the relationship.

The exploration of resistance reveals the narratives, metaphors, and symbols that form the basis of the internal working model related to the processes you are working on. For example, a person may have resistance to being known because that spells danger, but not to knowing the partner, because to know is to have power in this person's mind. This could be a part of an antisocial working model, but it need not entail an antisocial personality. This working model systematically distorts processes of the Sound Marital House and will appear as resistance in exercises at the Love Map level.

6. *No resistance?* When resistance does not occur, have the couple engage in another 6-minute interaction, during which the therapist is again quiet. Follow this by processing the session.

7. *Homework.* Design a homework task that will generalize the intervention to the couple's everyday life. Ultimately you are trying to change the way they move through time together.

I repeat that this outline is intended to provide an overall structure for treatment, which should be used flexibly. It is important that the couple be able to tell their own stories and not inhibited from raising issues and concerns that are not part of the therapist's overall therapeutic plan. In the rare follow-up studies that have been reported in the marital therapy literature (e.g., Jacobson, Schmaling, & Holtzworth-Monroe, 1987), the rigidity of the sessions has been a major complaint of couples.

Label Destructive Patterns: Don't Ignore Them! Build in the Antidotes!

One of the first things that I think therapists need to do is to label and try to stop destructive interaction patterns. This means directly telling people about the Four Horsemen of the Apocalypse, helping them to identify these behaviors, and explaining to them that these behaviors are consistent predictors of divorce. It also means not proceeding with the work of therapeutic change while ignoring these behaviors. That is, for example, do not ignore a spouse's contempt and try to empathize with the disappointment and hurt that may underlie the contempt. I suggest that you call it contempt and tell the couple that this behavior is unacceptable.

Wrong

Therapist: Why don't you each tell one another what your major complaints are right now. Mike, why don't you go first.

H: I don't even want to be here. All right, here goes. I am enraged about all the stuff I have to put up with. Jane wants to go to school to become a nurse. That will take two years of education. Two years in which she is away from our kids. She is being a goddammed selfish bitch and I won't put up with it. She can just take a hike. She will never get custody of her kids. I will see to it that she just loses her precious kids.

Therapist: You are very disappointed in this plan. You sound hurt.

H: Damn right I am. I am not going to take this crap from her. I work hard all the time and sacrifice in this awful job and I get no thanks at all. I am not going to be the only one sacrificing in this family.

Therapist: Tell me and Jane what you have been going through.

H: Jane is an irresponsible mother and a slut throughout all of this. I come home and the house is a mess, the kids are yelling and out of control. All I ask for is a little empathy and what do I get instead? She is constantly demanding. She wants to spend time with her girlfriends. She is spoiled rotten, if you ask me.

Therapist: Jane, why don't you tell Mike what you hear him saying. Can you reflect back the feelings you hear? Then we will switch roles and Jane will get her turn, with Mike as listener.

What is wrong with this scenario is that the therapist is ignoring Mike's contempt and belligerence. Mike's threats are being ignored. As the therapist uses empathy to get at what may be behind the contempt, he covertly sanctions this psychologically destructive, abusive behavior. Instead, I suggest that you react to it as you would to a child's playmate who turns out to be a bully and is physically aggressive. You would say something like, "In this house we don't hit. We use our words." Label destructive contemptuous or belligerent behavior; tell people it is corrosive of love. Offer alternatives.

Right

Therapist: Why don't you each tell one another what your major complaints are right now. Mike, why don't you go first.

Mike: I don't even want to be here. All right, here goes. I am enraged about all the stuff I have to put up with. Jane wants to go to school to become a nurse. That will take two years of education. Two years in which she is away from our kids. She is being a goddamned selfish bitch and I won't put up with it. She can just take a hike. She will never get custody of her kids. I will see to it that she just loses her precious kids.

Therapist: Let me just stop you here, Mike. Research has shown that there are some patterns of interaction in marriages that are very destructive of love. These are being contemptuous and insulting, and being threatening. I cannot let you interact like that here. I suggest that you don't do it at home either. Contempt and threats are part of a pattern of psychological abuse. Nothing is more destructive to love. So, please rephrase your complaints and try not to use these ways of expressing yourself.

Mike: Okay. Let me try. I am angry about Jane's desire to go to school to become a nurse. That will take two years of education. Two years in which she is away from our kids. I think this will harm the kids. They need a mother, and I need her too.

Therapist: So this plan has lots of elements of loss in your mind.

Mike: I feel like I am losing control here.

Therapist: This is partly an issue of who is in charge.

Mike: It's that, and it's about the commitment we made to raise the kids ourselves and not farm them out.

Therapist: Let's hear from Jane.

Jane: We had an agreement that things could change when all the kids were in school fulltime, and now they are. I am just bringing this up for discussion. I really want to go to school and become a nurse, and I think I can do it without hurting the kids. Mike is the one being selfish here.

Therapist: Name calling is contempt. Please refrain from this.

Jane: Yes, we're both doing it.

Mike: I work hard all the time and sacrifice in this awful job and I get no thanks at all. I am not going to be the only one sacrificing in this family.

Ostensibly there is not a great deal of difference between these two dialogues. However, in the second instance the therapist is calling the couple on patterns of dysfunctional behavior instead of ignoring these patterns and hoping that by getting at underlying feelings, they will go away by themselves. They won't go away.

When labeling dysfunctional behavior, try to build in the antidote.

- *Criticism:* The antidote is complaining without suggesting that one's partner is somehow defective.
- *Defensiveness:* The antidote is accepting responsibility for a part of the problem.
- *Contempt:* The antidote is creating a culture of praise and pride.
- *Stonewalling:* The antidote is self-soothing, giving listener backchannels, and staying emotionally connected.

INTERVENTION OVERVIEW

The Couple's Presenting Narrative of Their Dilemma

In the initial assessment the spouses need to tell their own stories of their marital dilemma, and its history, and they need to present their theories of what the problems are in their marriage. This seems to be an essential need of all couples coming for therapy. During this process it is important that the therapist listen fairly and nonjudgmentally to both spouses, periodically summarize what is heard (and ask if there is anything else still missing from this summary), and form therapeutic alliances with both people.

The Therapist's Healing Image of the Couple

As I absorb information from the Oral History Interview, and as I continue to work with a couple, I purposely let my mind develop a mental image of each spouse and of the relationship. For me, this internal image of the couple is critical for developing a healing stance toward them. I can't really identify the source of this image; it just comes to me when I let it. A part of this image usually contains an understanding of what healing needs to take place. During treatment this image changes. I talk about this image as I work with the couple and make the narrative of this image something the couple and I work on together.

Developing this image is a central part of many marital therapists' work. Jacobson and Christensen (1996) call it "the formulation." In her fascinating book on shamanism and modern medicine, *Imagery in Healing,* Jeanne Achtenberg (1985) discusses the healing image and its role in medicine and explores the mind-body relationships between these images and biological phenomena. So, the healing image is a very old idea, in magic and in treatment in general.

Designing a Marital Therapy: Using the Clinician's Checklist for Marital Assessment

The Clinician's Checklist for Marital Assessment (Table 4.1, pp. 115–116) is a guide for designing an individualized intervention for each couple. The first category, which asks, "Overall, where are they each in the marriage?" gives you a means for deciding whether you can or cannot work with the couple, and, if so, whether or not you need to consider this couple in a state of crisis.

The second category, "The Marital Friendship," refers to all interventions that deal with changing the setting conditions for dysfunctional conflict. You can help them rebuild positive aspects of their life together—joy, interest, affection, humor, delight in one another, knowledge of one another, emotional connection, and friendship.

The third part of the checklist is about sentiment override, and this is where I also note their perception of the interaction, particularly their partner's humor and anger, feeling flooded by the way the partner complains, and general diffuse physiological arousal.

The fourth part of the checklist concerns dealing with the way the couple regulates conflict: one for dealing with problems that can be solved and the other for dealing with the couple's relationship with perpetual conflict.

The fifth part of the checklist is about making the marriage one in which each person's life dreams can be known, honored, and supported (to varying degrees). It is also about individuation, because people who are not individuated are out of touch with their own life dreams. This part of the checklist is also about the couple's being able to create a shared meaning system; we use the Meanings Interview (Appendix C) to help with this task.

Finally, we deal with potential resistances that may be encountered. It is often possible to anticipate some of these resistances at the outset and use this information in treatment planning. However, resistances often arise in the process of trying to accomplish change itself, and usually arise once one is successful in creating the conditions for change.

The Therapeutic Contract

I use the Gottman 17-Areas Scale (see Appendix A) as a basis for building a therapeutic contract with a couple about where to begin. I use this scale as a revealed differences exercise. Both spouses write in a booklet about each item in the marriage, telling their partner how they see each area currently, and how they would like it to be. Then they read and discuss each other's responses.

MENU MODEL OF THE GOTTMAN MARRIAGE CLINIC

In the Gottman Marriage Clinic, after the assessment phase the couple is given a list of choices and is informed about each choice, its advantages and disadvantages, and its cost. This is a restaurant model of therapy rather than a standard clinic model where the couple gets a "one size fits all" method of change. In traditional clinical settings, clients generally get very little idea of what they can expect, and no choices. Their own preferences, financial priorities, time constraints, and hopes are ignored in this standard model.

Imagine a restaurant in which the menu read only "food," and there was a fixed price. (I am partial to this metaphor because my mother was trained as a chef, and I love to cook.) There has not been a single aptitude-by-treatment-interaction study in the marital therapy field. This is a study in which the therapy is changed to fit the particular needs of the marriage. I am sure that this is something every therapist has to do in every case, but as a field we have made no systematic approach to this important issue.

Treatment Format Options

All formats have a required summary session in which the therapist and couple decide where to go from there, and a one-month follow-up session scheduled in advance. The formats available are as follows:

- *Rapid initial dramatic change: One three-hour treatment on one specific issue.* This is an intensive clinical intervention with pre- and post-marital interactions on one specific (usually gridlocked) issue. It is designed to elicit maximal change in a short time. This option is useful when spouses have a very specific problem to work on. It is also useful for a reluctant spouse, who is willing to invest only a brief amount of time and money to see what may happen. Generally this format results in rapid, dramatic changes that are, unfortunately, in many cases temporary. The therapist should tell the couple that they can expect to have problems maintaining the changes and that the brief intervention is merely the start of a process. It is likely that a follow-up and a booster session or sessions will be required later. The major intervention used here is the Dreams-Within-Conflict one.

- *Weekend workshop followed by five individual sessions.* (This option is only possible when the workshops are offered; we now offer four workshops a year.) This format is appropriate for couples who want to see whether they can make some gains with a minimal investment of time and money; it is also an effective preventive approach to issues that are likely to surface.

- *One week, every day.* This is mostly for out-of-town couples, but it is also available for local couples who are able to check into a hotel and be away from work and children for an entire week (except, of course, for emergency contacts). The couple is seen for three hours every morning, with homework in-between. This is intensive, focused work on the marriage, and it can lead to dramatic changes, especially because they are removed from everyday stresses. Toward the end of this week issues of reentry and relapse are discussed.

- *Marital therapy.* Fourteen weeks or seven weeks with twice-a-week appointments. Following the treatment, the contract is negotiable for more sessions. The workshop is recommended prior to the therapy, if it is available.

- *Fading.* More intense and condensed initial marital therapy, combined with structured fading of the therapist toward the end of treatment. The Boegner and Zielenbach-Coenen (1984) study, which will be reviewed in Chapter 12, suggests that this format may produce greater change as well as less relapse.

- *Bibliotherapy.* The couple receives reading materials and telephone consultation for a total of three hours. The bibliotherapy option may also be used with couples when the workshops are not scheduled, as a supplement to therapy.

- *Divorce mediation.* An initial 10 sessions includes full mediation services, financial agreements, child custody arrangements, monitoring the couple's progress toward an amicable divorce, and telephone crisis negotiations. Follow-up for 6 months is also provided.

Short Courses and Therapeutic Modules

It is quite clear that improving spouses' communication will not necessarily result in their being able to budget their finances and develop an investment portfolio, nor will their sex life automatically improve, nor will all specific problems, or what may be called "content areas," automatically vanish. In addition to dealing with the processes of *how* they interact, we also need to address the particular problems that couples tend to have. I have found that the best format for covering these content areas is short courses or "brief treatment modules," followed up with five sessions with a therapist for individualizing the course for the couple. The goal of these short courses is very specific and often highly psychoeducational and didactic. If wider issues arise as the couple participates in these courses, an additional therapeutic contract may be established. Notice that we start with the two most common problems, sex and money. Any content issue can be the subject of marital gridlock, in which case the couple needs help uncovering and addressing the symbolic meaning of each issue.

- *Sex therapy* addresses the standard sexual dysfunctions (anorgasmia, dyspareunia, impotence, premature ejaculation, problems of desire, etc.)

- *Improving a dull but not dysfunctional sex life* integrates lovingness and intimacy with sexual activity.

- *Financial management* focuses on goal-setting, financial planning, investment, budgeting, and taxes.

- *Stress and time management* helps people manage work demands and still find time to sleep, eat, and spend time with loved ones.

- *Setting personal purposes in life* is a forum where people can explore life dreams, goal development, and career planning, and set a timeline to achieve them in a way that is consistent with whatever values they have for their marriage and family.

- *Maintaining marital intimacy after the baby arrives* is a very hot topic among young families.

- *Dual career issues* is a forum for exploring those areas such as competition, sharing housework, family planning, etc., that so often cause great havoc with couples.

- *Creating fun together* is a course that was developed in response to the need for modern families to *build* fun into their lives. Among some distressed couples this problem is quite serious, because the only way they actually come together is when they fight.

- *Creating a spiritual life together* addresses "spiritual" issues in its broadest sense, in terms of creating shared purpose and meaning. Religion can be a part of this, but this exploration is not restricted to formalized pathways of spiritual/religious practice.

- *The art of conversation* teaches couples how to rekindle the simple pleasure of talking to each other about a wide variety of topics, by providing tools for self- and partner-exploration, self-disclosure, emotional expressiveness, and becoming active listeners.

- *Male-female differences* explores what is really known about this confusing topic of gender differences, as well as what couples believe is true, and which gender styles they wish to establish in their own marriage.

- *Sharing power* explores issues of patriarchy, the history of male domination over women, the bases of misogyny, accepting influence from one another, as well as how marriages employing different power-sharing ideas can work. Peggy Papp's (1998) work on belief systems regarding gender issues is a guide for this module.

- *Creating community* explores the erosion of community and neighborhood in the United States and the resulting isolation. Families pay a serious price for this isolation, for it robs people of much needed social support as well as a chance to build meaning in their lives by caring about others.

- *Parent-child relations and emotion-coaching* teaches a Ginott-based approach that gives both the marriage and the child's emotional development a firm foundation. My book and accompanying video, *The Heart of Parenting,* is the basis for this module.

- *Honoring one another's life dreams and creating shared meaning* explores issues of individuation in relation to individual life dreams, and discusses how the marriage can accommodate these dreams.

- *Major life transitions* (to parenthood, aging parents, retirement) helps couples benefit from guidance and avoid the well-known pitfall of relationship deterioration that sometimes accompanies these normative transitions.

- *Transgenerational issues* examines the major problems of relating to kin in marriages.

- *Dealing with past traumas* (such as sexual or physical abuse or any situation that has produced a PTSD reaction) can burden a marriage while the affected party undergoes intensive treatment.

- *Dealing with a chaotic life* explores how to establish a sense of control and order in daily life so that spouses are able to plan and build rather than merely react to unexpected changes.

- *Jobs and career management issues* deal with a potpourri of common work-based conflicts: balancing work, family, and individual needs; working overtime, problems of hours not matching, shift switching, increased job demands creating excessive fatigue and/or depression; underemployment, low motivation for work, downsizing, and job loss.

- *Dealing with a chronic illness* (physical or mental), even one that is being managed and is no longer life-threatening, may have profound consequences for family and marital life. This course deals with these issues.

- *The issues of blended families* addresses those complex areas of adjustment that occur in blended families, especially when there are teenage children.

We are working on developing and standardizing these short courses, so that the therapist can pick and choose from a library of intervention modules to design an individualized program for a particular couple. Though these courses can probably be taught by non-therapists, a therapist is preferable because each of these areas of a couple's life is loaded with symbolic meaning. Take money, for example. Money is almost never just about money. It is about freedom, power, independence, love, security, competence, achievement, and so on. These are the underlying issues that are usually engaged by gridlocked conflict about money. They may also be engaged when a couple has been married for some time and still does not have any semblance of a budget, or a retirement plan, or an investment plan, and so on. Whether these courses are taught by therapists or non-therapists, they have to be followed up with at least five sessions with a therapist to individualize them for the couple.

SPECIFIC INTERVENTIONS, THERAPEUTIC MOMENTS, AND MARITAL WALNUTS

In the chapters that follow I will present interventions that highlight the changes that a couple can make in specific processes of the Sound Marital House. However, it is critical that these interventions be regarded as no more than a matrix that the therapist has in mind. They should not be an agenda that guides the therapy and prevents it from unfolding naturally.

Instead, what ought to guide the therapy are the moments that the couple brings into the session and displays for you in the process of interaction. I call these "marital walnuts." They are hard places in the process of interaction that demonstrate dramatically the problems in interaction the couple is confronting. Cracking these walnuts is the goal of marital therapy.

For example, in one case the wife raised the issue of her loneliness. She said that her husband doesn't respond to her when she needs him most. He responded by becoming defensive and talking about how tired he was at the end of a day when she typically wanted him to respond. The wife then softened her voice, began caressing the back of his neck, and said, "I know what pressure you're under right now." He sat there stiffly, arms folded across his chest, not looking at her. I asked him what he was feeling, and he said, "Oh, when she does something like this, I melt. It makes me feel great." I then asked her if she knew he was feeling that way, and she said, "No, I can't tell what he's feeling." I commented that his nonverbal behavior still looked defensive and turned away from her and asked him to tell her directly what he was feeling. He was able to do it, but with great difficulty. This moment revealed one of their walnuts.

My point here is that the best marital therapy flows from what the couple brings into a session. This is not to say that the therapist does not come into a session with a plan or an agenda. I always do, but this takes second place to what the couple brings in and shows me is their current and most pressing walnut. The greatest part of marital therapy is that the processes are right there for you to observe. The drama comes in staying in the here and now and focusing on the emotional moment. Here one can open and unfold the processes that form the basis of their hard walnut in attempting to connect. With support to both people, I explore the interactive processes, the thought processes, and, if necessary, the physiological processes involved in the walnut. When this works the walnut transforms into a closed flower bud that eventually opens into a flower. The defensiveness lowers, the attack retreats, and people can reach each other emotionally.

Enhancing the Marital Friendship

 *This chapter contains 14 interventions designed to change the lower levels of the Sound Marital House. They are suggested as specific interventions to use **within** a therapy session. Changing these processes, the theory suggests, changes the setting conditions that cause negative sentiment override. Positive sentiment overrides, the theory proposes, are responsible for effective repair during conflict resolution for conflicts that can be solved and for establishing a dialogue with perpetual conflict.*

THE FAILED BID

The fundamental dysfunctional unit of interaction at the heart of the marital friendship is the *failed bid*. Even in the most distressed marriages, partners keep making bids for one another's attention, interest, humor, affection, emotional support, solidarity, sex, and so on. The failed bid becomes the central event on which to focus the couple's attention for improving the marital friendship.

The Robinson and Price (1980) study showed that changing positive interaction is not merely a matter of changing behavior but of changing perception as well. Unhappily married couples under-detect their partner's positive interaction by 50% (compared to observers). Happily married couples and observers agree in the observations. The failed bid involves all three elements of the core triad of balance: interactive behavior, perception, and physiology.

What is the goal here? Is it to *eliminate* failed bids? No. Failed bids occur in all marriages. The goal is for people, on their own, to be able to repair failed bids when they do occur, to be able to recognize that this has occurred, understand it, and have a dialogue with the event. The Aftermath of Failed Bids Questionnaire (in Appendix D) is designed to formalize this process so that the couple learns to do what you would do normally as a therapist.

GOAL: COUPLE WILL BE ABLE TO PROCESS THEIR OWN INTERACTION AND MAKE IT BETTER

Most failed bids are not actively hostile retreats from intimacy but mindless responses in which people do not see the bid or have their own agenda that is not getting expressed. Using the Aftermath of Failed Bids Questionnaire makes processing failed bids a public endeavor the couple can follow and understand. In other words, the questionnaire gives spouses the structure they need for processing failed bids on their own, without me. Here are the steps in this processing:

- We examine the anatomy of bidding and turning away.
- I use the checklist in the questionnaire to examine: How did each person feel?
- We again learn that there are always two valid subjective realities in an interaction, and we describe these. We get them to validate a part of the partner's reality.
- We identify the triggers of bidding and turning away.
- We move toward Wile's admitting mode in which each partner acknowledges a contribution to the failed bid.
- We examine unexpressed needs in this interaction and how to improve the process of expressing these needs.
- We may examine the role of projection in the miscommuncation and take a look at each person's past.
- We look at Wile's "conversation they never had" and try to help them have that conversation in the session.
- We come up with one intervention that can make this better in the future.

THE INTERVENTIONS AND THEIR DESIGN

The interventions in this chapter are designed to change the spouses' knowledge of one another's psychological world (Love Maps), their Fondness and Admiration System, and the way they move through time together, prioritize how they choose to be together, and address the balances of engagement/disengagement and turning toward/turning away. These balances affect the setting conditions that have given rise to the gridlocks in the first place. These setting conditions do not involve conflict resolution, although they profoundly impact the degree of positive or negative sentiment override that is available, which, in turn, determines how the spouses handle minor everyday conflicts. Positive or negative sentiment override also determines the couple's ability to repair interaction during conflict resolution. Research suggests that if spouses are making an emotional connection—say, through listening sympathetically to their partner, even if only for 20 minutes a day—this alone will dramatically change the way they deal with conflict when it arises. They will be buffered by positive instead of negative sentiment override, so the way they react to each other's irritability will soften, and that will increase the chances that repair attempts will be successful.

Intervention 1. Love Maps: Introducing the Concept

Here the therapist is only sketching the outline of the couple's Love Maps by introducing the concept. In this intervention partners take turns selecting a card from the Love Maps deck. They try to answer the question on the card. For example, "Name your partner's least favorite relative." The listening spouse corrects the partner if necessary, but in a spirit of fun, not criticism.

Purpose

Spouses establish a baseline in their knowledge of one another and begin to become better known. Cognitive room begins to be allocated for the spouse and the marriage.

Exercise

Each spouse plays the Love Map Game. Love Map Card Items are included in Table 7.1.

Intervention 2. Love Maps: Generalizing to Everyday Life

This can take more than one session if all the exercises are used.

Purpose

The couple generalizes the expansion of cognitive room they gained by applying the Love Map Board Game to their everyday interactions.

Exercise

Spouses take turns using the form in Table 7.2 to interview their partner, asking the questions necessary to fill out the form.

Intervention 3: Three Additional Love Map Exercises

Purpose

The following exercises are structured conversations that the couple will have in the therapist's office. For each exercise, the couple is asked to have this same type of conversation once at home in the following week.

Exercise

Partners take turns as speaker and listener, discussing the most important recent and upcoming events in each one's personal life.

Table 7.1 Love Map Cards

1. Name your partner's two closest friends.
2. What is your partner's favorite musical group, composer, or instrument?
3. What was your partner wearing when you first met?
4. What are your partner's hobbies?
5. Where was your partner born?
6. What stresses are facing your partner in the immediate future?
7. Describe in detail your partner's day, either today or yesterday.
8. When is your partner's birthday?
9. What is the date of your anniversary?
10. Who is your partner's most favorite relative?
11. What is your partner's fondest dream, as yet unachieved?
12. What is your partner's favorite flower?
13. What is one of your partner's greatest disaster scenarios?
14. What is your partner's favorite time for making love?
15. What makes your partner feel most competent?
16. What is one thing that turns your partner on sexually?
17. What is your partner's favorite meal?
18. What is your partner's favorite way to spend an evening?
19. What is your partner's favorite color?
20. What personal improvements does your partner want to make in his or her life?
21. What kind of present would your partner like best?
22. What was one of your partner's best childhood experiences?
23. What was your partner's favorite vacation?
24. What is one of your partner's favorite ways of being soothed?
25. Who is your partner's greatest source of support (other than you)?
26. What is one of your partner's hobbies?
27. What is your partner's favorite sport to watch?
28. What is your partner's favorite sport to play?
29. What does your partner most like to do with time off?
30. What is one of your partner's favorite weekend activities?
31. What is your partner's favorite getaway place?
32. What is one of your partner's favorite movies?
33. What are some of the important events coming up in your partner's life and how does he or she feel about them?
34. What are some of your partner's favorite ways to work out?
35. What is your partner's favorite cologne or perfume?
36. Who was your partner's best friend in childhood?
37. What is one of your partner's favorite magazines?
38. Name one of your partner's major rivals or "enemies."
39. What would be an ideal job for your partner?
40. What is your partner's major fear?
41. Who is your partner's least favorite relative?
42. What is your partner's favorite holiday?
43. What is your partner's favorite kind of reading?
44. What is your partner's favorite TV show?
45. Who was your partner's best friend in childhood?
46. Who is your partner's favorite poet?
47. What is your partner's favorite side of the bed?

Table 7.1   Love Map Cards (*continued*)

48. What is your partner currently most sad about?
49. What is one of your partner's concerns, worries?
50. What medical problems does your partner worry about?
52. What is your partner's worst childhood experience?
53. Which people does your partner most admire in the world? Name two.
54. Name your partner's major rival or enemy.
55. Who is your partner's least favorite person you both know?
56. What is one of your partner's favorite desserts?
57. What is your partner's social security number?
58. What is one of your partner's favorite novels?
59. What is your partner's favorite romantic restaurant?
60. What are two of your partner's aspirations, hopes, wishes?
61. Does your partner have a secret ambition? What is it?
62. What foods does your partner hate?
63. What is your partner's favorite animal?
64. What is your partner's favorite song?
65. What is your partner's type of favorite tree?

Table 7.2   Real Map of Your Partner's Everyday Life

Ask your partner the questions you need answered to be able to fill in the information requested below.

The cast of characters in your partner's life

Who are your partner's friends?

Who are your partner's potential friends?

Who are the rivals, competitors, "enemies" in your partner's world?

What are recent important events? (What has occurred recently that is important to your partner?)

What are some important upcoming events? (What is your partner looking forward to?)

What are some current stresses in your partner's life?

What are some of your partner's current worries?

What are some of your partner's hopes and aspirations for self and others?

Exercise

Partners take turns as speaker and listener, discussing what they would like their lives to be like in 5 years (or the immediate future).

Exercise

Partners take turns as speaker and listener, discussing changes they would like to make to improve aspects in their personal lives (not related to the marriage)—for example, how to lose weight, get in shape, take classes, and so on. (This exercise was inspired by Tom Bradbury's work.)

Homework

Partners are asked to find one way of making contact mentally (simply thinking of one another) and actually making contact (e.g., a phone call or message) every day when they are apart—a way that is based on their knowledge of what is going on in their spouse's life that day. Then the partners talk about their day at the end of the day.

Intervention 4. Fondness and Admiration System: Introducing the Concept

Purpose

To reconnect partners with feelings of fondness and admiration and shift their focus to qualities that kindled their relationship in the past.

Exercise

Using the Gottman "I Appreciate . . . " Adjective Checklist in Table 7.3, instruct partners to select the three to five of the adjectives that have, at some time, characterized their partner's personality. They then share their responses and explain their choices. Next ask them to share a specific incident in which their partner exhibited this positive trait, telling the story of that event. Troubled couples tend to be somewhat vague about details of these events.

Intervention 5. Fondness and Admiration System: Building in Praise and Appreciation

Purpose

To evoke partners' feelings of fondness and admiration for one another and shift their focus to what they already have in their relationship rather than to what is missing. This intervention is aimed at increasing the amount of praise and appreciation that is expressed in the marriage.

Table 7.3   Gottman "I Appreciate . . ." Adjective Checklist

Instructions: It is very important to examine the positive aspects of your partner's personality. Many times when people are upset with one another they lose sight of all these positive aspects of the partner and of the relationship. If these positive areas of a partner or
of the marriage get acknowledged and discussed, change is often more possible and
exploring these areas that you appreciate may have positive consequences. For a few
moments, we'd like you to think about selected aspects of your partner's personality.
Even if there was only one instance of this characteristic in your partner's personality,
we'd like you to think about it. Circle three to five items that you think are characteristic,
even slightly, of your partner at times. For each item you check, briefly think of an actual
incident that illustrates this characteristic of your partner. You will then share this incident
with your partner.

1. Loving	37. Involved
2. Sensitive	38. Expressive
3. Brave	39. Active
4. Intelligent	40. Careful
5. Thoughtful	41. Reserved
6. Generous	42. Adventurous
7. Loyal	43. Receptive
8. Truthful	44. Reliable
9. Strong	45. Responsible
10. Energetic	46. Dependable
11. Sexy	47. Nurturing
12. Decisive	48. Warm
13. Creative	49. Virile
14. Imaginative	50. Kind
15. Fun	51. Gentle
16. Attractive	52. Practical
17. Interesting	53. Lusty
18. Supportive	54. Witty
19. Funny	55. Relaxed
20. Considerate	56. Beautiful
21. Affectionate	57. Handsome
22. Organized	58. Rich
23. Resourceful	59. Calm
24. Athletic	60. Lively
25. Cheerful	61. A great partner
26. Coordinated	62. A great parent
37. Graceful	63. Assertive
28. Elegant	64. Protective
29. Gracious	65. Sweet
30. Playful	66. Tender
31. Caring	67. Powerful
32. A great friend	68. Flexible
33. Exciting	69. Understanding
34. Thrifty	70. Totally silly
35. Future-thinking	71. Shy
36. Committed	72. Vulnerable

Table 7.4   Gottman Thanksgiving Checklist

Instructions: Select from the following list of items three qualities you really appreciate about your spouse. Then tell your spouse about the qualities you are thankful for. This can be a simple statement like, "I really like the way you are sensitive to my moods."

Husband Items	*Wife Items*
Her energy	His energy
How you feel about her strength	How sensitive he is to you
The way she is commanding	How he supports you and responds to
The way she lets you direct things	your mood
How sensitive she is to you	His ability to read you
How she supports you and responds to	How you feel about his strength
your moods	The way he is when the two of you make
Her ability to read you	decisions
How you feel about her skin	The way he lets you be yourself
How you feel about her face	How you feel about his skin
How you feel about her warmth	How you feel about his face
How you feel about her strength	How you feel about his warmth
How you feel about her hair	How you feel about his strength
How you feel about the way she touches you	How you feel about his hair
How safe you feel with her	How you feel about his touch
How you feel about her tenderness	How safe he makes you feel
How you feel about her imagination	His tenderness
How you feel about her eyes	His imagination
The way you trust her	The trust you feel
How you feel about her passion	How you feel about his passion
Her knowledge of you	How you feel about his knowledge of you
How you feel about her gracefulness	His gracefulness
The way she kisses you	The way he moves
Her playfulness	The way he kisses
Her competence as a wife	His affection
Her competence as a mother	His playfulness
What she is like as a friend	His humor
Her humor	How he looks in clothes
How she looks in clothes	His loyalty to you
Her loyalty	Anything else you like and appreciate
How you feel about her style	
Anything else about her	

Exercise

Using the Gottman Thanksgiving Checklist in Table 7.4, instruct partners to select three qualities that they most appreciate in their partner. They then share their responses and explain their choices.

Intervention 6. Fondness and Admiration System: Generalizing to Everyday Life

Purpose

To generalize the Fondness and Admiration System to the couple's everyday life.

Exercise

Partners are instructed to compose their own fondness and admiration checklist containing everything they value about their spouse. They are asked to memorize the list and rehearse it, or parts of it, daily. They are asked to develop new, flattering nicknames for each other (e.g., "The Human Dynamo," "The Hummingbird Lover"). They are instructed to express genuine appreciation for something their partner did at least once daily. They are asked to focus on what their partner is *adding* to their life that day and to make it a point to touch the partner (both verbally and physically) in a purely affectionate maner.

Intervention 7. Deepening Love Maps and Fondness and Admiration: Injury and Healing

Purpose

To deepen knowledge and understanding of one another about what injuries they have suffered, how they have coped with these, and what the implications are for the marriage.

Exercise

For the following exercise spouses will need paper and pen, and it might be helpful if they each had a notebook. Each writes his/her answers to the questions in Table 7.5 in a notebook, and then the partner reads these answers and they talk it over.

Table 7.5   Injury and Healing

Instructions: This exercise is designed to encourage you to write about some aspects of your life and personality that will help you and your spouse to understand you better. In your notebook, select any questions you wish and answer as candidly as you can.

What difficult events have you gone through in your life? Write down the psychological insults and injuries you have sustained—your losses, disappointments, trials and tribulations. Include periods of stress and duress, as well as quieter periods of despair, hopelessness, and loneliness that you have been through.

These traumatic or stressful events or periods might include your childhood as well as your adult life. They may involve periods of powerlessness, humiliating events or people, or traumas of molestation, abuse, rape, or torture. They may include previous, harmful relationships.

How have you coped with and gotten through these events and periods in your life? How have you endured? What were the lasting effects on you of going through these things?

How did you strengthen yourself and find healing? How did you redress your grievances? How did you revive and restore yourself?

How did you gird and protect yourself against this ever happening to you again? What were the means you established inside yourself for renewal, healing, and self-protection?

How do these injuries and the ways you protect and heal yourself affect your marriage today? What do you want your partner to know and understand about these aspects of yourself?

Intervention 8. Deepening Love Maps and Fondness and Admiration: Triumphs and Strivings

Purpose

To deepen knowledge and understanding of one another's history with the emotion of pride, their strivings, how they have coped with these, and the implications for the marriage.

Exercise

Each person writes his/her answers to the questions in Table 7.6 in a notebook, and then the partner reads these answers and they talk it over.

Table 7.6   Triumphs and Strivings

Instructions: This exercise is designed to encourage you to write about some aspects of your life and personality that will help you and your spouse to understand you. In your notebook, select any questions you wish and answer as candidly as you can.

What has happened in your life that you are proud of? Write down the psychological triumphs you have experienced in your life—your gains, times when things went even better than you expected, periods when you came through trials and tribulations even better off. Include those periods of stress and duress that you survived and mastered.

These events from your childhood or your adult life might include challenges you have met, even if these were challenges you created for yourself to meet. They may be periods of power, glorious events or fine people, events of closeness and intimacy, great times of friendship or even small events that still have a great deal of importance to you. They may include previous, very positive relationships, or positive moments within them.

How have you coped with and gotten through hard events and periods in your life? How have you endured? What glories and victories have you experienced? What were the lasting effects on you of going through these things?

What did you take from these positive events in your life? How have they affected the way you think of yourself and your capabilities? How have they affected your goals and the things you strive for? Did these events strengthen you?

What has been your history with the emotion of pride, and with praise? How did your parents show you that they were proud of you when you were a child? How have other people responded to your accomplishments?

What role does pride in your accomplishments play in your marriage? What role do your own strivings have in your marriage? Are your goals and strivings honored and valued? How so? What do you want your partner to know and understand about these aspects of yourself, your present, your future plans and goals, and your past?

Intervention 9. Deepening Love Maps and Fondness and Admiration: Mission and Legacy

Purpose

To deepen knowledge and understanding of one another's search for personal meaning, what they are both trying to accomplish in their lives, and how they wish to be remembered.

Exercise

Each person writes his/her answers to the questions in Table 7.7 in a notebook, and then the partner reads these answers and they talk it over.

Intervention 10. Work on the Fondness and Admiration System That Is in Your Own Head

Purpose

Changing how spouses think about the story of their relationship in seven weeks.

Exercise

The couple is asked to follow the instructions on Table 7.8.

Table 7.7 Mission and Legacy

Instructions: *This exercise is designed to encourage you to write about some aspects of your life and personality that will help you and your spouse to understand you better. In your notebook, select questions you wish to answer and do so as candidly as you can.*

Imagine that you are standing in a graveyard looking at your own tombstone. Think of the epitaph you would like to see there. Imagine your own obituary in the newspaper following your death. Write this obituary of yourself. It does not have to be brief. How do you want people to think of your life, to remember you?

Next, write the mission statement for your life. What are you trying to accomplish? What is your larger struggle? What is your dream? What legacy would you like to leave this world when you die?

What are your life dreams? What is it that you definitely want to do in your life that you have not yet fulfilled? This can be creating something or an experience that you want to have. Examples are learning to play the banjo, climbing a mountain, and so on.

We are all involved in becoming the person we most want to be like. In that struggle we all have our own "demons" to fight and overcome. What kind of person would you like to be? What have been your struggles in trying to become that person? What demons in yourself have you had to fight?

Table 7.8 Building the Fondness and Admiration System

Instructions: The following list of affirmations contains relationship-enhancing thoughts and actions that can replace the distress-maintaining ones that lead to the Distance and Isolation Cascade. Try to genuinely think about and rehearse these positive thoughts about your partner and your relationship and do the tasks suggested in italics. Do one a day.

Week 1

1. I am genuinely fond of my partner. *List one characteristic you find endearing or lovable.*
2. I can easily speak of the good times in our marriage. *Pick one good time and write a paragraph about it.*
3. I can easily remember romantic, special times in our marriage. *Pick one such time and think about it.*
4. I am physically attracted to my partner. *Think of one physical attribute you like.*
5. My partner has specific qualities that make me proud. *Write down one characteristic that makes you proud.*

Week 2

1. I feel a genuine sense of "we" as opposed to "I" in this marriage. *Think of one thing that you both have in common.*
2. We have the same general beliefs and values. *Describe one belief you both have.*
3. We have common goals. *List two such goals.*
4. My spouse is my best friend. *What secret about you does your spouse know?*
5. I get lots of support in this marriage. *Think of a time that you got really good support.*

Week 3

1. My home is a place to come for support and recovery. *List a time when your spouse helped you reduce stress.*
2. I can easily recall the first time we met. *Describe it on paper.*
3. I remember many details about deciding to get married. *Describe it in a paragraph.*
4. I can recall our wedding and honeymoon. *Describe one thing about them you enjoyed.*
5. We divide up household chores in a fair way. *Describe one way that you do this on a regular basis.*

Week 4

1. We plan things and have a sense of control over our lives together. *Describe one thing you both planned together.*
2. I am proud of this marriage. *What are you proud of?*
3. I am proud of my family. *Be specific about a time you felt this pride.*
4. There are some things I don't like about my partner, but I can live with them. *What are these minor faults?*
5. This marriage is a lot better than most I have seen. *Think of a marriage you know that's awful.*

Week 5

1. I was really lucky to meet my spouse. *List one benefit being married to your spouse conveys to you.*
2. Marriage is sometimes a struggle, but it's worth it. *Think of one difficult time you weathered together.*
3. There is a lot of affection between us. *Plan a surprise gift for your mate for tonight.*
4. We are genuinely interested in one another. *Think of something to do or to talk about together that would be interesting.*
5. We find one another to be good companions. *Plan an outing together.*

Table 7.8 Building the Fondness and Admiration System (*continued*)

Week 6

1. There is plenty of good loving in my marriage. *Think of a special trip you took together.*
2. My partner is an interesting person. *Plan something to ask your mate about that interests both of you.*
3. We respond well to one another. *Write a love letter to your spouse and mail it.*
4. If I had it to do over again, I would marry the same person. *Plan an anniversary (or other) getaway.*
5. There is a lot of mutual respect in my marriage. *Take a class together (sailing, ballroom dancing, etc.).*

Week 7

1. Sex is usually quite satisfying in this marriage. *Plan an evening of massage.*
2. We have come a long way together. *Think of all you have accomplished as a team.*
3. I think we can weather any storm together. *Reminisce about having made it through a hard time.*
4. We enjoy each other's senses of humor. *Rent a comedy video. Watch it together.*
5. My mate can be very cute. *Get very dressed up for an elegant evening together.*

Intervention 11. Emotional Bank Account: Introducing the Concept

Purpose

To introduce spouses to the concept of the emotional bank account and the idea of turning toward versus turning away, so that they can evaluate the strengths they wish to build in their marriage.

Exercise

The spouses fill out the Gottman Areas of Strength Checklist (Appendix A) independently, and then they spend another 15 minutes filling out this form by consensus. Instruct the partners to avoid arguing about whether or not an area is, or is not, a strength. One can always build strength in an area that is not strong.

Intervention 12. Emotional Bank Account: Generalizing to Everyday Life

Purpose

To enhance the couple's ability to create a peaceful home by learning how to have a stress-reducing conversation on a daily basis. Recall that Jacobson et al. (1987) found that stress spillover was the single discriminator between those couples who maintained change and those who relapsed two years after marital therapy. Therefore, this is probably the most important "deposit" that a couple will make to their emotional bank account, the most important part of turning toward one another.

Exercise

The stress-reducing conversation: Tell the couple that this exercise deals with the management of daily external stress, like job stress. Ask spouses to commit to having a conversation like this one every day, for at least 20 minutes, at the end of the day. Ask the spouses to *discuss a recent or upcoming stress in each of their lives that is not related directly to a marital issue (like an upcoming visit to in-laws or a business venture).* They take turns, allowing about 15 minutes for each.

Contrary to sterotypes, both men and women have a tendency to give support by trying to come up with solutions to the problem (Notarius & Herrick, 1988). I typically tell both men and women, "No, you do not have this responsibility to solve the problem. Give up this responsibility. Unburden yourselves. Your partners are not dumb and can come up with their own solutions." Men, in particular, need to understand that they can gain enormous mileage just by listening and being understanding. This is an eye-opener for most men. But for both men and women the basic principle is: *Understanding must precede advice.*

It is important for women to separate themselves from the stresses that their husbands are describing. Advise them, "Try not to think of this stress as *our* problem. Don't respond to your partner's stresses with complaint and criticism of your own. Just listen and be understanding."

In the last 5 minutes of the exercise, ask the partners to discuss how and when they could build in this kind of conversation into each day. See Table 7.9 for rules and suggestions for having this conversation. Give them a copy of the table.

Intervention 13. Emotional Bank Account: Generalizing to Everyday Life

Purpose

To change the way the couple moves together through time by finding the right balance of turning toward versus turning away.

Exercise

Have the couple fill out the Gottman Turning Toward During Everyday Events Checklist in Appendix A. In this checklist they indicate what things they wish to be doing more together, when they want their partner to turn toward them more. After filling it out separately, ask them to discuss their responses and come up with a consensus.

Table 7.9   Deposits to Your Emotional Bank Account, or Ways to Earn Marital Points

Giving Support:

- SHOW GENUINE INTEREST: Ask questions. Clarify details.
- COMMUNICATE UNDERSTANDING: "What a bummer! I'd be stressed out, too. I can understand why you feel that way."
- US AGAINST OTHERS: "That guy is a total jerk!"
- SOLIDARITY: "This is our problem and we will face it together."
- MY OWN EXPERIENCE IS SIMILAR: "I can understand because . . . "
- AFFECTION: "Come here and let me hold you. I'm totally on your side."
- LISTEN: Don't rush to suggest solutions right away. Listening is most important! "We'll figure this out eventually."

Requiting Emotions:

- INTEREST: "Tell me more about that." Ask questions.
- EXCITEMENT: "Wow! This is really hot stuff! Let's do it!"
- SADNESS: "Yeah, that is really so sad."
- FEAR: "That is something that would have me worried, too."
- IRRITATION AND ANGER: "I can see why you'd be annoyed here."
- DON'T: Stonewall, ignore your partner, fail to respond, get defensive, criticize, or side with the enemy (even if you think the enemy is partly right—support is much more important right now).

Intervention 14. Physiological Soothing

Purpose

To teach partners how to make the marriage feel like a port in a storm, where each can get support and solace from the everyday stresses of the world.

Exercise

Give the couple a copy of the written relaxation instructions in Table 7.10. They are to take turns reading these to each other in your office, at a point when they appear to be quite stressed, in a state of DPA, or feeling flooded. They can also do this at home, at the end of the day, while playing CDs that they find relaxing. Later they should also ask their partner for suggestions of what they can do physically to make their partner feel soothed (e.g., stroking partner's hair, foot massage, holding partner).

Table 7.10   Gottman Relaxation Instructions

Instructions: Keep your voice relaxed and even, speaking in a soothing monotone. Be sensitive to expressions of voice or face that show your partner's discomfort, and respond to these cues, trying to make your partner as comfortable as possible. Okay, find a position that is comfortable for your partner. Now have your partner sit back or lie down and try to get comfortable. Ask your partner, "Comfortable?" (If not, make adjustments.)

Okay. Just listen to the music and let your mind drift, as if you were on a cloud, floating very lazily and very relaxed through the air, mind drifting. Now let's begin. Concentrate on my voice and try to do everything I say. Close your eyes. Now let's start with your arms. Tense your arms, your biceps, and your shoulders, really tense them. Now hold the tension (count to 10), and now let it go, let go of the tension, let all the tension flow out as if it were a liquid flowing out of your arms, let it all out, let it all flow out. Feel the floor (or the chair) pressing up on your arms, feel them getting heavy, heavy, as if they are becoming like a lead weight, feel them now heavy, very heavy. Now they are getting this warm, heavy feeling, getting very warm.

Now let's move to your hands. Tense your hands, really tense them. Now hold it (count to 10), and now let it go, let go of the tension, let all the tension flow out as if it were a liquid flowing out of your arms, let it all out, let it all flow out. Feel the floor (or the chair) pressing up on your hands, feel them getting heavy, heavy, as if they are becoming like a lead weight, feel them now heavy, very heavy. Now they are getting this warm, heavy feeling, getting very warm. Both arms and hands are getting heavy and warm. Listening to the music and letting your mind drift, on a cloud, floating and very relaxed, mind drifting.

Now let's move on to your legs. Tense your legs and thighs and lower back, really tense them all. Now hold it (count to 10), and now let it go, let go of the tension, let all the tension flow out as if it were a liquid flowing out of your legs and lower back, let it all out, let it all flow out. Feel the floor (or the chair) pressing up on your legs and back, feel them getting heavy, heavy, as if they are becoming like a lead weight, feel them now heavy, very heavy. Now they are getting this warm, heavy feeling, getting very warm. Both arms and hands and legs and thighs are getting heavy and warm.

Move on to your feet. Tense your feet, really tense them both. Now hold it (count to 10), and now let it go, let go of the tension, let all the tension flow out as if it were a liquid flowing out of your feet, let it all out, let it all flow out. Feel your feet getting heavy, heavy, as if they are becoming like a lead weight, feel them now heavy, very heavy. Now they are getting this warm, heavy feeling, getting very warm. Both arms and hands and legs and thighs and feet are getting heavy and warm.

Let's move on to your abdomen. Tense your abdomen and middle back, really tense them. Now hold it (count to 10), and now let it go, let go of the tension, let all the tension flow out as if it were a liquid flowing out of your abdomen and back, let it all out, let it all flow out. Feel the floor (or the chair) pressing up on your abdomen and back, feel them getting heavy, heavy, as if they are becoming like a lead weight, feel them now heavy, very heavy. Now they are getting this warm, heavy feeling, getting very warm. Both arms and hands and legs and thighs and abdomen and back are getting very heavy and warm. Listening to the music and letting your mind drift, on a cloud, floating and very relaxed, mind drifting.

Table 7.10   Gottman Relaxation Instructions (*continued*)

Move on to your chest. Tense your chest and upper back, really tense them. Now hold it (count to 10), and now let it go, let go of the tension, let all the tension flow out as if it were a liquid flowing out of your chest and back, let it all out, let it all flow out. Feel the floor (or the chair) pressing up on your back, feel your chest and back getting heavy, heavy, as if they are becoming like a lead weight, feel them now heavy, very heavy. Now they are getting this warm, heavy feeling, getting very warm. Both arms and hands and legs and thighs and abdomen and chest and back are getting very heavy and warm.

Move on to your neck. Tense your neck. Now hold it (count to 10), and now let it go, let go of the tension, let all the tension flow out as if it were a liquid flowing out of your neck and back, let it all out, let it all flow out. Feel the floor (or the chair) pressing up on you, feel your neck getting very relaxed and warm. Arms and hands and legs and thighs and abdomen and chest and back and neck are getting very heavy and very warm. Listening to the music and letting your mind drift, on a cloud, floating and very relaxed, mind drifting.

Move on to your face. Tense the muscles of your brow region. Now hold the tension (count to 5), and now let it go, let go of the tension, let all the tension flow out as if it were a liquid flowing out of your forehead, let it all out, let it all flow out. Now tense the muscles around your eyes and upper nose. Now hold the tension (count to 5), and now let it go, let go of the tension, let all the tension flow out as if it were a liquid flowing out, let it all out, let it all flow out. Now let's move on to your cheeks and mouth. Tense the muscles of your cheeks and compress your lips together hard. Now hold this tension (count to 5), and now let it go, let go of the tension, let all the tension flow out as if it were a liquid flowing out of your face, let it all out, let it all flow out. Now let's move on to your jaw. Bite down hard and hold this tension. Hold the tension (count to 5), and now let it all go, let go of the tension, let all the tension flow out as if it were a liquid flowing out of your face, let it all out, let it all flow out. Now let's move on to your speech and vocal region. Now hold the tension (count to 5), and now let it go, let go of the tension, let all the tension flow out as if it were a liquid flowing out of your speech region, let it all out, let it all flow out. Go back and relax your forehead, eye, nose, cheeks, mouth, jaw and speech region. Let all the residual tension flow out.

Feel the floor (or the chair) pressing up on you, feel yourself all heavy, very heavy now, all warm, and relaxed. Look through your body for any residual tension, and let it go, let go of it all. Just listen to the music and let your mind drift, as if you were on a cloud, floating very lazily and very relaxed through the air, mind drifting.

Chapter 8 🦋

Solving What Is Solvable

 There is a two-pronged approach to the regulation of conflict, one for solvable and one for gridlocked issues. There are five skills for solvable problems, which are covered in this chapter.

I take a two-pronged approach to problem-solving in marriage: (1) functional problem-solving for resolvable problems, and (2) establishing a dialogue with perpetual problems. Some marital problems do, in fact, get solved by some couples. We have identified the functional aspects of the problem-solving process when this happens and found that there are several useful things that we can teach couples in this regard.

Not uncommonly, couples will select a gridlocked perpetual problem instead of a solvable problem for the first prong of these conflict regulation interventions. Therapists need to help them identify a situationally specific solvable problem. If it turns out that the problem is a perpetual gridlocked problem, start over. It is sometimes the case that all of a couple's problems are perpetual and gridlocked. In that case go right to the second prong of conflict regulation.

SETTING UP THE CONFLICT DISCUSSIONS

Setting up the discussion is the trickiest part of these conflict regulation interventions. It is important for the couple to understand the difference between solvable and perpetual gridlocked problems. Any issue can be a gridlocked issue or a solvable one. It depends entirely on how long the issue has lasted and whether the partners wind up feeling attacked, hurt, and basically rejected whenever they discuss the issue. The questionnaire in Table 8.1 illustrates perpetual issues in terms of fundamental differences in personality or needs of the spouses. The questionnaire in Table 8.2 illustrates a solvable problems checklist. I ask the cou-

Table 8.1 Perpetual Issues

Perpetual problems are usually either: (1) fundamental differences in your personalities that repeatedly create conflict, or (2) fundamental differences in your lifestyle needs. Needs are basic to your own identity, to who you are as a person. This is a problem you have had for a long time that keeps arising. Perpetual issues are gridlocked if, during the discussion, you always feel under attack and basically unaccepted when you express your positions.

Instructions: In your marriage you may have some gridlocked perpetual issues. Look over the following list and check each item that is a gridlocked issue between you. There may be some very basic differences between the two of you, but they may not have led to grid-locked conflict. In that case, circle the item; these circled items indicate strengths of your marriage.

1. ☐ *Differences in neatness and organization.* One person is neat and organized and the other is sloppy and disorganized.
2. ☐ *Differences in emotionality.* One person is very emotionally expressive and the other is not so expressive. One person also values exploring one's emotions more than the other.
3. ☐ *Differences in wanting time together versus time apart and alone.* One person wants more time alone than the other, who wants more time together. These reflect basic differences in wanting autonomy versus interdependence.
4. ☐ *Differences in optimal sexual frequency.* One person wants more sex than the other.
5. ☐ *Differences in preferred lovemaking style.* There are differences in what the two people want from lovemaking. For example, one sees intimacy as a precondition to making love, while the other sees lovemaking as a path to intimacy.
6. ☐ *Differences in approaching finances.* One person is much more financially conservative and a worrier, while the other wants to spend a lot more than the other, and has a philosophy more of living for the moment.
7. ☐ *Differences with respect to kin.* One person wants more independence from kin, and the other wants more closeness.
8. ☐ *Differences in how to resolve conflict.* One person likes to openly discuss conflicts while the other would prefer to avoid them more.
9. ☐ *Differences in how to approach household chores.* For example, one person wants equal division of labor, while the other does not.
10. ☐ *Differences in how to raise and discipline children.* One person is more involved with the children than the other.
11. ☐ *Differences in how to raise and discipline children.* One person is stricter with the children than the other.
12. ☐ *Differences in how to raise and discipline children.* One person wants more gentleness and understanding used with the children than the other.
13. ☐ *Differences in punctuality.* One person is habitually late, and to the other it is important to be on time.
14. ☐ *Differences in preferred activity level.* One person prefers active physical recreation, while the other is more passive and sedentary.
15. ☐ *Differences in being people-oriented.* One person is more extraverted and gregarious than the other.
16. ☐ *Differences in preferred influence.* One person prefers to be more dominant in decision-making than the other.
17. ☐ *Differences in ambition and the importance of work.* One person is far more ambitious and oriented to work and success than the other.

Table 8.1   Perpetual Issues (*continued*)

18. ☐ *Differences with respect to religion.* One person values a religious orientation more than the other.
19. ☐ *Differences with respect to drugs and alcohol.* One person is far more tolerant of drug and alcohol use than the other.
20. ☐ *Differences in independence.* One person feels a greater need to be independent or connected than the other.
21. ☐ *Differences in excitement.* One person feels a greater need to have life be exciting or adventurous than the other.
22. ☐ *Differences in preferred style of life.* Partners have major differences in the way they choose to live life on an everyday basis.
23. ☐ *Differences in values.* Partners have major differences in what they value in life.
24. ☐ *Others: You supply them here:*

ple to fill these out and identify an "easy" problem, one that is not gridlocked but on which they disagree to some extent, as well as one gridlocked problem.

Beware of the fact that *any* issue, no matter how specific or trivial it seems, can have huge symbolic meaning that is truly at the core of the person's sense of self. These are the issues that become perpetual issues and that sometimes become gridlocked. I knew a couple once who exemplified this point. He traveled a great deal and was a book editor. At home he worked a great deal at his desk. His wife ran a business from her home, and when he was gone she became lonely and somewhat afraid, so she suggested getting a puppy. She loved dogs and had one as a child. She also saw this as kind of preliminary to becoming parents. He didn't want a dog, but he waffled on the issue a bit, and she finally surprised him by getting a puppy when he was out of town. He was furious and felt betrayed because they had not made this decision together. He became adamant. He would accept no responsibility for the dog, would not walk it, would not clean up its messes. She hoped he would just fall in love with the puppy and soften with time. But he did not. The dog took a dump beneath his desk and he refused to clean it up. So did she, and they had a bitter fight about this. That pile of dog doo stayed under his desk for five years, while the marriage deteriorated. I am not making this up. This issue had profound symbolic meanings to both people, and they never got over the dog doo issue.

Solvable problems are usually more specific and situational, but that is a very rough guide. I suggest that the therapist have the couple fill out the questionnaire in Table 8.1. After that, ask them to identify an "easy" problem, one that is not a gridlocked issue, but still an issue on which they disagree to some extent.

RESOLVING PROBLEMS THAT CAN BE RESOLVED: THE FIVE SKILLS

The following discussion assumes that the therapist has helped the couple work through the Gottman Areas of Change Checklist or the Gottman Areas of Disagreement Scale (both in Appendix A) and has identified at least one issue in

Table 8.2   Solvable Problems Checklist

Instructions: Any problem can be a solvable or a perpetual issue, and any problem can be gridlocked or not. In the following list please try to select issues that are as SPECIFIC as possible for identifying a solvable problem in your marriage. Do NOT pick a perpetual or gridlocked issue, one that is a repeating source of great pain for you. Please check only those items that describe how you would like things to be in your marriage. Fill out this form individually. Select all that apply.

Housework: I would like my spouse to do the following:

Run errands to the cleaners
Wash windows
Plan the food menu
Go grocery shopping
Cook dinner
Set the table
Help out when I am tired
Clean up after dinner
Clean the kitchen
Clean the bathrooms
Put out clean towels
Keep counters clean
General tidying up
Take out garbage and trash

Do recycling
Do the laundry
Fold the laundry
Iron
Put the clean clothes away
Sweep kitchen and eating areas
Vacuum
Wash and wax floors
Make the beds
Defrost and clean refrigerator
House plant care
Straighten and rearrange closets
Others (you write in):

Errands: I would like my spouse to do the following:

Legal matters (e.g., wills)
Get the car serviced
Put gas in the car
Sort incoming mail
Write letters
Take phone messages
Communicate important events
    that have occurred during the day
Return phone calls or e-mail
Change light bulbs
Repair appliances
Shop for clothing
Home repair
Remodel
Do home maintenance
Buy furniture

Redecorate home
Buy items for the home
Buy new appliances
Sew and mend
Straighten kitchen cabinets
Do yard and garden work
Do lawn, tree, shrubbery maintenance
Run errands to the bank
Get people presents
Keep in touch with kin
Plan travel
Get house ready for guests
Party preparations
Take photos or videos
Work on the family photo album
Others (you write in):

Finances: I would like my spouse to do the following:

Carry more weight financially
Pay the bills
Balance the checkbook
Spend less money on self
Save more money
Spend more money on some things
Buy me gifts
Do the taxes
Be more frivolous

Be less frivolous
Do long-range financial planning
Earn more money
Have a more stable and financially
    productive work life
Plan major purchases (cars, etc.)
Have and manage investments
Others (you write in):

Table 8.2   Solvable Problems Checklist (*continued*)

In-laws: I would like my spouse to do the following:

Take my side in issues that arise
  with in-laws
Call in-laws more often
Call in-laws less often
Visit in-laws more
Visit in-laws less
Stand up to in-laws more

Help me be more accepted by
  spouse's family
Show more respect toward in-laws
Give in-laws less power than they now have
Be stronger with in-laws
Others (you write in):

Children: I would like my spouse to do the following:

Decide to have a child or have
  more children
Decide to *not* have a child or to *not*
  have more children
Buy children gifts
Take children to school
Pick children up from school
Child care after school
Child meals and lunches
Spend time with kids
Family outings with kids
Be more loving toward kids
Pediatrician visits
Dentist, orthodontist visits
Help with child homework
Do child baths
Take more responsibility with
  child discipline

Discuss differences in discipline
Bedtime with kids
Deal with a sick child
Handle child crises
Deal with a child's everyday emotions
Be emotionally closer to our children
Go to teacher conferences
Deal with the schools
Do special kid events
Care more about our kids
Plan kid birthday and other parties
Go to kid lessons
Be less involved with our children
Arrange kid play dates
Shop for kids' stuff
Others (you write in):

Relationship and Communication: I would like my spouse to do the following:

Prepare for holidays
Plan vacations
Plan getaways
Plan romantic dates
Stay emotionally connected
Talk to me more at the end of the day
Cuddle more
Show more respect
Be more complimentary toward me
Watch TV or listen to music together
Criticize me less
Share power in decision-making more
Ask me about my day
Bring me surprise personal gifts
Be verbally affectionate
Plan quiet evening at home
Bring home flowers
Help us be more of a team in
  this marriage
Contact me during the day

Be more considerate of me
Be more interested in me
Be less sad
Be less irritable and angry
Have more general conversation
  (for example, at dinner)
Have sex more often
Support me when I am worried or sad
Plan a romantic evening
Notice how I look
Be more romantic or passionate
Help me be less stressed
Talk more about feelings
Talk about religious or spiritual beliefs
Try new things sexually
Initiate lovemaking
Reminisce
Be less passive
Talk more about basic values and goals
  in life

Table 8.2   Solvable Problems Checklist (*continued*)

Express appreciation for things
   I do or have done

Be physically affectionate (not
   related to sex)

Plan special time during weekends

Plan a special meal

Accept my initiations for lovemaking

Control own anger better

Plan dinner out

Go on family outings, drives, picnics

Talk about the relationship

Others (you write in):

Friends and Community: I would like my spouse to do the following:

Plan get-togethers with friends

Keep in touch with friends

Help make new friends

Help have a party with friends

Show caring toward people who
   are important to me

Spend an evening out with friends

Do good deeds

Be more involved with charity

Deal with problems with our friends

Help other people who need help

Do more politically

Be more involved with the church
   [temple, synagogue, mosque]

Be less involved with the church [temple,
   synagogue, mosque]

Build community in other ways

Others (you write in):

Fun: I would like my spouse to do the following:

Plan recreational outings

Go to garage sales with me

Go hiking with me

Go camping with me

Go to concerts with me

Go to the movies with me

Play music together

Sing together

Plan a picnic

Plan a walk in the park

Have a hobby

Go canoeing or kayaking with me

Go shopping with me

Rent a video and watch it together

Spend weekends doing more fun things

Have more fun in the evenings after work

Others (you write in):

Balancing Work and Family: I would like my spouse to do the following:

Work less

Work more

Develop own work or career interests
   more

Work less in the evenings

Not take work along when we go away

Not think about work so much

Be more understanding of how much my
   work demands

Be able to enjoy working when we are
   together

Not take stresses out on me

Be more understanding and supportive of
   my job stress

Help me unwind

Other (you write in):

Health and Fitness: I would like my spouse to do the following:

Take care of family medicine

Use drugs less

Drink alcohol less

Stop smoking

Deal with own psychological
   problems by getting help (for
   example, with depression)

Visit the doctor or dentist regularly

Attend to other health areas

Diet or eat more nutritiously

Help me diet or eat more nutritiously

Be less concerned with my weight

Help me be less concerned with my weight

Improve on exercise and fitness

Help me with my own health and fitness

Be less concerned with my health and
   fitness

Other (you write in):

the marriage that is not gridlocked but solvable. It also assumes the therapist has done a play-by-play interview, watched the couple try to resolve the issue, and then diagnosed the areas of intervention they will need.

Based on what we have learned from couples on a trajectory toward stable, happy marriages, the work on effective problem-solving in marriages includes the following four skills:

- softened start-up
- repair and de-escalation
- accepting influence
- compromise

Basic to all skills is a fifth skill:

- physiological soothing (making the marriage a port in a storm)

Intervention 1. Softened Start-up

Notice that this is an exercise a person does alone, not with the spouse.

Purpose

To change the way that partners begin the conflict discussion, so that it is softened rather than harsh.

Examples

1. *Topic:* You want your partner to express more affection toward you.

   - *Harsh start-up:* You never touch me.
   - *Softened alternative:* I loved it when you kissed me in the kitchen the other day. You are a natural-born kisser. Would you please do more of that?

2. *Topic:* Your partner's car has a new dent in it. You are concerned that your partner is not being a careful driver and worried about your partner's safety.

   - *Harsh start-up:* I saw that new dent. When are you going to stop being so reckless?
   - *Softened alternative:* I saw that new dent. What happened? I am really getting worried about your driving, and I want you to be safe. Can we talk about this?

3. *Topic:* Your partner has not been paying enough attention to you.

   - *Harsh start-up:* You are so oblivious to me!
   - *Softened alternative:* I have been missing you lately and I'm getting a little lonely.

What leads people to decide to soften their start-up? It has to be an internal dialogue in which what wins is friendship and sympathy and understanding of the other's current life situation. For example, suppose that I am having a very bad day but still doing a lot to help with the children, household chores, errands, and so on. Meanwhile, my partner has been having breakfast with a friend and probably having a good time. The internal dialogue that leads me to not even raise this as an issue, or to do it in a softened way, may run something like this:

> I'm having a bad day, doing a lot more that my partner is doing. That really annoys me. But still, my partner is really pretty terrific. My partner does help a lot, but today is one of those days when things are not so balanced. But that's okay. My partner deserves this day off. That's because my partner has been under a lot of stress lately. But I wish I had been asked. That makes me mad. This got dumped on me at the last minute. Still, if I were asked I would have said okay, have breakfast with your friend, you deserve that day off. Do I need to be a sultan who is asked for permission? Cool out, enjoy your day as much as you can, and don't make a big deal out of this. I hope my partner is enjoying the day.

These internal dialogues in which partners decide on the course of softened start-up do not mean that they never raise issues. On the contrary. It just means that they raise them (not store them up for later and try to adapt to a bad situation) in a way that minimizes their partner's defensiveness.

Exercise

Clients are given the rules for softened start-up (Table 8.3) and the exercise in Table 8.4. They are asked to fill out the form (Table 8.4) individually.

Intervention 2. Repair and De-escalation

Purpose

To formalize the repair process. Of the 130 Seattle newlywed couples we studied who were high on the Four Horsemen (in the first few months of marriage) but repaired effectively during the interaction, 83% wound up in happy and stable marriages. Repair is absolutely critical in the regulation of conflict. Repair is a natural process, and this exercise leads naturally to the therapist's reframing repair attempts as just that (they are not really recognized by many distressed couples as repair attempts).

Here we start by formalizing a naturally occurring process. It is hard to refuse a repair attempt when both are holding the Gottman Repair Checklist (Table 8.5). The spouses are learning here how to be their own therapist, how to select their own interventions for repairing negativity. I think that this may be the most important part of the whole conflict resolution process.

Exercise

The couple discusses and resolves one issue in their marriage. They should not pick a gridlocked issue. The spouses take 5 minutes to become familiar with the Gottman Repair Checklist. Then they use the checklist in their discussion. They

Table 8.3   Rules for Softened Start-up

- **Be concise.**

It's harder to hear a complaint if it goes on and on, if it seems like a lengthy diatribe, even if it is about one thing. You usually don't need a lot of examples. Just describe the complaint, be brief, and then stop.

- **In the initial start-up complaint sentence, complain but don't blame.**

Let's assume you have a complaint to make or a gripe you want to discuss with your partner. Complaining is okay, but criticizing is not. Take the BLAMING out of the complaining. Talk about what you are feeling, and how you perceive things, presenting these as your *perceptions,* not as absolute truth.

- **Start with something positive.**

Posing problems in a positive context can often make it easier for your partner to hear a complaint. Think of a time when this issue was better and express appreciation of your partner's actions during that time. For example, instead of saying, "You are not affectionate when we watch TV," say, "I liked it the last time you held me during that romantic movie. I wish you would do that more often."

- **Make statements that start with "I" instead of "you."**

Child psychologist Haim Ginott (and later Thomas Gordon) noticed that statements that start with the word "I" instead of the word "you" are less likely to be critical and to make the partner defensive. Try to state what you are feeling in this particular situation with a complaint sentence that starts with the word "I." Instead of saying, "YOU are not listening to me," just rephrase this as "I would like it if you'd listen to me."

- **Describe what is happening, don't evaluate or judge.**

Instead of accusing or blaming, just describe what you see happening. For example, instead of saying "You don't help clean up," say "I seem to be winding up doing all the housecleaning today."

- **Talk clearly about what you need.**

Instead of asking your partner to guess what you need or to read your mind, just say it explicitly. For example, instead of saying "This dining room is a total mess," say "I'd appreciate it if you would clean your stuff off the dining room table."

- **Be polite.**

Make requests politely, adding such phrases as "please" and "I would appreciate it if . . . ." Politeness can go a long way, and it is contagious.

- **Express appreciation.**

If your partner has, at some time, been better in this situation, then ask for what you need and couch it within an appreciation of what you partner did right in the past and how much you miss that now.

- **Don't store things up.**

While being specific is better than launching a global criticism, storing things up so that you have a barrage of complaints in the "chute" is not a good idea.

- **Restate your feelings in terms of the more vulnerable emotions.**

Emotions that make you want to withdraw from the world, like sadness and fear, also convey your vulnerability, and this may be easier for your partner to respond to than the emotions

Table 8.3 **Rules for Softened Start-up** (*continued*)

associated with resentment. At times, there may be a softer emotion "behind" your harder emotion. For example, behind your anger or resentment there may be hurt, disappointment, fear, or insecurity. If you can rephrase your anger and resentment in terms of these more vulnerable emotions, sometimes they are easier for your partner to hear. For example, instead of saying "It makes me mad when you don't pay attention to me at parties," see if it makes sense to you to say, "I get lonely (or insecure) when you don't pay attention to me at parties."

---

are told to announce to their partner that they are making a repair attempt before making it. They can refer to the repair attempt by number, as in, "I'm making a repair attempt. It's the one under 'I FEEL,' number 6." Or they can just say it. (Nancy Dreyfus [1992], who invented this general approach in her "Flash Cards for Real Life," told me that she gets her best results when she does not permit couples to read the repair attempts. This probably eliminates the usual negative affect with which most repair attempts are delivered, making their acceptance more likely.) They continue the discussion for 15 minutes.

The job of the receiver of a repair attempt is to try to *accept* the repair attempt. This means that the receiver needs to find that part of the repair attempt that he or she can agree with right now. The process also involves accepting influence. The receiver is to try to view the interruption of the conversation (from the repair checklist) by the partner as an attempt to make things better.

After the exercise the checklist can go on the couple's refrigerator, where it will be easily acessible when needed. (The checklist can be cheaply laminated at a copy shop.) One of my couples not only put the repair checklist on their refrigerator but also tended to discuss issues by the appliance. One day their 3-year-old pulled his mom toward the refrigerator when the two of them were having a disagreement.

Intervention 3. Flooding and Self-Soothing

Purpose

To teach couples how to recognize when one of them feels flooded during a conflict and how to ritualize taking a break, during which they self-soothe.

Before we begin the exercise, I talk with the couple about diffuse physiological arousal (DPA) and the importance of physiological soothing. I explain why it is that the physiological state of one's body affects a myriad of factors—the ability to listen, access to recently learned behaviors and ways of thinking, and the ability to creatively solve problems—leading to reliance on over-learned behavior patterns and ways of thinking and, in particular, on fight-or-flight routines. I describe DPA as an aversive state related to flooding, which begins the Distance and Isolation Cascade. Most people recognize this state.

Table 8.4 Gottman Exercises on Softened Start-up

Instructions: In the items below a situation is described and an example of harsh start-up is given. Supply a softened alternative. This is not a test. Sample answers are given below, but try not to peek.

1. *Topic:* In-laws. Your mother-in-law is coming to visit this evening. You are upset with the way she criticizes how you discipline your children. You want your partner to back you up when you tell your mother in-law that it hurts your feelings when she does this.

   Harsh start-up: Your mother is a wart on the back of humanity.

   Your softened alternative:

2. *Topic:* Housework. You wish that your partner would either cook or take you out to dinner tomorrow night.

   Harsh start-up: You never take me anywhere, and I am sick of doing all the cooking.

   Your softened alternative:

3. *Topic:* Parties. You sometimes get shy in social situations. You think that your partner ignores you and spends time with other people when you go to parties. Tonight there is a party and you want your partner to spend time with you.

   Harsh start-up: I just know that tonight, once again, you will be flirting shamelessly at the party, and I am sick of it.

   Your softened alternative:

4. *Topic:* Sex. You are upset that you and your partner have not made love in some time. You are feeling unsure whether your partner finds you attractive. You wish that the two of you could make love tonight.

   Harsh start-up: You are so cold to me!

   Your softened alternative:

5. *Topic:* Finances. You want your partner to ask for a raise.

   Harsh start-up: You are too wimpy to get a raise for your own family.

   Your softened alternative:

6. *Topic:* Recreation.

   Harsh start-up: You have no idea how to have a good time. You are a workaholic.

   Your softened alternative:

7. *Topic:* Finances. You wish that the two of you could save more money.

   Harsh start-up: You have got to stop being such an impractical spendthrift.

   Your softened alternative:

Table 8.4   Gottman Exercises on Softened Start-up (*continued*)

8. *Topic:*   Finances. You wish your partner would spend more money on surprise presents for you.

   Harsh start-up: You are such a miser. When was the last time you spontaneously bought me anything?

   Your softened alternative:

Sample softened start-up answers:

1. I am worried that your mom is going to be critical of me tonight and that you won't back me up.
2. I am very tired of cooking. It'd be real nice if you took us all out.
3. I am feeling very shy tonight again. Please spend time with me and make it easier for me to talk to other people. You are so good at that.
4. I am really missing you lately and I feel very attracted to you. How about making love?
5. I'd love it if you would get a raise soon. What about if we talked about a plan for getting one?
6. I really want to spend some fun time with you this weekend. How about not working and let's do something fun together? There's a great new movie I'd really like to see.
7. I am feeling anxious about our savings. Let's come up with a savings plan, okay?
8. I am feeling very deprived lately, and I would love it if we surprised one another with a present "out of the blue" this week. What do you think?

I find that it is also useful to give couples a mini-lecture on sex differences in DPA, pointing out the evolutionary basis for the fact that during and after conflict discussions men tend to remain vigilant and rehearse distressing-maintaining thoughts, while women exercise their capacity for self-soothing and rehearse relationship-enhancing thoughts. I also summarize the current research on these evolutionary differences (Levenson & McCarter, 1996) noted in Chapter 2.

I stress to couples that these differences are nobody's fault. They are just part of what we inherited as a species. And these gender differences do not matter very much in situations that do not provoke contempt and disgust. But in marriage, where conflict is inevitable, they matter a great deal. So those couples who have learned to "soothe the savage male"—and this means both male self-soothing and wife soothing the male—are way ahead of the game in terms of marital stability and happiness.

Now, this does not mean that flooding isn't important for women. Women need to learn when they are flooded and be able to take a break and calm down, as is true for men. In fact, there is evidence that chronic flooding in marriages is very bad for the physical health of *both* husbands and wives.

Finally, I talk about *the pursuer-distancer pattern*, since it is so common. I describe this as a pattern that begins with one partner, usually the woman, starting the conversation, bringing up an issue, trying to come to some resolution of a problem in the marriage that she thinks is creating emotional distance, while the partner (usually the husband) doesn't really want to talk about it and may not

Table 8.5 Gottman Repair Checklist

I Feel

1. I'm getting scared.
2. Please say that more gently.
3. Did I do something wrong?
4. That hurt my feelings.
5. That felt like an insult.
6. I'm feeling sad.
7. I feel blamed. Can you rephrase that?
8. I'm feeling unappreciated.
9. I feel defensive. Can you rephrase that?
10. Please don't lecture me.
11. I don't feel like you understand me right now.
12. Sounds like it's all my fault.
13. I feel criticized. Can you rephrase that?
14. I'm getting worried.
15. Please don't withdraw.

Sorry

1. My reactions were too extreme. Sorry.
2. I really blew that one.
3. Let me try again.
4. I want to be gentler toward you right now but I don't know how.
5. Tell me what you hear me saying.
6. I can see my part in all this.
7. How can I make things better?
8. Let's try that one over again.
9. What you are saying is . . .
10. Let me start again in a softer way.
11. I'm sorry. Please forgive me.

Get to Yes

1. You're starting to convince me.
2. I agree with part of what you're saying.
3. Let's compromise here.
4. Let's find our common ground.
5. I never thought of things that way.
6. This problem is not very serious in the big picture.
7. I think your point of view makes sense.
8. Let's agree to include both our views in a solution.

I Need To Calm Down

1. Can you make things safer for me?
2. I need things to be calmer right now.
3. I need your support right now.
4. Just listen to me right now and try to understand.
5. Tell me you love me.
6. Can I have a kiss?
7. Can I take that back?
8. Please be gentler with me.
9. Please help me calm down.
10. Please be quiet and listen to me.
11. This is important to me. Please listen.
12. I need to finish what I was saying.
13. I am starting to feel flooded.
14. Can we take a break?
15. Can we talk about something else for a while?

Stop Action!

1. I might be wrong here.
2. Please, let's stop for a while.
3. Let's take a break.
4. Give me a moment. I'll be back.
5. I'm feeling flooded.
6. Please stop.
7. Let's agree to disagree here.
8. Let's start all over again.
9. Hang in there. Don't withdraw.
10. I want to change the topic.
11. We are getting off track.

I Appreciate

1. I know this isn't your fault.
2. My part of this problem is . . .
3. I see your point.
4. Thank you for . . .
5. That's a good point.
6. We are both saying . . .
7. I understand.
8. I love you.
9. I am thankful for . . .
10. One thing I admire about you is . . .
11. I see what you're talking about.
12. This is not your problem, it's OUR problem.

even think there is really a problem. The way the issue is brought up and pursued by the speaker has a very negative effect on the listener, who winds up doing one or both of two things: running away and/or escalating the conflict and rejecting all influence from the speaker. The pattern gets progressively worse over time, and it usually leads one or both people to become flooded.

Flooding Intervention A. Take a break

Purpose

To introduce a "withdrawal ritual" into the marriage. After describing the basic pattern of DPA, I show people how to take their heart rates and I describe what constitutes a "good" break: It must be at least 20 minutes long and truly relaxing; it cannot involve rehearsing distress-maintaining thoughts like "I don't have to take this," or "I'm going to get even." When taking this break, partners need to schedule a time to get back together. In our marriage experiments we have discovered that just interrupting spouses' conflict discussion and having them read magazines side by side while we tell them that we are "setting up the equipment again" significantly reduces heart rate and makes the next interaction on the conflict topic much more positive. *One of the most important things you can do for a couple is to help them create this "time out" procedure for themselves in their marriage.* Make sure that they return to the issue after the break.

Exercise

Have the couple discuss the following questions. There is to be no blaming.

- What makes me (you) feel flooded? What are the feelings inside me when this happens? What am I thinking, usually?
- How do I (you) typically bring up issues or complaints?
- Do I (you) store things up?
- Is there anything I can do that soothes you?
- Is there anything I can do to soothe myself?
- What signals can we develop for letting the other know when one of us is feeling flooded? Can we take breaks? (This is the most important part of this exercise.)

Flooding Intervention B. Imagining and Self-Soothing

Purpose

To give partners a reliable tool for self-soothing during times of flooding. In analyzing the interactions of the 130 Seattle newlyweds we studied, self-soothing turned out to be one of the best predictors of outcome in the marriage, particularly the male's ability to self-soothe.

Exercise

Take the couple through an imaging exercise using the following steps. Tell them: "When you are feeling tense and find yourself going into DPA, use the repair attempt in which you tell your partner you want to take a short break to calm yourself down. Here's what to do during those times. There are four steps of soothing yourself."

- The first step is to get control of your breathing. When you are getting flooded, you will find yourself either holding your breath a lot or breathing shallowly. Change your breathing so that it is even by taking deep, regular breaths. Take your time inhaling and exhaling. Do six breaths a minute.

- The second step is to notice areas of tension in your body. Now intentionally contract and then relax these muscle groups. For example, become aware of your face, particularly your forehead and jaw muscles, then your neck, shoulders, arms, and back. Intensify the tension, then let it flow out (next 2 steps).

- The third step is to let the region become heavy, to feel as if you are weighted down and leaden.

- The fourth step is to imagine the region becoming comfortably warm. This gets more blood to flow into the tense region and begins the process of deep relaxation.

- My wife, Julie, adds a fifth step. Think of a personal image that brings all four steps into focus and memory. For example, my own personal image is a place on Orcas Island where the loudest sound is the wind in the trees. It is near an eagle rookery, and two eagles soar majestically over the trees and sea. That image is very soothing for me, and it calls forth all four steps of self-soothing. Focus your attention on one calming vision or idea. It can be a very specific place, like a forest or a beach. Imagine this place as vividly as you can as you calm yourself down.

Biofeedback

I use biofeedback equipment in the Ring area of my office. These machines have a simple, comfortable finger sensor and provide a large beat-by-beat readout (on a desktop unit) of heart rate and oxygen consumption. They also have an alarm that can be set anywhere you like. I set mine at 95 to 100 beats a minute. When they beep, I suggest that people may need to engage in some self-soothing. I have two BCI-3040 pulse oximeters ($600 each, from Narco Medical in Fargo, North Dakota). The subject just sticks a finger in a small tube (plethysmograph). Sports companies like Polar or Sports Instruments manufacture watches (I recently bought two for $69 each, from Recreational Equipment Incorporated) that give heart rate and have an alarm. It is necessary to use a chest band with these units. It is also possible to obtain a watch unit that uses a finger plethysmograph for about $26 per unit by calling 732-842-4402 and asking for the Finger Heart Rate monitor. If you don't want to use equipment, you can teach the couple how to take their heart rate by pressing on the carotid artery pulse. Start by getting their baseline physiology when they are closing their eyes and relaxing (say, listening to music). Then measure their physiology during emotional interaction in your office. Look at the increase in heart rate. If it is not high, this is a strength in the marriage. However, if it increases about 15 bpm, this suggests that soothing is important in this marriage. Also look for how much recovery toward baseline they make in five minutes after the discussion ends. For a more sophisticated biofeedback setup, call J&J Engineering at 530-872-9602.

Intervention 4. Accepting Influence

Purpose

To get both partners to yield a bit and find their common ground so that they can arrive at a compromise position on the issue.

The idea of accepting influence is to help spouses find those parts of their partner's position that they can understand and with which they can agree. For conflicts that are not gridlocked, this involves partners' learning that sharing or relinquishing influence is an asset in the marriage. If saving face is an issue, use the Gottman Accepting Influence training audiotapes (available from the Seattle Marital and Family Institute's Marriage Clinic). These are used individually.

The therapist can also use our *video recall methodology* to explore special moments. The therapist plays these specially selected moments for the clients and then asks questions, like: What were you each thinking and feeling here? What did you wish had happened? (This elicits their goals.) You can also use the questionnaire on Innocent Victim and Righteous Indignation Scale in Appendix B.

Exercise

In this exercise the spouses work together to try to develop a common way of thinking about the issue and to start constructing a compromise that they can both live with. They will each be asking their partner these questions:

- How can we understand this issue? Can we develop a compromise view here?
- What are our common feelings or the most important feelings here?
- What common goals do we have here?
- What methods can we agree upon for accomplishing these goals?

These strategies will usually work with solvable problems; however, when we are dealing with a perpetual problem other strategies are required. These are discussed in the next chapter.

Chapter 9 &

Living with the Inevitable

 The hub of the interventions for gridlocked problems is the Dreams-Within-Conflict interview, which focuses on the symbolic meaning of people's entrenched positions and the personal goals of creating meaning. It is also designed to deal with emotional withdrawal in marriages by helping people feel entitled to their complaints.

ESTABLISHING A DIALOGUE WITH PERPETUAL PROBLEMS

We have discovered in our study of long-term happy marriages that when people stay married for a long time, they learn to become mellower about each other's faults. They become more accepting of each other, and they communicate this acceptance. A big part of marital gridlock is that usually both people feel criticized and *unaccepted by their partner.*

This is the point that Neil Jacobson and Andrew Christensen (1996) are making with their acceptance-oriented therapy. A central part of accepting influence is uncovering and understanding the *meaning* of each person's position in the conflict, finding out what things mean to each of them

The Dreams-Within-Conflict Interviews

In this part of the therapy there is one major intervention, with two parts. The first part of this intervention involves breaking up the couple's logjam by uncovering the dreams that underlie each person's entrenchment in an uncompromising position. Each of the two positions involves metaphors, stories, hopes, and dreams, and these first need to be uncovered and expressed in a safe marital climate. The second part of this intervention is changing the influence patterns in the marriage so that both people can proceed to honor one another's dreams.

234

Even if the spouses are not in a state of crisis, they are probably in a state of intense pain due to the fact that they are deadlocked on some central issues in their marriage. Because of the average delay of six years between couple's first detecting that there is something seriously wrong with their marriage and getting any kind of help (Buongiorno & Notarius, 1992), many marriages have compounded problems when they come to see you. Couples experiencing gridlock on a problem over a period of years typically have passed through a number of conflictual stages, beginning with *dreams in opposition,* moving on to *entrenchment of positions, fears of accepting influence, vilification,* and, finally, *emotional disengagement.* Eventually, one of two states will be observed: the "hot" state, in which all Four Horsemen of the Apocalypse are active, or the state of "affective death," in which partners exhibit high levels of fatigue and emotional distance and apathy and low levels of humor and affection.

The Dreams-Within-Conflict interviews explore, in the conjoint context, the symbolic meaning of each person's position and his/her fears of accepting influence on this issue. Behind the position and the resistance to accepting influence are metaphors and narratives that go way back into the person's past, perhaps into the family of origin.

Revealing the dreams behind the entrenched positions and assuring that each understands the meaning of the partner's positions and resistances is not sufficient, however. The marital interaction has to shift from one in which two dreams are locked in opposition, to one in which both partners are dedicated to making *both* of their dreams a reality. Based on our data, the final step is one of changing the power configuration of the standoff so that *the husband* accepts influence from *his wife.* That is because, among young couples today, women are already accepting influence from their husbands at a high rate. So the basic principle is: I work toward both people accepting influence from one another and honoring one another's life dreams. The issue is not who the spouses believe should be dominant, or who they think should be in charge in the marriage, but rather how can they convey honor and respect for both.

In our data, emotionally intelligent husbands were found in only 35% of newlywed marriages. By "emotional intelligence" I mean that there is a balance of power, and respect and honor are conveyed.

In our interventions, usually the husband winds up realizing that he must yield to win on this issue, that he does not want to have a marriage in which he has been successful in killing his wife's dream. It is our observation that the wife has usually yielded a considerable degree of power to the husband in the five-stage process of entrenchment, so we help women stay strong and firm regarding their dreams. Based on our data, this intervention should result in a shift toward equity in the power balance of the relationship.

In this second part of this intervention, the therapist may run into considerable resistance from the husband. Some of this male resistance has a sociological and cultural base. You may also run directly into the fact that men in our culture are under enormous demands that they change. The breadwinner role has been lost, and the family model of the 1950s is no longer the way things are. Women mostly work, and increasingly at jobs that provide not only income but also self-esteem and psychological and economic power. Women are unwilling to settle for a bad marriage anymore, and men are feeling this.

In addition to these sociological forces of change, husbands who strongly resist accepting influence from their wives may have fears of losing control, losing face, and other catastrophic scenarios connected to yielding to some part of their wife's position. These fears may have a long history for the husband, and the husband may require special soothing and training. For husbands for whom this intervention implies a loss of face, we have developed training audiotapes that they can use at home alone so that they can learn and rehearse the response of accepting influence and becoming more agreeable.

This intervention is broken down into several parts. In the first part the partners listen to one another's dreams and discover the symbolic meaning underlying their positions on a gridlocked issue.

Intervention 1. Recognizing Strengths

Purpose

To help partners become aware of the adaptation they have already made but not congratulated themselves for.

Exercise

Partners have already accepted a great deal of what they can't change in their marriage. Have each person ask their partner these questions:

- What adaptations has each of us already made in our marriage? Are there parts of one another's personalities that are not ideal but to which we have already made adjustments?
- Are one person's feelings more important on this issue than the other's?
- Is it possible to have some kind of trade-off, for example, across issues, with one person "winning" on one issue and the other person "winning" on another issue?
- How can we further adapt to this?
- Can we minimize the importance of the issue, emphasize common ground, laugh about this, accept one another's foibles?
- Is it okay for this problem to never be fully resolved?

Example

Even seemingly small and trivial issues can have great symbolic value. Here is one example of how to unlock the symbols and meanings within each person's positions. This conversation is a composit of several conversations.

A wife complains that her husband leaves his clothes all over the house and she has to pick them up. She gets angry and he reluctantly agrees to pick them up, but then he never seems to really get around to it. They have had this issue for years, but recently it has come to a head.

W: Why won't you do it? I am not your servant.

H: What does this mean to you, when I leave my clothes around?

W [*crying*] Don't you love our home? Why do you trash it when I work so hard to build it? Don't you cherish what we have, what I am trying to build?

H: What are you trying to build?

W: To me, a home has to be neat.

H: Tell me the story of that. Where does this idea come from? What does it mean to you?

W: My parents were slobs! They drank like fish and the house was chaotic. Disorder spells chaos to me. Order means a peaceful home.

H: So that's what you're trying to build? A peaceful home?

W: Yes, exactly. Okay, let's switch. You talk. What does leaving clothes around the house mean to you? Tell me the story behind your side of all this.

H: I'm exhausted at the end of the day, worn down. All day long I have to follow someone else's rules. A home ought to be a place where you can be free of rules, a place to unwind and be yourself.

W: Tell me more about rules and what this means to you.

H: By telling me to pick up these few clothes I scatter around, you are making more rules for me to have to follow, trying to control me like others always do. You join the enemy. I'm trying to shed my false skin, and you are not letting me do that.

W: So, for you, a home is a place to be free.

H: Yes. But not just free. It's a place without pretensions, not a place to show others, but a place where I can be myself.

W: Free to be yourself, unbound and unfettered. Is there a history to this? Tell me the story of this.

H: My mother kept the sofas and chairs in the living room covered with plastic and she still didn't like us kids to get on the furniture. We stayed out of the living room because it was for company. If we tracked mud into it, holy hell broke loose. She gave us tons of rules. I had to follow the rules or she'd blow up. I hated that house.

W: So a very neat home means it's your mother all over again?

H: All over again.

This conversation is just a beginning, and there are still many avenues left unexplored, hot words and phrases (like *servant* and *cherish what we have* for the wife, *rules* and *enemy* for the husband). The therapist's job is to pursue these loaded words and phrases to find out more about the stories in each person's position, discovering the metaphors behind them. Many of these notions and images go back to childhood and the primary family of origin. The therapist can search for the resonant word, phrase, or idea that has symbolic value beyond the conflict, and then ask the client what these words mean to him/her. In this example the therapist could ask the wife, "What does 'servant' mean to you?" or ask the husband, "What is it about 'rules' that gets to you?"

Metaphors may underlie these loaded words or phrases that relate to latent catastrophic scenarios or to myths about the other person that need to be challenged. These may as yet be unarticulated. What are they? Where do they come from? Explore words repeated or stressed, ideas that are emphasized. Find a word spoken with a particular tone indicating that it is loaded with meaning for the person. Look for words that are commonly laden with meaning, like *love*. Deep emotions may be tied to such words. Ask questions, like, "What does it take for you to feel loved?" or "Was there a time in your life when you felt very loved?" or "How did your parents show you that they loved you?" Ask questions that are genuine in revealing your interest.

Intervention 2. Imagining Others' Dreams

Purpose

To help partners recognize the dream within the gridlocked position in *someone else's conflict*.

Exercise

Following is a sampling of gridlocked issues that other people have had in their marriages. In this exercise, see if you can imagine and identify a dream within each position. Make up a story, or narrative, for each side of the gridlock. In each case imagine that this is *your* position and that it is very hard for you to yield on it. Think of what your position might mean to you. Also think about how this dream relates to your own past life history. Doing this exercise will eventually help you with your own gridlocked conflict. The narratives are for the first two issues.

Examples

1. I want to save money so that we can have an investment portfolio for our later years. My partner wants to spend money and not "live for tomorrow." My partner objects to having a sizable savings plan. I think that my partner is impractical and thoughtless.

Here's a story that illustrates the dream within this conflict: I grew up living with my grandmother, who was a fine person. However, she and my mother just did not get along. In her later years my grandmother had very little control over her own life, and she had to endure a lot of indignities just so she could have a roof over her head. I feel that I am a lot like her. When I become old, I want to have the control over my life that she never had. I want to be able to live as I want to live, not extravagantly, but with dignity and some measure of control. This will require planning and setting money aside. But I feel I need to do this to be secure right now that everything will be okay when I become old.

2. I want to spend a reasonably large portion of our income, close to 10%, on charitable contributions. My partner objects to this because we do not have much of a savings plan ourselves. My partner thinks my insistence on this is impractical and thoughtless.

Here's a story that illustrates the dream within this conflict: My family, the Johnsons, have a heritage of giving money to the poor and of spending part of every week doing something for the poor. My mother ran a soup kitchen, for example. I have always worked in a soup kitchen in our local church. I decided long ago to tithe, and that is a part of my identity. It is my link to my family tradition. I can't give in on this issue because I would be betraying something that I believe in. I would be betraying myself. My dream is to lead a moral life in what I see as a basically selfish and cruel world.

For the items below fill in the blanks with "narratives" of your own.

3. My partner is overly neat and tidy, in my opinion. I like a certain amount of order and neatness in our home, but not as much as my partner insists upon. I find myself constantly trying to find things after my partner has cleaned up. I think my partner is being inconsiderate and overly controlling, and I am tired of this.

Here's my story that illustrates the dream within this conflict:

4. I like a certain amount of order and neatness in our home. I find myself constantly cleaning up my partner's messes. I think my partner is being inconsiderate, and I am tired of this.

Here's my story that illustrates the dream within this conflict:

5. My partner has an issue with jealousy. At parties and other places I think that it is the time to meet new people, and I find this very interesting. My partner hangs on and is overly shy. My partner claims that I look at other people and flirt, but this isn't true at all. I find this insulting and it makes me angry. I don't know how to reassure my partner and I am tired of trying. This is eroding trust between us.

Here's my story that illustrates the dream within this conflict:

6. I have an issue with jealousy. At parties and other places I think that my partner looks at other people and flirts. I find this insulting and demeaning. I have brought this up repeatedly but my partner doesn't change.

Here's my story that illustrates the dream within this conflict:

7. My partner is an overly emotional person and claims that I am far too unemotional. This difference between us makes me feel that my partner is overly sensitive, overreactive, and out of control at times. I think that being rational is usually the best approach to strong emotional situa-

tions, not getting more emotional. My partner claims that I am hard to read and too distant.

Here's my story that illustrates the dream within this conflict:

8. I am a very emotional person and my partner is far too unemotional. This difference between us makes me feel that my partner is cold and fake at times, not really present. Many times I have no idea what my partner is thinking or feeling. I am frustrated by this difference between us.

Here's my story that illustrates the dream within this conflict:

9. My partner needs a lot of time alone, but I think it is important to spend our free time doing things together. I find it hard to get this need met, and I feel like my partner really doesn't have too much interest in being with me. My partner calls me "dependent" for wanting to be intimate in this marriage.

Here's my story that illustrates the dream within this conflict:

10. I need a lot of time alone, but my partner keeps wanting to spend all of our free time doing things together. I find this dependent and cloying and resent not getting enough time just to do things that I like, by myself or with friends.

Here's my story that illustrates the dream within this conflict:

11. My partner likes to have sex much more often than I do. I don't know what to do when my partner keeps approaching me for sexual intimacy. I don't know how to say "no" in a gentle way. This pattern makes me feel like an ogre. I don't know how to deal with this.

Here's my story that illustrates the dream within this conflict:

12. I like to have sex much more often than my partner. I keep getting my feelings hurt when I approach my partner for sexual intimacy and get turned down. This pattern makes me feel unattractive and unwanted. I don't know how to deal with this.

Here's my story that illustrates the dream within this conflict:

13. We have different styles of making love. When we try to talk about these differences, I keep feeling inadequate. It seems to me that my partner has so many conditions that must be met before we can make love that this will never happen, or it will always be fraught with problems.

Here's my story that illustrates the dream within this conflict:

14. We have different styles of making love. When we try to talk about these differences, I keep feeling frustrated. I try to explain the things I need for sex to feel more like making love, but these things seem never to get through to my partner.

Here's my story that illustrates the dream within this conflict:

15. Money has been a gridlocked conflict of ours for some time. I think that my partner is far too stingy when it comes to money and doesn't believe in spending enough on just enjoying life and having fun. I also resent not having more personal freedom and control when it comes to money.

Here's my story that illustrates the dream within this conflict:

16. Money has been a gridlocked conflict of ours for some time. I think that my partner is impractical when it comes to money and spends far too thoughtlessly and selfishly.

Here's my story that illustrates the dream within this conflict:

17. My partner likes to stay in much closer touch with our families than I do. To me, family connections are great sources of stress and disappointment. I have broken away from my family and I want much greater distance.

Here's my story that illustrates the dream within this conflict:

18. I like to stay in much closer touch with my family than my partner does. To me, family connections are very important. My partner wants greater independence from both of our families than I do.

Here's my story that illustrates the dream within this conflict:

19. I am far more introverted than my partner is. I like to spend a lot of quiet time alone. My partner wants to have dinner parties fairly often, have people over a lot, and be more connected to friends than I do. This has been a continual issue between us.

Here's my story that illustrates the dream within this conflict:

20. I am far more extraverted than my partner. I like to have dinner parties fairly often, have people over a lot, and be more connected to friends than my partner does. My partner is more of a loner, more solitary. This has been a continual issue between us.

Here's my story that illustrates the dream within this conflict:

21. My partner believes in stricter discipline of our children than I do. I am accused of being soft, of spoiling them. I believe that love and understanding are the way to approach kids, but my partner was raised a different way and does not agree with my philosophy about raising children.

Here's my story that illustrates the dream within this conflict:

22. I believe in stricter discipline of our children than my partner does. I can't stand kids who are selfish, rude, misbehaved, or disrespectful. I think my partner is soft on our kids and spoils them. I believe that "tough love" best prepares kids for success in the world.

Here's my story that illustrates the dream within this conflict:

23. My partner places much more importance and emphasis on career than on family and this keeps causing great conflict between us. We tend to do very little together as a couple or family because of this.

Here's my story that illustrates the dream within this conflict:

24. My career is very important to me. My partner places much more importance and emphasis on family than I do, and this keeps causing great

conflict between us. I think we do enough things together as a couple and family, but my partner constantly complains about this.

Here's my story that illustrates the dream within this conflict:

Below are some sample narrative dreams from others' gridlocked positions:

3. My partner is overly neat and tidy, in my opinion. . . .

Growing up, my parents were very strict disciplinarians. They wouldn't take any disagreement in the home. They saw this as insubordination. As a result of this I became somewhat of a rebel. I freely admit that I have a problem with authority, and that's why I decided to build my own business. I think of a home as a place where I can be myself, and that means not following any rigid set of rules. I want my kids to challenge authority and think for themselves, not simply learn to be obedient. I myself want to be free in my home, free to be myself, even if that means being a bit sloppy at times.

4. I like a certain amount of order and neatness in our home. . . .

I grew up in a totally chaotic home. There was nothing I could count on as a child. I never knew who was driving me to school or picking me up. My mom would sometimes forget to pick me up, and I hated her for that sometimes. Then I would get home and there would often be no dinner, and no clean clothes. It fell on my shoulders to create all the order and sense of responsibility for my younger sibs. I resented having to do all that. My parents just weren't fully mature. Well, I want to provide a much healthier family environment for my kids and family. To me, order means predictability, security, and peacefulness. I want that for my kids. When the house is a mess, it takes me back to the chaos of my youth.

5. My partner has an issue with jealousy. . . .

I must admit that I have always liked parties, especially dancing. It is my place to unwind. I enjoy meeting new people, and finding people to dance with. I like dancing with my partner as well, but I like to feel free to meet lots of new personalities at a party. I really do not flirt, nor do I have any interest in anyone but my spouse. It's just that parties are my only way of really satisfying my gregarious and wild side. I really don't want to be responsible for anyone else when I go to a party. My dream is a dream of freedom and exploration.

6. I have an issue with jealousy. . . .

I have always wanted to be able to feel that I was "enough" for someone special in my life. That is my dream: To feel truly attractive and desirable to my partner. I want my partner to be interested in ME, in knowing me and finding out what I think, wanting to know what I am like inside. I would find it incredibly romantic if I could go to a party with my spouse and my partner didn't even notice that there was anyone else there, had eyes only for me, and spent hours in rapt conversation and dancing with just me, and if that were totally satisfying for my partner.

7. My partner is an overly emotional person and claims that I am far too unemotional. . . .

I grew up in a family where everyone was a debater. We loved to argue with one another. My dad always asked a question, challenged me, and then took a contrary position to mine. Then the debate was on. It was no holds barred, and we all loved it. But getting emotional was illegal in this debating context. Once someone got emotional, the argument was over. So staying in emotional control was highly prized in my family. It still is. That's why I can do the job I have so well. It requires a cool head, and getting emotional is not an asset. So maybe I should be more emotional but it's not in my makeup. I think of it as a weakness, not a strength.

8. I am a very emotional person and my partner is far too unemotional. . . .

I am just an emotional person and that's all there is to it. I think that's what life is all about, feeling things, being in contact, responding. That's what "responsible" ought to mean, "response able," or able to respond. That's the highest value for me. I respond to everything around me, to great art, to architecture, to children, to puppies, to competition in athletics, to sad movies, to everything. To be emotional just means being alive. And if I can't share my emotions with the person I love, then what's the point? The marriage is doomed to seem dead, fake, and lonely.

9. My partner needs a lot of time alone. . . .

I am dependent, but I think that's a strength. I need to be needed and I need a lot of intimacy in my closest relationships. Relationships are not about doing things separately. I like a certain amount of aloneness and I need some time just to be with my kids, for work, for my hobbies and for my friends. But I think that fundamentally a marriage is about contact, not time apart. I want my life entwined with my partner's. That kind of intimacy and shared purpose is deeply fulfilling. I am lonely in this marriage and I don't think that's right.

10. I need a lot of time alone. . . .

I have just a certain amount of energy, and I apportion that energy to my painting, my child, and my partner. That's it for me. To paint, to really be able to paint from the soul, which is very important to me, requires a great deal of time alone. I admit that this may be selfish, but I need it unless whatever I do be superficial. I cannot create, I cannot find that "red line" inside me where my anguish lives unless I spend a great deal of time alone. What do I do when I am alone? I can't even begin to tell you, except to say that I drift in an aimless and rambling way that leads to nowhere in particular. But I can't even begin to go there with someone else.

11. My partner likes to have sex much more often than I do. . . .

I was sexually mistreated long ago. I had no control over this and it was quite horrible, but it did happen. I know my partner is not to blame for many of the feelings I now have. But I feel that sex can be okay only if it is on my terms. In my marriage there has been a lot of healing and gentleness, but I probably will never get over these feelings of having gone through a real trauma. I need to be able to have sexual closeness on my terms only.

12. I like to have sex much more often than my partner. . . .

My dream is to have my partner initiate sexual encounters with me and somehow be "swept away" by passion, I guess to really be totally attracted to me. I know I am not especially much to look at, but on some days I am not too bad. I periodically want my partner to feel that I am simply irresistible.

13. We have different styles of making love. . . .

To me, sex ought to be an expression of affection and great closeness. It ought to flow naturally from these things. Otherwise it seems contrived and artificial to me. I have found sex to build the relationship when it has these qualities, so I keep looking for this right combination of intimacy and romance. I want passion and I also want gentleness and closeness.

14. We have different styles of making love. . . .

I wish our sex were more erotic and sensual. Sometimes I just want sex to be "easy" and very natural. I want to be desired and not just play a role of having to manage romance. Sometimes a passionate "quickie" seems just right. It can ease tension and draw us closer together. Lots of times romance seems phony and contrived to me, like I am acting in a play. I would love my partner to be so carried away with passion and desire for me that we just do it because it must be. I also have some fantasies I would like to share with my partner, but I am afraid to bring them up.

15. Money has been a gridlocked conflict of ours for some time. . . .

Life is too short to just save for the future all the time. I know that a certain amount of that is necessary, but I want to have some sense that I am not just living for tomorrow. I don't want to feel that life is passing me by. And that's what I often feel, that I am not special enough to "waste" money on. I want to feel special and very alive. This comes, I suppose, from always having to scrimp when I was poor. But now I make a good income and I don't have to live like that anymore.

16. Money has been a gridlocked conflict of ours for some time. . . .

I want to enjoy life, but within limits. To me, the problem with the world is greed. People never seem to be able to have enough "stuff" or get enough money. Just look at Americans on vacation, with all their things, campers, motorcycles, boats, cars. I don't want to want things. I want to be satisfied with just a small amount of things and a small amount of money. I honestly don't need very much to be happy. So I see myself as kind of a monk who has a purpose in life, and I do have that. A monk can be satisfied with very little, contented, counting all the blessings in life, and there are so many. So I believe in saving and spending very little. To me, that's how one should lead a moral life. Where does this come from? I think it comes from my father, who also was very frugal. Thanks to him, our family always did well, and when he died my mom was well provided for. I respect what he accomplished.

17. My partner likes to stay in much closer touch with our families than I do. . . .

It took me a great deal of effort to get away from a very dysfunctional family. My parents were very cold and distant. My sister wound up in a mental hospital and my brother became a drug addict. I was the only one who escaped. I escaped by becoming very distant from my family and becoming very close to my friends. Friendships have always meant a lot to me and continue to be very important. But I am wary of being close to my partner's family. I see a lot of dysfunctional patterns and they scare me. I want us to form our own family traditions and maintain our own independence.

18. I like to stay in much closer touch with my family than my partner does. . . .

To me, a feeling of an extended family has always been very important. I can recall many a Sunday when my mother would have twenty or thirty family members visit. The coffee and pastries would keep coming all afternoon, and there would be lots of good stories, and card playing, and lots of laughter. Then there would be great food for dinner. Even during the hard times, my mother always was able to stretch the soup, and it stayed thick and hearty. I have always wanted to have this family feeling of community, closeness, and great comfort in my own family.

19. I am far more introverted than my partner is. . . .

I really value quietness and peace. My best times as a child growing up were, frankly, times when I was in nature. As I grew up, I came to love solo backpacking and mountain climbing. Today I still need to spend lots of time alone in my wood shop. I really enjoy working with my hands and making beautiful furniture. I like people, but only after I have had a lot of solitude. My partner is far more socially skilled than I am and I appreciate those qualities. But I can't be as outgoing as my partner. Where does all this come from? As far as I can tell, it's just my nature. My family was very social and I participated in many family events growing up, but they let me have my solitude, and I appreciated that.

20. I am far more extraverted than my partner. . . .

I am just a people person. I have a job doing TV production in which I coordinate many talented people in a team in which I get things done, and the whole process is very dynamic. I love the excitement. I love working with artists and enjoy eccentric, interesting, creative people. At home I really believe in opening our home to people, making our home a place where very interesting people will want to come for food, good conversation, and intellectual and emotional nourishment. To me, a lot of very interesting things happen in such a home. Now I also want my children to be exposed to this type of home. I think it can be very fulfilling for them.

21. My partner believes in stricter discipline of our children than I do. . . .

In my family we were allowed a lot of freedom to develop our own individual personalities. We could decide what our interestes were, and we were encouraged to develop on our own. My parents were very understanding of our feelings, and we were never hit. We had discipline, but it was based on reasoning and on love and understanding. My parents were always very flexible. We had rules, but we problem-solved so that things stayed flexible. I think that is the way to raise kids, with love and understanding. I hate an authoritarian approach because I want my kids to be able to think for themselves.

22. I believe in stricter discipline of our children than my partner does. . . .

My family believed in "tough love." In my family all the kids had chores to do and we earned our own allowances. The older kids had more responsible and more difficult chores to do and were a model for the younger kids. No one whined in my family. We just did our chores and that was that. I think that the discipline was one of the best things in my growing up. It also gave our family a feeling of working together toward a common goal. Whenever one of us kids messed up, we knew what was coming to us, and we took our punishment without complaining. This was not a cold family. It was very warm and loving. We were raised with good values. We just all worked hard on the farm and helped out, because it was the right thing to do. I believe that kind of thing is sorely needed in today's world. It's good for families and good for kids.

23. My partner places much more importance and emphasis on career than on family. . . .

To me, being a husband and father are the most important things I have ever done, and the most challenging. I am the family chef, and I take this job very seriously. I love shopping, planning meals, and cooking, and seeing every one in the family happy and healthy. That's where I get my real kicks. I do really enjoy my work as well, but I must admit it is secondary. I am married to a very dedicated career woman. She is a great wife and mother as well. But I am very upset about many of the choices she makes that take her away from the family. We are doing less and less together as a family and the kids are growing. I am afraid she is missing it all. I know I am missing her.

24. My career is very important to me. . . .

I love being a lawyer. To me, it is all about the pursuit of justice. In my work I am trying to make the world a better place, to be able to help people lift up the yoke of oppression that injustice is a part of. I feel like a champion for freedom and liberty in my work. It is really a crusade for me. So I really see my "family" as all the clients who come into my office. I also value my family. I tend to view them as my real source of sanity and love in this bitter world. I try to do all I can to balance work and family. But my work is my true passion, my "calling," and my major source of identity in my life.

Intervention 3. Dreams Within Conflict

Purpose and Pitfalls

To uncover the unacknowledged dreams underlying fixed positions on conflict issues. This is a powerful exercise, and it often requires a great deal of therapist support and work on symbolic meanings. In our workshops, we have discovered that about 10–20% of the couples who go through this exercise run into trouble. Some people are unaware that they have, in fact, given up their dreams over time. Some people are aware of the loss but place the blame on their partner, accepting no responsibility for the decision not to pursue their own dreams. The effect of this exercise on these people is to make them angry at their partner. There are resultant feelings of disappointment, hurt, and disgust with the conditions that have led them to give up pursuing their dreams. Instead, people need to take responsibility for these things and go from here. This exercise is not about airing resentments; such an attitude will ruin the spirit of the exercise.

Table 9.1   Dreams Within Conflict—Sample Dreams

1. A sense of freedom	19. Asking God for forgiveness
2. The experience of peace	20. Exploring an old part of myself I have lost
3. Unity with nature	21. Getting over a personal hangup
4. Exploring who I am	22. Having a sense of order
5. Adventure	23. Being able to be productive
6. A spiritual journey	24. A place and a time to just "be"
7. Justice	25. Being able to truly relax
8. Honor	26. Reflecting on my life
9. Unity with my past	27. Getting my priorities in order
10. Healing	28. Finishing something important
11. Knowing my family	29. Exploring the physical side of myself
12. Becoming all I can be	30. Being able to compete and win
13. Having a sense of power	31. Travel
14. Dealing with my aging	32. Quietness
15. Exploring a creative side of myself	33. Atonement
16. Becoming more powerful	34. Building something important
17. Getting over past hurts	35. Ending a chapter of my life
18. Becoming more competent	36. Saying goodbye to something

Exercise

The couple works on a core (preferably gridlocked) marital issue. They discuss a core problem area in their marriage, *but they do not, under any circumstances, try to solve it.* First, the spouses look over the checklist in Table 9.1, which lists dreams that people sometimes have (or have lost) that could underlie the position they have taken on this issue. Second, they explain and share this with their partner. The husband will start as the speaker for 20 minutes, and the wife will be the listener. After 20 minutes, they switch roles. They will be asking each other these questions:

- What do you believe about this issue?
- What do you feel about it? Tell me all of your feelings about it.
- What do you want to happen?
- What does this *mean* to you?
- How do you think your goals can be accomplished?
- When you look over the list of *sample dreams,* what symbolic meaning do you find for your position?

Speaker's job: It is the speaker's job to say honestly what this position means to him or her, what the *dream* might be behind the position, and to tell the story of what this dream means—where it comes from and what it symbolizes. The speaker must be as clear as possible so that the partner understands.

Listener's job: It is the listener's job to just listen, the way a friend would listen. A good line is "Tell me the story of that. I'd like to understand what this means to you." The listener contributes to this climate by suspending judgment and acting like someone who wants to hear the partner's story and the dream behind the story—just *hear* it and not judge it. The listener is not to try to solve this problem. It is much too soon for that. First the spouses have to end the opposition of dreams and become one another's friend instead of one another's fiend. The listener is to try to understand the meaning of the partner's dream, to ask questions and to convey genuine interest. Then, if possible, he/she will tell the partner that he/she supports the dream, will try to make it happen in their lives, and will try to be a part of this dream.

The bottom line about life dreams is this: You don't want to have the kind of marriage in which you win and are influential in the marriage but wind up crushing your partner's dream. You want the kind of marriage in which you are supporting one another's dreams. If your dreams connect, so much the better.

Both men and women need to stay with the feelings evoked by this exercise. Women are better at this, usually, than men. It is important for both people to explore the meanings of their dreams with each of them. What is the story of these dreams? Where do they come from?

Example

Here are two ways a husband might respond to his wife's dream.

> W: What getting a small cabin in the forest means to me is very hard to describe. It goes back to when I would run out of my parents' house whenever there was conflict and an awful thing had happened to me. I would go to a beautiful park near home and receive comfort just by sitting in an old tree. Since then the forest has always meant peace and solace to me. It's the one place I feel close to God.

Don't:

> H: I know all that, but it's simply not practical. I am the only realist in this marriage.
> W: Forget it.
> H: Gladly.

Do:

> H: Tell me more about what it means to you, how you imagine this cabin. Can you see it in your mind? What would it be like for you to have the cabin? What would it do for your life?

The implicit reframing in this exercise: Marital therapists have discovered that most marital conflict is defined by each spouse in terms of negative things they want the partner to stop doing. *If only my partner would stop doing X,* each of them thinks, *we would be happy.* In the behavioral marital therapies, therapists attempt to change this way of thinking by getting spouses to describe what positive things they wish to see amplified in the marriage, instead of what negative things they wish to see disappear. By focusing solely on the positive, these therapists hope to get people to be more accepting of, and positive about, one another. However, this attempt is often doomed because the symbolic meaning of the negative interactions is ignored.

In this Dreams-Within-Conflict exercise, we are saying, in effect, that grid-locked conflict on this issue could be resolved if each person were to understand what the partner's position meant symbolically. We are saying, *search for the dream behind the conflict. Forget about the conflict, and go after the hidden dream. Then try to understand and support your partner's dream. The conflict then vanishes. Discuss all the feelings surrounding this issue. Don't stay hidden.*

Intervention 4. Honoring One Another's Dreams

Purpose

To help the couple find a way of honoring both people's life dreams within the gridlocked conflict. Honoring can mean many things, but it always means supporting and respecting. Various levels of honoring are possible. Some may be able to provide only understanding of their partner's dream. Some may be able to honor the dream by providing understanding plus financial support. Some may be able to join the partner wholeheartedly, on all levels.

Exercise

Change the influence processes so that the couple move toward honoring both people's life dreams. The spouses will describe their core gridlocked issue with the goal of changing gridlock to dialogue. Have the couple do this exercise in three steps.

- First, define the minimal core areas that you cannot yield on.
- Second, define areas of greater flexibility that are not so "hot" emotionally.
- Third, come up with a temporary compromise and a plan.

Example

She wants a cabin in a forest. It is very important to her for many symbolic reasons. The cabin is a respite from a very crazy work life she leads. It is also a place she can feel close to nature and at peace. He feels that they cannot afford this, that it is highly extravagant, given their salaries. He wants financial security, which has a lot of symbolic meaning for him. He is afraid that he will be poor when he is old, like some of his relatives. One of his big goals in life is avoiding humiliation when he is old. They have already discussed the symbolic meaning of their stands on this gridlocked issue.

Step 1. They define the *minimal* core areas that they cannot yield on. She wants at least a three-room cabin on about two acres of forest land. He wants at least $30,000 as a start-up for long-term financial investment.

Step 2. They define their areas of flexibility. She says that *time* is an area of flexibility for her. She would like to have the cabin within the next three years. She is also flexible on the location and size of the cabin, and how much land they buy. But she wants to be close to a forest.

Step 3. They come up with the temporary compromise, so that both dreams are going to be realized. He says that he can see saving half of the extra money he is going to be earning in the next three years for the down payment on the cabin and some for the investment start-up fund. She says that she can take on some extra work to pay the mortgage, once they buy the cabin.

The couple realize that the perpetual problem may never go away in this marriage. She is always going to be the visionary, having ideas for things like cabins and great trips, and he is going to worry about their financial security, their retirement fund, and so on. But they can establish a dialogue around these types of differences between them. That is the goal of this exercise. Over time the dreams of this couple changed as they continued the dialogue on the issue. Eventually the cabin also became a place he liked to go to, and it was no longer just him going along with her dream. She also came to respect the idea of long-term financial investment and joined in the planning. For this intervention to be successful, however, this kind of meshing of dreams is not necessary. The goal is moving from gridlock to dialogue.

Intervention 5. Handling the Most Common Resistance to This Intervention

Purpose

To deal with potential resistances to changing the influence patterns in the marriage by recasting them as fears of accepting influence.

Exercise

Discuss fears of accepting influence. In discussing a gridlocked issue, we try to get each person to talk about the *symbolic meaning* of his/her position. As we do this, we often run into catastrophic expectations people have of accepting their partner's dreams. A part of this reaction usually involves fear of accepting influence from the partner, fear of truly sharing power in a relationship. Fear of losing control is usually part of the mix. In this exercise spouses take turns discussing their *fears* of accepting influence on this issue.

It is important to help people try to understand where these fears come from in their own past. This often involves having people investigate their own scenarios of disaster in relationships and ponder the origins of these scenarios.

The speaker's job: Talk to your partner about your dream, and be *genuine* about what you are afraid of in helping to make your partner's dream come true. Don't give up your dream for the sake of peace between the two of you. Argue for what you really want. But don't be mean-spirited. Accept those parts of your partner's ideas that you can live with. You will win by also letting your partner be influential.

The listener's job: Ask about your partner's fears. There is probably some scenario of potential catastrophe in your partner's head. Learn what this is and then try to soothe the fear. Help make the plan a reality, one that you can feel good about sharing. It is your job to give a great deal in this conversation. You will get your turn when your dream is discussed.

DREAMS-WITHIN-CONFLICT CASE

While I have emphasized changing the setting conditions that give rise to the dysfunctional patterns, which is really operating on the friendship in the marriage, there is a great deal of power in interventions at the level of meaning and culture. The case described here dramatizes an intervention I call making life dreams come true.

This case was part of a TV show we did with "Dateline NBC." The entire assessment and intervention happened in one working day. The show was, however, never aired on television. The couple selected by the producer to be profiled had been married less than one year. Still, the husband scored in the unhappily married range on the Locke-Wallace, saying that he was not sure, if he had it to do over again, whether he would marry the same person, and his scores on the Weiss-Cerreto indicated that he was seriously thinking about separation and divorce. The wife's scores were lower than would be expected of a newlywed, but not as distressed as her husband's.

Nevertheless, the Oral History Interview revealed a couple who had a lot of affection and admiration for one another. They sat very close together and she had her hand on his left shoulder and chest almost all the time in a lovely gesture of intimacy. They were animated and happy telling the story of their romance, with a lot of we-ness and spontaneous expressions of admiration for one another. In Katie's life prior to meeting Harry, owning a horse had played a major role. She said that, during a particularly difficult part of her childhood, she learned to ride, met a horse named Marigold, and became an accomplished competitive jumper. She had very strong feelings about this part of herself. She said that Marigold was a "mutt," and so was she, but that together they were champions. Katie's family was a close, middle-class Italian-American family. An important step toward commitment for this couple involved bringing Katie's horse from Los Angeles to Seattle. Harry originally was very much in favor of this step, and he supported Katie's athletic competition actively at first. He went to the barn with her, went to her meets, and so on.

Harry came from a large, tight-knit Irish-American family. His mother had an explosive temper and she terrorized the entire family with the threat of her rages. His father was a very quiet and passive man who was intimidated by his wife. During their courtship Harry's mother was diagnosed with cancer, and she died before they married. In many ways the wedding was a healing event for Harry's family. Harry and Katie paid for it, they made it a lavish affair, and everyone enjoyed it greatly. But as a result of that expense they began their marriage about $20,000 in debt. This situation was intolerable for Harry.

First Marital Conflict Discussion

Their first marital interaction in the lab was about the financial problems they felt they were facing. Harry began talking, was directive in defining the problem, and became quite domineering—a shift from the cooperative and warm style he had displayed in the Oral History Interview. Katie had already leased out half of

Marigold to a young girl who was sharing some of the expenses. Katie had agreed to cut back drastically on her time with Marigold as well as her time showing and jumping. It was clear that this was but a temporary solution to the financial problems, and that Marigold was, in fact, on the way out. They both agreed that Katie was the "irresponsible" and "unrealistic" one in the marriage and that Harry was the realist. Marigold was a luxury for Harry that had to go, while for Katie she was a necessity. She seemed to feel very guilty about her need for the horse and was making efforts to change and adapt to this upcoming loss.

During the conversation there was almost no positive affect. Katie's face was very tense and drawn, and her heart rate was 120 beats a minute. Harry's was normal. We were very surprised about the lack of affect in this conversation.

Pre-intervention Conversation

H: Okay, what do you want to talk about in terms of finances? Where do you . . . ? In that last conversation we had, I think it was pretty clear that we had to make some changes. Where do you think we stand on that?

W: I think that we stand about halfway there. I think we are moving in the right direction. I think that . . . um . . . [*sigh*] that without making radical changes we have gotten halfway there. There is still room to make changes and we need to do that. My way of dealing with the problem was to find a way to make it happen and I did for now, with regard to Marigold, and I think that's a good step for both of us. Maybe not the answer that you would have wanted, but a good in-between. Um, and I think. . . .

H: [*nervous laugh, not reciprocated*] "The answer that you would have wanted." That sounds like I'm dictating everything.

W: No, no. I don't mean that at all. I mean the logical side. If I say Harry's the logical one and Katie is the. . . . [*pause*] illogical one, when it comes to spending money on a horse, I mean that we need to understand that we feel differently—that for me it's a need and for you it's a luxury.

H: Right, right.

W: I think that we've made some good progress and I think you've been really good about it all. I think you have been more supportive and I think that is probably a good start for you. For us.

H: Right. I don't quite understand what a "lease" is all about. What does that mean in terms of boarding and training and vet bills and . . .

W: It means that they pay half of . . .

H: . . . everything.

W: Well, no. It means that she pays for her lessons.

H: Right.

W: I pay for turnout, which is less than half of training.

H: Right.

W: And we split the board and we split shoes.

H: Do we split vet bills?

W: Not maintenance.

H: Okay.

W: No. And this may turn out to be a month-to-month thing, or it may work longer-term. At this rate I don't think we can look at it as a permanent fix, but it's definitely getting us over a hump.

H: Right. And are they encouraged thus far? It's not that one day they are going to show up and say, "We're not happy with Marigold"?

W: As of now everything is really positive.

H: Good.

W: So that's a good in-between.

H: Huh, yeah.

W: I mean, it's certainly a good in-between for me. It helps me to take a step back. It takes some of the time burden off, which I think helps us as well.

H: Um-hmm.

W: It helps because I think it's twofold. Not only does it . . .

H: Yeah, I do like the time we spend together as opposed to the time we spend apart. I think that has been good lately.

W: Yeah, I do too. It has taken a lot of pressure all the way around. Is it ideal for me? No.

H: Right.

W: I mean, I'd like to be able to do the whole nine yards with Marigold.

H: Right.

W: So, I think that we have come a long way, and while I don't think the problem is resolved, I also don't know if it's even a resolvable issue. But I certainly think it's an issue in progress and something that's going to change. Over the next couple of years it's going to come and go depending on the situation, on whether she is leased, on whether we find a home for her, on whether, at some point, there is another horse, or whatever.

H: Right, right, right.

W: We're just gonna have to play it by ear, and I think that you have come a long way in trying to understand how important it is to me. And I think that's good.

H: Good.

W: I think we almost need to say that, okay this is a good resolution for right now, and this is helping, and let's revisit it, but for right now this is the best we can do.

Our Brief Interventions

My colleague Dr. Sybil Carrére and I intervened with them as follows. We told them that we were genuinely puzzled by their first conversation. Here was Katie making plans to give up Marigold when they had just finished telling me how important she was to Katie and to the movement of this relationship toward commitment. What was going on?

Harry said that the horse was just impractical, that she cost too much, and that it was purely a question of money, that she had to go, and that was all there was to it. We asked them to tell one another what their "dreams" were behind the horse and financial issue. We asked them *not* to try to convince one another about the validity of his/her position but to just tell one another what these meant to each of them.

Katie had no trouble telling Harry what Marigold meant to her. She satisfied so many parts of who she was. She was an athlete and she loved to compete and win. She loved having such great rapport with so large and powerful an animal. She loved the motion of riding and jumping together, the feeling of communication between them. She loved all the small aspects of the sport, the tending to the animal, the grooming, and so on. She loved horses, but it was also clear that she loved this particular horse very much, that Marigold was very special to her.

For Harry this conversation was much more difficult. His "dreams" were less defined. He mentioned financial security in general terms and then talked about having once owned a motor boat and wanting one again. He also wanted to build a small cabin on some land his family owned and that his father could build it with him for just about the amount that they were in debt. The process of building the cabin with his father was also important to him.

In their second marital interaction, the same themes as we had detected in the first conversation resurfaced. Harry said that he felt as if he was doing all the compromising in this marriage, that he was not ever going to get to actualize any of his wishes in the marriage, and all because of her unrealistic "Marigold thing." While this conversation was more emotional, once again there was no positive affect, and the patterns of physiological arousal and tension were the same as in the first conversation. After this second conversation, we all went to lunch.

After lunch, Sybil and I worked separately with Harry and Katie. She decided to work with Katie on restating the importance of Marigold to her in a gentle but firm way. She also asked her to think about what Harry's fears might be about accepting influence from her. Katie decided that Harry needed to be reassured that if it came to choosing between him and the horse, she would, of course, choose Harry. Sybil told her that we had discovered that women were all too willing to give up their dreams for relationships, much to their later regret.

I worked separately with Harry. I told him that by keeping his dreams vague, he was maintaining power in the relationship. Katie had already given up half of her dream, but he had not even articulated his. I explored what his dreams were and what they were related to. They had a lot to do with establishing closeness with his father, and there was a residual fear that Harry might turn out like his father and Katie might turn out like his mother. He was determined not to let that happen. I also told him that, based on our research, he could not afford to have a marriage in which he succeeded in crushing his wife's dreams, that it would be a Pyrrhic victory: He would win the battle but lose the war. He would risk losing his wife.

The Third Conversation

W: I want to go back and talk about your not understanding my need, the desire and the dream I have. I can understand that it's a pretty different desire. But I think what I want to talk about is your making an effort to share that with me. Ideally, for me to fulfill my dream, I would want you to be a big part of it—to share it with me and to enjoy it with me—to realize that you play a part in that. You definitely do. I want you to realize that when Marigold and I do well, it's because you are there. More than just financially.

H: [*laughs*]

W: That's what you're thinking.

H: [*laughs*]

W: But more than just financially, that you play a big part in who I am, especially in who I am now. I think the reason that last show was so fulfilling is because you're a part of my life now, and you weren't before. To be able to have both is wonderful. And we've talked about it at home, that you worry about what I would choose, and I would never choose Marigold over you. If we had to make that decision, there's no doubt in my mind . . . .

H: Yeah, but we don't have to make that decision. I mean, so . . .

W: [*big smile comes over her face*]

H: . . . work out the Marigold thing, I would think, where I could support you on that um . . . what?

[*Both of them are grinning very wide Duchenne grins now.*]

W: I think that's great. [*Her heart rate rapidly drops from 120 bpm to 80 bpm here.*]

H: I mean, I think there's a way to work this out so that we are working toward you and Marigold and me being a team. And we also support me. I mean, I never have very clearly defined what it is that I want. There's sort of this innocuous cabin or boat. It really never has been nailed down which one. But the part of the reason I don't think we have ever nailed that down is that, in my mind, we can't have both, and we need to figure out a way that we can do both. Obviously, you have made some sacrifices in leasing Marigold and getting rid of the car—well, we haven't gotten rid of it yet . . . .

W: No, but we will.

H: And maybe we can start working toward both of our dreams a little bit. I think what would probably help me in supporting Marigold and you is to recognize that I have these goals and dreams and so on and so forth.

W: I think that it will make you feel like you're working for a reason, not just to keep your head above water.

H: Um-hmm.

W: And it would give me something to share with you.

H: Um-hmm.

W: And it would give you something to share with me, that we could work together on, and we could both pursue our dreams together without guilt.

H: Right.

W: Because we're pursuing this together for both of us, that we can both share.

H: Right.

W: We could do that.

H: What's interesting about this is, I was—you have got to admit—I was pretty damn excited about Marigold initially.

W: [*laughs*] Oh, you were.

H: And I don't know what it is that changed. I think that's one thing that was really hard for me and the times that I sat back and went "What changed?" This isn't what I thought . . .

H: Right.

W: We never talked about it, but this isn't what I thought our married life was going to be like. I thought that we had filled in that empty gap, and now all of a sudden the rules have changed, and this huge part of me [the horse part] needs to go away. And I thought, this isn't what I thought I was getting into.

H: Well, you said that.

W: Yeah.

H: You said that I misled you.

W: I didn't mean that you misled me but that I *felt* misled.

H: Right.

W: I don't think it was something that you did intentionally.

H: Right.

W: But the end result is the same, except that I'm not angry at *you*. I'm just angry in general.

H: Right. So, it's obvious that I was extremely happy about the horse and, you know, Marigold and your riding and something changed. I think that maybe if we found out what that was, you know between you and me, maybe we could move forward on this. A lot of what I don't understand about this is I don't understand, you know, everything about a horse that there is. You know, when I used to go out to the barn with you I was fascinated. I don't know when it changed. A lot of it has to do with the finances.

W: Right.

H: You know, I wasn't getting help at home with those bills, at all, I mean, so when it came the time to pay all the bills, I took care of all the bills and you had all the fun. Now it wasn't that way before, so I think if we can get past those hurdles, then we can pursue your Marigold situation, I mean I . . .

W: Okay, we also need to sit down come up with a plan on how we can move forward toward putting in place what it takes to achieve your dream too—our dream, I mean I want a cabin someday, too. Or a boat. And where you put your priorities on those two things. I would back either one 100%. Either one. Whatever makes us happy and gives us something to work on for you and ultimately for us, I think that's great. And I think we can do that.

H: I think it's doable.

W: And maybe at first the steps we take aren't going to be as great as the ones we take a year from now. But I think once we start taking steps, it's going to help. It's going to give you something to hold on to, and to work towards, and to feel assured that I see you have needs and dreams too, and it's not just about me being spoiled and needing to fulfill this want in myself, however you look at it. I think we can do that.

H: I think it's doable.

W: And that's much more positive. I mean, I giggled, but it was because I think we can do this. And your voice of reason, or realism, or pessimism [*laughs and he laughs too*] is good for us. It's definitely good for us. It keeps me in check.

H: But it also always makes me look like the bad guy.

W: Yeah, but if you can be a realist without being a pessimist—because I hear pessimism about what we can't do, we can't do, we can't do . . .

H: I know, I know, I know. That's very true. I do that.

W: And we say what we *can't* do now, but what *can* we do to make it happen? Or okay, so we can't have an 80' boat now but we can have an 8' foot boat. But whatever it is, let's live a positive life. I mean, I am going to be a dreamer, I'm always going to be a dreamer. And there are going to be dreams, when all is said and done, that don't come true, but dreaming is an awful lot of fun.

H: So, does it take me coming out to the barn with you to make you realize or recognize that I am supporting you?

W: Every once in a while. Do you have to go out every day? No.

H: Right.

W: I want you to want to go out to the barn.

H: You've got to make it worth my while.

[*Both laugh a lot.*]

W: Well, somebody gave me that advice before. Let's talk about that later.

[*Both laugh.*]

When Harry said that he understood what Marigold meant to her, and he thought that they could work toward her goals as well as his, Katie smiled a complete smile for the first time. (This is called a "Duchenne" smile, after the French anatomist, and is easily observable: It involves both raised upper lip corners and eye corner wrinkles.) For the first time in the day her heart rate returned from its elevated 120 beats per minute to 80.

Note that both of them acknowledged that this was a crisis in their lives. She admitted to being angry all the time and in despair that this big part of *herself* had to "go away." This is in sharp contrast to the content of the first conversation, in which they told one another that all is okay, that they were making an adjustment to this financial situation and it will be all right, not ideal, but all right. In this third conversation there was a sense that she is entitled to her complaints about giving up Marigold. After the conversation she said, "I feel like I got my friend back."

Epilogue

As we continued to follow Harry and Katie, this unanimity about their dreams eroded. At around six months after our intervention we found that Harry had reasserted his demand that the horse had to go if they were to have any financial security. They had fought a great deal about all this. He finally agreed that they would have a horse in their lives again after they had reestablished security, perhaps in two years. Katie agreed to this and said that she felt good about the agreement.

At two years post-intervention we checked up on them again and found that they had resolved the issue entirely on their own. Katie had sold Marigold but still had a continuing relationship with her. She decided she needed a younger horse for what she now wished to accomplish in jumping competitively, so she had leased a horse for that purpose. They now said that they never fought about money.

This case dramatizes the complexity of the kind of alliance spouses need to create around their life dreams, hopes, and aspirations. In this case, and others we are working with, figuring out how to mesh these life dreams and, what is probably most important, to feel like one's spouse is one's ally in the things that really matter in life, is a very powerful and constructive way to approach conflict and its resolution. It also integrates the friendship part of the marriage with the conflict resolution part.

Life Dreams and Shared Meanings

 In this chapter we arrive at the attic of the Sound Marital House. Each family is a unique culture and has a unique way of creating meaning, complete with its own symbols, metaphors, and narratives. Most important for marital outcomes is the way the marriage enables both people to feel that the relationship supports their life dreams.

In most marital conflicts we are actually dealing with what things *mean* to the individuals in the partnership. In Chapter 4 and Appendices B and C, we have reviewed the Meanings Interview and shared the Shared Meanings Questionnaire. Here I suggest that the therapist consider a series of interviews with the couple that are aimed at changing two existential factors: (1) discrepancies on the listed dimensions between spouses, and (2) discrepancies between ideal and actual realizations of their values.

Remember that this interview is about the family *culture*. In the intervention phase of this interview, we have the spouses identify aspects of these areas that they want to change. After asking the couple about the rituals, roles, and symbolic meanings in their lives, we explore common ground as well as differences between them in each of these categories and ask them if they want to make any changes. Then we do four interventions, which follow the same format. For each intervention the couple is given these instructions:

1. Begin by getting a personal notebook for each of you and taking one question you'd like to think about from those below. Then separate and write your thoughts about the question in your answers.

2. Read one another's answers.

3. Discuss your answers with one another.

4. Discover your areas of common ground, areas that you can build upon.
5. Discuss your differences as well.
6. Find ways to honor both of your values, philosophies, and dreams.
7. Although in many areas you can have separate needs, you can still find ways to be supportive of one another in these areas.
8. Where you differ fundamentally, find ways of being respectful, of honoring the differences between you.
9. Write out, if you like, your own "family constitution," your shared philosophy of life.

Intervention 1. Building Shared Meaning in Family Rituals

Purpose
Build or strengthen shared meaning around rituals.

Exercise
Proceed with the intervention using the questions in Table 10.1.

Intervention 2. Building Shared Meaning in Family Roles

Purpose
To build or strengthen shared meaning around roles.

Exercise
Following the instructions, the spouses explore a question from Table 10.2.

Table 10.1   Family Rituals

1. How do we or should we eat together at dinner? What is the meaning of dinnertime? How was dinnertime done in each of our families growing up?
2. How should we part at the beginning of each day? What was this like in our families growing up? How should our reunions be?
3. How should bedtime be? What was this like in our families growing up? How do we want this time to be?
4. What is the meaning of weekends? What was this like in our families growing up? What should they be like?
5. What are our rituals about vacations? What was this like in our families growing up? What should these mean?
6. Pick a meaningful holiday. What is the true meaning of this holiday to us? How should it be celebrated this year? How was it celebrated in each of our families growing up?
7. What rituals do we each use to feel refreshed and renewed? What is the meaning of these rituals?
8. What rituals do we have when someone is sick? What was this like in our families growing up? How should it be in our family?

Table 10.2 Roles

1. How do you feel about your role as a husband or wife? What does this role mean to you? How did your father or mother view this role? How are you similar? How are you different? How would you like to change this role?
2. How do you feel about your role as a father or mother? What does this role mean to you? How did your father or mother view this role? How are you similar? How are you different? How would you like to change this role?
3. How do you feel about your role as a son or daughter? What does this role mean to you? How did your father or mother view this role? How are you similar? How are you different? How would you like to change this role?
4. How do you feel about your role as a worker (your occupation)? What does this role mean to you? How did your father or mother view this role? How are you similar? How are you different? How would you like to change this role?
5. How do you feel about your role as a friend to others? What does this role mean to you? How did your father or mother view this role? How are you similar? How are you different? How would you like to change this role?
6. How do you feel about your role in your community? What does this role mean to you? How did your father or mother view this role? How are you similar? How are you different? How would you like to change this role?
7. How do you balance these roles in your life?

Intervention 3. Building Shared Meaning in Family Goals

Purpose

To build or strengthen shared meaning around goals.

Exercise

The couple chooses a question or task from Table 10.3.

Table 10.3 Goals

1. Write a "mission statement" of what your purpose in life is.
2. Write your own obituary. What would you like it to say?
3. What goals do you have in life for yourself, for your spouse, for your children? What do you want to accomplish in the next five to ten years?
4. What is one of your life dreams that you want to fulfill before you die?
5. What legacy do you want to leave after you die?
6. We often fill our time with things that demand our immediate attention, putting out the "fires," so to speak. But what are the truly important things in your life that are great sources of energy and pleasure that you really need to block out time for, the important things that keep getting postponed or crowded out?

Intervention 4: Building Shared Meaning in Family Symbols

Purpose

To build or strengthen shared meaning in the marriage by looking at symbols.

Exercise

The couple explores a question from Table 10.4.

CASE EXAMPLE

Presenting Picture Before Interview or Interaction

My wife Julie and I did this intervention with a couple. The wife scored in the normal range of marital satisfaction but the husband scored in the very unhappy range (57, his score, was 3 standard deviations below the mean, so it was very low). Also, on the divorce proneness scale, his score was a 4, which is just at the cutoff. Hers was a zero. This suggests that not only is he unhappily married but quite likely to leave the marriage, since persistent thoughts about divorce are predictive of divorce. The wife was 5 months pregnant.

Oral History Interview

Issues and weaknesses.   Based on our scoring of this interview and our previous data, this husband was very low in *fondness/affection.* They sat without touching, though during the interview she touched him, but he did not reciprocate. They were both low in *we-ness.* Even when talking about the baby, they both referred to it as *"my* son." In terms of *cognitive room* for the relationship, she was high and he was low. They were very high on *chaos,* which means that things keep happening to them that they have to adjust to, rather than feeling in control of their lives.

Strengths.   Neither of them was very negative toward the other. They were very high on *gender role stereotypy,* which means that they both subscribe to the idea that men and women should have traditional roles (he works, she is a house-

---

Table 10.4   Symbols

---

1. Who is your family in the world? What do you value about being [supply your last names]?
2. What are some stories about your family that go way back in history, stories you are proud of and want to be a part of the tradition your family continues?
3. What does a home mean to you? What qualities must it have for you? What was home like in your families growing up?
4. What is your philosophy of how to leave a meaningful, good life? How are you putting this into practice, or failing to?
5. What is the role of spirituality in your lives? What was this role in your families growing up? How should this be in your family?

---

wife and mother). They were reasonably high on thinking that conflict is worth it, that you learn from it and get stronger and better (we call this *glorifying the struggle*). They were not very volatile.

First Conversation

The major issues were *her jealousy* and *religion*. He is an agnostic and she is a Catholic, and she revealed that she had been thinking seriously of having the baby baptized. He expressed shock that he had to come to this laboratory to discover this and felt some betrayal that these considerations were going on behind his back, in her conversations with her father. Although he was emotionally expressive, he was actually also very supportive and gentle with her. She, too, was reassuring. They began moving toward discussing a compromise.

The conversation was quite unsatisfying. They were very rational and there was no humor and little affection between them. They were not affecting one another or trying to understand what this issue was all about, why it had surfaced at all, and what it meant to each of them.

After this first conversation my question was, What is the symbolic meaning of religion (or agnosticism) to them, especially in terms of their own primary families?

Intervention

We suggested that they discuss what religion means to each of them: what its presence in her baby's life would mean to her and what its absence would mean to him. Here we are instructing them to talk about the symbolic meaning of each of their positions, *not to solve the issue*. We asked each of them to just listen, not to try to persuade, or be persuaded by, one another.

The wife began the discussion, but it was clear to us after a minute that she did not understand our intervention, so we explained the intervention again. Then we restarted the timer; this time it was clear to us that they understood the intervention.

Second Conversation

The wife began the discussion again, describing that her beliefs had carried her through very hard times when her family was not there for her at all and yet she felt the comfort of God's love. This was very emotional for her; at first she stifled her tears but then began crying openly. He encouraged her to continue when she described herself as silly and handed her a Kleenex. He listened with great compassion for the suffering she had endured in the past, when her family was not there for her but the Church was. He told her that he now understood and that the conversation had become much more profound for him.

He then talked about how his father *was* there for him and that he does not want the Church to be between them and their son. They then began talking about how they can have a family that honors both visions for their son.

Throughout their interaction it was clear that both of them are strong individuals who will not relinquish their own beliefs, but who would like to find some way of being together on this issue.

This second conversation was clearly much more affective in tone. She cried, and he responded with compassion and empathy. Our analysis of the interaction showed that there was a dramatic increase in sadness from the wife in the second conversation and another decrease in dominance from him. The mathematical model also showed that they moved one another in a positive direction on the second conversation, while on the first conversation the opposite was true: They had moved one another in a more negative direction.

Both spouses showed a great deal of physiological arousal during both conversations. The intervention seemed to remove a block to their emotions, which now flowed more freely. It also affected the influenced stable steady state, which was now more positive than the uninfluenced stable steady state. Before we intervened, the influenced stable steady state was more negative than the uninfluenced. For a very short time we were successful in reversing the effects of emotional distancing that had been created by seemingly irreconcilable differences in meanings and values.

Debriefing. We strongly recommended therapy for this couple, pointing out how much they had gained from just our brief intervention, and how much more they could expect to gain with a therapist we had trained. We explored their feelings about this idea and then gave them a therapist's phone number to call, if they wished.

The problem we expect to have with our brief interventions is that, although they may produce very dramatic changes in a very short time, these changes do not last very long. In fact, part of the design of this research is to provide a method to study the occurrence of relapse.

We think we have begun a process of creating a shared meaning and unlocking the marital gridlock, but the process must continue for it to have a lasting impact on the marriage. This problem of the relapse of intervention effects is our biggest challenge in the marital therapy area. It is that problem that we have under the "microscope" in our laboratory.

Chapter 11 🙚

Resistance to Change

 This chapter presents an approach to thinking of resistance to change in terms of the Sound Marital House theory in conjunction with a concept from attachment theory, the "internal working model" a person has about specific processes in marital relationships.

Resistance to change emerges from a systematic distortion of specific processes in the Sound Marital House. Uncovering these processes is an essential part of marital therapy. Rather than thinking of resistance as an impediment to changing a specific process of the Sound Marital House, its emergence marks a breakthrough, since it will lead the therapist to an exploration of the person's internal working model about this process. For this exploration to occur, the therapy must provide a safe place in which to reveal what has been concealed.

Resistance is based on the therapist's lack of understanding about how to make change feel safe and ego-syntonic, and to make therapy feel like a positive, personal growth experience. The key to unlocking resistance is exploring the person's meaning system, honoring each person as the profound philosopher of his or her life, and serving as an ally to both clients in this very personal life journey.

INTERNAL WORKING MODELS AND THE SOUND MARITAL HOUSE

I want to move away from just applying labels to describe people's pathology. While these labels can be helpful at times, the biggest problem with labeling someone as "borderline" or "narcissistic" or "antisocial" is that the label doesn't automatically suggest something active that you can do as a therapist to deal with the problem or the resistance.

What makes dealing with resistance difficult is that it is usually the product of what attachment theorists call an "internal working model" of relationships and, in particular, a working model that represents a distortion in the proper working of various components of the Sound Marital House. I have already talked some about this source of resistance to change in marital therapy. The Resistance Interview in Appendix D outlines questions to uncover this model.

Individual psychopathology as a source of resistance has been the primary concern of both analytically-oriented marital therapies and systems-oriented marital therapies. The best integration of these approaches that I have seen is William Pinsof's (1995) book. Pinsof makes the brilliant point that the selection of the form of individual or family therapy ought to be based, *not on the symptoms initially presented but on the nature of the resistance the therapist encounters.* Then he tells the therapist how to do this.

I take another approach to this source of resistance. Recall our work with the mathematical model, in which there are uninfluenced stable steady states (reflecting, in part, what each spouse brings to the interaction before being influenced by the partner) and the influenced stable steady state. Resistance due to individual psychopathology is manifested in two ways.

- First, psychopathology renders the *uninfluenced steady state* highly negative in the first place: This person brings into a marital interaction a very negatively balanced set of behaviors and thoughts, as well as high levels of physiological arousal. Examples of this are: (1) The person's past abuse history leads to an interpretation of bids for intimacy as attempts to dominate, control, and injure; (2) depression and despair set expectations so low that pessimism characterizes the individual's expectations at the start of every interaction; or (3) the person has paranoid levels of jealousy.

- Second, psychopathology distorts the way the person influences and accepts influence. The person's internal working model of relationships militates against we-ness and cohesion in the interaction. Examples: (1) antisocial working models; (2) borderline working models; (3) narcissistic working models (or heightened senses of entitlement); (4) drug and alcohol dependence. Direct confrontation of the working model and its self-defeating nature is essential, as well as exploration of why it is there at all. In each type of psychopathology specific themes will emerge. Hence, I am going to suggest that we need to look at how various psychopathologies, and prior histories, affect the Sound Marital House. The solutions will involve attempting changes at each level of the Sound Marital House to reveal a client's or marital system's specific resistance to change.

I have created two questionnaires to evaluate the depressed and antisocial internal working models of relationship, which can be found in Appendix D. I am not saying that when people have these models, or pieces of them, that they have these psychopathologies. Rather, my point is that it may be helpful to think of these models more specifically, in terms of how they distort particular processes of the Sound Marital House.

The Depression/Low Self-Esteem Internal Working Model

Below I have answered questions as they would be answered by women with the depression internal working model. This, in effect, turns this interview into a self-report scale that the clinician can administer to assess the strength of this depression/low self-esteem internal working model (see Appendix D for the scale).

Love Maps

To know someone else:

    a. It is scary to get to know someone because then I might find out that I really am worthless.

    b. If my partner gets to know me well, he (she) will discover that most people are better than me in some way.

To be known by someone:

    a. When I get close to someone, I am afraid they will find out the true me and not like me.

    b. I expect rejection if I get too close.

    c. If someone sees the real me, that person will choose another.

Solution: Explore narratives about the client's sense of self, searching for variability. Find a perspective for rewriting these narratives.

Fondness and Admiration System

To be thought of with fondness and admiration by another:

    a. I don't believe it when people pay me a compliment.

    b. I have rarely believed it when someone is proud of me.

To think of someone else with fondness and admiration:

    a. No one would value my being proud of them.

    b. If I showed I admired him (or her), he (or she) would just make fun of me.

Solution: Explore the client's past history with admiration and pride in self, as well as with criticism, neglect, and humiliation. Examine the self-critic in the client and explore these internal dialogues. Work to build in rituals of genuine appreciation in the marriage, on the way to creating a culture of pride and admiration.

Turning Toward Versus Turning Away

To turn toward another:

    a. I don't want to keep giving because it probably will turn him (or her) off.

    b. He (or she) will find me repulsive if I keep being too nice.

Having someone turn toward you:

   a. I don't believe that I will ever be truly loved for who I am.

   b. I don't think that anyone can really find me attractive.

   c. I don't think that anyone can really find me interesting.

   d. I don't think anyone really, truly cares about me.

Solution: Begin by examing how needs are expressed by the client and how these are translated into bids for emotional connection. See section in Chapter 12 on building rituals of connection.

Positive Sentiment Override

Having enough positive sentiment toward another that it can override that person's being negative:

   a. I always expect people to revert to selfishness—that's human nature.

   b. As soon as someone is nasty, I have trouble remembering all the past nice things they did.

Someone else trusts you enough so that your negativity is overridden by positive feelings:

   a. No matter how much you do for someone else, they will always want more.

   b. As soon as I am in a bad mood and show it, his (or her) love for me will disappear.

Solution: The "chip on the shoulder" that characterizes negative sentiment override needs to be examined, especially its history. Then work to build into thought processes of both spouses a familiarity with the defensiveness of negative sentiment override so that a dialogue can be established with this perpetual problem.

Dialogue with Perpetual Problems

Being able to accept someone else, despite his/her shortcomings, and be amused by his/her failings rather than enraged by them:

   a. I tend to focus on people's flaws.

   b. I see mostly the dark side of human nature.

Being able to believe that you are accepted by someone else, despite your own shortcomings, and have that person be amused by your failings rather than enraged by them:

   a. I find it hard to believe that someone will overlook my faults.

   b. No one has really ever truly accepted me.

Solution: Self-acceptance is the key to this issue. Consider supplementing couples' therapy with individual therapy or continue to do individual therapy in a couple's context.

How Complaints Are Raised

With softened gentleness:

> a. When I get upset, I find it hard to be gentle.
>
> b. I usually come on too harshly with my complaints.

Being able to respond to another's gentleness:

> a. When my partner complains in a nice way, I find it hard to respond.
>
> b. I don't believe it when my partner is upset and is still being nice.

Solution: Irritability with one's self is often the basis of this negativity toward complaints. Part of the problem may also be stockpiling grievances. See the Marital Poop detector intervention for lowering the threshold of negativity.

Accepting Influence

Being able to influence someone else, be persuasive, but yield to win:

> a. I am never very good at persuading my partner that I am right.
>
> b. Why try to be persuasive when you will only fail?

Accepting influence from another:

> a. I find it hard to give in once I have made up my mind.
>
> b. I can be very stubborn, but I think it's necessary.

Solution: Set up standards for success in the area of influence. Use some of the team-building tasks in Chapter 13 as a safe context for building influence processes.

Being Able to Repair an Interaction

Being able to offer a repair:

> a. I am not good at being able to make things better between us once they have gone sour.
>
> b. When I am upset, I can't think of how to make it better.

Accepting someone else's attempt at repair:

> a. When I am in a bad mood, it's hard for me to let someone try to make things better.
>
> b. My partner's attempts to repair things between us usually seem hollow to me.

Solution: Success at repair and awareness of these expectations will turn this issue into a perpetual issue instead of an impediment to effective repair. Start small. Praise small accomplishments.

Being Able to De-escalate and Calm Down

Being able to self-soothe:

a. I have a lot of trouble calming down when I am upset.

b. I can nurse a bad mood or grudge for a long time and can't get myself out of it.

Being able to soothe one's partner:

a. When my spouse is upset, I am no good at calming him (or her) down.

b. I am not good at creating peace once it is gone.

Solution: Systematic application of relaxation, soothing, and care for oneself.

Being Able to Compromise

Being able to propose a compromise solution:

a. I am not very likely to think of some way of compromising.

b. When we disagree, I find myself sticking to my guns.

Accepting another's compromise solution:

a. When my partner suggests compromise, I get even more stubborn.

b. When my partner suggests that I give in a little if he (she) will, I simply refuse to budge.

Solution: Support the client's smallest solutions and ideas. Use the context of the consensus exercises in Chapter 13, like the Paper Tower exercise.

Creating Shared Meaning

Supporting your partners dreams, even if they are different from your own:

a. If my partner wants things in life that are different from what I want, I feel lonely and abandoned.

b. I think it's a bad sign if you and your partner are different in what you want out of life.

Supporting your own dreams, even when they are different from your partner's and developing them within the context of the relationship:

a. I want my marriage to support my interests even if they are not my spouse's interests.

b. I think it's healthy to develop my own dreams and interests in life, different from my spouse's.

Solution: These issues are best worked on by supplementing marital with individual therapy. These are often issues of failures in individuation. They come, at times, from neglecting to honor one's own dreams.

The Antisocial Internal Working Model

Below I have answered questions as they would be answered by someone with the antisocial internal working model. This, in effect, turns the interview into a self-report that the clinician can administer to assess the strength of the antisocial internal working model.

Love Maps

To know someone else:

    a. It is important to know about someone else because that knowledge is power.

    b. If you really can read someone, you can usually get what you want from them.

To be known by someone:

    a. If my partner gets to know me well, he (she) will use that knowledge to manipulate me toward her (his) ends.

    b. When I get close to someone, I am afraid they will know too much about me.

Solution: The issues of trust and safety must be explored. Use the Injury and Healing intervention (Table 7.5). Be careful, because this may be a powerful intervention.

Fondness and Admiration System

To be thought of with fondness and admiration by another:

    a. When people pay me a compliment, I wonder what they want.

    b. When someone is proud of me, I think they are out to get something from me.

To think of someone else with fondness and admiration:

    a. I think most people's accomplishments are usually hype and phony.

    b. If I showed someone I admired him (or her), I'd be making myself too vulnerable.

Solution: Explore the client's past history with admiration, pride, and success in life. Use the Triumphs and Strivings intervention (Table 7.6).

Turning Toward Versus Turning Away

To turn toward another:

    a. I don't want to spend too much time with any one person.

    b. When I am being very nice, I am usually after something.

Having someone turn toward you:

    a. I don't believe that anyone ever truly loves me for who I am.

    b. When someone finds me interesting, I feel like I have the upper hand.

    c. In this world usually no one really truly cares about anyone else.

Solution: Explore the client's history with directly asking for something out of need. This may be an area of past injury and present vulnerability. Experiment with small steps toward this in the marriage.

Positive Sentiment Override

Having enough positive sentiment toward another that it can override that person's being negative:

    a. I always expect people to revert to selfishness because that's what I would do.

    b. As soon as someone starts becoming nasty, I will turn against them.

Someone else trusts you enough so that your negativity is overridden by positive feelings:

    a. When you do things for others, they will just take advantage of you.

    b. I put on bad moods sometimes just to throw people off guard.

Solution: Consider using the Injury and Healing intervention (Table 7.5) to explore how these expectations guard against further psychological injury.

Dialogue with Perpetual Problems

Being able to accept someone else, despite his (or her) shortcomings, and be amused by his (or her) failings rather than enraged by them:

    a. Everyone in this world is mostly out to get what they can.

    b. I can't tolerate too much closeness.

    c. I am basically not that fond of people.

Being able to believe that you are accepted by someone else, despite your own shortcomings, and have that person be amused by your failings rather than enraged by them:

    a. No one will ever overlook my faults, so I try to keep them hidden.

    b. No one has really ever truly accepted me and I don't blame them.

Solution: The goal is to turn this issue of distance and closeness into a perpetual problem in this marriage. The client needs to stay in control of distance and closeness. Treat the client like someone who has a post-traumatic stress disorder around this issue. Explore why.

How Complaints Are Raised

With softened gentleness:

    a. When I get upset, I come on like a ton of bricks because of the element of surprise attack.

    b. If I didn't come on strong, people would walk all over me.

Being able to respond to another's gentleness:

    a. When my partner complains in a nice way, I see it as a weakness.

    b. When my partner is upset and still trying to be nice, I know I have the upper hand.

Solution: The underlying issue is a strong sense of powerlessness. What is required is not usually anger management, but an understanding that power lies in effective communication.

Accepting Influence

Being able to influence someone else, be persuasive, but yield to win:

    a. I can always con anyone at any time and persuade them I am right.

    b. Why not try to be persuasive, since it is so easy?

    c. If you don't control others, they will try to control you.

Accepting influence from another:

    a. I am not going to let my spouse influence or control me in any way.

    b. I can be very stubborn, but I can't let anyone walk all over me.

Solution: This is the most difficult part of the antisocial internal working model. It is the crux of it, in my experience. The client needs to learn that one can only be powerful by yielding power on some things, while still maintaining one's stand on other things. That is, it's not an all or none matter. Use the consensus tasks of Chapter 13 (like the Gottman Island Survival Problem) as a context for exploring this point.

Being Able to Repair an Interaction

Being able to offer a repair:

    a. Once things have gone sour between us, I just couldn't care less.

    b. When I am upset, I come on strong so that I will be in charge.

Accepting someone else's attempt at repair:

    a. It's hard for me to let my spouse try to make things better between us, unless he (or she) gives in.

    b. My partner's attempts to repair things between us are never going to work.

Solution: Once again, success with small repair attempts may affect this view.

Being Able to De-escalate and Calm Down

Being able to self-soothe:

    a. I don't usually really get upset, but I like to act upset for the effect it has.

    b. I can put on a show of being in a bad mood just to get the upper hand.

Being able to soothe one's partner:

a. When my spouse is upset, I wouldn't even bother calming him (or her) down.

b. I am good at creating upset in my partner if it helps me stay in control.

Solution: Self-soothing is not very difficult for this client to learn. The issue is that acting upset has worked in the past as a way of controlling and manipulating others. Explore this and where it comes from. Empathy is central in soothing one's partner, and marital therapy is a good context for building empathy. Use the stress-reducing conversation as a context for empathy work, not marital conflict.

Being Able to Compromise

Being able to propose a compromise solution:

a. I refuse to think of some way of compromising.

b. When we disagree, I become impatient and just want to win the argument.

Accepting another's compromise solution:

a. When my partner suggests a compromise, I get mad and stubborn.

b. When my partner suggests that I give in a little if he (or she) will, I see that as an attempt to manipulate me.

Solution: Again, the key issue is accepting influence. Explore the idea of a core part of the problem that one doesn't yield on, but other parts one is willing to yield on. Think of the individual audiotapes for accepting influence (available from our institute; see Appendix E).

Creating Shared Meaning

Supporting your partner's dreams, even if they are different from your own:

a. If my partner wants things in life that are different from what I want, it's fine with me, as long as it doesn't cost me my freedom.

b. I don't much care about my partner's goals in life.

Supporting your own dreams, even when they are different from your partner's, and developing them within the context of the relationship:

a. I demand that my marriage support my interests even if they are not my spouse's interests.

b. My own dreams and interests in life have got to be central in my marriage.

Solution: Use the exercises on shared values and meaning in Chapter 10 to explore the common base of agreement that may already exist in this marriage. Use the Mission and Legacy intervention (Table 7.7). This will be doing individual therapy in a couple's context. This will be a difficult part of the Sound Marital House for this internal working model because it means getting very close, trusting, and being a true team player.

Previously Abused Woman's Internal Working Model of Relationships

The basis for this section is an interview I did with my wife, Dr. Julie Schwartz Gottman, about a type of patient she has worked with for many years, the previously abused woman. I asked her to summarize her clinical experience with these kinds of clients and how their internal working model affects marital therapy. This section is offered as an illustration of how the interview can be a guide for understanding resistance in a variety of clients.

What does it mean to the abused woman to know someone?

She is going to be hypervigilant. She is going to try to know everything she can possibly know about her partner, particularly regarding his sexual behavior, the cues as to when he may become sexual. She will be aware of attempts by the other person to control her, aware of his interest in other women. She will have a sexualized sense of the other.

What does it mean to her to be known?

The sexually abused woman will be frightened to be known because deep down she believes she is bad or evil or worthless. She thinks if someone really knows who she is, he will abandon her. Also, she will be frightened about being known sexually and may hide her own sexual abuse history from the spouse. Emotional intimacy may be the big barrier to being known. The perpetrator had a very close, dependent relationship with her, so the prospect of emotional intimacy brings terror. She may shut down sexually once she becomes really close.

What does it mean to her to be thought of with fondness and admiration by another?

She will not believe it. She will always discount or rebuff it either through her internal self-talk or externally to the partner, which will be frustrating for him because he will often be genuinely trying to compliment her. She will believe that he is fond of her because she acts like the maid. She'll cook all the meals, she'll do the laundry, etc., and she will figure that her partner is just complimenting her because he is appreciative of her maid duties. And she'll think that he wants her to do more, so she will look at the compliment as a manipulation.

What does it mean to her to think of someone else with fondness and admiration?

It's rare that a sexually abused woman will admire a man, period—her partner or really anybody else. She may idealize the partner in some ways but that it usually pretty short-lived. After he becomes sexually threatening to her, following emotional intimacy, she is more likely to vilify him than express admiration and fondness. The only fondness and admiration that a sexually abused woman will often feel, particularly if she hasn't had therapy, is for her partner if he is nonsexual. If she has no sexual contact with him, then she will feel fond and grateful, but she will also feel very guilty.

What does it mean to turn toward another characteristically and want to be with that person?

That is not an experience that is familiar or comfortable to the sexually abused woman. Crossing the threshold toward intimacy with the partner, she will be agitated and threatened, almost repelled, by his sexuality. The desire to be with the other person will be brief. She will sense the threat and really want to pull back. She may be minimally interested, but often she carries a lot of narcissism because she has been injured so early. She can't be wholeheartedly interested in her partner if she perceives the partner to be a perpetrator. She will care about what the partner has to say, but mostly from the position of hypervigilance.

What does it mean to her to have someone turn toward her?

A sexually abused woman will feel totally threatened and overwhelmed. She won't trust it but will assume that the man just wants sex. Attraction, of course, feels threatening on a sexual level. She won't believe her partner is interested in her; she will feel he is trying to manipulate her into having sex.

What does it mean to her to have enough positive sentiment toward another that it can override that person's being negative?

That actually can happen, but only following a great deal of treatment in which the image and behavior of the original perpetrator are separated from the partner. With or without individual treatment, it is important for the partner to be totally nondemanding sexually. She will often criticize her partner as a way of keeping distance between them, not necessarily openly but in her own mind. She works to keep negative sentiment override alive and well so that she can maintain interpersonal distance.

What does it mean to her to have someone else trust her enough so that her own negativity is overridden by positive feelings?

She is often very grateful for that, but it will make her uncomfortable in terms of the increased closeness. Consequently, she will escalate her negativity to reestablish a more distant and comfortable interpersonal space.

What does it mean to her to be able to accept someone else, despite his/her shortcomings, and be amused by his/her failings rather than enraged by them?

The sexually abused woman is rarely amused by anything the partner does. She feels too threatened by him. It is possible at the end of treatment, but without treatment there is a lot of disrespect and criticism for failings of the partner, which keeps that interpersonal distance in place.

What does it mean to her to be able to believe that she is accepted by someone else, despite her own shortcomings, and have that person be amused by her failings rather than enraged by them?

She will not believe it. Her shortcomings are evidence to her of her badness, so when she fails she will believe that her partner is seeing her utter worthlessness. She believes that her partner really wants to reject and abandon her.

What does it mean to her to be able to raise a complaint with softened gentleness?

That will be hard for her to do, but she will try because she feels so guilty for coming on harshly.

What does it mean to her to be able to respond to another's gentleness?

She will *only* be able to respond when the partner is gentle. Otherwise she will immediately become flooded, because her threshold for stimulus overload is very low. She will hear correction in a normal tone of voice as yelling. If the partner is actually yelling, she will be out the door and down the street.

What does it mean to her to be able to influence someone else, be persuasive, but also yield to win?

It will be critically important for her to be able to influence her partner so that she can maintain some kind of control in the relationship. Otherwise she will feel sexually threatened.

What does it mean to her to be able to accept influence from another?

This will be extremely difficult, if not impossible, without treatment. Accepting influence is confounded with being molested by the perpetrator. In her past male perpetrators have actually been very complimentary and persuasive, as they have tried to bribe her with gifts, win her confidence, and manipulate her into being the victim. So she will be very sensitive to any attempt to influence her and be very threatened by that as an attempt to control her.

What does it mean to her to be able to offer a repair?

She will often try to make repairs because conflict is very threatening to her. She may, however, back away and seek distance. She may not be able to process well enough to compose a repair.

What does it mean to her to accept her spouse's attempt at repairing things?

She won't trust it and will probably sabotage it. If the partner repeats it several times, she may calm down enough to accept it. She will almost never accept a repair on the first attempt.

What does it mean to her to be able to self-soothe?

She has to shut out the partner completely to calm down. She has experienced living with the perpetrator for periods between the abuse and she is often waiting, hypervigilant, for things to escalate again. The self-soothing period will have to last several hours at least, not the usual 20 minutes; she will often shut down completely for days at a time

What does being able to soothe her partner mean to her?

The abused woman also fears abandonment, so by way of forestalling that calamity, she will often placate her partner. This creates the back-and-forth motion of increasing and decreasing interpersonal distance. If he starts stonewalling, she will go out of her mind and feel abandoned, even offering sex when she does not want this.

What does it mean to her to be able to propose a compromise solution to a marital problem?
She may believe in a compromise solution intellectually but it will be extremely hard for her to do it emotionally. She is usually too flooded to do this in the face of conflict.

What does it mean to her to be able to accept another's compromise solution?
If the other person is doing the thinking, she may be able to accept it.

What does it mean to her to accept and support her partner's dreams, even if they are different from her own?
She will likely be threatened by them, but she might go along with them to avoid abandonment.

What does it mean to her to have her own dreams and develop them within the context of the relationship?
First of all, it is very difficult for a sexually abused woman to have any dreams because she has had to deny her own needs. She won't be in touch with her own needs, let alone dreams. She doesn't know who she is. Once she develops dreams she will battle for them, and if the partner doesn't support them, she will throw him out.

It is important to distinguish two states of prior abuse. When she remembers the abuse, she will avoid her partner or use alcohol or drugs to numb herself before sex so she doesn't feel anything. Sex will usually be unsatisfactory for her and the partner will feel like she is not present. She will conduct herself sexually that way if there is a fear of abandonment. She may be obese and stuff herself before and after sex to tolerate it. However, when there is no awareness or only growing awareness, sex will be extremely difficult. She will be in touch with the terror and have dyspareunia or freeze, curl up in fetal position, and cry. She may have panic symptoms, migraines, or gastric problems.

How is the partner separated from the perpetrator in therapy? First the partner has to agree to not have sex for some time, period. There has to be an emotional intimacy they can both tolerate. Out of that emotional connection a sexual relationship can grow. The abuse victim gets to have total control over the progression of the sexual relationship. She defines the first step, the second step, etc. She defines what will trigger her so that the couple can avoid those triggers. She controls the timing of it, how long it will last, what behaviors and positions are allowed, etc.

OTHER SOURCES OF RESISTANCE

Resistance Due to Disorders of Individuation

The absence of personal fulfillment, definition, and development leads individuals to confuse fusion with intimacy and militates against building the lower levels of the Sound Marital House.

Solution: The therapist needs to help the spouses establish an awareness of their own needs as individuals, coming together to build we-ness from a position of self-understanding and knowledge. A helpful metaphor is the airlines' instruction to put on your own oxygen mask before helping another. In many forms of marital therapy, individuation work involves work with the primary family, either directly or in terms of projections within the marriage. These transgenerational approaches can be helpful when there are serious issues with individuation and fusion.

Resistance Due to Relationship Pathology

Although disorders are generally conceptualized in terms of individuals, we see a great deal of what could be called "relationship pathology" that is not based on individual pathology. These are marital arrangements that are dysfunctional for the partners and lead to increasing distance and isolation. Examples are open sexual relationships in which rejections and betrayals are constant sources of conflict.

Solution: The couple needs to be educated regarding the consequences of their choices (e.g., the effects on trust of a sexually "open" marriage).

Resistance Due to the Absence of Community

The absence of community in people's lives lowers the levels of support and the ability to give to others and to be involved with others. They are isolated socially, unconnected to a caring community of other people. In times of transition these supports can be critical for helping the couple.

Solution: Help the partners find a community where they feel comfortable and accepted. Point out that partners can't fulfill every single one of their spouse's needs. Other people are needed to supplement and support the couple's fulfillment.

Resistance Due to the Need for Social Change

The therapist works with families in a political and social context. There are forces beyond the therapist's control that deeply affect families. Examples are social policies that affect the workplace and militate against family cohesion (for example, punishing dads who choose their kids' soccer match on Sunday over playing golf with clients), social policies that affect crime and safety, the availability of jobs, and wealth and its distribution. Increasingly in the U.S.A. community is dying. There is an absence of extended family, formal and informal friendship networks, and a male mentorship system. The concept of a family wage is dying, along with safety nets for medical support and retirement. The workplace is designed to militate against families, and this is especially true during times of major family stress and life-cycle changes (transition to parenthood, adolescent children, caring for aging parents).

Solution: Policy needs to be changed on a national level. But the therapist can help make the couple aware of these social and political forces that operate against families. For example, data suggest that if they choose family over work, they will earn less. If they choose work over family, they will earn more and their lives will have less meaning and fulfillment. A balance is clearly necessary, and the therapist can help the couple sort out these choices.

C h a p t e r 12 ❧

Avoiding Relapse

 In this chapter I discuss the two things I want to make sure are established before I terminate with a couple. I then set up a follow-up interview 3 to 6 months after termination.

I feel most comfortable ending treatment with a couple when, at a minimum, I think they can process a marital argument that has failed, and when they have firmly established some rituals of emotional connection. By a failed marital argument I mean that they have had a fight that has left them feeling hurt, rejected, and alienated from their partner.

THE FAILED MARITAL ARGUMENT

Goal: The couple will be able to process their own interaction and make their next conversation better.

Before I terminate therapy I want to be confident that the couple can process a marital argument without me. So in my office I use the Aftermath of a Marital Argument Questionnaire (Table 12.1) as a guide for couples. I will have them move from the "corner" portion of my office to the "Ring." Recall that the Ring is where I videotape the spouses talking to one another (with biofeedback). I do not speak for 6 to 10 minutes. Then we move back to the corner to process the interaction. I use video recall to help the spouses process the interaction without starting the fight again. The processing is systematic. Here together we examine:

- *Feelings.* I use the "I feel" part of the Aftermath Questionnaire. What was each person feeling? What were the unstated "I statements"? Look at all the emotions, including uncertainty, that each person was experiencing.
- *The anatomy of the defend/attack mode* (see Figure 12.1). How were their needs and issues raised? What is the anatomy of each person's

Table 12.1   Aftermath of a Marital Argument Questionnaire

Instructions: This form is a guide for processing and evaluating what happened in your last marital argument. It is designed to try to increase understanding between the two of you. The idea here is that there is no absolute "reality" in a marital conflict, but only two "subjective realities." This form is designed to help you get at these.

Answer each item, filling out the form individually. Then discuss with your partner how you filled out each item.

How did you feel?

Negative Feelings:

1. During the argument I felt defensive.	A Great Deal	Definitely	A Little	Not at All
2. During the argument my feelings got hurt.	A Great Deal	Definitely	A Little	Not at All
3. I felt excluded.	A Great Deal	Definitely	A Little	Not at All
4. I felt angry.	A Great Deal	Definitely	A Little	Not at All
5. I felt sad.	A Great Deal	Definitely	A Little	Not at All
6. I felt misunderstood.	A Great Deal	Definitely	A Little	Not at All
7. I felt criticized.	A Great Deal	Definitely	A Little	Not at All
8. I felt like my partner didn't even like me.	A Great Deal	Definitely	A Little	Not at All
9. I was afraid.	A Great Deal	Definitely	A Little	Not at All
10. I was worried.	A Great Deal	Definitely	A Little	Not at All
11. I felt I was right and my partner was wrong.	A Great Deal	Definitely	A Little	Not at All
12. I felt out of control.	A Great Deal	Definitely	A Little	Not at All
13. I felt righteously indignant.	A Great Deal	Definitely	A Little	Not at All
14. I felt unfairly picked on.	A Great Deal	Definitely	A Little	Not at All
15. I felt unappreciated.	A Great Deal	Definitely	A Little	Not at All
16. I felt unattractive.	A Great Deal	Definitely	A Little	Not at All
17. I felt neglected.	A Great Deal	Definitely	A Little	Not at All
18. I felt disgusted.	A Great Deal	Definitely	A Little	Not at All
19. I was disapproving.	A Great Deal	Definitely	A Little	Not at All
20. I was morally outraged.	A Great Deal	Definitely	A Little	Not at All
21. I felt taken for granted.	A Great Deal	Definitely	A Little	Not at All
22. I felt like leaving.	A Great Deal	Definitely	A Little	Not at All
23. I was overwhelmed with emotion.	A Great Deal	Definitely	A Little	Not at All
24. I felt excluded.	A Great Deal	Definitely	A Little	Not at All
25. I felt powerless.	A Great Deal	Definitely	A Little	Not at All
26. I felt like I had no influence.	A Great Deal	Definitely	A Little	Not at All
27. I felt like my opinions didn't even matter.	A Great Deal	Definitely	A Little	Not at Al
28. I had no feelings at all.	A Great Deal	Definitely	A Little	Not at All
29. I had no idea what I was feeling.	A Great Deal	Definitely	A Little	Not at All
30. Other feelings (write in):				

Table 12.1   Aftermath of a Marital Argument Questionnaire (*continued*)

Positive Feelings:

1. During the argument I felt calm.	A Great Deal	Definitely	A Little	Not at All
2. During the argument I felt loved.	A Great Deal	Definitely	A Little	Not at All
3. During the argument I felt appreciated.	A Great Deal	Definitely	A Little	Not at All
4. During the argument I felt respected.	A Great Deal	Definitely	A Little	Not at All
5. During the argument I felt happy.	A Great Deal	Definitely	A Little	Not at All
6. During the argument I felt powerful.	A Great Deal	Definitely	A Little	Not at All
7. During the argument I felt loving.	A Great Deal	Definitely	A Little	Not at All
8. During the argument I felt kind.	A Great Deal	Definitely	A Little	Not at All
9. During the argument I felt in control.	A Great Deal	Definitely	A Little	Not at All
10. During the argument I felt like we were making progress.	A Great Deal	Definitely	A Little	Not at All
11. During the argument I felt connected to my partner.	A Great Deal	Definitely	A Little	Not at All
12. During the argument I felt optimistic.	A Great Deal	Definitely	A Little	Not at All
13. Other feelings (write in):				

What were the triggers?

Events Related to Inclusion

1. I felt excluded.	A Great Deal	Definitely	A Little	Not at All
2. My partner was not interested in me.	A Great Deal	Definitely	A Little	Not at All
3. I was being ignored.	A Great Deal	Definitely	A Little	Not at All
4. I was not important to my spouse.	A Great Deal	Definitely	A Little	Not at All
5. I felt cold toward my spouse.	A Great Deal	Definitely	A Little	Not at All
6. My partner was not happy to see me.	A Great Deal	Definitely	A Little	Not at All

Others (write in):

Events Related to Affection

1. I felt no affection from my partner.	A Great Deal	Definitely	A Little	Not at All
2. My partner was cold toward me.	A Great Deal	Definitely	A Little	Not at All
3. I definitely felt rejected.	A Great Deal	Definitely	A Little	Not at All
4. I was criticized.	A Great Deal	Definitely	A Little	Not at All
5. I felt no affection toward my partner.	A Great Deal	Definitely	A Little	Not at All
6. I felt that my partner was not attracted to me.	A Great Deal	Definitely	A Little	Not at All

Others (write in):

Events Related to Influence

1. I had no power in this discussion.	A Great Deal	Definitely	A Little	Not at All
2. I felt helpless to affect how the conversation went.	A Great Deal	Definitely	A Little	Not at All
3. I felt there was a lack of respect toward me.	A Great Deal	Definitely	A Little	Not at All

Table 12.1 Aftermath of a Marital Argument Questionnaire (*continued*)

4. My sense dignity was being compromised.	A Great Deal	Definitely	A Little	Not at All
5. My partner was being domineering.	A Great Deal	Definitely	A Little	Not at All
6. I could not persuade my partner at all.	A Great Deal	Definitely	A Little	Not at All

Others (write in):

Do these feelings relate to your past?

Some self-examination is necessary here to identify where the triggers come from in your own past. What issues are you particularly sensitive about, and what is the origin of these sensitivities?

When people are under prolonged periods of stress, old patterns of thought and behavior can emerge, old sensitivities can become heightened, and the fighting in the marriage is a symptom of older patterns. This section is designed to help you see what potential past events may have set the conditions for the fighting.

How I have been responding lately when stressed? What sensitivities, thoughts, and feelings have I had lately in my marriage:

They come from the way I was treated in my family growing up (explain):

They come from a previous relationship (explain):

They come from past injuries I suffered (explain):

They come from really hard times I endured (explain):

They come from traumas I experienced (explain):

They come from basic fears and insecurities I have (explain):

They come from things and events I have not yet resolved or put aside (explain):

They come from unrealized hopes I have (explain):

They relate to ways I was treated in the past by other people (explain):

They relate to things I have always thought about myself (explain):

Table 12.1   Aftermath of a Marital Argument Questionnaire (*continued*)

They relate to old "nightmares" or "catastrophes" I have worried about (explain):

Other (explain):

Summarize in writing how you saw this argument and what the subjective reality was for you. Share your subjective reality and try to see how your partner's subjective reality might make sense, given your partner's perspective.

Try to communicate (in writing) your understanding of your partner's subjective reality in this argument.

It is essential that each of you attempt to give some credence to the other's subjective reality. Try to do that right now in your mind.

In moving from a defensive or attacking, critical posture, there is a need to first understand YOUR part in all of this. It is natural for each of us to make the fundamental error that it is all our partner's fault. Actually, because it is all a cycle, it is the *fault* of neither. What is necessary is to be able to move BOTH of you out of the defensive or attacking pattern into a more productive pattern. This starts by EACH OF YOU admitting some role (however slight at first) in creating this argument.

Admitting Your Role

It is essential that you each take some responsibility for what happened. That cannot happen easily unless you have first calmed yourself down physiologically. Recall the five steps of self-soothing: Breathing evenly and deeply, tensing and then relaxing muscle groups, making the muscle groups heavy, making the muscle groups warm, and, finally, summarizing all of this in a personal image of tranquility and peace. Second, you have to let go of thoughts that maintain the distress, thoughts of feeling misunderstood and of either righteous indignation or innocent victimhood. Take some time, allowing at least 20 minutes for this to happen. Then fill out the rest of this form.

Calmer? YES   NO

If NO, go back and calm down some more.

If YES, you are calmer, now try to admit to yourself what role you may have had in this argument.

1. I have been very stressed and irritable lately.	YES, DEFINITELY	MAYBE A LITTLE
2. I have not expressed much appreciation toward my spouse lately	YES, DEFINITELY	MAYBE A LITTLE
3. I have taken my spouse for granted.	YES, DEFINITELY	MAYBE A LITTLE
4. I have been overly sensitive lately.	YES, DEFINITELY	MAYBE A LITTLE
5. I have been overly critical lately.	YES, DEFINITELY	MAYBE A LITTLE
6. I have not shared very much of my inner world.	YES, DEFINITELY	MAYBE A LITTLE
7. I have not been emotionally available.	YES, DEFINITELY	MAYBE A LITTLE

Table 12.1   Aftermath of a Marital Argument Questionnaire (*continued*)

8. I have been more typically turning away.	YES, DEFINITELY	MAYBE A LITTLE
9. I have been getting easily upset.	YES, DEFINITELY	MAYBE A LITTLE
10. I have been depressed lately.	YES, DEFINITELY	MAYBE A LITTLE
11. I would say that I have a chip on my shoulder lately	YES, DEFINITELY	MAYBE A LITTLE
12. I have not been very affectionate.	YES, DEFINITELY	MAYBE A LITTLE
13. I have not made time for good things between us.	YES, DEFINITELY	MAYBE A LITTLE
14. I have not been a very good listener lately.	YES, DEFINITELY	MAYBE A LITTLE
15. I have not asked for what I need.	YES, DEFINITELY	MAYBE A LITTLE
16. I have been feeling a bit like a martyr.	YES, DEFINITELY	MAYBE A LITTLE
17. Other:		

Overall, my contribution to this was:

How can you make this better in the future?
What one thing could your spouse do, and what one thing could you do next time to avoid this problem?

It's easier to start here, so we will. What one thing could your spouse do differently?

It's harder to do this, but try it. What one thing could you do differently?

Now share your form with your spouse and talk about the argument without starting the argument again.

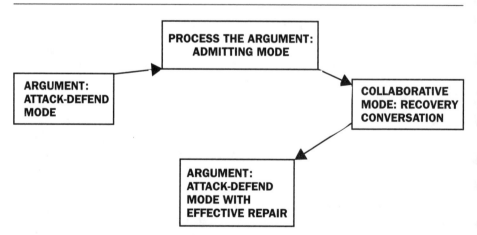

Figure 12.1   Four modes of marital arguments as four stages of therapy with respect to the regulation of conflict (modified from Wile, 1996). In the first mode, couples are only capable of being in an argumentative mode (the Four Horsemen are present) and their repair is ineffective. In the second admitting mode, couples are able to process the argument and take responsibility for hurting one another. In the third, collaborative mode, they can recover from the hurt feelings and the righteous indignation of the argument. In the fourth mode they are able to effectively repair the argument during the argument, even when the Four Horsemen are present.

defensiveness? There are many ways of acting defensively (e.g., cross-complaining, whining) and therefore many ways of feeling defensive. What is going on in the defensive person's mind and body? What is the constellation of the defensiveness? Does this anatomy have a history?

- *Two subjective realities.* It is important to see that in any failed marital argument there are always two valid subjective realities. I think, as does Jerry Lewis, that an important goal in all processing is getting both people to realize that there are always at least two partially valid ways of seeing any interaction. Ask, "Is there any part of your partner's reality you can understand?"

- *Identifying the triggers.* What set each person's defensive, sad, or critical, hurt, or angry (and so on) feelings off? Are these familiar triggers for that person?

- *Moving to admitting mode.* I use video playback to help with this transition. Just watching the tape and asking people what they noticed usually accomplishes a valuable transformation of getting out of the fight and becoming a viewer. It also helps most people see their own role in the discussion. But, even without videotape, the Aftermath Questionnaire helps in this transformation by requiring people to think about their role.

- *Expressing needs.* What was each person's needs in this situation? How did they express their needs? Are they from "the land of Indirect"? I joke that in the land of Indirect people use their right hand over the back of their heads to scratch the left side of their nose. In the land of Indirect people never really come out and just say what they need. They often don't even know themselves what they need. How can they be more direct about our needs?

- *Projection.* Is there some sense in which they are responding to their partner as they have in the past in other relationships?

- *The conversation they never had.* Dan Wile (1996) helps couples have what he calls "the conversation they never had." This is the discussion they really needed to have instead of the awful one they wound up having. In the early stages of therapy I speak for each person in Wile fashion. Then, using the Aftermath of a Marital Argument Questionnaire, I have them do it in processing the fight. They need to be calm before they can do this.

- *Intervention.* Can they come up with one idea for making this continuing dialogue on this issue better next time? In the beginning of treatment I am usually the source of these ideas. But before I have them get back into the ring, I first ask about how they understand this idea and how they can make this intervention ego-syntonic (not phony).

- *The next interaction.* Therapist: Be still. As you observe, think of one tool—only one—you can offer people who have been getting hit in the head for 6 to 10 minutes.

BUILD IN RITUALS OF EMOTIONAL CONNECTION

Goal: The couple will have reliable ways of connecting emotionally.

Earlier we examined the couple's family rituals, both formal and informal. This approach is entirely consistent with the approach taken by Doherty's (1997) book, *The Intentional Family,* which emphasizes formal and informal rituals of connection in families.

There are alarming statistics about the percentage of U.S. families who do not regularly eat dinner together. Less than 33% of U.S. families eat dinner together regularly, and over half of these have the TV on during dinner. TV is well known to kill conversation. The typical amount of conversation that parents have with their children is 35 minutes a week. This does not include conversation such as "Get your coat on, we're leaving for school." Dual career couples tend to converse less than 2 hours a week. Yet the average U.S. child watches 4 hours of TV a day.

Doherty argues for building meaningful rituals of connection in families both for informal events (such as partings, homecomings, bedtimes) and for more formal events (such as birthdays, anniversaries), and for holidays (Thanksgiving, Christmas, Kwanza, Passover, Ramadan). He suggests that these rituals be scripted so everyone knows who is doing what where, how the ritual begins, continues, and is exited.

In my practice I have modified this approach to have people review how these events were handled and mishandled in their own primary family. This can reveal a great deal of ambivalence about the ritual and projections around unresolved conflict. For example, when creating a ritual around birthdays, I ask people to describe birthday disasters in their childhood, and a great birthday as well. These narratives often reveal the dynamics of current conflicts. They can then be a lead-in to designing and scripting the ideal birthday ritual.

Doherty suggests that these rituals be scripted, so that everyone knows how the ritual is orchestrated. That makes it more likely that it will actually happen and become a family tradition with some meaning.

Today many couples leave important events of emotional connection as the very last thing they "do" in a busy schedule. Because of this, these emotional connections rarely happen, usually through no intention to actively avoid one another, but because people don't make time for them. By building these events in as rituals (formal or informal), they become dependable times from which people can derive contact, connection, and meaning in their families.

Intervention: Building Rituals

The idea here is to build in a set of rituals of connection surrounding informal but significant daily events. Ask the couple to discuss and build rituals for each of the following. Script these carefully so both know what they are supposed to do when. This includes entry into the ritual, the ritual (roles), and its ending. Here is a list of some of the events that can be ritualized for connection. I don't try to build all of these in, just a few that the couple considers to be adequate.

- *Leave-taking.* Don't leave without knowing at least one thing that is going to happen in your partner's life that day.

- *Reunions.* When returning home there is an affectionate greeting. There is a loving kiss that lasts at least several seconds (not a peck on the cheek).

- *Mealtimes.* Come together at meals and share the events of the day. Each person gets a chance to talk. Make meals an environment of peace, affection, support, and attention. Avoid conflict during dinners.

- *Eating out.* Eating out can be a special event that can turn an ordinary end of a day into a celebration or romantic event. Eating in a favorite restaurant can become a family tradition and ritual with considerable meaning.

- *After-meal coffee or tea.* Doherty and his wife Leah created a tradition after dinner in which their children played or did homework while the two of them talked. They all cleaned up after dinner and then Bill made the coffee and brought it out to Leah in the living room, and they talked for about an hour. It was a time of peace and connection.

- *The reunion stress-reducing conversation.* Each person gets a turn to talk about what was stressful that day (not about the relationship), and to receive support.

- *Bedtimes.* Going to bed is a time when there can be cuddling, physical affection, letting go of tension and irritability. Don't go to sleep without a kiss (not a perfunctory one).

- *Morning rituals.* For many families mornings are chaotic times, but this need not be the case at all. They can be times of connection when everyone is sent off with positive wishes and a good spirit.

- *Dates and getaways.* These are times when the couple gets a baby sitter and does something alone, on their own, including talking to one another. No kids are to be present. In our child-centered families these dates and getaways (like for a weekend to a bed-and-breakfast inn) become very rare. We recommend weekly dates and weekend getaways 3 times a year.

- *When one person is sick.* Rituals surrounding getting sick and being taken care of can be very important to people. Often spouses have very different ideas about how they want to be treated when they are sick.

- *Celebrations of a triumph.* How does this family deal with pride and praise, celebrate successes, and acknowledge and reward achievement? I recommend that the family build what I call a culture of praise. By this I mean that it is possible to search for things to be thankful for and pleased about, even if these are only small and everyday things.

- *Rituals surrounding bad luck, failure, fatigue, or exhaustion.* How does this family heal, support, or renew itself?

- *Rituals surrounding entertaining.* Again, the idea of a home and bringing friends into it can lead to important rituals of connection for a couple and for children.

- *Rituals surrounding keeping in touch with kin and friends.* Family events, reunions, and so on can play a vital role in families.

- *Rituals surrounding initiating and refusing lovemaking, and talking about it.* These are often very important events that get left for the very end of the day when partners are exhausted and have little left for tenderness or for facing potential rejection. The famous sex therapist Lonnie Barbach says that couples often think these events should be "spontaneous," and so they avoid any scripting or planning. However, if they think back to their courtship they recall that romantic dates were often planned, even the attire, perfume, place to go to, music and wine for the return to his or her apartment, and so on. Once married, suddenly these events become an afterthought and, hence, a casualty of being married. This has led to the old saw that marriage is the cure for lust.

- *Vacations.* The way people introduce a need for a vacation, an idea for a vacation, how they plan the trip, and what the vacation itself is like (do people take work to do? Are they available to the office? How separate are they, how together? etc.).

There are rituals of connection that surround somewhat more formal events, such as anniversaries, birthdays, and so on. Then there are the more formal events and holidays that tend to be rich in emotional significance and may involve extended family or community. These constitute a yearly holiday cycle, which can be imbued with profound meaning.

Doherty also talks about rituals of passage like circumcisions, bar and bat mitzvahs, weddings, and funerals. These meaningful events punctuate the family life cycle and are usually community events as well.

As I noted, I have found it helpful to go back to each person's primary family and ask about the rituals of connection surrounding these events. I try to elicit rich narratives about these events. I ask about the typical ritual, and then ask about the worst and the best such event. For example, I ask people to recall their worst birthday experience growing up. One reason I ask these questions is that there are often unresolved conflicts or traumas surrounding these events and these get played out in the marriage and keep leading to disappointment, defensiveness, and hurt. These reactions may be projections onto a hapless spouse, but they are attributed to that spouse's character. In this exploration I also try to uncover the central elements that each person needs for these rituals to have meaning and for becoming pleasant events they anticipate with pleasure.

The therapist can expect to encounter considerable resistance to creating these rituals of connection. This resistance will reveal blocks to intimacy in this marriage. They are worth exploring in their own right. However, today in the U.S. people in untroubled marriages have great difficulty finding time for connecting, and they are postponing fun as well. So a precursor to building these rituals of emotional connection is helping people rebuild their schedules so interaction is a priority. It is helpful to have each person make a list of what he/she values in the week, and then schedule time for it. Steven Covey and his colleagues talk about this cogently in their book, *First Things First* (1995). They present the metaphor of a bottle that one fills with large rocks. The large rocks are the list of one's central priorities (e.g, reading, spending time with my daughter, talking to my wife, seeing my mother, teaching, writing, cooking). There is still room in the bottle for smaller rocks (things of lower priority), then gravel, and then sand. However, most people tend to fill their schedules with the sand first. They are putting out fires all day, and the small things crowd out the important priorities. There is no room for the gravel or the large rocks.

Once the rituals of connection are in place, this is only part of the picture. There will be times when people miss one another, when rituals are ignored. There will be arguments and failed bids. It is very helpful to use the Aftermath of a Marital Argument Questionnaire (Table 12.1) to help people process these unfortunate events and insure that they don't happen very often.

Chapter 13

Putting It All Together: Working as a Team and Terminating Therapy

 This chapter describes how to solidify the marital friendship, conflict regulation skills, and the ability of the couple to function as a team. Finally, prior to termination the couple's marital poop detector is reset to lessen the likelihood of relapse.

Kissinger once said that power is an aphrodisiac. This may have been true for him, but our research (Gottman, 1994a,b) suggests that in marriages, for women, the aphrodisiac is the couple being able to work together as a team, with affection, support, emotional connection, and respect. Women even find men doing housework erotic, not because housework is intrinsically erotic, but because it spells male emotional engagement and friendship. In our work on the Sound Marital House questionnaires we found that, for women, the marital friendship was strongly related to good sex, romance, and passion. The same thing was true for men. We agree with Peggy Papp, who recently said (personal communication, 1998) that "men and women are from Earth."

In our research work with couples on the transition to parenthood (Shapiro, Gottman, & Carrére, unpublished) we asked the question, "What aspects of the marriage in the first few months after the wedding will predict the couple's adaptation to the transition?" We were attempting to predict whether a couple would be in the group in which the wife's marital satisfaction plummeted after the baby arrived or in the group where it was maintained. The answer turned out to be the dimensions of marriage we have reviewed so far, particularly the couple's ability to work together as a team, a sense of "we-ness" (assessed in our Oral History Interview) rather than "me-ness." Belsky and Kelly's (1994) summary of Belsky's longitudinal work on the transition to parenthood echoed this theme. They noted the importance of the spouses' being able to work together as a team and their ability to regulate conflict. One important part of this skill was the equitable distribution of household chores, childcare, and the management of closeness in the marital relationship itself. Another important study on the transition to parenthood by Cowan and Cowan (1992) confirmed these processes as central to managing the transition.

This chapter addresses these we-ness dimensions of marriage. Working as a team puts it all together.

PUTTING IT ALL TOGETHER

Intervention 1. Working as a Team: The Paper Tower

I have used the Paper Tower exercise for many years, but never in research. I have always found it to be clinically diagnostic of the distribution of power in the marriage, and I have found that it reveals both the strengths and the issues the marriage is facing. Often we use it in our 6-month follow-up couples workshop. Here I suggest its use as an intervention for getting people to focus on the dimensions of working together as a good team.

Purpose

To help the couple work as a team by turning toward versus turning away from one another, and giving and accepting influence in an equitable sharing of power on a task that is unrelated to marital issues. This exercise also prepares the couple for a change in their conflict resolution patterns and introduces the metaphor of a marriage as building something together.

Exercise

This is intended to be a low-threat exercise. In the therapist's office the couple is given a box containing assorted materials such as newspapers, construction paper, tape, sparkly glue, cellophane, magic markers, straws, string, stapler, magic markers, crayons, and so on. (I have generally found that the more you put in the box, the more interesting it will be.) They are instructed to build a paper tower. It must be tall, strong, and beautiful, and it has to be able to stand unsupported. They can earn up to a total of 20 points for size, and up to a total of 20 points for strength, and up to a total of 50 points for beauty. This point system favors beauty, so the artist is favored slightly over the engineer. That is intentional, because the engineer-type tends to dominate on this kind of task, but here the point system favors the artist, so the smart engineer will utilize the team's artistic resources. The therapist can suggest that they create a crest or flag of the marriage for the tower.

The points are awarded by the therapist, who also gives the spouses feedback on how they worked together as a team. It is helpful to revisit the emotional bank account idea within the context of this exercise, pointing out that often the most influential team member is the one who draws out the other, asks questions, and gives support, rather than the one who dominates. In one variation of this exercise, the therapist gives the couple feedback halfway through the exercise, and the partners attempt to improve their functioning as a team, using the feedback. Point out strengths, praise what is positive, be specific, and give as little feedback as possible (people hear a lot of even very good feedback as criticism).

Intervention 2. Consensus Decision-Making and Team-Building

Purpose

To improve partners' skills in problem-solving as a team, compromising, and accepting and giving influence on a problem unrelated to their relationship.

Exercise

First, partners do the task described in Table 13.1 individually, and then they do it again but by a consensus discussion.

Intervention 3: The Gottman Island Survival Problem

Purpose

To give the couple another chance of working on a consensus task after feedback from the mountain survival problem. It can also be used to focus on the experience of accepting influence.

Exercise

The therapist suggests that the couple use this joint decision-making task as an opportunity to work on accepting influence: "The themes of this exercise are to evaluate your ability to extend inclusion, to accept influence, and share power." They are given 30 minutes to do the Gottman Island Survival Problem (Table 13.2), 10 minutes to do the task individually and 20 minutes for consensus decision-making.

In this exercise the spouses are trying to do two things: (1) give and accept influence, and (2) create a positive and cooperative emotional tone in the discussion. They are to try not to dominate each other. The therapist observes which tactics they use are influential. How do they include or exclude the other person? How do they work together as a team? Finally, what is the emotional tone in the discussion: Were they having fun? If not, what emotions were evident? Observe, then talk about it with the couple. A form for guiding the therapist's observations is included as Table 13.3.

Intervention 4. Negotiating Marital Power: Who Does What in the Marriage?

Purpose

To help couples negotiate their ideas about gender roles in marriage. There is no right or wrong solution. The important thing is the perception of fairness. The issue is respect.

Table 13.1   Gottman Mountain Survival Problem

Your plane has crash-landed on a high snowy mountaintop in the Swiss Alps. The two of you are the only survivors, and one of you is somewhat injured. You have no idea of exactly where you are. You think that there is some chance that people may know of the plane's distress, but you are not sure. A storm appears to be on the way. You decide that you both need to descend the mountain. Rank order the following items for their survival value according to your plan, with a 1 for the most important item, a 2 for the next most important item, and so on. First rank order these individually, on your own. Think of your reasoning for your rankings. Then develop a consensus ranking by discussing the problem and your rationale for the rankings.

1. Oxygen tanks
2. Radio (one-way)
3. Water
4. Skis
5. Matches
6. Shovel
7. Backpack
8. Toilet paper
9. Tents
10. Sleeping bags
11. Knife
12. Snowshoes
13. Lantern
14. Cook stove
15. Long rope
16. Walkie-talkie
17. Freeze-dried food
18. Dental floss
19. Boots
20. Flares
21. Compass
22. Regional aerial maps
23. A gun with six bullets
24. Camera and film
25. First aid kit

Exercise

Fill out the questionnaire in Table 13.4 individually and then again through discussion, trying to arrive at consensus. (Peggy Papp has couples read books like Arlie Hochschild's *The Second Shift*, which is about gender inequality, for purposes of discussion. That would be a good thing to do in preparation for this task.)

THE MARITAL "POOP DETECTOR": RESETTING THE NEGATIVITY THRESHOLD

The final part of the therapy program involves changing the couple's influence functions, particularly the negative threshold for changing things when they start

Table 13.2   Gottman Island Survival Problem

Your cruise ship sank in the Caribbean and the two of you awaken to find yourself on a tropical desert island. You are the only survivors, and one of you is somewhat injured. You have no idea of exactly where you are. You think that there is some chance that people may know of the ship's distress, but you are not sure. A storm appears to be on the way. You decide that you need to prepare to survive on this island for some time and also make sure you will rendezvous with a potential rescue party. There is a bunch of stuff from the ship on the beach and you make an inventory of this stuff. First select the 10 most important items. Then rank order these 10 items for their survival value according to your plan, with a 1 for the most important item, a 2 for the next most important item, and so on. First rank order these individually, on your own, and then develop a consensus ranking by discussing the problem.

1. Two changes of clothing
2. AM-FM and short-wave radio receiver
3. Water, 10 gallons
4. Pots and pans
5. Matches
6. Shovel
7. Backpack
8. Toilet paper
9. Two Tents
10. Two Sleeping bags
11. Knife
12. Small life raft, with sail
13. Sun block lotion
14. Cook stove and lantern
15. Long rope
16. Two walkie-talkie sender-receiver units
17. Freeze-dried food for seven days
18. Change of clothing
19. One fifth of whiskey
20. Flares
21. Compass
22. Regional aerial maps
23. A gun with 6 bullets
24. Fifty packages of condoms
25. First aid kit with penicillin
26. Oxygen tanks

---

going bad. By resetting their thresholds of the marital poop detector, they actually notice and intervene with each other sooner than before therapy. The negativity threshold is that point where a partner's negativity begins to have an impact on the spouse. As I mentioned in Chapter 2, this finding came from longitudinal research with newlyweds, in which the wife was the key spouse in the detection of negativity. In marriages that eventually wound up happy and stable, the wife noticed and reacted to her husband's negativity at a much lower level of negativity than in marriages that wound up either divorced or unhappy and stable. It is my hypothesis (currently being tested) that this negativity threshold is related to early repair of the marriage.

Table 13.3   Gottman Island Survival Problem Observer Evaluation Form

As you observe partners interact in this exercise, notice, in particular, the following factors.

Were they both effective at influencing each other?

Were they both effective at being able to accept influence?

Was there a dominance struggle? Was there competitiveness?

Did either sulk or withdraw?

What were their emotions and actions during this task?

anger:
sadness:
tension:
contempt (one-upmanship?):
amusement or laughter:
interest:
affection (appreciation):
kindness:

Did they both feel included in this task?

Did they both work well as a team?

Did they each have fun?

Let us consider the case of a couple we have followed for the past six years, from the first few months of the newlywed phase through the birth of two children. Here is a summary of an interview I recently did with them. The most stressful event they had been through in the two and a half years since we had last seen them was the birth of their second child. One day Brett said that he was lying on the bed and realized that there were now two people between himself and his wife (literally and figuratively). He became depressed and felt very distant from the whole family. When Gail suggested that they needed a few things at the local store, he was eager to volunteer to do the errand because it meant a drive by himself away from the family. A few days later he and Gail and the two kids were on the couch and he was very quiet. She said, "What's going on with you?" He said, "Oh, I'm having a pity party." This was a very gentle way of introducing his issue. He told Gail gently that he was feeling neglected.

His issue led to Gail's venting her feelings. She said that she had no time at all to herself anymore, with two children needing her constantly, and she was sorry but until she got some time to herself a little bit, she would be unable to respond to Brett's needs. I asked, "What happened then?" Gail said, "Oh, he was great. He just took Elissa to the mall immediately and they were gone several hours. He could see how much more desperate I was than he was. He did this consistently for over a month! After that amount of time—it took that long—I

Table 13.4   Gottman Form for "Who Does What in the Marriage?"

Instructions: For the following items, please describe your perception of how things currently are handled and then how you would like them to be. What is your philosophy about who should do what? Who generally does what? Are things shared as you would like them to be, or could things be closer to your ideal?

	Currently Fine	*Could Be Better*
Running errands to the cleaners	☐	☐
Washing windows	☐	☐
Planning the food menu	☐	☐
Going grocery shopping	☐	☐
Cooking dinner	☐	☐
Setting the table	☐	☐
Cleanup after dinner	☐	☐
Cleaning the kitchen	☐	☐
Cleaning the bathrooms	☐	☐
Putting out clean towels	☐	☐
Keeping counters clean	☐	☐
General tidying up	☐	☐
Getting the car serviced	☐	☐
Putting gas in the car	☐	☐
Sorting incoming mail	☐	☐
Paying the bills	☐	☐
Balancing the checkbook	☐	☐
Writing letters	☐	☐
Taking phone messages	☐	☐
Returning phone calls or e-mail	☐	☐
Saving money	☐	☐
Taking out garbage and trash	☐	☐
Recycling	☐	☐
Doing the laundry	☐	☐
Folding the laundry	☐	☐
Ironing	☐	☐
Putting the clean clothes away	☐	☐
Sweeping kitchen and eating areas	☐	☐
Vacuuming	☐	☐
Washing and waxing floors	☐	☐
Changing light bulbs	☐	☐
Repair of appliances	☐	☐
Making the beds	☐	☐
Defrosting and cleaning refrigerator	☐	☐
Shopping for clothing	☐	☐
Planning travel	☐	☐
Home repair	☐	☐
Remodeling	☐	☐
Home maintenance	☐	☐
Buying furniture	☐	☐
Redecorating home	☐	☐
Buying items for the home	☐	☐

Table 13.4 Gottman Form for "Who Does What in the Marriage?" (*continued*)

	Currently Fine	Could Be Better
Buying new appliances	☐	☐
Sewing and mending	☐	☐
Straightening kitchen cabinets	☐	☐
Yard and garden work	☐	☐
Lawn, tree, shrubbery maintenance	☐	☐
Errands to the bank	☐	☐
House plant care	☐	☐
Straightening and rearranging closets	☐	☐
Getting house ready for guests	☐	☐
Party preparations	☐	☐
Buying children gifts	☐	☐
Taking children to school	☐	☐
Picking children up from school	☐	☐
Childcare after school	☐	☐
Child meals and lunches	☐	☐
Spending time with kids	☐	☐
Family outings with kids	☐	☐
Pediatrician	☐	☐
Dentist, orthodontist	☐	☐
Child homework	☐	☐
Child baths	☐	☐
Child discipline	☐	☐
Bedtime with kids	☐	☐
Dealing with a sick child	☐	☐
Handling child crises	☐	☐
Dealing with a child's emotions	☐	☐
Teacher conferences	☐	☐
Dealing with the schools	☐	☐
Special kid events	☐	☐
Kid birthday and other parties	☐	☐
Kid lessons	☐	☐
Kid play dates	☐	☐
Shopping for kids' stuff	☐	☐
Getting people presents	☐	☐
Keeping in touch with kin	☐	☐
Preparing for holidays	☐	☐
Planning vacations	☐	☐
Planning getaways	☐	☐
Romantic dates	☐	☐
Planning quiet evening at home	☐	☐
Planning weekends	☐	☐
Planning a special meal	☐	☐
General conversation	☐	☐
Planning a romantic evening	☐	☐
Initiating lovemaking	☐	☐
Planning dinner out	☐	☐
Family outings, drives, picnics	☐	☐

Table 13.4   Gottman Form for "Who Does What in the Marriage?" (continued)

	Currently Fine	Could Be Better
Financial planning	☐	☐
Major purchases (cars, etc.)	☐	☐
Managing investments	☐	☐
Talking about the relationship	☐	☐
Get together with friends	☐	☐
Keeping in touch with friends	☐	☐
Doing the taxes	☐	☐
Legal matters (e.g., wills)	☐	☐
Family medicine	☐	☐
Drugs and other health areas	☐	☐
Exercise and fitness	☐	☐
Recreational outings	☐	☐

had finally gotten some time alone and I was ready to turn to him again." Brett added, "And she did." After a month, Gail and Brett began talking about how to be closer with two children instead of one. Brett and Gail found ways to change their marriage and find time for just the two of them.

This approach is the model of resetting the negativity threshold, which we call "the marital poop detector." Go over the Marital Poop Detector questionnaire with clients (Table 13.5) and talk about how to use it to gently bring up an issue with one's partner (softened start-up). It is important that emotional distance not turn into quiet resentments that lead to silent negative attributions that get rehearsed every day when the two of them are apart. This can erode the Fondness and Admiration System very slowly, almost imperceptibly. We want them to monitor the occurrence of emotional distance and to talk it over soon and on their own.

There clearly needs to be some formalized time when the couple can get away from kids. This can be done with a baby-sitting cooperative they work out with a few other couples. The "date" should be considered sacrosanct, not to be broken, even when they are tired. Going out for coffee or a drive and talk in the car is fine—just keep the date.

MORE INTENSE AND RAPID TREATMENT COMBINED WITH FADING

There is some evidence that the timing of the intervention may make a major difference in long-term outcome in marital therapy. Boegner and Zielenbach-Coenen (1984) wrote:

> One main strategy for fostering maintenance of change is the gradual shift from therapist control to self-management during the course of therapy. The concept is that couples increase expertise and autonomy during treatment, gaining the competence to cope with their own problems during and after therapy. (p. 27)

Table 13.5   Marital Poop Detector

Instructions: Use this questionnaire to assess how things went in your marriage today (or lately), and whether you want to *gently* bring up an issue that will draw the two of you closer. Check as many as you think apply.

1. I have been irritable lately.
2. I have been feeling emotionally distant.
3. There has been a lot of tension between us.
4. I find myself wanting to be somewhere else.
5. I have been feeling lonely.
6. My partner has seemed emotionally unavailable to me.
7. I have been angry lately.
8. We have been out of touch with each other.
9. My partner has little idea of what I am thinking lately.
10. We have been under a great deal of stress and it has taken its toll on us.
11. I wish we were closer right now.
12. I have wanted to be alone a lot lately.
13. My partner has been irritable lately.
14. My partner has been emotionally distant.
15. My partner's attention seems to be somewhere else.
16. I have been emotionally unavailable to my partner.
17. My partner has been angry lately.
18. I have little idea of what my partner is thinking lately.
19. My partner has wanted to be alone a lot lately.
20. We really need to talk.
21. We haven't been communicating very well lately.
22. We have been fighting more than usual.
23. Lately small issues escalate.
24. We have been hurting one another's feelings lately.
25. There hasn't been very much fun or joy in our lives lately.
26. My partner seems to have no time or energy for me lately.
27. I have been feeling sorry for myself lately.
28. We have had little time or energy for physical affection.
29. We are not making love very much.
30. I wish my partner would touch me more often.

These authors also used an accelerated time schedule for the beginning of the intervention, using more frequent and longer sessions, while at the end of treatment they used longer sessions with scheduled "vacations" from therapy. The context for their experiment was the Munich Marital Therapy Clinic; they used the entire combined intervention (behavior exchange, training in problem-solving, and crisis management—see Hahlweg, Schindler, Revenstorf, & Brengelmann, 1984) and compared it to a format with fading and a waiting list control group. There were 6 couples in each of the two treatments and 12 couples in the waiting-list condition. Only questionnaires were used to evaluate treatment. The authors were the therapists; they were graduate students at the time, with two years of therapy experience. Despite this fact and the small number of subjects in each of the treatment conditions, this study is, in my view, one of the most important in the marital therapy literature.

There were 14 units or sessions of weekly therapy in the standard behavioral therapy in the Munich study. In the fading condition the authors conducted some longer sessions that combined units. Each of their fourth, fifth, and sixth sessions lasted 1½ hours and combined two of the standard units. Their seventh session lasted 3½ hours and combined four of the standard units. After the seventh session, the couple had a two-week break from therapy, and after the eighth session they had a 3-week break from therapy. During the break the therapist telephoned the couple once a week to check on the homework assignments. There was a follow-up at 2 months and again at 8 months after termination of the therapy.

Thus, in the fading condition two things happened. The clients received exactly the same therapy as the standard condition. They just received it in fewer sessions—9 instead of 14 weeks. Furthermore, there were two scheduled vacations from therapy, during which the therapist maintained telephone contact with the couples.

Both treatment groups did far better than the waiting-list control group. This is no surprise, due to the fact that distressed couples deteriorate massively in no-treatment control groups. However, the interesting thing about this study was the comparison between the two treatment groups. The scales used were: quarreling, tenderness, communication, problem severity, and general happiness. Tenderness was the only scale whose use surprised me, since working on tenderness was not part of either intervention.

At follow-up, couples in the intervention with fading, compared to those in the standard intervention, reduced their quarreling significantly more. The fading couples remained stable at the 8-month follow-up, while the standard treatment couples relapsed to pretreatment level. The fading procedure resulted in more tenderness after treatment than the standard treatment, but both groups relapsed at 8 months on this measure. The fading procedure resulted in less relapse in communication scores and ratings of problem severity at 8 months than the standard treatment. In terms of general happiness, at 8-month follow-up, the fading procedure couples scored in the happy range, while the couples in the standard treatment procedure scored in the unhappy range.

The evidence suggests that a condensed treatment with fading resulted in greater initial effects and less relapse than the standard treatment. The authors speculated that a more rapid and intense tackling of the couples' problems, combined with phased withdrawal of the therapist, initially gave them more hope for change and finally more of a sense of autonomy and confidence than the standard schedule, in which they came to rely on the therapist for maintaining changes. These methods have yet to be tested again in marital therapy, but this study suggests to me that they should become standard clinical practice.

When to Terminate Therapy: Successful Cases

I suggest that therapy can be terminated before this is a great marriage. The goal of marital therapy is to change the trajectory of the marriage, not its final state. That goal can be left to the couple to accomplish over a period of years. The goals of therapy can be considered as met when the spouses have the tools to make their last conversation better on their own. This means that they can effectively repair failed bids and that they can effectively repair a marital argument. They do not necessarily have to be able to do this while they are having the failed bid or the marital argument. If they can process the failure and make things better on their own, then the therapist can consider termination.

A more conservative approach is to consider termination when the following goals of the therapy are mostly met.

The setting conditions have changed.

- The Love Map has been created and it is getting used and updated regularly.
- The Fondness and Admiration System has been activated or reactivated.
- The couple has created positive sentiment override and its maintenance through re-setting the stable steady state of turning toward versus turning away.

The markers of dysfunction are reduced.

- The overt markers of divorce have been significantly and meaningfully reduced, particularly negative sentiment override, the Four Horsemen, or emotional disengagement.

The couple is dealing effectively with solvable problems.

- They are using softened start-up.
- They are accepting influence.
- They are using positive affect in the service of de-escalation.
- They show effective repair and de-escalation.
- They are handling any flooding well by applying methods of physiological soothing.
- They can move to compromise.

The couple has moved from gridlock to dialogue with perpetual issues.

- There is some positive affect (amusement) with the perpetual problem instead of emotional disengagement or the Four Horsemen.
- Partners feel basically liked and accepted, not rejected.
- They can honor and accept one another's dreams, to some degree.

The couple has the tools to avoid relapse.

- The couple has the tools, without the therapist, to make the next conversation better than their last—not just conflict conversations, but also conversations that involve previously failed bids.
- The threshold of the marital poop detector has been lowered significantly, and this is being used to deal with incipient signs of discord or emotional distance in a timely fashion.

- Rituals of emotional connection have been firmly established.
- The therapist feels that the couple will seek therapeutic help when things get tough (this is what John Reid calls the "dental model" of marital therapy, periodic checkups and prophylactic work).

THE MAGIC FIVE HOURS A WEEK

From following up the couples who have taken our weekend workshops (about 900 so far), we have been able to generate a hypothesis that the couples who continue to make progress after these workshops appear to be doing a number of things to restructure five hours a week of their time together. I have put these tips together into a hypothesis I call the "magic five hours." Here is what the amalgam of advice seems to be saying:

- *Partings.* Don't part in the morning without knowing one interesting thing that will happen in your spouse's day. (2 minutes a day × 5 working days: total 10 minutes)
- *Reunions.* Take 10 minutes to talk about your day (the stress-reducing conversation). Partners alternate in actively listening. Rule: Support and understanding must precede advice. (20 minutes a day × 5 days: total 1 hour 40 minutes)
- *Admiration and appreciation.* Find some way every day to genuinely communicate affection and appreciation toward your spouse. (5 minutes a day × 7 days: total 35 minutes)
- *Affection.* Kiss, hold, grab, touch each other. Play is good. Make sure to kiss each other before going to sleep and follow the admonition in Ephesians, "Do not let the sun set on your wrath." (5 minutes a day × 7 days: total 35 minutes)
- *Love Maps and arguing.* Take at least 2 hours a week for a marital date. During this date couples do a number of things, such as updating their Love Maps, turning toward one another, discussing conflictual issues, repairing failed bids, and often just asking one another how each is. Some think of questions to ask their spouses (e.g., "How are you thinking of changing the bedroom these days?" or "What would be your idea of a great getaway?" or "How are you thinking about your work these days?").

WHEN TO TERMINATE THERAPY: UNSUCCESSFUL CASES

Consider terminating when the Fondness and Admiration System is dead. Discuss the possibility of divorce with the couple. This sad piece of advice is all I have to offer at this point in my work. I don't know yet how to rekindle a marriage when there is no more fondness and admiration present. In most cases psychological abuse has taken over the now-dead Fondness and Admiration System, and the marriage is doing more harm than good to the spouses and to any children who may be a part of, or a witness to, these processes. Under these circumstances moving the couple toward a structured separation or divorce can be a positive event. My goal would be to move the spouses toward an amicable divorce through mediation, and to help them learn to co-parent in a cooperative and nonhostile fashion.

There are many reasons for these failures we can understand. The couple may have chosen one another poorly. Some mismatches are not solvable. Some dreams are incompatible. Some personalities result in so many perpetual problems that life is not pleasant. The cost-benefit analysis of one or both people doesn't add up to togetherness. Or the couple may have waited too long to seek treatment. There may have been too many betrayals in this relationship that

Table 13.6   Relapse Questionnaire

Instructions: We would like to see if you feel that any gains you made in treatment have relapsed or are in the process of relapsing. Please give your frank evaluation of the following items by circling either "DOING FINE" or "A PROBLEM NOW" for each item.

1. Communicating regularly (talking).	DOING FINE	A PROBLEM NOW
2. Maintaining emotional connection.	DOING FINE	A PROBLEM NOW
3. Physical affection.	DOING FINE	A PROBLEM NOW
4. Our sexual relationship.	DOING FINE	A PROBLEM NOW
5. Giving appreciations.	DOING FINE	A PROBLEM NOW
6. Talking about issues.	DOING FINE	A PROBLEM NOW
7. Conflict resolution.	DOING FINE	A PROBLEM NOW
8. Having regular fun.	DOING FINE	A PROBLEM NOW
9. Handling finances.	DOING FINE	A PROBLEM NOW
10. Work-family balance.	DOING FINE	A PROBLEM NOW
11. Our spiritual connection.	DOING FINE	A PROBLEM NOW
12. Respect in the marriage.	DOING FINE	A PROBLEM NOW
13. Knowing one another (Love Maps).	DOING FINE	A PROBLEM NOW
14. Flooding.	DOING FINE	A PROBLEM NOW
15. Recurring thoughts about divorce.	DOING FINE	A PROBLEM NOW
16. Handling children.	DOING FINE	A PROBLEM NOW
17. Housework and childcare.	DOING FINE	A PROBLEM NOW
18. Issues of power and respect.	DOING FINE	A PROBLEM NOW
19. Overall marital quality.	DOING FINE	A PROBLEM NOW
20. Issues of commitment.	DOING FINE	A PROBLEM NOW

21. Please give a description of how you see things in your marriage right now:

Check here if you wish to be called for an additional session:

_____   Marital session
_____   Individual session

Best times to reach you and phone numbers:

have resulted in bitterness, unforgivable resentment. The couple may have incompatible values. One function of therapy may have been to bring the couple to the brink of realizing that they would be better off apart. The goal of treatment then becomes negotiating an amicable divorce.

There are also those reasons for unsuccessful couples therapy that are harder to understand. They are best thought of as failures of the treatment, because this conclusion will lead us to design better interventions. Right now the biggest challenge is for therapies that deal with specific issues and comorbid psychopathologies. Examples are marital therapy when there is clinical depression, alcohol or other substance abuse, physical violence, an extramarital affair, previous abuse history or other traumas, sexual problems, a variety of parenting and/or child problems, or chronic physical illness (see Halford & Markman, 1997).

IN ALL CASES EXPECT RELAPSE: FOLLOW-UP SESSIONS

I advise scheduling regular follow-up reunion sessions every 6 months for a least 2 years. Use periodic phone call assessments. The Locke-Wallace and the Weiss-Cerreto inventories are adequate for assessing the current status of the marriage. Our Relapse Questionnaire is shown in Table 13.6. If you have concerns after scoring the questionnaire, call the couple in for a "reunion" meeting, as advised by Carlson and Sperry (1993).

Emotion and Meta-emotion

 The topic of emotion, emotion expression, and people's thoughts and feelings about the basic emotions comes up extremely often in working with couples. There is a lot of confusion in this area and myths about gender differences that are not helpful. It is my view that the concepts involved with meta-emotion clarify a great deal of the confusion in this area. People's feelings about emotion in general and specific emotions, their metaphors, and their philosophies are easily accessible and can be easily understood using the concepts explored in this chapter.

It is remarkable how often a couple's basic issues come down to two very different philosophies and life experiences about the expression and experience of emotion. Emotion and how people feel about expressing it appear to be central to almost all the therapy we do with couples. We have found a very effective way to explore the topic using our Meta-Emotion Interview and examining people's history, metaphors, and philosophy about each of the emotions.

Most of the time, meta-emotion mismatches fall along gender-stereotyped lines. Women are more likely to value the expression of emotion and see this as a road to intimacy, whereas men have a philosophy of emotion that emphasizes concealment, particularly of fear and sadness. Women are more likely to value expression and introspection when they feel sad or afraid, whereas men are more likely to believe that dwelling on these emotions is a waste of time or even potentially harmful. Men are more likely to hold a philosophy that positive thinking should supplant negative emotions. In the longitudinal study we began in 1986 we found that these mismatches alone create problems for marriages and predict divorce with 80% accuracy (Gottman et al., 1996).

We now ask people to think about the experiences they had with the following emotional states during their growing-up years:

- *Anger:*   When you got angry as a child; your parents' reaction to you; how they showed anger toward one another and toward you.

- *Sadness:*   When you expressed sadness, hurt, or disappointment as a child; how your parents expressed their own sadness, grief, and hurt.

- *Fear:*   How your parents dealt with your fears, and with their own; how they approached danger and safety.

- *Love:*   How your parents showed you that they loved you; how you showed it to them; what affection was like in your family growing up; how it is in your own marriage.

- *Pride:*   Your parents' pride in you; your own pride in yourself; how the two of you show one another that you are proud of one another.

- *Joy* (includes excitement):   How your parents showed delight and joy in life; how they responded to your joy and enthusiasm; how the two of you express joy.

People do not differ very much across the planet in their spontaneous expression and experience of emotion. They *do* differ greatly in how much awareness they have about the emotions they experience in their lives, how they think and feel about the basic emotions, how much they monitor their own emotions, how much they permit themselves to express emotion, and how well developed their language is for describing emotion. The language people have for emotion is very closely allied with the richness of their emotional experience. The emotion lexicon is not very difficult to develop in people. It can start with people keeping an emotion diary and having a list of emotion words in their wallet.

We can understand this area of people's lives on two levels. One level is general and analyzes people in terms of their philosophy toward emotion and its expression in general. Here people differ vastly in terms of whether they are dismissing of emotion or ready to explore it. There are huge implications of these two very general styles, both for marriages and for parent-child relationships. The second level concerns the way people feel about the specific emotions and is, in many ways, more interesting. A person can seem to be an emotionally expressive person, except, say, for a particular emotion, like sadness. She has essentially decided that she will never be sad, or that she will transmute any sad feelings into another emotion, like happiness or anger. This also has vast implications for the way this person relates to her own internal experience of sadness and loss and for the way she relates to others when they are sad.

George Lakoff (1993) suggested that, to understand how someone thinks about some aspect of his/her life, study his/her metaphors about it. As we go through some of these metaphors for sadness and anger, we can imagine the implications of having these metaphors for dealing with one's child's sadness or anger. In this chapter I will explore these areas of a person's emotional world and discuss what they may mean for marriages; in the next chapter I will look at the implications for parent-child relationships.

A CASE OF META-EMOTION MISMATCH

This case demonstrates what I call the "Timothy Smith intervention," based on some research he did on hypertension in marriage. This intervention is particularly effective in getting an emotionally disengaged male to confront how he feels about his wife's emotionality. In the Smith intervention both people are told to argue tooth and nail for their points of view, very much as they would in a debate. They each think of counter-arguments that their spouse would be likely to raise and how to effectively destroy those counter-arguments. Smith got a lot of hostility and increased blood pressure from his intervention, so I modified his intervention just a little. I said, "Don't be a brick wall. Accept influence on smaller points. To be really influential give a bit on more peripheral points in favor of winning on the big points. Don't be unreasonable, but be strong and active." This turned out to change the intervention considerably.

This intervention was originally designed to be used with a control group. I thought that it would be the opposite of the validation (active listening) intervention. But my version of the Smith intervention appears to work like a charm for most couples who are facing emotional disengagement due to meta-emotion mismatch. It is far better than the active listening intervention.

In the following case, we will see pre- and post-intervention conversations. The second is the kind of conversation the therapy needs to make happen so the couple can deal with mismatches. They are talking about the mismatch itself. She is lonely and he is scared by their differences. This is a remarried couple. Each of them has two children, and all four children live with the couple all the time. They have been married for two years.

The Pre-intervention Conversation

I haven't included this conversation, but if you were to watch this videotape, you would see in this conversation characteristics of a couple in the early stages of emotional withdrawal. There is almost no positive affect. There is very little facial expressiveness, and their voices are somewhat flat, without the rises and falls of inflection that characterize engagement. They seem detached, not very interested in what they are discussing. Yet, they are also telling one another that everything is okay. They are trying to adapt to a situation in which they really are quite unhappy but do not feel entitled to their complaints. Some inexperienced clinicians to whom I have shown this interaction say that they would not think anything was wrong with this couple. Indeed, the spouses are saying that everything is fine. The clue that everything is not fine is the near absence of any positive affect.

The Post-intervention Conversation

This conversation was dramatically different from the first one. The husband, who was very quiet and passive in the former conversation, has become very active here in getting to the point.

H: Do you understand the . . . well, I'm the one that selected *pacing* as the conflict in our marriage. Did you understand what I meant by that?

W: Uh-huh. I think so.

H: We've had this discussion before. There are different styles. For me, it's led into conflict because I don't like feeling pressured into going faster than I want to, or doing something that I don't want to do, or doing it out of obligation. I know I do a lot of things out of obligation, but I don't like being put in a position where I have to do that. It has something to do with the pacing, that, um . . . my observation is that you're a more intense person and react more emotionally, and, um . . . more quickly, but with more emotion, more intensity behind it. As we were talking before, I'm more deliberative and act in my own sweet time, I guess. I have to figure out the proper reaction. I think that there's validity in both styles, but *I like to honor my style* because I think that, particularly in this last year, there's been a lot of stress in our marriage, with blending our families and having the four kids and scheduling and how hectic it was. I need to hold onto that slowness, I guess, to have some sense of control over the situation. *There's so much emotion going on already, that to me it works better to react with less emotion, to sort of tone it down.* [emphasis mine]

Here the husband says that he thinks his style of dealing with stressful situations in their marriage ought to be "honored" more than it is. He thinks that his style is slower, calmer, and that things *work better with less emotion. That's the key to his points.*

W: But what emotions are you feeling? I mean, you're feeling some of the emotions yourself, but that you'd like to show them less?

His wife, very gently, but also in more animated fashion, talks about emotion, not as an all-or-none thing (you are emotional or not emotional), but as highly differentiated.

H: Um, yes, I am feeling emotions but it's a strategy I use, a natural strategy to not show them so much, to not react or overreact so emotionally. I guess I'm afraid that an emotional reaction to an emotional situation will only bring up more emotion!

He is beginning to express his philosophy that expressing emotion when things are already emotional is like throwing gasoline on an open flame. His wife senses this.

W: And then?

H: And then, I don't know. I guess that's where I feel uncomfortable and I don't know where it's going to lead. It doesn't seem to have any direction or purpose.

Here is the meta-emotional belief that introspection about emotion is purposeless and unhelpful.

W: Well, how do you know if it never gets that far? It's pretty hard to say, isn't it? But, are you saying that over this last year, you purposely didn't have emotions, or you tried to "honor your style" because it seemed to work better . . . because there was already so much emotion? So when I'm having a lot of emotion, you can't have so much emotion because it will add too much emotion and the whole thing can blow up sky high? Is that . . . .

H: Yeah. That's pretty accurate.

She picked up on his hidden explosion metaphor when she said "blow sky high." He agrees that this is what he wants to avoid. This crystallizes a problem that she has been feeling in their relationship: that she down-regulates her emotional expressions for his sake.

W: Yeah, you know, I was thinking in listening to you here that I've been doing what I did growing up—tailoring my emotions so that I don't have them as often. I mean, it's caused me a lot of anxiety to repress my feelings and try to be more logical and rational and go in a room by myself and not get . . . I don't know, it would be nice to . . . it would be nice for me to have more reaction from you.

She is stating her case, and now she backs up how productive she thinks it is for him to be emotionally expressive.

W: Just even the littlest things, like lately with you reacting more to Matthew. . . . I mean, your face changes, you show more emotion, because this is a challenge to you that I can't do, and I can't solve the problem, and I don't have to deal with it. It just, I don't know, it feels good. Not only is it a relief but it feels like you're participating more in life. You know, sometimes I'm left alone doing it [parenting]. I guess I've felt better in the last few weeks just because you've been coming more in my direction, for whatever reasons, whatever feelings you got, coming from a feeling, an emotion that you had, and that feels really good. It's like you're more vulnerable, like there's something you need from me, not just the other way around. I've been in distress and I've had these feelings, and it's not great to feel like that—I mean, to feel that loneliness.

H: Yeah, well, the last few months are a good example. I feel freer to express my emotions because the rest of my life is more stable. So now it feels like it's okay.

He is telling her that he can only express emotion when things are calm. That won't do for her.

W: Yeah, but you can't . . . you mean that the minute our kids react, I'm not going to get any kind of attention anymore? You're going to get all focused on holding down the fort, so to speak, emotionally, keeping everything stuffed down there so that. . . . I think I react sometimes so that I don't rock the boat, so that you won't withdraw your love for me. That doesn't really work because then underneath that, I feel like it's too high a price to pay sometimes, for me, too much stuffing so that you won't, you know. . . . Well, what's going to happen if you *have* to feel more and express more, and come out more because you have to do it? What's going to happen? Obviously, I think something bad, too.

Notice how understanding and accepting she is being even though she is still confronting this perpetual issue. They have all the skills they need to establish a dialogue with this issue. Now he brings up feeling competitive with her.

H: Well, part of what's going on is I . . . you're so much better at expressing your emotions. I think you are. You verbalize so much better, that I feel at a disadvantage to you, so I don't . . . it's like we get into a competition almost.
W: Oh.
H: And if you're expressing emotion, then I feel I have to match your emotion, and I can't do it, so it's like I don't even want to try. Whereas when things are more neutral, and there isn't a lot of emotion going on, if I express emotion—like that's setting the tone—then you can easily match that or exceed it and I don't feel so bad. But when you're the one that is expressing a lot of intense emotions, um . . .
W: You feel competitive that you can't, so you don't.

Notice how understanding they are being with one another even in the face of confrontation. There is a lot of affection in their interaction, and soon there will be humor as well.

H: Yeah. I can't . . . [*turning toward therapist*] I mean, does she want me to react to the same level of intensity she is? I can't do it.
W: Well, who says that's what I want?
H: I don't know. [*Both laugh.*]

Here we see the emergence of some amusement about their differences.

W: Well, I understand what you're saying. I can see that. I've learned those dynamics.

She is understanding, but this raises another issue for her.

W: But I don't . . . it puts me at an unfair advantage because then I'm the one who has to change my behavior, because my options are, change my behavior or I won't get a reaction. Your options are, wait till I change my behavior, then feel free to come out. Um, that's what sometimes just feels not equitable, like I have to do all the compromising. I think it was apparent last year because I said that, I have to compromise so much with my reactions to my teenager. I have to try all these techniques that go against my very nature, which is not totally healthy all the time, and these are good techniques, but it's a lot of stress to feel like, oh my god, I have to . . .

Now here comes the big issue for their marriage:

> W: . . . and if I want support from my husband, I have to tone myself
> way down so that he can feel comfortable enough to kind of come out
> and, um, I don't know. . . . It's been better these last few weeks
> because I went through, um . . . there is so much torment when you're
> gone, fantasizing just how this is not going to work, this pacing, this
> whole thing, this whole . . . the problem is, I don't know how I can
> tone myself down all the time. I can't guarantee that. And I like the sta-
> bility and I like some equanimity, too. The price I have to pay for it
> sometimes seems so great, and I feel like I'm the one who's done more
> of the work to change my behavior. It would be nice to have you do
> some more.

She is very worried about having brought this up.

> W: How does that feel to even have me say that? It seems like I don't say
> that anymore. I don't know . . .
> H: Yeah, well that's . . .
> W: It's taboo.
> H: Huh?
> W: It's taboo. It's one of the taboos. You don't ask people to . . .
> H: Yeah, well, it does cause anxiety in me because it feels like I'm being
> asked to change or do something that I'm uncomfortable doing. I
> understand your point when you say that you feel like you're the one
> who has to do all the work then in changing. Your choices are to be
> your natural self and be disappointed because you're not getting the
> reaction that you're looking for, or, um, letting go . . .

Here he has communicated to her that he understands her dilemma. But he
is going to argue about it as well.

> H: I mean, you're not totally giving up who you are, I don't think. But not
> bringing it up to me is not being totally dishonest to yourself. You've
> still got other people who you can talk to, um, I don't know . . . bring
> it up in a different context, more of . . . an element of style rather
> than substance, unless you're saying the way in which you release your
> emotions and express yourself is so intertwined with who you are that
> you can't do it a different way. Because that makes a big difference to
> me. I mean, it's not my natural self to even talk about my feelings and
> emotions, but I'm willing to, you know, if approached a certain way,
> and I think you have to get used to saying things exactly the right
> way. I think definitely there is a wrong way and a right way of
> doing it.
> W: Well, I'd like to be approached a different way, too. The right way for
> me. You have a right way for you that works, that I've been searching
> for, and I'd like you to do that for me, too.
> H: Well, um, I don't know what has worked well the last couple of

months—whether it's the absence of crises elsewhere in our lives that's not pulling us off in different directions and we can focus more on us, just maybe probably letting it go to try to figure it out and solve it and . . . then our more natural feelings toward each other come out.

W: Well, I don't think, for me, it's so much a global thing as you were saying earlier—that you feel that so much of these pressures have eased that you feel you can do more, and I'm sure that's true. But to me, I feel like the real control is not waiting for everything to be perfect and then focusing on some of the positive things. I was alone for those days when you were gone, and that was good because I could really feel and honor my feelings for those days when you were on Mt. Rainier. I could cry when I wanted to, I could eat when I wanted to, I could do everything the way I wanted to without compromising for my children or you, because getting feedback is important to me.

H: I think that's good.

W: It was good, it was good, but it's . . .

Now they begin to realize that this will be one of their perpetual problems.

H: It was good for me too, because the other person can't do everything for you. I'll never meet your expectations.

W: Well, I know.

H: And you will never meet all of mine.

W: It's amazing how many more you meet when two things happen: You lower your expectations, and also you have a chance to feel how you feel. Because you don't like to be pressured to feel a certain way. I don't like to be pressured to *not* feel, to *not* show anything, to make everything seem neutral. I know that your ultimate goal is probably so that . . .

Now all this has made it possible for him to ask her some basic questions about herself that he has never explored with her.

H: Why do you feel so much?

W: Why?

H: No, really. Because you have such high expectations?

W: No, I don't think it's all that. I think it's being *aware* and sensing things. To me, it feels alive. It doesn't feel bad to cry. It doesn't feel bad to feel things. What feels bad is to have a block in front of those feelings, like it's not okay. That feels bad, you know.

He is more aware of her negative feelings, and he thinks her feeling so much is an indication that something is wrong. He suspects that she may just be pessimistic, and that's why she has so many feelings. He thinks this comes from her expectations being too high.

H: It seems like a lot of your feelings stem from a disappointment in the way things are, or turn out, with the kids and so forth.

W: No, some are positive.

Now he also tries to become more understanding of her perspective.

H: And, unfortunately, you've been saddled with three, four males. Out of six people in the family there are four males who tend to show less emotion, and I think that it would be interesting if it was the other way around, if there were more girls in the family.

W: Well, Leah isn't exactly a . . .

H: Yeah, she doesn't show a lot of emotion either.

W: She's very . . . she's the most reticent.

H: You stick out because you're, by far, the one who shows the most emotion.

W: I think one time we were talking about it before how—if you were more participatory, expressed more of yourself, that would set the tone more.

In this second conversation both people have felt free to admit that the differences between them in the area of emotion have been very stressful. She has been trying to tone herself down so he won't get scared, but she has ended up feeling lonely. He has been terrified of how emotional she gets and feeling competitive with her at the same time. They both want to find a balance between their two styles. All this was hidden in the first conversation. Will this problem now be solved? No, I think not. These issues are so fundamental that this will always be a perpetual issue in this marriage. But now they have started a dialogue on the issue, instead of the trajectory they were on—emotional disengagement.

OTHER SOURCES OF MISMATCHES: EMOTION METAPHORS

Most of my research with meta-emotion and emotion metaphors was done in the context of longitudinal research on the relationship between marriage, parenting, and emotional and social development in children. Only recently have we extended the meta-emotion work to couples and included the emotions of fear, pride, and love in our interview. Therefore, the summary that follows is based in large measure on the longitudinal work with people about their history with the specific emotions of sadness and anger, and how it relates to their parenting. In the meta-emotion interview we also explore feeling out of control with respect to either sadness or anger. One scale of our meta-emotion coding system contains items that assess the parents' feeling out of control, with either sadness or anger. For both sadness and anger, the items on this scale are: The person has difficulty regulating the intensity of the emotion, the emotion occurs often, the emotion is difficult to get over, the emotion has been a problem or a concern, the person thinks this emotion can be dangerous, and the person has needed help with this emotion. Some of our subjects said that they avoided the emotion of anger or sadness and structured their lives to do so, but this was too small a percentage of subjects to study, and the dimension does not seem to be the same as suppression. We have grouped all of the reactions to sadness and anger into three categories: positive, somewhat but not entirely positive, and negative.

Sadness Metaphors

Positive Sadness Metaphors

Those people who have positive metaphors for sadness say that it is productive, that it is there for a reason, that sadness informs you about some aspect of your life, that it makes you slow down and reflect. They say that sadness is good because it means you can feel and empathize, that it is sometimes pleasant to feel sad in some movies, and that there is such a thing as a "good cry." For example, one husband said:

> I do think that sadness can hit you and there could be a very positive reason for that happening when it does. You could be going through very fast times, and sadness could be a reason to slow down and to think about what you're doing or where you've been or what's happening to you.

The views of this man's wife were similar:

> I think sadness is real important. I think that if you don't feel sadness at some point, you're missing a big part of the importance of life.

Another woman talked about sadness as a healing experience:

> I don't think you can ignore your feelings. Maybe I tend to overdo it, you know, but I just don't like to ignore them. *It's kind of a cleansing thing.* You know, if you ignore your problems, they're just going to come back and bother you later, so if you feel sad, deal with it, find out why you feel sad.

One woman talked about the positive aspects of feeling sad and mentioned the "good cry."

> I have a good cry at the drop of the hat. I mean, I could watch a sad movie and cry [*laughs*] and just cry—quietly, you know.

Somewhat But Not Entirely Positive Sadness Metaphors

In contrast to these people, others had metaphors for sadness that were not positive but not negative either. One husband viewed sadness as if it were a limited positive resource, like the amount of money in a checking account. He was concerned that sadness not be "spent" on trivial matters . . .

> . . . like losing a toy or tearing a page in a book or something like that is not something to waste your time being sad on. You save sadness for, you know, [*laughs*] the death of a pet, or something like that.

This man, who was a father, reacted to his daughter's sadness in a very complex manner, ignoring some expressions entirely and being very supportive during others. His responsiveness conveyed to her some amount of judgment, that he did not approve of her being sad on this occasion because it is not important enough in his eyes, but he did approve on other occasions. What will she learn from this philosophy of her father's about being sad?

Other ambivalent responses to sadness depended on factors such as how long the sadness lasted. One man said:

You know, when somebody has a death in their family or a major crisis in their family, you've got every right to sit around and get yourself together. But, for my own case, I wouldn't want that to be a prolonged period of time. I wouldn't, you know, sit in the corner in a sack cloth for six months or something.

This man went on to say that, contrary to the prevailing view, in his view being sad is okay for men and boys, as long as it is over in due time.

I think that it's okay to be sad. Maybe that's part of the thing, maybe that's something that, especially for men in America, it hasn't been okay for them to be for a long time. I think that maybe that's part of the way I was brought up—it's okay to be sad but it's not something to dwell on forever, it's something that you have to pull yourself out of eventually.

Negative Sadness Metaphors

Other people were far less ambivalent in their negativity toward sadness. Some viewed sadness as toxic. An example was one husband who feared that sadness was just the beginning of a major pathological condition:*

I: What do you think would happen if you stay sad?
H: I don't know. I've never been there. I don't know. It would be poor judgment, I guess.
I: Do you ever see other people when they get really sad?
H: Um-hmm. We had a schizophrenic skitzo living near us, so we knew from what she was like—we could see that she was always, you know, didn't smile much.
I: Um-hmm, um-hmm. So what do you think it did to her?
H: Almost killed her. [*pause*] It almost killed her.
I: So it's a really bad thing.
H: Must be.

Some people view sadness as appropriate particularly when a death has occurred. One man said:

When I think about sadness, the first thing that comes to mind is death. A loved one dying, you feel sad. A kid may feel that way more toward an animal or a possession. When I was a kid I remember my grandpa died, and it was really the first death in the family. I was in fifth grade. It was the same month as John Kennedy's death. Both of those things affected me in being sad. Then I looked at my parents and saw how they were handling it. It's part of life. Going to the funeral, they said, "Eric, you're mature enough to go to the funeral." And I was really thankful that they felt that way toward me rather than keep me home with a baby sitter. They let me go and it was my first experience. I felt sadness but then I felt very—not relieved—I felt a part of the family, that I could go to the funeral and look at my grandpa lying there. That was the first experience I ever had with it. I guess I'm relating deaths to sadness [*laughs*], but I don't really know of anything of late that I've been really sad about.

*I = interviewer; H = husband; W = wife; F = father; M = mother.

When discussing their children, some parents see sadness as unproductive, as a state to be altered and changed. One father equated sadness with depression:

Oh, nothing good can ever come out of depression unless you come out of depression. A depressed mood to me is a useless time. It's when you're doing nothing constructive whatsoever. You're feeling sorry for yourself, if nothing else.

One father felt it best not to react at all when his daughter is sad.

I classify myself as a realist in the scheme of life. I try to look at things and see them, at least as close as I can, as what they are. She's sad. What am I going to do? Am I going to go tickle her chin or cheer her up? I don't know if that's really what you need to do. I think a lot of times people need to work out their own problems.

Some parents viewed sadness in themselves as a time when they wanted to be alone and not talk to anyone about their feelings:

The times that I've really been sad about things, I've always kept it to myself. [*laughs*]

In treatment it is important to explore the history of these feelings and metaphors toward sadness because they greatly affect the way people conduct themselves in everyday life, even around moments that involve minor disappointments or losses. What happens when husband and wife have a very different set of metaphors about sadness? In one example we saw recently, a man who was an emergency room physician was married to a woman who had a chronic problem with depression. Rather than viewing her problem medically, he saw it as malingering. He told her that he saw people every day whose problems were far worse than her own, that she was making a mountain out of a molehill. He didn't want to listen to her being sad; he wanted her to cheer up. He had no respect for her struggles with her own sadness; he was simply fed up with her. The effect this had on her was to make her feel more alone and more worthless.

Anger Metaphors

Positive Anger Metaphors

We have found that many metaphors in the Meta-Emotion Interview suggest that anger is viewed by some as energizing. One woman said that anger gave her motivation: "I feel anger just gets me to say things that I've been wanting to say." This sentiment was also reflected by another woman:

[*sigh*] I think it's invigorating at first, because I'll find myself saying, well, to hell with it, I'm angry, let it all hang out. And [*laughs*] I'll just go off and I'll say what I feel, but then after a while I don't feel really good about that I've done it, that I've let go.

This idea of anger as positive because it makes it possible to let go of some built-up pressure was expressed in the following excerpt:

Well, you know, if you're working on something that doesn't go right, you get real mad, and I think it *lets off some steam* and kind of clears your head once it's over with. And it kind of relaxes you once it's over with.

A commonly expressed view was that anger was productive in that it showed people they could not push the angry person around. As one man said, "It wasn't that wrong because it made a point that I can't be pushed around so much."

At a minimum many people expressed the idea that anger is positive because it requires one to have contact with people, that it entails communication. For example, one woman said:

> I think if you're angry about something, then it calls for communication. You're angry, you need to communicate with somebody or about some issue or something that's making you angry, and to do it in such a way that it's going to help the situation and not make it worse.

Somewhat But Not Entirely Positive Anger Metaphors

Some expressed the view that anger, *if controlled,* was acceptable and even positive. One man said: "I mean, it's right to have anger but kind of control it." This idea was reinforced by a woman who said that, for her, not expressing anger was to court an embarrassing explosion:

> And my sister was the sweetest thing. She still is. She's just as sweet as she can be. She takes so much, I wouldn't take half of the stuff she takes on one given day, you know. She has a real picky, picky husband now. She takes and she takes and boy, you think, wow, why is she letting him get away with these things? And then, when she decides to let loose, it is so [*laughs*] embarrassing for you sitting there with him, till you feel so badly for him.

This view was often expressed as a "hydraulic" metaphor, that is, if unexpressed, the pressure of the anger would have to come out somewhere else. For example, one mother said, about her children:

> Yeah, they see me get angry quite often with other things and I try not to, you know. I don't like arguing in front of them because I feel that that would make them more nervous. I try not to get angry in front of them. I try to calm down. But if I get angry I try to calm down, you know, before, but things will pop up [*laughs*], if I get angry with something else.

Negative Anger Metaphors

The most common negative set of metaphors accompanying anger involved *fire* and *explosion.* Here's an example: "I don't like it, because I think, 'This is the only way that I can get something done.' I don't like it. *I don't like blowing up.* [*laughs*] It makes me feel bad afterwards."

Some parents view the expression of anger as destructive:

> She's learning with sadness, too, but anger is for a four-year-old just so much more exciting than it is to sit down and cry. Maybe because it shows a lot more different things; it shows destruction. If she's being destructive, I don't like it.

This father explains that when he was younger, anger did imply his being destructive.

The following comment from a father describes anger as uncivilized:

It gets back to reasoning. You know, you ought to be able to reason and talk with people. *Civilized people should be able to reason things out without getting hostile toward each other.*

Some parents equate anger with aggression. When this father was asked what he wanted to teach his child about anger, he immediately connected it to teaching her to avoid becoming aggressive:

I just think, we're just trying to bring her up to be ready to deal with things as they come up. She's starting school next year. You know, all little kids at one time or another might have a problem with other little kids because they do things to hurt each other. We want her to realize that that could happen and for her to not automatically turn around and strike back and hurt them back. Maybe if she has a problem to go to someone, an authority, you know, rather than just taking matters into her own hands.

We were surprised by the fact that many parents expressed the view that *a child's anger should be punished, regardless of whether it involves misbehavior.* The mother in the following excerpt suggests that she has some ambivalence about how she supports her child's sadness but punishes his anger:

I'm just sort of realizing that maybe there is some kind of a double standard between letting him cry, that's okay, but with anger, the message I give is "Don't have it. Go upstairs, get rid of it, and then come down and be pleasant." I can deal with the crying, I can say, "Poor Max," and stroke his head, but when he's mad I don't say, "Poor Max," and stroke his head, I say, "Take it somewhere else. I don't want to hear it." I don't know. It's kind of interesting.

In our interviews we heard a fair number of very negative views of anger that had to do with extreme bodily functions. One parent had such a negative view of the expression of anger that he used the metaphor *when people get angry they are relieving themselves on others.* Another called it mastication, chewing on others; another said that it was vomiting on others; another that it was drowning. Some parents expressed the view that anger was best left unexpressed, or that anger and hurt always go together, or that people who were angry should be quarantined, or that it was shameful if people saw you angry, or that if a person were healthy he/she would show no anger. Clearly, these negative concepts about anger will affect the way a parent responds to the child's anger. Many of our parents used a variety of punishments, such as spanking and time-out, solely for the child's expression of anger (not misbehavior).

Overall Emotion Philosophy

General philosophy of emotion fell into three categories: those in favor of emotional expression, those opposed to it, and those advocating finding a balance between positive and negative emotions. The positive philosophy contends that it is important to get emotions "out of your system." Some expressed the concept that emotions are always there, a part of life, and that a "constructive pattern" of dealing with them is needed. Those who opposed expressing one's emotions said that negative emotion must be endured, plowed through, overcome, or simply waited out because the *passage of time* alone will solve emotional problems.

A common point of view we saw in our data was that negative emotion must be *balanced* by positive emotion. Or the philosophy might be expressed that to get over a negative emotion, just get on with life's routines. Another view was to accentuate the positive instead of harping on the negative, and some saw positive emotion as an antidote to the toxicity of negative emotion. A pragmatic, problem-solving view of the expression of emotion in cost-benefit terms was expressed. Common elements of the balance philosophy are the idea of not losing control and the idea that one can change one's feelings at will.

Summary on Discrepancy in Emotion Philosophy

The issue in marriages is usually the discrepancy between spouses about these meta-emotions. People who agree on generally being dismissing about particular emotions do not seem to have any conflict in their marriages in this realm. One cannot then decide that people *ought* to have particular attitudes about each emotion.

In general, though, the philosophy of emotion that has proven most productive with children is that the way to deal with an emotion is *through* the emotion. To use science fiction language, the emotion is the "wormhole" for passing through the experience. Emotions do have a purpose and a meaning—they inform us about what we are experiencing, and they provide a direction in our lives.

In couples therapy it is useful for people to at least understand how and why they have created their own culture about emotion in their marriage and family. The conjoint Meta-Emotion Interview can facilitate the acquisition of this insight and understanding.

Chapter 15 🐚

Buffering Children from Marital Conflict

 This chapter describes our longitudinal work researching children's emotional and social development and the development of emotional intelligence. Our work with meta-emotion and emotion-coaching is described in this chapter as one method for buffering children from the deleterious consequences of continued marital hostility, in which the children are used to get at one's marital partner or ex-partner. The brilliant clinical work of Haim Ginnot is reviewed as central to our research findings.

For the past 15 years my laboratory has been investigating the degree to which marital discord is transferred to the developing child. We have been searching for buffers against the deleterious effects of marital conflict on children. The question that motivated this research was, Is there anything that parents in an ailing marriage can do to buffer their children? Our longitudinal research suggests one possible answer to this question.

EMOTION-DISMISSING VS. EMOTION-COACHING PARENTS

In brief, in our meta-emotion interviews we discovered two basic types of parents: *emotion-dismissing* (ED) and *emotion-coaching* (EC). Emotion-dismissing parents:

- Don't notice lower-intensity emotions in kids or self.
- View negative affects as toxins.
- Want a cheerful child and see an unhappy child as a failing of their parenting.

- Want to protect their child from ever feeling any negative affect.
- Believe that staying in a negative affect state a long time is harmful, and are impatient with negative affect.
- Believe in accentuating the positive in life.
- Will try to distract, cheer up, tickle, use food, etc., to change the child's negative affect quickly.
- See examining the negative affect as a waste of time or potentially destructive.
- Don't have a very detailed language for emotions.

Here are some examples. One emotion-dismissing father in our studies said about his son: "If one of his friends took his toy or hit him, I say, don't worry about it, he probably didn't mean it or he'll give it back, but just don't dwell on it. Roll with the punches." Another father said about his daughter, "If she is sad I try to find out her needs. I say, 'What do you need? Do you need to go outside? Do you need to watch TV? Do you need to eat something?' Just respond to her needs. But usually she is never sad." This is distraction carried to an extreme.

Being raised by emotion-dismissing parents has profound consequences. One story that was particularly poignant came from an interview I recently conducted. I asked the woman if there was anything special about her marital relationship. By way of answering my question, she told of recently unpacking a "smiley face" calendar from her childhood and explained that her parents would put a smiley face sticker on the day's box if she had been cheerful that day. If she earned 20 smiley faces a month, she could get some special toy. She said that her husband seemed to be interested in being with her no matter what mood she was in. Even if she were depressed or in a crabby mood, he still wanted to listen to her and be near her. That was a first in her life. (By the way, she grew up to be a professional football cheerleader.)

Emotion-coaching parents have entirely different meta-emotions. Here are their characteristics:

- They notice lower-intensity affects in their kids.
- They see the negative affects as an opportunity for intimacy or teaching.
- They see the child's experiencing negative affect as healthy or even part of the growth of the child.
- They are not impatient with the negative affect.
- They communicate understanding and empathy.
- They help the child verbally label feelings.
- If there is misbehavior, they try to understand the feelings that underlie the misbehavior.
- Finally, they set clear limits on behavior, problem-solve with the child, and discuss with the child what he/she can do in certain situations.

We now think that these differences have implications for how the child's brain processes what are called the "withdrawal emotions" (sadness, fear, and disgust). They are called withdrawal emotions because they make you want to withdraw from the world, unlike joy, interest, affection, and anger, which make you want to interact with the world. Emotion-coaching, we think, adds a sense of control and optimism to the experience of the withdrawal emotions. The child is still sad or afraid but feels more in control and feels more optimistic about things as well. This may have profound implications for how the child's autonomic nervous system bounces back from physiological arousal, as mediated by the vagus nerve.

Thanks to a brilliant undergraduate honors thesis by Vanessa Kahen, we found that in *the teaching situation* ED parents and EC parents teach in very different ways. Table 15.1 summarizes these dramatic differences.

Let me share a story that shows the profound impact of such teaching experiences on a child. I recently read a book called *Sons on Fathers* (Keyes, 1992), a collection of reminiscences about fathers written by their very successful sons. One chapter was written by Christopher Hallowell. His major memory of his dad was an incident that happened when Christopher was about six years old. His father called him into his woodshop and said, "Son, today I am going to teach you how to make a box. If you can build a box, you can build anything in the woodshop." His father showed him how to use the angle vises, and so on. Young Christopher then worked by himself for a long time, and he built a box that he recalled was a bit shaky, but it even had a lid on it, and he proudly showed it to his dad. His dad said, "Son, this is a wobbly box. If you can't build a box, you'll never be able to build anything." To this day the young man, who is also now a father, keeps that box on his dresser table. He wrote that he cannot open the lid of the box without seeing his father's face in the lid saying to him, "You'll never be able to do anything." His father actually never said that, but Christopher's memory is very powerful indeed.

There is another story that Haim Ginott told about a little boy named Stuart. Ginott was in a school one morning when an elementary school teacher told him

Table 15.1 Differences in Teaching Styles of EC and ED Parents

Emotion-Coaching	Emotion-Dismissing
1. Give child very little information, enough to get started, in a calm manner.	1. Give child lots of information in an excited manner.
2. Are not involved with the child's mistakes.	2. Are very involved with the child's mistakes.
3. Wait for the child to do something right, then praise child's performance specifically.	3. Wait for the child to make a mistake and then criticize child's performance.
4. Give child a bit more information ("scaffolding").	4. Then they escalate the criticism to: insults, trait labels, intrusiveness, belittling, and mockery.

that today she was going to read a very compassionate poem to the class. She was having some trouble getting the class to sit down. Stuart was clowning around when she said, "Stuart! What is wrong with you? Do you need a special invitation to sit down, or are you just naturally slow?" Stuart finally sat down, and Ginott said that the teacher then read this very sensitive poem to the class, but Stuart was not listening because he was busy planning the details of his teacher's funeral. This example also illustrates the idea that *process is everything in the area of emotion.* You can only teach respect respectfully, and you can only teach compassion by being compassionate. That's how children learn. They learn both parts of the role—the way they feel and your part also.

Emotion-dismissing parents can be very warm, but this dimension of emotion-dismissing or -coaching has nothing to do with warmth. We have seen many parents, in response to their child's sadness, say, very warmly, "Sweetheart, cheer up. Just put a smile on your face. Now that's better, isn't it?" A parent can be very caring and affectionate and still be dismissing of a child's negative emotions.

THE CONTRIBUTION OF HAIM GINOTT

Ginott was, in my view, our most brilliant child psychologist. Whereas most other parenting approaches focus on noncompliant children and discipline, Ginott noted that if we were completely successful with these approaches we would produce only *obedient children.* Also, he claimed, we would produce children whose morality was what Selma Fraiberg (1959) called a "bookkeeping" mentality, evaluating actions in terms of rewards and punishments. A purely external reward and punishment approach to morality interferes with the normal development of conscience, which is based on identifying with the parent. When contemplating an immoral act, like hitting a younger child, the child sometimes goes through reasoning along the lines of: "What will it cost me? What will I gain? Oh, well, it's worth it." Morality becomes a cost-benefit analysis. There is no internal code based on empathy, ethics, values, or justice.

Ginott disagreed with many books on parental discipline that advised parents to be unemotional when disciplining their child. In emotion-coaching, the basis of discipline can be the parent's genuine anger or disappointment with the child when the child has done something the parent thinks is wrong. However, the anger should not get translated into insulting or belittling comments. The strong emotional bond formed through emotion-coaching is disrupted by these parental emotions following the child's misbehavior, and the child wants to set things right again, to reestablish closeness. Hence, Ginott argued that the parent should not be unemotional when disciplining a child, but use these real emotions (in a non-insulting manner) to let the child know how the parent feels. The parent's anger and disappointment are the parent's most powerful tools in discipline, Ginott counseled.

Ginott taught us that the most important moments to focus on in parent-child interaction are those moments when the child is emotional. This was a very big conceptual break from the psychoanalytic stress on projection through play.

The child is not asked to recreate an event and then to discuss it. Many teachers who seek to teach children about emotion do so by taking a calm group of kids and asking them about when they felt angry. Ginott argued that this is not how kids learn about anger. They learn about it when they are actually angry. Then, when they are angry once again, they will have access to this learning. Learning about emotion is state-dependent.

But, more importantly, Ginott gave us a complete approach to parenting, not just an approach to discipline. These insights have been corroborated by our research. What were some of his insights?

1. He asked, "What is different about the language I must use with children?" He answered, "We avoid expressions that judge a child's character or ability. We describe what we see, what we feel."

Criticism: "I see the milk spilled, here is a rag.   *Not:* "You are so clumsy, clean it up or else" (self-fulfilling prophecy)

Praise: (A girl draws something and asks if it is good.)   *Not:* "This is wonderful. You are a talented artist."
"I see a purple house and lots of flowers. It makes me feel like I am in the country."

One of his insights was that nonspecific praise can be as harmful as negative labeling of a child's character. Here is an example. For 20 minutes, during a car ride, Jason was quiet in the back seat of the car while Mom, Dad, and the baby rode in the front seat. Mom then turned around to Jason and said he was her perfect angel. Jason then proceeded to dump the full ashtray on his mom's head. She did not understand his behavior. After she had been so nice to him, he was mean to her. But the truth is that Jason was quiet for the past 20 minutes because he was trying to imagine how the family could get into a car accident that would kill only the baby but leave him and his parents alive. He had been silently planning the baby's death when his mom called him a little angel. Nonspecific praise can raise a child's anxieties by setting standards that are unreachable. So the child tries to act so as to relieve us of our unreasonable expectations.

2. Process is everything. We can only teach kindness kindly. We can only teach respect by being respectful. We can only teach politeness by being polite with our children. You can't say, "You stupid idiot, I said to be polite!" This is probably the most important principle that Ginott espoused. A lot of this has to do with empowering a child. I have seen many parents dramatize to a child his or her own powerlessness. Kids are very aware that they are small and powerless. They worry about it all the time and think constantly about how old they are, about what they couldn't do last year but can do now. They want to be bigger, more competent, more capable, but they still want their parents to take care of them. So they feel somewhat ambivalent about growing up.

Empowering a child is very important if we want children who will eventually be independent and able to think for themselves. Parents can still set limits and yet empower their children by offering them real choices. It is a strange thing, but I have noticed that the building blocks of self-concept involve honoring a child's small preferences. These often begin around food. A young child is unlikely to say, "When I grow up I will study astronomy and theoretical physics." Instead the child is likely to say, "I'm not eating this. I hate it when the peas and the mashed potatoes touch." This is a test of a small bit of self. The child is saying, "I think that I'm the kind of kid who likes separate food. Let's see what my mom says about that." It's as if the child is trying on a self-concept as he or she might try on a new shirt and then look in the mirror. The child whose mom says "okay" and then takes the plate and rearranges the peas and the potatoes so they don't touch can then say, "Hey, I am the kind of kid who likes separate food and this is okay with my mom, and it's me." The child is saying, "I am acceptable this way." These little experiments with self-concept that empower the child do not create an obnoxious child. They lead to a child who will later say to herself, "I'm the kind of kid who likes a challenge on the monkey bars and then I do it."

3. Parents do enormous harm by invalidating children's emotions, getting children to doubt their own instincts.

Child: "My finger hurts."

Parent: "A scratch can hurt."   *Not:* "It couldn't hurt; it's just a little scratch."

Child: "It's hot."

Parent: "It's hot in here for you."   *Not:* "Don't be silly. It's freezing in here."

We have discovered that even in disciplining children, the basic Ginott principle holds: *Words of understanding must precede words of advice.*

Parents, especially dads, were very confused about what effect they would have if they were understanding of a child's fear, especially fear in boys. Emotions do not vanish by being banished; research shows that they intensify physiologically if their expression is suppressed. Kids do not become wimps if Dad understands their fear. Say, "Show me those scary shadows," not, "Don't be a wimp."

A parent who sits with a sad child and is also sad and not impatient with the sadness communicates many profound things to the child:

- Being sad will not kill you. It's okay to be sad.
- You are not alone. I understand and also feel what you feel.
- It makes sense to feel what you feel. Trust your feelings.
- Even with these feelings, you are acceptable.

A parent who sets limits by communicating real feelings of anger and disappointment (without insult) also communicates a great deal to the child. Discipline becomes part of sharing the values of the family and being close;

these values are internalized. Emotional communication becomes two-way and real.

A parent who involves the child in the solution to a problem and not just in the problem also communicates a great deal:

- You have good ideas.
- You can solve problems.
- I trust your capability.
- You can be part of the solution, not just part of the problem.

Our Research Findings in Light of Ginott's Views

What did we find in our research? We found that children with EC parents have:

- Greater ability to calm their hearts after emotional upset (higher vagal tone).
- Greater ability to focus attention.
- Higher math and reading scores at age 8, even controlling age for IQ at age 4.
- Fewer behavior problems as rated by teachers.
- Better relations with other kids.
- Fewer infectious illnesses.

These differences were only amplified as we followed the children into adolescence.

We had to conclude that the children are really developing an emotional intelligence, as Dan Goleman (1995) has called it, because the very "skills" EC teaches in early childhood become a liability in middle childhood in the face of peer teasing and peer entry situations. The worst thing that a middle-childhood kid can say in response to teasing is "I don't like it when you do that." Talking about one's feelings and calling attention to oneself become a liability in middle childhood. When we make tape recordings of middle-childhood kids talking to their friends, the major thing they are worried about is avoiding embarrassment. In effect, they act with their peers (not in private) as if they have had an "emotion-ectomy."

The amazing thing is that kids who have been emotion-coached early know this and act accordingly. They have the ability to "psych out" social situations and analyze them appropriately. At each major developmental period this "psych-out" involves different processes being prominent. In adolescence it involves using friendships and love relationships for self-exploration. Again, kids who are emotion-coached do well with these developmentally appropriate tasks. So learning the skills of emotion-coaching is not learning a set of splinter skills; rather it involves learning a kind of emotional intelligence. These children become better social problem-solvers.

TRAINING PARENTS TO BE EMOTION-COACHING

These ideas do not usually involve social skill training of parents. We do not need a very detailed and time-consuming treatment program to teach parents to become emotion-coaching. The skills are usually in the repertoire of the parents, *in how they treat guests.* When a guest leaves an umbrella, we say:

"You forgot your umbrella. Here it is."

Not: "What is wrong with you? If you keep forgetting things, you will never succeed in life. What am I, your slave?"

When a guest spills some wine, we say:

"The wine spilled. No problem."

Not: "You are so clumsy. You have ruined my best tablecloth. I can never invite you again. If you keep being careless, you will become a criminal and probably be executed."

So, if emotion-coaching is as easy as I say it is, and the skills are in most people's repertoire already, why don't they do it? This is a great question. We have found that the major obstacle to parents' being able to follow the rule "understanding must precede advice" is a natural parental concern about various problems they worry about in each child; this leads parents to want to draw a moral lesson in every situation. We call this the *parental agenda.* These parental agendas are usually very healthy. Dad worries that his son is not very generous, or Mom worries that her daughter is too impulsive, and so on. Then, when a situation arises that dramatizes this parental worry, it is quite natural for the parent to try to draw out a moral lesson from this disastrous situation.

Here's an example supplied by Alice Ginott-Cohen, Haim Ginott's widow. It is Christmas and a mother warns a 4-year-old child she considers somewhat "spacey" to pay attention and stay close to her in the department store. Otherwise he might get lost. Of course, he does get lost. After 45 frantic minutes the parent and child are reunited by the store detective. What has been going on in the child's mind during this time? The separation has activated one of the terrors of this age. The boy is thinking, "I bet this is how kids wind up in orphanages. I just know it, they are going to take me and put me in an orphanage and I'll never see my parents or my dog or my house again. My life is over." When the mother and child get together again, she is very likely to say:

"I am never taking you anywhere again. You are never leaving your room. Didn't I tell you to stay close to me? Why are you so spacey?"

Instead the mother could say:

"Come over here. That must have been very scary. Were you scared? Tell me. [*pause while Mom listens*] Yes, I don't blame you for being scared. I was scared. Now let's calm down. [*then later*] That was so awful, let's talk about how we can prevent that from happening again. Any ideas?"

When I was in graduate school, I leaned against a loose railing on my friend Steve Asher's porch, and fell and broke my elbow. After 5 hours of surgery, I called my parents. My father was very quiet, and then he said, "How many times have I told you, *Don't lean.*" Indeed, that was a parental agenda of his when I was growing up. He had to find a moral lesson in the event. It is a parental urge.

To help parents become better emotion coaches I recommend *The Heart of Parenting* and my training videotape. We have also used this training approach in an 8-session small group for parents, in which we begin by having parents talk about their own experiences with anger, fear, and sadness in growing up and their own meta-emotions. From there we lead into role-playing an ED response and an EC response to actual emotional situations that parents report each week. They write these on index cards, and we role play them, with someone other than the parent who wrote the index card playing the role. We discuss, in this context, various developmental issues, including obtaining cooperation from children.

What Have We Added To Ginott?

We have added two qualities to Ginott's thinking—*specificity* and *simplification*—by delineating the five steps of emotion-coaching:

- Developing an awareness of less intense emotions in self and child.
- Viewing the expression of these emotions as an opportunity for intimacy or teaching.
- Communicating empathy and understanding of the emotions, even if these emotions underlie misbehavior.
- Helping the child label the emotions.
- Setting limits on behavior (not feelings or wishes) and problem-solving.

Second, we have supplied research data on the concept of meta-emotion and how people's metaphors about emotion shape their parental response to the child's emotions.

Third, we have discovered the father's importance in the child's emotional development. In all our path models, the father's variables were much more powerful in predicting child outcomes than the mother's. This is because there was three times the variability in the father's behavior than in the mother's. Fathers were capable of doing great harm as well as great good in their children's emotional and social development. Mothers tended to be more positive and have less variability. This research confirms the importance of recognizing and supporting emotionally intelligent fathers, that is, fathers who make a Love Map of their child's world, the child's daily schedule, friends, preferences and routines, and so on. I have designed a board game for parents called Kid Love Maps that parallels the marital Love Map Board Game.

Fourth, we discovered that when parents are emotion-coaching, there is no tradeoff between the marriage and the parenting. They are all of one fabric. In fact, we are beginning to find in our clinical work that training parents in EC helps marriages. Parents who are EC with their children become EC in their marriage. Also, fathers who are involved with their children's emotional worlds are more involved in the family in general, and the partnership between spouses is enormously strengthened.

Fifth, we have expanded and corroborated Ginott's interest in teaching kids. We already discussed the two styles of teaching we discovered with Vanessa Kahen's coding of our parent-child teaching interaction. These results parallel Ginott's ideas in working with teachers. Derogatory parenting, labeling the child's character, intrusiveness, and so on, have very strong negative effects on child outcomes.

Sixth, our focus on the child's regulatory physiology is entirely new, as is the seventh contribution we have made, which is a focus on attention. Attention is turning out to be the most sensitive lead indicator for the development of school failure and, in fact, for the development of a wide range of child psychopathology.

Seventh is our emphasis on the child's peer world. We are very interested in the development of the child's social competence, and emotional intelligence is our key construct in understanding this important developmental outcome. It has proven to be the best predictor of adult functioning we can obtain from childhood assessments.

Finally, we have discovered that emotion-coaching buffers children from nearly all the negative consequences of a hostile or a dissolving marriage, including impaired school performance and peer relations and avoiding the development of behavior problems and infectious illnesses. It does not buffer children from sadness and anxiety in their daily moods. We think that it takes only one parent to be an emotion coach for these effects to be obtained, although we also discovered that discrepancies between parents in philosophy of emotion-coaching are highly predictive of divorce.

Afterword

Here is my vision. To continually grow and develop, to keep serving the needs of families, and to avoid stagnation and dogmatism, the Marriage Clinic needs to be a wedding of the research and clinical worlds. To my knowledge this kind of marriage clinic has never been built before. It needs to be a place where both kinds of knowledge, scientific and clinical, can be honored and can affect one another. The Marriage Clinic in Seattle is designed to provide research (both basic and applied) for education, clinical training, and supervision, as well as service delivery.

To accomplish these goals, we insist on the accountability of the clinical services. We use a method that has worked effectively in industry, called "evolutionary operations," or EVOP. In a factory, for example, an EVOP committee decides on a variant (call it "Brand-X") of the standard operating procedure (SOP). Then the two methods of production, SOP and Brand-X, are alternated until a sequential statistical test can decide which of the two methods of production is best. If it turns out to be Brand-X, then Brand-X becomes the new standard operating procedure (SOP). In our clinic there is an ongoing seminar in which cases are discussed, supervision is provided, and more theoretical discussions are held, with invited speakers and the discussion of new papers. Based on the discussions and deliberations in this seminar, the EVOP committee decides on a new Brand-X, and the process continues.

In the Marriage Clinic 10% of all the clinical hours are research hours. This is not enough to strongly affect the clinic's income, but it is enough for research. Therapists either do SOP or Brand-X marital therapy, and treatment adherence is monitored by taping and blind-coding a random proportion of the sessions.

The EVOP committee consists of the clinical director (Julie Gottman), therapists, and staff directly interested in research, including the research director (John Gottman). It is important that all participants feel that they have an investment in both the clinical work and the research.

In addition to these functions, the Marriage Clinic in Seattle plans to network with other such clinics so that there can be a frank exchange of ideas, including presentations of treatment successes and failures, video teleconferencing supervision, and two-week clinical sabbaticals in Seattle. A small proportion of the fees generated by the Marriage Clinic are used to fund basic and applied research and the development of products for educational uses (in therapy, clinical training, and public education). The Marriage Clinic is part of the Gottman Institute, which also has a nonprofit arm, the Gottman Research Institute (GRI). The GRI can submit and administer research grants, as well as educational grants. We are also trying to build a research endowment for the GRI.

Appendix A
Assessment Instruments: The Basic Questionnaires

What follows is my selected library of questionnaires you may find useful in your practice. Do not expect to use these scales in every case.

1. Marital Satisfaction: Locke-Wallace Marital Adjustment Test.

2. Weiss-Cerreto Marital Status Inventory (included with permission from Dr. Robert Weiss, October, 1996).

3. SCL-90. I use standardized questionnaires for the assessment of psychophathology and to decide whether conjoint marital therapy is contraindicated. Use whatever scales you prefer. I have included the SCL-90 here as an example.

4. Scales to assess for marital violence: It is estimated that between 30% and 50% of clinic couples have had some incidence of violence, so that it becomes important to assess this dimension in every case.

    For physical violence, I use the (Straus-Gelles) Conflict Tactics Scales (CTS). For emotional abuse, I use the Waltz-Rushe-Gottman Emotional Abuse Questionnaire (EAQ).

5. Gottman Love and Respect Scale.

6. Gottman Marital Style Questionnaire.

7. Distance and Isolation Questionnaires.

8. Gottman Areas of Disagreement Scale.

9. Gottman Areas of Change Checklist: Solvable Problems. This questionnaire can also be used in two additional ways:

    ■ As a follow-up and assessment of relapse.

    ■ As a marital contract exercise (we do this in the 6-month follow-up workshop). In this case, we add to each item a question of how they wish this area of their marriage would be. Each person is asked to first fill out the questionnaire alone; and then the spouses discuss it and arrive at consensus.

10. Gottman 17-Areas Scale

11. Gottman Turning Toward During Everyday Events Checklist.

12. Gottman Areas of Strengths Checklist.

13. Krokoff-Gottman Enjoyable Conversations Scale. This is useful for setting up a conversation to assess how much positive affect the partners can demonstrate.

LOCKE-WALLACE MARITAL ADJUSTMENT TEST

Check the dot on the scale line which best describes the degree of happiness, everything considered, of your present marriage. The middle point, "happy," represents the degree of happiness which most people get from marriage, and the scale gradually ranges on one side to those few who are very unhappy in marriage, and on the other, to those few who experience extreme joy or felicity in marriage.

●   ●   ●   ●   ●   ●   ●

| Very Unhappy | Happy | Perfectly Happy |

State the approximate extent of agreement or disagreement between you and your mate on the following items. Please check each column.

	Always Agree	Almost Always Agree	Occasionally Disagree	Frequently Disagree	Almost Always Disagree	Always Disagree
Handling family finances						
Matters of recreation						
Demonstrations of affection						
Friends						
Sex relations						
Conventionality (right, good, or proper conduct)						
Philosophy of life						
Ways of dealing with in-laws						

Check one:

When disagreements arise, they usually result in: (a) husband giving in _____ (b) wife giving in _____ (c) agreement by mutual give and take _____

Do you and your mate engage in outside interests together? (a) all of them _____ (b) some of them _____ (c) very few of them _____ (d) none of them _____

In leisure time do you generally prefer: (a) to be "on the go" _____ (b) to stay at home _____ ?

Does your mate generally prefer: (a) to be "on the go" _____ (b) to stay at home _____ ?

Do you ever wish you had not married? (a) frequently _____ (b) occasionally _____ (c) rarely _____ (d) never _____

If you had your life to live over again, do you think you would: (a) marry the same person _____ (b) marry a different person _____ (c) not marry at all _____ ?

Do you ever confide in your mate: (a) almost never _____ (b) rarely _____ (c) in most things _____ (d) in everything _____ ?

LOCKE-WALLACE MARITAL ADJUSTMENT TEST (*continued*)
Marital Adjustment Test Scoring Key

Check the dot on the scale line which best describes the degree of happiness, everything considered, of your present marriage. The middle point, "happy," represents the degree of happiness which most people get from marriage, and the scale gradually ranges on one side of those few who are very unhappy in marriage, and on the other, to those few who experience extreme joy or felicity in marriage.

0	2	7	15	20	25	35
•	•	•	•	•	•	•

Very Unhappy   Happy   Perfectly Happy

State the approximate extent of agreement or disagreement between you and your mate on the following items. Please check each column.

	Always Agree	Almost Always Agree	Occasionally Disagree	Frequently Disagree	Almost Always Disagree	Always Disagree
Handling family finances	5	4	3	2	1	0
Matters of recreation	5	4	3	2	1	0
Demonstrations of affection	8	6	4	2	1	0
Friends	5	4	3	2	1	0
Sex relations	15	12	9	4	1	0
Conventionality (right, good, or proper conduct)	5	4	3	2	1	0
Philosophy of life	5	4	3	2	1	0
Ways of dealing with in-laws	5	4	3	2	1	0

Check one:

When disagreements arise, they usually result in: (a) husband giving in __0__ (b) wife giving in __2__ (c) agreement by mutual give and take __10__

Do you and your mate engage in outside interests together? (a) all of them __10__ (b) some of them __8__ (c) very few of them __3__ (d) none of them __0__

In leisure time do you generally prefer: (a) to be "on the go" _____ (b) to stay at home _____ ?
Does your mate generally prefer: (a) to be "on the go" _____ (b) to stay at home _____ ?
(stay at home for both, 10 points; on the go for both, 3 points; disagreement 2 points)

Do you ever wish you had not married? (a) frequently __0__ (b) occasionally __3__ (c) rarely __8__ (d) never __15__

If you had your life to live over again, do you think you would: (a) marry the same person __15__ (b) marry a different person __0__ (c) not marry at all __1__ ?

Do you ever confide in your mate: (a) almost never __0__ (b) rarely __2__ (c) in most things __10__ (d) in everything __10__ ?

WEISS-CERRETO
MARITAL STATUS INVENTORY

We would like to get an idea of how your marriage stands right now. Please answer the questions below by circling TRUE or FALSE for each item with regard to how things stand right now. For items that are true, please indicate what year the item began to be true.

FALSE TRUE Year:_____ 1. I have made specific plans to discuss separation or divorce with my spouse. I have considered what I would say, etc.

FALSE TRUE Year:_____ 2. I have set up an independent bank account in my name in order to protect my own interests.

FALSE TRUE Year:_____ 3. Thoughts of divorce occur to me very frequently, as often as once a week or more.

FALSE TRUE Year:_____ 4. I have suggested to my spouse that I wished to be separated, divorced, or rid of him/her.

FALSE TRUE Year:_____ 5. I have thought specifically about divorce or separation. I have thought about who would get the kids, how things would be divided, pros and cons, etc.

FALSE TRUE Year:_____ 6. My spouse and I have separated. This is a (check one) ____ trial separation or ____ legal separation.

FALSE TRUE Year:_____ 7. I have discussed the question of my divorce or separation with someone other than my spouse (trusted friend, psychologist, minister, etc.).

FALSE TRUE Year:_____ 8. I have occasionally thought of divorce or wished that we were separated, usually after an argument or other incident.

FALSE TRUE Year:_____ 9. I have discussed the issue of divorce seriously or at length with my spouse.

FALSE TRUE Year:_____ 10. I have filed for divorce, or we are divorced.

FALSE TRUE Year:_____ 11. I have made inquiries of nonprofessionals as to how long it takes to get a divorce, grounds for divorce, costs involved, etc.

FALSE TRUE Year:_____ 12. I have contacted a lawyer to make preliminary plans for a divorce.

FALSE TRUE Year:_____ 13. I have consulted with a lawyer or other legal aid about the matter.

FALSE TRUE Year:_____ 14. I have considered divorce or separation a few times, other than during or after an argument, although only in vague terms.

SCL-90

Below is a list of problems and complaints that people sometimes have. Please read each one carefully. After you have done so, select one of the numbered descriptors that best describes HOW MUCH DISCOMFORT THAT PROBLEM CAUSED YOU DURING THE PAST WEEK, INCLUDING TODAY. Place the number in the space to the right of the problem. Respond to each problem listed. Please read the following example before beginning.

EXAMPLE

DESCRIPTORS

0 = Not at all
1 = A little bit
2 = Moderately
3 = Quite a bit
4 = Extremely

In the previous week, how much were you distressed by:

Body aches: __3__

In this case the respondent experienced body aches quite a bit (3) in the previous week. Please proceed with the questionnaire.

IN THE PREVIOUS WEEK, HOW MUCH WERE YOU DISTRESSED BY:

Headaches

Nervousness or shakiness inside

Repeated unleasant thoughts that won't leave your mind

Faintness or dizziness

Loss of sexual interest or pleasure

Feeling critical of others

The idea that someone else can control your thoughts

Feeling others are to blame for most of your troubles

Trouble remembering things

Worried about sloppiness or carelessness

Feeling easily annoyed or irritated

Pains in heart or chest

Feeling afraid in open spaces or on the streets

Feeling low in energy or slowed down

Thoughts of ending your life

Hearing voices that other people do not hear

Trembling

Feeling that most people cannot be trusted

Poor appetite

Crying easily

Feeling shy or uneasy with the opposite sex

Feelings of being trapped or caught

Suddenly scared for no reason

Temper outbursts that you could not control

Feeling afraid to go out of your house alone

Blaming yourself for things

Pains in lower back

Feeling blocked in getting things done

Feeling lonely

Feeling blue

Worrying too much about things

Feeling no interest in things

Feeling fearful

Your feelings easily being hurt

Other people being aware of your private thoughts

Feeling others do not understand you or are unsympathetic

Feeling that people are unfriendly or dislike you

Having to do things very slowly to insure correctness

Heart pounding or racing

Nausea or upset stomach

Feeling inferior to others

Soreness of your muscles

Feeling that you are watched or talked about by others

Trouble falling asleep

Having to check and double-check what you do

Difficulty making decisions

Feeling afraid to travel on buses, subways, trains

Trouble getting your breath

Hot or cold spells

Having to avoid certain things, places, or activities because they frighten you

Your mind going blank

Numbness or tingling in parts of your body

A lump in your throat

Feeling hopeless about the future

Trouble concentrating

Feeling weak in parts of your body

Feeling tense or keyed up

Heavy feelings in your arms or legs

Thoughts of death or dying

Overeating

Feeling uneasy when people are watching or talking about you

Having thoughts that are not your own

Having urges to hurt, injure, or harm someone

Awakening in the early morning

Having to repeat the same actions, such as touching, counting, washing

Sleep that is restless or disturbed

Having urges to break or smash things

Having ideas or beliefs that others do not share

Feeling very self-conscious with others

Feeling uneasy in crowds, such as shopping or at a movie

Feeling everything is an effort

Spells of terror or panic

Feeling uncomfortable about eating or drinking in public

Getting into frequent arguments

Feeling nervous when you are left alone

Others not giving you proper credit for your achievements

Feeling lonely even when you are with people

Feeling so restless you couldn't sit still

Feelings of worthlessness

The feeling that something bad is going to happen to you

Shouting or throwing things

Feeling afraid you will faint in public

Feeling that people will take advantage of you if you let them

Having thoughts about sex that bother you a lot

The idea that you should be punished for your sins

Thoughts and images of a frightening nature

The idea that something serious is wrong with your body

Never feeling close to another person

Feelings of guilt

The idea that something is wrong with your mind

CONFLICT TACTICS SCALES (CTS)*

No matter how well a couple gets along, there are times when they disagree on major decisions, get annoyed about something the other person does, or have spats or fights because they're in a bad mood or for some other reason. A couple may also use many different ways to settle their differences. Listed below are some things that you or your spouse may have done when you had a dispute. First, rate how many times you have done any of these things in the last year. Second, rate how many times your spouse has done any of these things in the last year. Then rate whether you or your spouse has ever done any of these things.

| | You in the Past Year | | | | | | | | Spouse in the Past Year | | | | | | | | Ever Happened | | |
---	Never	Once	Twice	3-5 times	6-10 times	11-20 times	More than 20	Don't know	Never	Once	Twice	3-5 times	6-10 times	11-20 times	More than 20	Don't know	Yes	No	Don't know
a. Discussed the issue calmly	0	1	2	3	4	5	6	X	0	1	2	3	4	5	6	X	1	2	X
b. Got information to back up (your/his or her) side of things	0	1	2	3	4	5	6	X	0	1	2	3	4	5	6	X	1	2	X
c. Brought in or tried to bring in help to settle things	0	1	2	3	4	5	6	X	0	1	2	3	4	5	6	X	1	2	X
d. Insulted or swore at the other one	0	1	2	3	4	5	6	X	0	1	2	3	4	5	6	X	1	2	X
e. Sulked and/or refused to talk about it	0	1	2	3	4	5	6	X	0	1	2	3	4	5	6	X	1	2	X

	You in the Past Year									Spouse in the Past Year									Ever Happened		
	Never	Once	Twice	3-5 times	6-10 times	11-20 times	More than 20	Don't know		Never	Once	Twice	3-5 times	6-10 times	11-20 times	More than 20	Don't know		Yes	No	Don't know
f. Stomped out of the room or house (or yard)	0	1	2	3	4	5	6	X		0	1	2	3	4	5	6	X		1	2	X
g. cried	0	1	2	3	4	5	6	X		0	1	2	3	4	5	6	X		1	2	X
h. Did or said something to spite the other one	0	1	2	3	4	5	6	X		0	1	2	3	4	5	6	X		1	2	X
i. Threatened to hit or throw something at the other one	0	1	2	3	4	5	6	X		0	1	2	3	4	5	6	X		1	2	X
j. Threw or smashed or hit or kicked something	0	1	2	3	4	5	6	X		0	1	2	3	4	5	6	X		1	2	X
k. Threw something at the other one	0	1	2	3	4	5	6	X		0	1	2	3	4	5	6	X		1	2	X
l. Pushed, grabbed or shoved the other one	0	1	2	3	4	5	6	X		0	1	2	3	4	5	6	X		1	2	X
m. Slapped the other one	0	1	2	3	4	5	6	X		0	1	2	3	4	5	6	X		1	2	X

	You in the Past Year								Spouse in the Past Year								Ever Happened		
	Never	Once	Twice	3-5 times	6-10 times	11-20 times	More than 20	Don't know	Never	Once	Twice	3-5 times	6-10 times	11-20 times	More than 20	Don't know	Yes	No	Don't know
n. Kicked, bit, or hit with a fist	0	1	2	3	4	5	6	X	0	1	2	3	4	5	6	X	1	2	X
o. Hit or tried to hit with something	0	1	2	3	4	5	6	X	0	1	2	3	4	5	6	X	1	2	X
p. Beat up the other one	0	1	2	3	4	5	6	X	0	1	2	3	4	5	6	X	1	2	X
q. Threatened with a knife or gun	0	1	2	3	4	5	6	X	0	1	2	3	4	5	6	X	1	2	X
r. Used a knife or gun	0	1	2	3	4	5	6	X	0	1	2	3	4	5	6	X	1	2	X
s. Other	0	1	2	3	4	5	6	X	0	1	2	3	4	5	6	X	1	2	X

To score the behavior of the respondent, add the answer numbers under "You in the past year" as follows. Negotiation scale = the sum of items a, b, and c. Psychological Aggression scale = sum of items d, e, f, h, i. Physical Assault (violence) scale = sum of items j through s (but see note 2). To score the behavior of the spouse, do the same for the items under "Spouse in the past year."

Notes: (1) Item g ("cried") is not scored on any of the scales. (2) The scoring procedure given above is the one used for this book. The scoring procedure recommend by Straus differs in two ways. (A) Item j (threw or smashed something) is scored as part of the Psychological Aggression scale. (B) Instead of summing the answer numbers, they are converted to the midpoints of each category (0, 1, 2, 4, 8, 15, and 25) and these midpoints are summed.

*From Straus (1979). A revised version of the CTS for use with couples is in Straus, Hamby, Boney-McCoy, & Sugarman, 1986. A revised version to measure parent-to-child behavior is in Straus, Hamby, Finkelhor, Moore, & Runyan (1998). Versions to use for adult-recall or child-report are in Straus, 1999.

WALTZ-RUSHE-GOTTMAN EMOTIONAL ABUSE
QUESTIONNAIRE (EAQ)

Read each statement and circle the word that best describes the frequency with which each behavior occurs.

Social Isolation Subscale

I have to do things to avoid my partner's jealousy.

       Never   Rarely   Occasionally   Very Often

My partner tries to control who I spend my time with.

       Never   Rarely   Occasionally   Very Often

My partner disapproves of my friends.

       Never   Rarely   Occasionally   Very Often

My partner does not believe me when I talk about where I have been.

       Never   Rarely   Occasionally   Very Often

My partner complains that I spend too much time with other people.

       Never   Rarely   Occasionally   Very Often

My partner accuses me of flirting with other people.

       Never   Rarely   Occasionally   Very Often

In social situations my partner complains that I ignore him.

       Never   Rarely   Occasionally   Very Often

My partner is suspicious that I am unfaithful.

       Never   Rarely   Occasionally   Very Often

My partner acts like a detective, looking for clues that I've done something wrong.

       Never   Rarely   Occasionally   Very Often

My partner checks up on me.

       Never   Rarely   Occasionally   Very Often

My partner keeps me from going places I want to go.

       Never   Rarely   Occasionally   Very Often

My partner keeps me from doing things I want to do.

       Never   Rarely   Occasionally   Very Often

My partner says I act too seductively.

       Never   Rarely   Occasionally   Very Often

My partner keeps me from spending time at the things I enjoy.

       Never   Rarely   Occasionally   Very Often

My partner threatens to take the car keys if I don't do as I am told.

       Never   Rarely   Occasionally   Very Often

My partner threatens to take the money if I don't do as I am told.

Never   Rarely   Occasionally   Very Often

My partner threatens to take the checkbook if I don't do as I am told.

Never   Rarely   Occasionally   Very Often

My partner prevents me from leaving the house when I want to.

Never   Rarely   Occasionally   Very Often

My partner disables the phone to prevent my using it.

Never   Rarely   Occasionally   Very Often

My partner disables the car to prevent my using it.

Never   Rarely   Occasionally   Very Often

My partner threatens to pull the phone out of the wall.

Never   Rarely   Occasionally   Very Often

My partner forcibly tries to restrict my movements.

Never   Rarely   Occasionally   Very Often

My partner acts jealous.

Never   Rarely   Occasionally   Very Often

My partner keeps me from spending time with the people I choose.

Never   Rarely   Occasionally   Very Often

Scoring.   Here's how to find out whether the client is being emotionally abused through isolation: Score 1 point for every "Never" circled, 2 points for every "Rarely" circled, 4 points for every "Occasionally" circled, and 5 points for every "Very Often" circled. If the client scored between 51–67, the client is being emotionally abused through isolation. If the client scored 68 or greater, the emotional abuse is severe.

Degradation Subscale

My partner tries to catch me at inconsistencies to show that I'm lying.

Never   Rarely   Occasionally   Very Often

My partner tries to convince other people that I'm crazy.

Never   Rarely   Occasionally   Very Often

My partner tells other people that there is something wrong with me.

Never   Rarely   Occasionally   Very Often

My partner says things to hurt me out of spite.

Never   Rarely   Occasionally   Very Often

My partner has told me that I am sexually unattractive.

Never   Rarely   Occasionally   Very Often

My partner tells me that I am sexually inadequate.

Never   Rarely   Occasionally   Very Often

My partner insults my religious background or beliefs.

     Never   Rarely   Occasionally   Very Often

My partner insults my ethnic background.

     Never   Rarely   Occasionally   Very Often

My partner insults my family.

     Never   Rarely   Occasionally   Very Often

My partner talks me into doing things that make me feel bad.

     Never   Rarely   Occasionally   Very Often

My partner tells me that no one else would ever want me.

     Never   Rarely   Occasionally   Very Often

My partner humiliates me in front of others.

     Never   Rarely   Occasionally   Very Often

My partner makes me do degrading things.

     Never   Rarely   Occasionally   Very Often

My partner questions my sanity.

     Never   Rarely   Occasionally   Very Often

My partner tells other people personal information or secrets about me.

     Never   Rarely   Occasionally   Very Often

My partner swears at me.

     Never   Rarely   Occasionally   Very Often

My partner verbally attacks my personality.

     Never   Rarely   Occasionally   Very Often

My partner has insulted me by telling me that I am incompetent.

     Never   Rarely   Occasionally   Very Often

My partner ridicules me.

     Never   Rarely   Occasionally   Very Often

My partner forces me to do things that are against my values.

     Never   Rarely   Occasionally   Very Often

My partner questions whether my love is true.

     Never   Rarely   Occasionally   Very Often

My partner compares me unfavorably to other partners.

     Never   Rarely   Occasionally   Very Often

My partner intentionally does things to scare me.

     Never   Rarely   Occasionally   Very Often

My partner threatens me physically during arguments.

> Never   Rarely   Occasionally   Very Often

My partner warns me that if I keep doing something, violence will follow.

> Never   Rarely   Occasionally   Very Often

Our arguments escalate out of control.

> Never   Rarely   Occasionally   Very Often

I'm worried most when my partner is quiet.

> Never   Rarely   Occasionally   Very Often

My partner drives recklessly or too fast when he is angry.

> Never   Rarely   Occasionally   Very Often

Scoring. Here's how to find out whether the client is being emotionally abused through degradation: Give the client 1 point for every "Never" circled, 2 points for every "Rarely" circled, 4 points for every "Occasionally" circled, and 5 points for every "Very Often" circled. If the client scored between 73–94, the client is being emotionally abused through degradation. If the client scored 95 or greater, the client is being severely emotionally abused.

Sexual Coercion Subscale

My partner makes me engage in sexual practices I consider perverse.

> Never   Rarely   Occasionally   Very Often

In bed my partner make me do things I find repulsive.

> Never   Rarely   Occasionally   Very Often

My partner is not sensitive to me during sex.

> Never   Rarely   Occasionally   Very Often

My partner pressures me to have sex after an argument.

> Never   Rarely   Occasionally   Very Often

My partner intentionally hurts me during sex.

> Never   Rarely   Occasionally   Very Often

I feel pressured to have sex when I don't want to.

> Never   Rarely   Occasionally   Very Often

Even against my will, violence is a part of our sex life.

> Never   Rarely   Occasionally   Very Often

Scoring. Here's how to find out whether the client is being abused through sexual coercion: Give the client 1 point for every "Never" circled, 2 points for every "Rarely" circled, 4 points for every "Occasionally" circled, and 5 points for every "Very Often" circled. If the client scored between 14–18, the client is being sexually abused through sexual coercion. If the client scored 19 or greater, the client is being severely sexually abused.

Property Damage Subscale

My partner threatens to hurt someone I care about.

Never   Rarely   Occasionally   Very Often

My partner intentionally damages things I care about.

Never   Rarely   Occasionally   Very Often

My partner threatens to break things that are valuable to me.

Never   Rarely   Occasionally   Very Often

My partner damages things in our home.

Never   Rarely   Occasionally   Very Often

My partner threatens to destroy my property.

Never   Rarely   Occasionally   Very Often

My partner does cruel things to pets.

Never   Rarely   Occasionally   Very Often

My partner threatens to hurt animals I care about.

Never   Rarely   Occasionally   Very Often

Scoring.   Here's how to find out whether the client is emotionally abused through property damage. Give 1 point for every "Never" circled, 2 points for every "Rarely" circled, 4 points for every "Occasionally" circled, and 5 points for every "Very Often" circled. If the client scored between 15–21, the client is being emotionally abused through property damage. If the client scored 22 or greater, the client is experiencing severe emotional abuse.

Julia Babock devised the scoring for this questionnaire.

GOTTMAN LOVE AND RESPECT SCALE

Self-Test:
Is There Enough Love and Respect in Your Marriage?

Answer "yes" or "no" to each of the following statements, depending on whether or not you mostly agree or disagree. Take the test on behalf of your partner also, if necessary.

1. My spouse seeks out my opinions.
YOU: Yes No   YOUR PARTNER: Yes No

2. My spouse cares about my feelings.
YOU: Yes No   YOUR PARTNER: Yes No

3. I don't feel ignored very often.
YOU: Yes No   YOUR PARTNER: Yes No

4. We touch each other a lot.
YOU: Yes No   YOUR PARTNER: Yes No

5. We listen to each other.
YOU: Yes No   YOUR PARTNER: Yes No

6. We respect each other's ideas.
YOU: Yes No   YOUR PARTNER: Yes No

7. We are affectionate toward one another.
YOU: Yes No   YOUR PARTNER: Yes No

8. I feel that my partner takes good care of me.
YOU: Yes No   YOUR PARTNER: Yes No

9. What I say counts.
YOU: Yes No   YOUR PARTNER: Yes No

10. I am important in our decisions.
YOU: Yes No   YOUR PARTNER: Yes No

11. There's lots of love in our marriage.
YOU: Yes No   YOUR PARTNER: Yes No

12. We are genuinely interested in one another.
YOU: Yes No   YOUR PARTNER: Yes No

13. I just love spending time with my partner.
YOU: Yes No   YOUR PARTNER: Yes No

14. We are very good friends.
YOU: Yes No   YOUR PARTNER: Yes No

15. Even during rough times, we can be empathic.
YOU: Yes No   YOUR PARTNER: Yes No

16. My spouse is considerate of my viewpoint.
YOU: Yes No   YOUR PARTNER: Yes No

17. My spouse finds me physically attractive.
YOU: Yes No   YOUR PARTNER: Yes No

18. My partner expresses warmth toward me.
YOU: Yes   No   YOUR PARTNER: Yes   No

19. I feel included in my partner's life.
YOU: Yes   No   YOUR PARTNER: Yes   No

20. My spouse admires me.
YOU: Yes   No   YOUR PARTNER: Yes   No

Scoring: If the person checked "yes" to fewer than seven items, then it is likely he or she is not feeling adequately loved and respected in the marriage.

GOTTMAN MARITAL STYLE QUESTIONNAIRE

Answer "yes" or "no" to each of the following statements, depending on whether or not you mostly agree or disagree. Take the test on behalf of your partner also, if necessary.

Part I
Is the Conflict Avoider Style of Marriage Right for You?

1. I often hide my feelings to avoid hurting my spouse.
YOU: Yes   No   YOUR PARTNER: Yes   No

2. When we disagree, I don't believe there is much point in analyzing our feelings and motivations.
YOU: Yes   No   YOUR PARTNER: Yes   No

3. When we disagree, we often solve the problem by going back to our basic beliefs about the different roles of men and women in marriage.
YOU: Yes   No   YOUR PARTNER: Yes   No

4. We have a lot of separate friends.
YOU: Yes   No   YOUR PARTNER: Yes   No

5. It is important to attend a church or synagogue regularly.
YOU: Yes   No   YOUR PARTNER: Yes   No

6. Many marital conflicts are solved just through the passing of time.
YOU: Yes   No   YOUR PARTNER: Yes   No

7. We each do a lot of things on our own.
YOU: Yes   No   YOUR PARTNER: Yes   No

8. During a marital conflict, there is not much to be gained from figuring out what is happening on a psychological level.
YOU: Yes   No   YOUR PARTNER: Yes   No

9. Our religious values give us a clear sense of life's purposes.
YOU: Yes   No   YOUR PARTNER: Yes   No

10. When I'm moody, I prefer to be left alone until I get over it.
YOU: Yes   No   YOUR PARTNER: Yes   No

11. I don't feel very comfortable with strong displays of negative emotion in my marriage.
YOU: Yes   No   YOUR PARTNER: Yes   No

12. We turn to our basic religious or cultural values for guidance when resolving conflicts.
YOU: Yes   No   YOUR PARTNER: Yes   No

13. I just accept most of the things in my marriage that I can't change.
YOU: Yes   No   YOUR PARTNER: Yes   No

14. We often agree not to talk about things we disagree about.
YOU: Yes   No   YOUR PARTNER: Yes   No

15. In our marriage there is a fairly clear line between the husband's and wife's roles.
YOU: Yes   No   YOUR PARTNER: Yes   No

16. We just don't seem to disagree very much.
YOU: Yes   No   YOUR PARTNER: Yes   No

17. When we have some difference of opinion, we often just drop the topic.
YOU: Yes   No   YOUR PARTNER: Yes   No

18. We hardly ever have much to argue about.
YOU: Yes   No   YOUR PARTNER: Yes   No

19. A lot of talking about disagreements often makes matters worse.
YOU: Yes   No   YOUR PARTNER: Yes   No

20. There are some personal areas in my life that I prefer not to discuss with my spouse.
YOU: Yes   No   YOUR PARTNER: Yes   No

21. There is not much point in trying to persuade my partner of my viewpoint.
YOU: Yes   No   YOUR PARTNER: Yes   No

22. There's not much to be gained by getting openly angry with my spouse.
YOU: Yes   No   YOUR PARTNER: Yes   No

23. Thinking positively solves a lot of marital issues.
YOU: Yes   No   YOUR PARTNER: Yes   No

24. In marriage it is usually best to stick to the traditional values about men and women.
YOU: Yes   No   YOUR PARTNER: Yes   No

25. I prefer to work out many of my negative feelings on my own.
YOU: Yes   No   YOUR PARTNER: Yes   No

26. Going over a lot of negative feelings in a marital discussion usually makes things worse.
YOU: Yes   No   YOUR PARTNER: Yes   No

27. If you just relax about problems, they have a way of working themselves out.
YOU: Yes   No   YOUR PARTNER: Yes   No

28. When we talk about our problems, we find they just aren't that important in the overall picture of our marriage.
YOU: Yes   No   YOUR PARTNER: Yes   No

29. Men and women ought to have separate roles in a marriage.
YOU: Yes   No   YOUR PARTNER: Yes   No

Scoring: Total up the number of items checked "yes." If the number is greater than 8, you probably feel comfortable with a conflict-avoider marriage philosophy.

COMFORT WITH AN AVOIDER PHILOSOPHY (CHECKED EIGHT OR MORE YES)
              YES   NO
You
Your Partner

Part II
Are You Comfortable with a Volatile or Validator Style of Marriage?

1. I think it's a good idea for my partner and me to have a lot of separate friends.
YOU: Yes   No   YOUR PARTNER: Yes   No

2. I believe in honestly confronting disagreements, whatever the issue.
YOU: Yes   No   YOUR PARTNER: Yes   No

3. We often do things separately.
YOU: Yes   No   YOUR PARTNER: Yes   No

4. The feeling of togetherness is central to our marriage.
YOU: Yes   No   YOUR PARTNER: Yes   No

5. Marriage partners should be direct and honest no matter what the results.
YOU: Yes   No   YOUR PARTNER: Yes   No

6. I feel quite comfortable with a strong expression of negative feelings.
YOU: Yes   No   YOUR PARTNER: Yes   No

7. Sometimes I enjoy a good argument with my spouse.
YOU: Yes   No   YOUR PARTNER: Yes   No

8. The most important aspect of marriage is companionship.
YOU: Yes   No   YOUR PARTNER: Yes   No

9. Jealousy is sometimes an issue in our marriage.
YOU: Yes   No   YOUR PARTNER: Yes   No

10. It is important to be a separate individual in a marriage.
YOU: Yes   No   YOUR PARTNER: Yes   No

11. I think we should argue but only about important issues.
YOU: Yes   No   YOUR PARTNER: Yes   No

12. We often eat separately.
YOU: Yes   No   YOUR PARTNER: Yes   No

13. Our marriage is based on being one another's best friend.
YOU: Yes   No   YOUR PARTNER: Yes   No

14. I enjoy trying to persuade my spouse when we have a disagreement.
YOU: Yes   No   YOUR PARTNER: Yes   No

15. The religious and other beliefs we share are basic to our marriage.
YOU: Yes   No   YOUR PARTNER: Yes   No

16. I believe in keeping our marriage very romantic.
YOU: Yes   No   YOUR PARTNER: Yes   No

17. We often look back at our photo albums together.
YOU: Yes   No   YOUR PARTNER: Yes   No

18. We cultivate a sense of we-ness in our marriage.
YOU: Yes   No   YOUR PARTNER: Yes   No

19. We share all things personal and emotional in our marriage.
YOU: Yes   No   YOUR PARTNER: Yes   No

20. All the spaces in our home are shared spaces.
YOU: Yes   No   YOUR PARTNER: Yes   No

21. I would never take a separate vacation from my spouse.
YOU: Yes   No   YOUR PARTNER: Yes   No

22. At times I enjoy expressing anger.
YOU: Yes   No   YOUR PARTNER: Yes   No

23. I believe it is important to fight even about small matters.
YOU: Yes   No   YOUR PARTNER: Yes   No

24. I enjoy working out our values through thorough arguments.
YOU: Yes   No   YOUR PARTNER: Yes   No

25. There is nothing personal that I do not share with my spouse.
YOU: Yes   No   YOUR PARTNER: Yes   No

26. I am comfortable only with a moderate amount of emotional expression.
YOU: Yes   No   YOUR PARTNER: Yes   No

27. It is essential to have a strong sense of togetherness in marriage.
YOU: Yes   No   YOUR PARTNER: Yes   No

28. Keeping a certain amount of distance in a marriage helps the romance.
YOU: Yes   No   YOUR PARTNER: Yes   No

29. A strong sense of traditional values is good for a marriage.
YOU: Yes   No   YOUR PARTNER: Yes   No

30. There are few issues in a marriage worth arguing about.
YOU: Yes   No   YOUR PARTNER: Yes   No

Scoring: In the *Validator* and *Volatile* columns below, put a check next to the number of each question you answered "yes" to above. Next, separately add up all the check marks in each column. Divide each sum by 15. This will give you percentage scores for your comfort level with each style. For example, you may wind up with a 53% score on the *Volatile* scale and an 80% score on the *Validator* scale. This suggests that you are mostly comfortable with a validator philosophy of marriage, although there are elements of the volatile type with which you are also comfortable.

VOLATILE	VALIDATOR
1	4
2	8
3	11
5	13
6	15
7	17
9	18
10	19
12	20
14	21
16	25
22	26
23	27
24	29
28	30

Volatile Total/15 = Volatile %
Validator Total/15 = Validator %

	VOLATILE		VALIDATOR	
	YES	NO	YES	NO
You				
Your Partner				

THE DISTANCE AND ISOLATION QUESTIONNAIRES

A. Self-Test Flooding

1. At times, when my partner gets angry I feel confused.	Yes	No
2. Our discussions get far too heated.	Yes	No
3. I have a hard time calming down when we discuss disagreements.	Yes	No
4. I'm worried that one of us is going to say something we will regret.	Yes	No
5. My partner gets far more upset than is necessary.	Yes	No
6. After a fight I want to keep away for a while.	Yes	No
7. There's no need to raise one's voice the way my partner does in a discussion.	Yes	No
8. It really is overwhelming when an argument gets going.	Yes	No
9. I can't think straight when my partner gets so negative.	Yes	No
10. I think, "Why can't we talk things out logically?"	Yes	No
11. My partner's negative moods come out of nowhere.	Yes	No
12. When my partner's temper gets going, there is no stopping it.	Yes	No
13. I feel cold and empty after one of our fights.	Yes	No
14. When there is so much negativity, I have difficulty focusing my thoughts.	Yes	No
15. Small issues suddenly become big ones for no apparent reason.	Yes	No
16. I can never seem to soothe myself after one of our fights.	Yes	No
17. Sometimes I think that my partner's moods are just crazy.	Yes	No
18. Things get out of hand quickly in our discussions.	Yes	No
19. My partner's feelings are very easily hurt.	Yes	No
20. When my partner gets negative, stopping it is like trying to stop an oncoming truck.	Yes	No
21. All this negativity drags me down.	Yes	No
22. I feel disorganized by all this negative emotion.	Yes	No
23. I can never tell when a blowup is going to happen.	Yes	No
24. When we have a fight, it takes a very long time before I feel at ease again.	Yes	No

Scoring: If a person answered "yes" to more than eight statements, this is a strong sign that that person is prone to feeling flooded during conflict with the spouse.

B. Self-Test: How Lonely Is Your Marriage?

1. Marriage is a lot lonelier than I thought it would be.	Yes	No
2. We're not as close as I wish we were.	Yes	No
3. I feel an emptiness in this marriage.	Yes	No

4. I often feel bored when we do things together.	Yes	No
5. I feel very restless and sad even when we're together.	Yes	No
6. Lots of times I don't know what to do with myself.	Yes	No
7. At times I feel bored and restless in this marriage.	Yes	No
8. I long for someone I can be close to.	Yes	No
9. I feel so lonely it hurts.	Yes	No
10. Something is missing from my marriage.	Yes	No
11. I wish people would call me more often.	Yes	No
12. I often wish I had someone to be with.	Yes	No
13. I don't feel that I'm an important part of someone's life.	Yes	No
14. I don't feel that I belong to anyone.	Yes	No
15. I often feel emotionally isolated.	Yes	No
16. I feel abandoned in this marriage.	Yes	No
17. There is no one I can turn to.	Yes	No
18. I often feel left out.	Yes	No
19. No one knows me.	Yes	No
20. No one understands me.	Yes	No
21. There is often no one I can talk to.	Yes	No
22. I often feel a great need for companionship.	Yes	No
23. I have become very withdrawn in this marriage.	Yes	No
24. I feel disconnected.	Yes	No

Scoring: If a person has answered "yes" to eight or more of the questions, he/she may have reached the end of the Distance and Isolation Cascade.

C. Self-Test: Can You Work Things Out?

1. Talking things over with my partner only seems to make them worse.	Yes	No
2. I'd rather just keep things to myself.	Yes	No
3. I am a very private person about my feelings.	Yes	No
4. When I'm in a bad mood, I'd much rather just go off by myself.	Yes	No
5. I don't see much point in discussing my troubles with my partner.	Yes	No
6. Talking about our problems only gets them more muddled.	Yes	No
7. There are some people you just can't talk to, and my partner's one of those.	Yes	No
8. I'd rather try to work out our marital problems alone.	Yes	No
9. Our conversations about our problems never seem to get anywhere.	Yes	No
10. I don't place a lot of faith in delving into my problems with my spouse.	Yes	No

11. I have given up on trying to talk things out.   Yes   No

12. I don't see any potential gain in trying to talk things over
    with my partner.   Yes   No

Scoring: If the person answered "yes" to four or more of these statements, he/she has given up working things out with the spouse. This attitude almost inevitably leads to the next step in the Distance and Isolation Cascade.

D. Self-Test: Do You Lead Parallel Lives?

1. We don't eat together as much as we used to.   Yes   No

2. Sometimes it seems we are roommates rather than a
   married couple.   Yes   No

3. We have fewer friends in common than we used to.   Yes   No

4. We seem to do a lot more things separately.   Yes   No

5. It seems that we have fewer and fewer interests in common.   Yes   No

6. Sometimes we can go for quite a while without ever talking
   about our lives.   Yes   No

7. Our lives are more parallel than connected.   Yes   No

8. We often don't talk about how our separate days went.   Yes   No

9. We don't spend very much time together anymore.   Yes   No

10. We spend a lot of our free time apart.   Yes   No

11. We don't set aside much time just to talk.   Yes   No

12. I don't think we know each other very well anymore.   Yes   No

13. We don't have dinner together very much anymore.   Yes   No

14. We rarely go out on dates together.   Yes   No

15. A lot of good times these days are with people other than
    each other.   Yes   No

16. We seem to be avoiding each other.   Yes   No

17. We are like two passing ships, going our separate ways.   Yes   No

Scoring: If the person answered "yes" to five or more of the statements, then he/she and the spouse may well be leading parallel lives. Realizing that the situation has deteriorated to this extreme is the first step toward rediscovering one other.

GOTTMAN AREAS OF DISAGREEMENT SCALE

This form contains a list of topics that many couples disagree about. We would like to get some idea of how much you and your spouse disagree about each area.

In the first column please indicate how much you and your spouse disagree by placing a number from 0 to 100 next to each item. A zero indicates that you don't disagree at all, and a 100 indicates that you disagree very much.

In the second column, please write down the number of years, months, weeks, or days that this has been an area of disagreement

For example:

We disagree about . . .	How much?	How long?
Alcohol and drugs	90	2 ½ years

This indicates that alcohol and drugs are something you disagree about very much and that this has been a problem for about 2 ½ years.

We disagree about	How much?	How long?
Money and finances		
Communication		
In-laws and kin		
Sex		
Religion		
Recreation and having fun		
Friends		
Alcohol and drugs		
Children		
Jealousy		
Lifestyle		
Philosophy of life		
Basic values		
Our goals		
Emotional expression		
Issues of power		
Independence and dependence		
Household chores and childcare		
Politics		
Balancing career and family		
Handling stresses		

Please feel free to write down any other areas of disagreement:

GOTTMAN AREAS OF CHANGE CHECKLIST: SOLVABLE PROBLEMS

Circle a number of any issue that represents an area in your marriage that you think requires some change. If it is a very serious problem, circle a "5," if it is only a small problem circle a "1," and use the numbers in-between 5 and 1 to indicate the severity of the problem in your view (1 = small problem, 5 = major problem).

1. I would like us to talk to each other more.	1 2 3 4 5
2. I would like our sex life to become more satisfying.	1 2 3 4 5
3. I would like us to have more independence in this marriage.	1 2 3 4 5
4. I would like it if we were more organized.	1 2 3 4 5
5. I would like it if my spouse spent more time with me.	1 2 3 4 5
6a. Our problems center on doing household chores.	1 2 3 4 5
6b. I do too much of the work.	1 2 3 4 5
7. I would like my spouse's relationships with our children to improve.	1 2 3 4 5
8. I would like my spouse's relationships with our families to improve.	1 2 3 4 5
9. I would like us to go to church, mosque, or synagogue together.	1 2 3 4 5
10. I would like us to have more fun together on weekends.	1 2 3 4 5
11. I would like to have fewer problems with my jealousy.	1 2 3 4 5
12. I would like to have fewer problems with my partner's jealousy.	1 2 3 4 5
13. I would like my partner to have fewer problems with alcohol and drugs.	1 2 3 4 5
14. I would like us to have more friends in common.	1 2 3 4 5
15. I would like to be consulted on important decisions.	1 2 3 4 5
16. I would like my partner to show more physical affection toward me.	1 2 3 4 5
17. I want us to go out on more "dates" together.	1 2 3 4 5
18. I would like my partner to watch less television and talk to me more instead.	1 2 3 4 5
19. I want us to make love more often.	1 2 3 4 5
20. I want more help with the finances.	1 2 3 4 5
21. I would want to receive more appreciation for what I do.	1 2 3 4 5
22. There's an extramarital affair that we need help getting over.	1 2 3 4 5
23a. I would like for us to have fewer problems with in-laws.	1 2 3 4 5
23b. I would like to get more support from my spouse about in-law problems.	1 2 3 4 5
24. I would like us to agree more about saving money.	1 2 3 4 5
25. I would like it if our lives were less chaotic.	1 2 3 4 5
26. I would like it if we had fewer disagreements about spending money.	1 2 3 4 5

27. I would like our lives to be less stressful. 1 2 3 4 5

28. I would like us to have more fun than we do. 1 2 3 4 5

29. We don't have enough of a social life. 1 2 3 4 5

30. I would like us to talk over a major upcoming decision. 1 2 3 4 5

31. I don't feel that my partner listens to me when I am upset. 1 2 3 4 5

32. I don't feel supported in this marriage. 1 2 3 4 5

33. I don't feel that my partner is very affectionate. 1 2 3 4 5

34. I would like to have a (or another) child. 1 2 3 4 5

35. We don't take enough vacations. 1 2 3 4 5

36. List your own issue: 1 2 3 4 5

GOTTMAN 17-AREAS SCALE

How Are Things Changing, or Not Changing, in Your Marriage?

To be of assistance to you, to responsibly track our workshop participants, and to design future workshops, we would like to know how you think things are, or are not, changing in your relationship. Please take the time to read each area we have outlined of your life together, and tell us if this area is fine or needs improvement. Put an X in the box that you think applies to your relationship right now. Then, at the end of each area, add comments, and, if things are fine, briefly tell us how you are managing this area of your lives. If things are not fine, tell us the obstacles you currently see to improving this area of your relationship. This information is completely confidential.

1. Staying emotionally connected ☐, or becoming emotionally distant ☐

Check all the specific items below:

Just simply talking to each other. Not a problem ☐ A problem ☐

Staying emotionally in touch with each other. Not a problem ☐ A problem ☐

Feeling taken for granted? Not a problem ☐ A problem ☐

Don't feel my spouse knows me very well right now. Not a problem ☐ A problem ☐

Spouse is (or I am) emotionally disengaged. Not a problem ☐ A problem ☐

Spending time together. Not a problem ☐ A problem ☐

Comments, and if things are fine, tell us how you are managing this area of your lives. If things are not fine, tell us the obstacles you see to improving this area of your relationship.

2. Handling job and other stresses effectively ☐, or experiencing the "spillover" of non-marital stresses ☐

Check all the specific items below:

Helping each other reduce daily stresses. Not a problem ☐ A problem ☐

Talking about these stresses together. Not a problem ☐ A problem ☐

Talking together about stress in a helpful manner. Not a problem ☐ A problem ☐

Spouse listening with understanding about my stresses and worries. Not a problem ☐ A problem ☐

Spouse takes job or other stresses out on me. Not a problem ☐ A problem ☐

Spouse takes job or other stresses out on the children or others in our life. Not a problem ☐ A problem ☐

Comments, and if things are fine, tell us how you are managing this area of your lives. If things are not fine, tell us the obstacles you see to improving this area of your relationship.

3. Handling issues or disagreements well ☐, or gridlocking on one or more issues ☐

Check all the specific items below:
Differences have arisen between us that feel very basic. Not a problem   ☐
   A problem   ☐

These differences seem unresolvable. Not a problem   ☐   A problem   ☐

We are living day-to-day with hurts. Not a problem   ☐   A problem   ☐

Our positions are getting entrenched. Not a problem   ☐   A problem   ☐

It looks like I will never get what I hope for. Not a problem   ☐   A problem   ☐

I am very worried that these issues may damage our relationship. Not a problem   ☐
   A problem   ☐

Comments, and if things are fine, tell us how you are managing this area of your lives. If things are not fine, tell us the obstacles you see to improving this area of your relationship.

4. The marriage is romantic and passionate ☐, or it is becoming passionless; the fire is going out ☐

Check all the specific items below:
My spouse has stopped being verbally affectionate. Not a problem   ☐   A problem   ☐

My spouse expresses love or admiration less frequently. Not a problem   ☐
   A problem   ☐

We rarely touch each other. Not a problem   ☐   A problem   ☐

My spouse (or I) have stopped feeling very romantic. Not a problem   ☐   A problem   ☐

We rarely cuddle. Not a problem   ☐   A problem   ☐

We have few tender or passionate moments. Not a problem   ☐   A problem   ☐

Comments, and if things are fine, tell us how you are managing this area of your lives. If things are not fine, tell us the obstacles you see to improving this area of your relationship.

5. Our sex life is fine ☐, or there are problems in this area ☐

Check all the specific items below:
The frequency of sex. Not a problem   ☐   A problem   ☐

The satisfaction I (or my spouse) get from sex. Not a problem   ☐   A problem   ☐

Being able to talk about sexual problems. Not a problem   ☐   A problem   ☐

The two of us wanting different things sexually. Not a problem   ☐   A problem   ☐

Problems of desire. Not a problem   ☐   A problem   ☐

The amount of love in our lovemaking. Not a problem   ☐   A problem   ☐

Comments, and if things are fine, tell us how you are managing this area of your lives. If things are not fine, tell us the obstacles you see to improving this area of your relationship.

6. **An important event (like the birth of a child, job loss, changes in job or residence, an illness, the death of a loved one) has occurred in our lives ☐. The marriage is either dealing with this well ☐, or it is not ☐**

   Check all the specific items below:

   We have very different points of view on how to handle things. Not a problem   ☐
   A problem   ☐

   This event has led my partner to be very distant. Not a problem   ☐   A problem   ☐

   This event has made us both irritable. Not a problem   ☐   A problem   ☐

   This event has led to a lot of fighting. Not a problem   ☐   A problem   ☐

   I'm worried about how this will all turn out. Not a problem   ☐   A problem   ☐

   We are now taking very different positions. Not a problem   ☐   A problem   ☐

Comments, and if things are fine, tell us how you are managing this area of your lives. If things are not fine, tell us the obstacles you see to improving this area of your relationship.

7. **Major issues about children have arisen (this could be about whether or not to have a child) ☐. The marriage is handling these well ☐, or it is not ☐**

   Check all the specific items below:

   We have very different points of view on goals for the children. Not a problem   ☐
   A problem   ☐

   We have different positions on *what to* discipline the children for. Not a problem   ☐
   A problem   ☐

   We have different positions on *how* to discipline the children. Not a problem   ☐
   A problem   ☐

   We have issues about how to be close to our children. Not a problem   ☐   A problem   ☐

   We are not talking about these issues very well. Not a problem   ☐   A problem   ☐

   There is a lot of tension or anger about these differences. Not a problem   ☐
   A problem   ☐

Comments, and if things are fine, tell us how you are managing this area of your lives. If things are not fine, tell us the obstacles you see to improving this area of your relationship.

8. **Major issues or events have arisen about in-laws, a relative or relatives ☐. The marriage is handling these well ☐, or it is not ☐**

   Check all the specific items below:

   I feel unaccepted by my partner's family. Not a problem ☐ A problem ☐

   I sometimes wonder which family my spouse is in. Not a problem ☐ A problem ☐

   I feel unaccepted by my own family. Not a problem ☐ A problem ☐

   There is tension between us about what might happen. Not a problem ☐ A problem ☐

   This issue has generated a lot of irritability. Not a problem ☐ A problem ☐

   I am worried about how this is going to turn out. Not a problem ☐ A problem ☐

   Comments, and if things are fine, tell us how you are managing this area of your lives. If things are not fine, tell us the obstacles you see to improving this area of your relationship.

9. **Being attracted to other people or jealousy is not an issue ☐, or spouse is flirtatious or there may be a recent extramarital affair ☐**

   Check all the specific items below:

   This area is a source of a lot of hurt. Not a problem ☐ A problem ☐

   This is an area that creates insecurity. Not a problem ☐ A problem ☐

   I can't deal with the lies. Not a problem ☐ A problem ☐

   It is hard to reestablish trust. Not a problem ☐ A problem ☐

   There is a feeling of betrayal. Not a problem ☐ A problem ☐

   It's hard to know how to heal this. Not a problem ☐ A problem ☐

   Comments, and if things are fine, tell us how you are managing this area of your lives. If things are not fine, tell us the obstacles you see to improving this area of your relationship.

10. **When disagreements arise, we resolve issues well ☐, or unpleasant fights have occurred ☐**

    Check all the specific items below:

    There are more fights now. Not a problem ☐ A problem ☐

    The fights seem to come out of nowhere. Not a problem ☐ A problem ☐

    Anger and irritability have crept into our marriage. Not a problem ☐ A problem ☐

    We get into muddles where we are hurting each other. Not a problem ☐ A problem ☐

    I don't feel very respected lately. Not a problem ☐ A problem ☐

    I feel criticized. Not a problem ☐ A problem ☐

Comments, and if things are fine, tell us how you are managing this area of your lives. If things are not fine, tell us the obstacles you see to improving this area of your relationship.

11. We are in synchrony on basic values and goals ☐, or differences between us in these areas or in desired lifestyle are emerging ☐

Check all the specific items below:

Differences have arisen in life goals. Not a problem ☐ A problem ☐

Differences have arisen about important beliefs. Not a problem ☐ A problem ☐

Differences have arisen on leisure time interests. Not a problem ☐ A problem ☐

We seem to be wanting different things out of life. Not a problem ☐ A problem ☐

We are growing in different directions. Not a problem ☐ A problem ☐

I don't much like who I am with my partner. Not a problem ☐ A problem ☐

Comments, and if things are fine, tell us how you are managing this area of your lives. If things are not fine, tell us the obstacles you see to improving this area of your relationship.

12. Very hard events (for example, violence, drugs, an affair) have occurred *within* the marriage ☐. We are handling these well ☐, or they seem to be hard for the marriage to deal with right now ☐

Check all the specific items below.

There has been physical violence between us. Not a problem ☐ A problem ☐

There is a problem with alcohol or drugs. Not a problem ☐ A problem ☐

This is turning into a marriage I hadn't bargained for. Not a problem ☐ A problem ☐

Our marriage "contract" is changing. Not a problem ☐ A problem ☐

I find some of what my partner wants upsetting or repulsive. Not a problem ☐ A problem ☐

I am now feeling somewhat disappointed by this marriage. Not a problem ☐ A problem ☐

Comments, and if things are fine, tell us how you are managing this area of your lives. If things are not fine, tell us the obstacles you see to improving this area of your relationship.

13. We work well as a team ☐, or we are not working very well as a team right now ☐

Check all the specific items below:

We used to share more in the family's workload. Not a problem   ☐   A problem   ☐

We seem to be pulling in opposite directions. Not a problem   ☐   A problem   ☐

Spouse does not share in housework or childcare. Not a problem   ☐   A problem   ☐

Spouse is not carrying weight financially. Not a problem   ☐   A problem   ☐

I feel alone managing this family. Not a problem   ☐   A problem   ☐

Spouse is not being very considerate. Not a problem   ☐   A problem   ☐

Comments, and if things are fine, tell us how you are managing this area of your lives. If things are not fine, tell us the obstacles you see to improving this area of your relationship.

14. We are coping well with issues of power or influence ☐, or we are having trouble in this area ☐

Check all the specific items below:

I don't feel influential in decisions we make. Not a problem   ☐   A problem   ☐

Spouse has become more domineering. Not a problem   ☐   A problem   ☐

I have become more demanding. Not a problem   ☐   A problem   ☐

Spouse has become passive. Not a problem   ☐   A problem   ☐

Spouse is "spacey," not a strong force in the marriage. Not a problem   ☐   A problem   ☐

I am starting to care a lot more about who is running things. Not a problem   ☐
   A problem   ☐

Comments, and if things are fine, tell us how you are managing this area of your lives. If things are not fine, tell us the obstacles you see to improving this area of your relationship.

15. We are handling issues of finances well ☐, or we are having trouble in this area ☐

Check all the specific items below:

I, or spouse, just doesn't bring in enough money. Not a problem   ☐   A problem   ☐

We have differences about how to spend our money. Not a problem   ☐   A problem   ☐

We are stressed about finances. Not a problem   ☐   A problem   ☐

Spouse is financially more interested in self than us. Not a problem   ☐   A problem   ☐

We are not united in managing our finances. Not a problem   ☐   A problem   ☐

There is not enough financial planning. Not a problem   ☐   A problem   ☐

Comments, and if things are fine, tell us how you are managing this area of your lives. If things are not fine, tell us the obstacles you see to improving this area of your relationship.

16. **We are doing well having fun together ☐, or we are not having very much fun together these days ☐**

    Check all the specific items below:

    We don't seem to have very much time for fun. Not a problem ☐ A problem ☐

    We try but don't seem to enjoy our times together very much. Not a problem ☐
      A problem ☐

    We are too stressed for fun. Not a problem ☐ A problem ☐

    Work takes up all our time these days. Not a problem ☐ A problem ☐

    Our interests are so different now that there are no fun things we like to do together. Not a problem ☐ A problem ☐

    We plan fun things to do but they never happen. Not a problem ☐ A problem ☐

    Comments, and if things are fine, tell us how you are managing this area of your lives. If things are not fine, tell us the obstacles you see to improving this area of your relationship.

17. **We are feeling close in the area of spirituality ☐, or we are not doing very well in that area these days ☐**

    Check all the specific items below:

    Sharing the same beliefs. Not a problem ☐ A problem ☐

    Agreeing about religious ideas and values. Not a problem ☐ A problem ☐

    Issues about the specific church, mosque, synagogue, etc. Not a problem ☐
      A problem ☐

    Communicating well about spiritual things. Not a problem ☐ A problem ☐

    Issues about spiritual growth and change. Not a problem ☐ A problem ☐

    Spiritual issues involving family or children. Not a problem ☐ A problem ☐

    Comments, and if things are fine, tell us how you are managing this area of your lives. If things are not fine, tell us the obstacles you see to improving this area of your relationship.

In case we omitted something, or an important area, please make your comments here.

GOTTMAN TURNING TOWARD DURING EVERYDAY EVENTS CHECKLIST

We would like to know how you feel about your spouse's participation during everyday events. During these events your spouse could either be turning away from you emotionally or toward you emotionally. We want you to assess in what areas you want more turning toward you. If an item is not an issue, circle NA.

From the list below, select the most important areas in your life where you would like your spouse to turn toward you more. Turning toward you means that you want greater connection with your spouse, emotionally. If you want more TURNING TOWARD YOU in an area, circle Y for "YES."

1. Reunion at the end of the day and talk about how the day went. Y   NA

2. Staying in touch with kin, e.g., calling parents (Mom, Dad, Grandmas) or siblings and in-laws. Y   NA

3. Shopping for groceries, making the shopping list. Y   NA

4. Cooking dinner, baking. Y   NA

5. House cleanups. Y   NA

6. Shop together for presents for a friend (e.g., friend's wedding). Y   NA

7. Family goes out to breakfast Saturday or Sunday. Y   NA

8. Read morning paper together. Y   NA

9. Stress reduction conversations (not about the marriage). Y   NA

10. Help partner with a self-improvement plan (e.g., a new class, weight loss, exercise, a new career). Y   NA

11. Plan a dinner party. Y   NA

12. Have a dinner party. Y   NA

13. Do laundry. Y   NA

14. Fold laundry, put it away. Y   NA

15. Call your spouse during the workday. Y   NA

16. Think about your spouse during the workday. Y   NA

17. Going out on a date with your spouse (no kids). Y   NA

18. An overnight with spouse at a romantic place. Y   NA

19. Morning breakfast during work week. Y   NA

20. Morning bathroom rituals. Y   NA

21. Going to a church, mosque, or synagogue together. Y   NA

22. Yard work. Y   NA

23. Home repair. Y   NA

24. Car maintenance and washing. Y   NA

25. Shoveling the walk. Y   NA

26. Committee work in the community (e.g., volunteering). Y   NA

27. Physical workouts together. Y   NA

28. Weekend outings (e.g., picnic, drives). Y   NA

29. Time with kids—bedtimes, baths, homework. Y   NA

30. Time with kids alone (e.g., zoo, museum, out to dinners). Y   NA

31. Going to the kids' school (e.g., volunteering, teacher conferences). Y   NA

32. Time with kin (parents, in-laws, siblings). Y   NA

33. Entertaining visitors from out of town. Y   NA

34. Traveling together (plane, bus train, car). Y   NA

35. Long drives together. Y   NA

36. Rent video and watch it together. Y   NA

37. Order dinner in or take out. Y   NA

38. Watch TV together. Y   NA

39. Double dating with another couple or friends. Y   NA

40. Sports events on TV. Y   NA

41. Doing a favorite activity together (e.g., bowling, going to the zoo, amusement park, bicy-cling, hiking, horseback riding, camping, canoeing, sailing, boating, water skiing, swimming). Y   NA

42. Build a fire at home. Sit in front of the fire and talk or read. Y   NA

43. Listening to music. Y   NA

44. Going to a concert. Y   NA

45. Going dancing together. Y   NA

46. Going to a night club or jazz club. Y   NA

47. Going to the theater. Y   NA

48. Going out to eat. Y   NA

49. Kid's birthday party. Y   NA

50. Taking kid to lessons. Y   NA

51. Kid's sporting events. Y   NA

52. Going to a kid performance (recital, play, etc.). Y   NA

53. Paying the bills. Y   NA

54. Writing letters or cards. Y   NA

55. Buying clothes for self or kids. Y   NA

56. Family medical events (taking kids to the doctor, dentist, or emergencies). Y   NA

57. Working at home, but still being together in some way. Y   NA

58. Going to a community event (e.g., church auction). Y   NA

59. Going to a party. Y   NA

60. Driving to or from work together. Y   NA

61. Major milestone child-oriented events (confirmations, graduations, games, recitals). Y   NA

62. Major milestone non-child-oriented events (e.g., celebrating successes). Y   NA

63. Any celebrations. Y   NA

64. Shopping: Buying things together that the house needs or you both need. Y   NA

65. Having kids' friends over. Y   NA

66. Buying toys for kids. Y   NA

67. Planning vacations. Y   NA

68. Taking vacations. Y   NA

69. Making plans, dreaming. Y   NA

70. Walking the dog. Y   NA

71. Sewing, knitting, crocheting. Y   NA

72. Reading out loud together. Y   NA

73. Playing a board game or a card game. Y   NA

74. Putting on plays or skits together. Y   NA

75. Doing errands together on a weekend. Y   NA

76. Hobbies: e.g., painting, sculpting, making music. Y   NA

77. Talk while drinking (alcohol, coffee or tea). Y   NA

78. Going out to your favorite bar or haunt. Y   NA

79. Time to just talk without interruptions. Y   NA

80. Time when I know I can have my spouse really listen to me. Y   NA

81. Visiting friends or family. Y   NA

82. Playing together. Y   NA

83. Philosophizing together. Y   NA

84. Gossiping (talking about other people). Y   NA

85. Going to a funeral. Y   NA

86. Helping a friend. Y   NA

87. Phone calls catching up with people you know. Y   NA

88. Visiting a sick friend. Y   NA

89. Doing other things to help other people out. Y   NA

GOTTMAN AREAS OF STRENGTHS CHECKLIST

Circle the issues that represent areas in your marriage in which you would like to build or increase strength. If it is already a strength in your marriage, *circle the item number* and *then skip the item.* If it is not a strength but you think it is very important to build strength in that area, circle a "5." Use the numbers in-between 5 and 1 to indicate the importance of the strength in your view (1 = important but not very important, 5 = very important).

I would like us to be able to say about our marriage:

1. We have very good communication.	1 2 3 4 5
2. We have a satisfying sex life.	1 2 3 4 5
3. We allow one another a lot of independence.	1 2 3 4 5
4. Our home is pretty well organized.	1 2 3 4 5
5. We are both very involved in this marriage and are a great team.	1 2 3 4 5
6. We both help out with household chores.	1 2 3 4 5
7. We both try very hard to be good parents and to have good relationships with our children.	1 2 3 4 5
8. We have good relationships with our families.	1 2 3 4 5
9. We have similar beliefs, basic values, and goals in life.	1 2 3 4 5
10. We have similar ideas about how to have a good time and enjoy life.	1 2 3 4 5
11. We are very good friends.	1 2 3 4 5
12. My partner gives me no reason for feeling jealous.	1 2 3 4 5
13. We are very good at helping each other to reduce stress.	1 2 3 4 5
14. I feel respected in this marriage.	1 2 3 4 5
15. I feel loved in this marriage.	1 2 3 4 5
16. I like what I am like in this relationship.	1 2 3 4 5
17. We admire one another.	1 2 3 4 5
18. I feel fairly confident that we could handle any problem we might face together.	1 2 3 4 5
20. I feel secure in this relationship.	1 2 3 4 5
21. We get along well with our in-laws.	1 2 3 4 5
22. We share similar views about basic religious or philosophical issues.	1 2 3 4 5
23. We agree on issues related to children.	1 2 3 4 5
24. We have similar views about money.	1 2 3 4 5
25. We manage pretty well with the daily stresses of our lives.	1 2 3 4 5
26. We have a lot of fun in life.	1 2 3 4 5
27. My partner knows and understands me.	1 2 3 4 5
28. I have all the independence I need.	1 2 3 4 5
29. I like where we are going in the future.	1 2 3 4 5
30. Our lives together have purpose and meaning.	1 2 3 4 5
31. We have a sense of adventure in our lives.	1 2 3 4 5

KROKOFF-GOTTMAN ENJOYABLE CONVERSATIONS SCALE

Below is a list of topics many couples enjoy talking about. We would like to get some idea of how enjoyable each topic is to you.

Please indicate how enjoyable each topic is by placing a number from 0 to 100 next to each item. A zero indicates that the topic is not at all enjoyable, and a 100 indicates that it is very enjoyable.

For example:

I enjoy talking to my spouse about. . .	How enjoyable?
The children	90

This indicates that you think that talking to your spouse about the children is very enjoyable.

I enjoy talking to my spouse about . . .	How enjoyable?
Other people we know	☐☐☐
Casual and informal types of things	☐☐☐
Political and current events	☐☐☐
Things that we have to get done around the house	☐☐☐
Things happening in town	☐☐☐
Silly and fun types of things	☐☐☐
Recreation, dates, dinners, parties	☐☐☐
Celebrations, holidays, special events	☐☐☐
Some good times we've had in the past	☐☐☐
The children (or grandchildren)	☐☐☐
Our views on different issues	☐☐☐
Our accomplishments	☐☐☐
Family pets	☐☐☐
Something we've recently done together	☐☐☐
Our sleep dreams	☐☐☐
Our dreams in life	☐☐☐
Our plans for the future	☐☐☐
Things we've seen on TV, heard, or read about	☐☐☐
Vacations we've taken	☐☐☐

Please feel free to write down any other conversations you find enjoyable.

Appendix **B**

The Sound Marital House Questionnaires

With my student Kim Ryan, I have designed and validated a comprehensive set of 15 self-report questionnaires that assess each important process in the Sound Marital House theory. These questionnaires are not a substitute for the Oral History, Meta-Emotion, and Meanings interview (see Appendix C), or for actually observing marital interaction. But they do offer a comprehensive snapshot of the couple's perception of each level of the Sound Marital House, and they are strongly related to Locke-Wallace marital satisfaction, the Weiss-Cerreto divorce proneness scale, and the SCL-90 psychopathology checklist. I suggest that this packet of questionnaires be given to spouses to take home prior to or after the first conjoint session. Make sure that they understand that they are to be filled out individually and that they are not to discuss how they filled them out with one another. Privacy is important in this process. This will help guarantee, to some degree, that their responses will be honest. Explain that you will share their responses as you move to a summary of the assessment.

There are four parts to the Sound Marital House:

1. Three levels that are about the marital friendship. These levels include Love Maps (knowing each other), the Fondness and Admiration System, and Turning Toward or Away (the "emotional bank account").

2. Positive or negative perspective. We will help you assess which kind of sentiment override partners use.

3. Regulation of conflict. In this level, we decide which of the couple's marital issues are perpetual problems and which are solvable situational problems. With regard to regulation of conflict, we will help assess Start-up (whether it is harsh), Accepting Influence, whether Repair Attempts are effective, and how good both spouses are at Compromise. With regard to perpetual problems, we will try to determine if the couple is in Gridlock, if the Four Horsemen of the Apocalypse have visited the marriage, whether they feel Flooded, whether they have assumed the position of

Innocent Victim, and if they are becoming Emotionally Disengaged and Lonely.

4. The couple's ability to honor one another's dreams and to create meaning together. This is important in its own right, and it also affects the basic marital friendship.

DEMOGRAPHIC INFORMATION SHEET

Please supply the information below. We realize that some of this information is very personal and sensitive, and we are asking you to trust us and report honestly. All information will be kept completely confidential. This demographic information sheet applies to you as an individual, not as a couple.

1. Date the questionnaire was completed: _____

2. Full name: _____

3. Spouse's full name: _____

4. Address: _____

   _____

5. Age: _____

6. Date of birth: _____

7. Sex   Male ☐ (1)   Female ☐ (2)

8. **Highest levels of education completed (check all those that apply):**

Less than high school	☐ (1)	Finished college (BA/BS Degree)	☐ (7)
Finished high school or equivalent	☐ (2)	Some graduate education	☐ (8)
Some college	☐ (3)	Professional Degree (e.g. Law)	☐ (9)
Two years of college	☐ (4)	Master's Degree	☐ (10)
Associate of Arts Degree	☐ (5)	Ph.D.	☐ (11)
M.F.A. Degree or equivalent	☐ (6)	Ed.D.	☐ (12)
Other advanced degree	☐ (13) please specify: _____		

9. **Ethnic or Racial Group Membership (check all that you feel apply):**

Caucasian or Euro-American	☐ (1)	Native American	☐ (5)
Black	☐ (2)	Hawaiian Islander	☐ (6)
African American	☐ (3)	Asian American please specify: _____	☐ (7)
Hispanic/Latino American	☐ (4)	Other please specify: _____	☐ (8)

**Religious Affiliation, if any
(please specify):** _____

10. **Current Personal Annual Income**

Less than $10,000	☐ (1)	Between $60,000 and $70,000	☐ (7)
Between $10,000 and $20,000	☐ (2)	Between $70,000 and $80,000	☐ (8)
Between $20,000 and $30,000	☐ (3)	Between $80,000 and $90,000	☐ (9)
Between $30,000 and $40,000	☐ (4)	Between $90,000 and $100,000	☐ (10)
Between $40,000 and $50,000	☐ (5)	Between $100,000 and $150,000	☐ (11)
Between $50,000 and $60,000	☐ (6)	Above $150,000	☐ (12)

11. **Your Occupation(s): Please briefly describe your occupation and what you do:** _____

_____

12. **Is this your first marriage?**   Yes ☐ (1)   No ☐ (2)   If no, which one?

13. **Full name of your couple's therapist:** _____

LOVE MAPS

Read each statement and place a check mark in the appropriate TRUE or FALSE box.

STATEMENT	RESPONSE			
I can name my partner's best friends.	True	☐ (1)	False	☐ (2)
I can tell you what stresses my partner is currently facing.	True	☐ (1)	False	☐ (2)
I know the names of some of the people who have been irritating in my partner's current life.	True	☐ (1)	False	☐ (2)
I can tell you some of my partner's life dreams.	True	☐ (1)	False	☐ (2)
I am very familiar with my partner's religious beliefs and ideas.	True	☐ (1)	False	☐ (2)
I can tell you about my partner's basic philosophy of life.	True	☐ (1)	False	☐ (2)
I can list the relatives my partner likes the least.	True	☐ (1)	False	☐ (2)
I know my partner's favorite music.	True	☐ (1)	False	☐ (2)
I can list my partner's three favorite movies.	True	☐ (1)	False	☐ (2)
My spouse is familiar with my current stresses.	True	☐ (1)	False	☐ (2)
I know the three times that have been most special in my partner's life.	True	☐ (1)	False	☐ (2)
I can tell you the most stressful thing that happened to my partner as a child.	True	☐ (1)	False	☐ (2)
I can list my partner's major aspirations and hopes in life.	True	☐ (1)	False	☐ (2)
I know my partner's major current worries.	True	☐ (1)	False	☐ (2)
My spouse knows who my friends are.	True	☐ (1)	False	☐ (2)
I know what my partner would want to do if he or she suddenly won the lottery.	True	☐ (1)	False	☐ (2)
I can tell you in detail my first impressions of my partner.	True	☐ (1)	False	☐ (2)
Periodically, I update my knowledge of my partner's world.	True	☐ (1)	False	☐ (2)
I feel that my partner knows me pretty well.	True	☐ (1)	False	☐ (2)
My spouse is familiar with my hopes and aspirations.	True	☐ (1)	False	☐ (2)

FONDNESS AND ADMIRATION SYSTEM

Read each statement and place a check mark in the appropriate TRUE or FALSE box.

STATEMENT	RESPONSE			
I can easily list the three things I most admire about my partner.	True	☐ (1)	False	☐ (2)
When we are apart, I often think fondly of my partner.	True	☐ (1)	False	☐ (2)
I often find some way to tell my partner "I love you."	True	☐ (1)	False	☐ (2)
I often touch or kiss my partner affectionately.	True	☐ (1)	False	☐ (2)
My partner really respects me.	True	☐ (1)	False	☐ (2)
I feel loved and cared for in this relationship.	True	☐ (1)	False	☐ (2)
I feel accepted and liked by my partner.	True	☐ (1)	False	☐ (2)
My partner finds me sexy and attractive.	True	☐ (1)	False	☐ (2)
My partner turns me on sexually.	True	☐ (1)	False	☐ (2)
There is fire and passion in this relationship.	True	☐ (1)	False	☐ (2)
Romance is something our relationship definitely still has in it.	True	☐ (1)	False	☐ (2)
I am really proud of my partner.	True	☐ (1)	False	☐ (2)
My partner really enjoys my achievements and accomplishments.	True	☐ (1)	False	☐ (2)
I can easily tell you why I married my partner.	True	☐ (1)	False	☐ (2)
If I had it to do all over again, I would marry the same person.	True	☐ (1)	False	☐ (2)
We rarely go to sleep without some show of love or affection.	True	☐ (1)	False	☐ (2)
When I come into a room, my partner is glad to see me.	True	☐ (1)	False	☐ (2)
My partner appreciates the things I do in this marriage.	True	☐ (1)	False	☐ (2)
My spouse generally likes my personality.	True	☐ (1)	False	☐ (2)
Our sex life is generally satisfying.	True	☐ (1)	False	☐ (2)

TURNING TOWARD OR AWAY

Read each statement and place a check mark in the appropriate TRUE or FALSE box.

STATEMENT	RESPONSE			
We enjoy doing even the smallest things together, like folding laundry or watching TV.	True	☐ (1)	False	☐ (2)
I look forward to spending my free time with my partner.	True	☐ (1)	False	☐ (2)
At the end of a day my partner is glad to see me.	True	☐ (1)	False	☐ (2)
My partner is usually interested in hearing my views on things.	True	☐ (1)	False	☐ (2)
I really enjoy discussing things with my partner.	True	☐ (1)	False	☐ (2)
My partner is one of my best friends.	True	☐ (1)	False	☐ (2)
I think my partner would consider me a very close friend.	True	☐ (1)	False	☐ (2)
We love just talking to each other.	True	☐ (1)	False	☐ (2)
When we go out, the time goes very quickly.	True	☐ (1)	False	☐ (2)
We always have a lot to say to each other.	True	☐ (1)	False	☐ (2)
We have a lot of fun together in our everyday lives.	True	☐ (1)	False	☐ (2)
We are spiritually very compatible.	True	☐ (1)	False	☐ (2)
We tend to share the same basic values in life.	True	☐ (1)	False	☐ (2)
We like to spend time together in similar ways.	True	☐ (1)	False	☐ (2)
We really have a lot of interests in common.	True	☐ (1)	False	☐ (2)
We have many of the same dreams and life goals.	True	☐ (1)	False	☐ (2)
We like to do a lot of the same things.	True	☐ (1)	False	☐ (2)
Even though our interests are somewhat different, I enjoy my partner's interests.	True	☐ (1)	False	☐ (2)
Whatever we do together we usually tend to have a good time.	True	☐ (1)	False	☐ (2)
My partner tells me when he or she has had a bad day.	True	☐ (1)	False	☐ (2)

NEGATIVE PERSPECTIVE

Fill this form out thinking about your immediate past (last 2 to 4 weeks), or a recent discussion of an existing marital issue. Read each statement and place a check mark in the appropriate TRUE or FALSE box.

IN THE RECENT PAST IN MY MARRIAGE, GENERALLY:	RESPONSE
I felt hurt.	True ☐ (1) False ☐ (2)
I felt misunderstood.	True ☐ (1) False ☐ (2)
I thought, "I don't have to take this."	True ☐ (1) False ☐ (2)
I felt innocent of blame for this problem.	True ☐ (1) False ☐ (2)
I thought to myself, "Just get up and leave."	True ☐ (1) False ☐ (2)
I was angry.	True ☐ (1) False ☐ (2)
I felt disappointed.	True ☐ (1) False ☐ (2)
I felt unjustly accused.	True ☐ (1) False ☐ (2)
I thought, "My partner has no right to say those things."	True ☐ (1) False ☐ (2)
I was frustrated.	True ☐ (1) False ☐ (2)
I felt personally attacked.	True ☐ (1) False ☐ (2)
I wanted to strike back.	True ☐ (1) False ☐ (2)
I felt like I was warding off a barrage.	True ☐ (1) False ☐ (2)
I felt like getting even.	True ☐ (1) False ☐ (2)
I wanted to protect myself.	True ☐ (1) False ☐ (2)
I took my partner's complaints as slights.	True ☐ (1) False ☐ (2)
I felt like my partner was trying to control me.	True ☐ (1) False ☐ (2)
I thought that my partner was very manipulative.	True ☐ (1) False ☐ (2)
I felt unjustly criticized.	True ☐ (1) False ☐ (2)
I wanted the negativity to just stop.	True ☐ (1) False ☐ (2)

START-UP

Read each statement and place a check mark in the appropriate TRUE or FALSE box.

WHEN WE DISCUSS OUR MARITAL ISSUES:	RESPONSE			
My partner is often very critical of me.	True	☐ (1)	False	☐ (2)
I hate the way my partner raises an issue.	True	☐ (1)	False	☐ (2)
Arguments often seem to come out of nowhere.	True	☐ (1)	False	☐ (2)
Before I know it, we are in a fight.	True	☐ (1)	False	☐ (2)
When my partner complains, I feel picked on.	True	☐ (1)	False	☐ (2)
I seem to always get blamed for issues.	True	☐ (1)	False	☐ (2)
My partner is negative all out of proportion.	True	☐ (1)	False	☐ (2)
I feel I have to ward off personal attacks.	True	☐ (1)	False	☐ (2)
I often have to deny charges leveled against me.	True	☐ (1)	False	☐ (2)
My partner's feelings are too easily hurt.	True	☐ (1)	False	☐ (2)
What goes wrong is often not my responsibility.	True	☐ (1)	False	☐ (2)
My spouse criticizes my personality.	True	☐ (1)	False	☐ (2)
Issues get raised in an insulting manner.	True	☐ (1)	False	☐ (2)
My partner will complain at times in a smug or superior way.	True	☐ (1)	False	☐ (2)
I have just about had it with all this negativity between us.	True	☐ (1)	False	☐ (2)
I feel basically disrespected when my partner complains.	True	☐ (1)	False	☐ (2)
I just want to leave the scene when complaints arise.	True	☐ (1)	False	☐ (2)
Our calm is suddenly shattered.	True	☐ (1)	False	☐ (2)
I find my partner's negativity unnerving and unsettling.	True	☐ (1)	False	☐ (2)
I think my partner can be totally irrational.	True	☐ (1)	False	☐ (2)

ACCEPTING INFLUENCE

Read each statement and place a check mark in the appropriate TRUE or FALSE box.

WHEN WE DISCUSS OUR MARITAL ISSUES: RESPONSE

Statement	Response
I find that I am really interested in my spouse's opinion on our basic issues.	True ☐ (1) False ☐ (2)
I usually learn a lot from my spouse, even when we disagree.	True ☐ (1) False ☐ (2)
I want my partner to feel that what he or she says really counts with me.	True ☐ (1) False ☐ (2)
I generally want my spouse to feel influential in this marriage.	True ☐ (1) False ☐ (2)
I can listen to my partner, but only up to a point.	True ☐ (1) False ☐ (2)
My partner has a lot of basic common sense.	True ☐ (1) False ☐ (2)
I try to communicate respect even during our disagreements.	True ☐ (1) False ☐ (2)
If I keep trying to convince my partner, I will eventually win out.	True ☐ (1) False ☐ (2)
I don't reject my spouse's opinions out of hand.	True ☐ (1) False ☐ (2)
My partner is not rational enough to take seriously when we discuss our issues.	True ☐ (1) False ☐ (2)
I believe in lots of give-and-take in our discussions.	True ☐ (1) False ☐ (2)
I am very persuasive and usually can win arguments with my spouse.	True ☐ (1) False ☐ (2)
I feel important in our decisions.	True ☐ (1) False ☐ (2)
My partner usually has good ideas.	True ☐ (1) False ☐ (2)
My partner is basically a great help as a problem-solver.	True ☐ (1) False ☐ (2)
I try to listen respectfully even when I disagree.	True ☐ (1) False ☐ (2)
My ideas for solutions are usually much better than my spouse's.	True ☐ (1) False ☐ (2)
I can usually find something to agree with in my partner's position.	True ☐ (1) False ☐ (2)
My partner is usually too emotional.	True ☐ (1) False ☐ (2)
I am the one who needs to make the major decisions in this marriage.	True ☐ (1) False ☐ (2)

REPAIR ATTEMPTS

Read each statement and place a check mark in the appropriate TRUE or FALSE box.

DURING OUR ATTEMPTS TO RESOLVE CONFLICT:	RESPONSE			
We are good at taking breaks when we need them.	True	☐ (1)	False	☐ (2)
When I apologize, it usually gets accepted by my partner.	True	☐ (1)	False	☐ (2)
I can say that I am wrong.	True	☐ (1)	False	☐ (2)
I am pretty good at calming myself down.	True	☐ (1)	False	☐ (2)
Even when arguing, we can maintain a sense of humor.	True	☐ (1)	False	☐ (2)
When my partner says we should talk to each other in a different way, it usually makes a lot of sense.	True	☐ (1)	False	☐ (2)
My attempts to repair our discussions when they get negative are usually effective.	True	☐ (1)	False	☐ (2)
We are pretty good listeners even when we have different positions on things.	True	☐ (1)	False	☐ (2)
If things get heated, we can usually pull out of it and change things.	True	☐ (1)	False	☐ (2)
My spouse is good at soothing me when I get upset.	True	☐ (1)	False	☐ (2)
I feel confident that we can resolve most issues between us.	True	☐ (1)	False	☐ (2)
When I comment on how we could communicate better, my spouse listens to me.	True	☐ (1)	False	☐ (2)
Even if things get hard at times, I know we can get past our differences.	True	☐ (1)	False	☐ (2)
We can be affectionate even when we are disagreeing.	True	☐ (1)	False	☐ (2)
Teasing and humor usually work with my spouse for getting over negativity.	True	☐ (1)	False	☐ (2)
We can start all over again and improve our discussions when we need to.	True	☐ (1)	False	☐ (2)
When emotions run hot, expressing how upset I feel makes a real difference.	True	☐ (1)	False	☐ (2)
Even when there are big differences between us, we can discuss these.	True	☐ (1)	False	☐ (2)
My partner expresses appreciation for nice things I do.	True	☐ (1)	False	☐ (2)
If I keep trying to communicate, it will eventually work.	True	☐ (1)	False	☐ (2)

COMPROMISE

Read each statement and place a check mark in the appropriate TRUE or FALSE box.

DURING OUR ATTEMPTS TO RESOLVE CONFLICT:	RESPONSE			
Our decisions often get made by both of us compromising.	True	☐ (1)	False	☐ (2)
We are usually good at resolving our differences.	True	☐ (1)	False	☐ (2)
I can give in when I need to, and often do.	True	☐ (1)	False	☐ (2)
I can be stubborn in an argument, and I'm opposed to compromising.	True	☐ (1)	False	☐ (2)
I think that sharing power in a marriage is very important.	True	☐ (1)	False	☐ (2)
My partner is not a very stubborn person.	True	☐ (1)	False	☐ (2)
I believe that one person is usually right and the other wrong on most issues.	True	☐ (1)	False	☐ (2)
We both believe in meeting each other halfway when we disagree.	True	☐ (1)	False	☐ (2)
I am able to yield somewhat even when I feel strongly on an issue.	True	☐ (1)	False	☐ (2)
The two of us usually arrive at a better decision through give-and-take.	True	☐ (1)	False	☐ (2)
It's not a good idea to give in too much, in my view.	True	☐ (1)	False	☐ (2)
In discussing issues, we can usually find our common ground of agreement.	True	☐ (1)	False	☐ (2)
No one ever gets what they want when there is a compromise.	True	☐ (1)	False	☐ (2)
My partner can give in, and often does.	True	☐ (1)	False	☐ (2)
I wait until my partner gives in before I do.	True	☐ (1)	False	☐ (2)
When I give in first, my partner then gives in too.	True	☐ (1)	False	☐ (2)
Yielding power is very difficult for my spouse.	True	☐ (1)	False	☐ (2)
Yielding power is very difficult for me.	True	☐ (1)	False	☐ (2)
Give-and-take in making decisions is not a problem in this marriage.	True	☐ (1)	False	☐ (2)
I will never compromise when I believe I am right.	True	☐ (1)	False	☐ (2)

GRIDLOCK

Read each statement and place a check mark in the appropriate TRUE or FALSE box.

WHEN WE DISCUSS OUR MARITAL ISSUES:	RESPONSE
The same problems keep coming up again and again in our marriage.	True ☐ (1) False ☐ (2)
We rarely make much progress on our central issues.	True ☐ (1) False ☐ (2)
We keep hurting each other whenever we discuss our core issues.	True ☐ (1) False ☐ (2)
I feel criticized and misunderstood when we discuss our hot topics.	True ☐ (1) False ☐ (2)
My partner has a long list of basically unreasonable demands.	True ☐ (1) False ☐ (2)
When we discuss our basic issues, I often feel that my partner doesn't even like me.	True ☐ (1) False ☐ (2)
My partner wants me to change my basic personality.	True ☐ (1) False ☐ (2)
I often keep quiet and withdraw to avoid stirring up too much conflict.	True ☐ (1) False ☐ (2)
I don't feel respected when we disagree.	True ☐ (1) False ☐ (2)
My partner often acts in a selfish manner.	True ☐ (1) False ☐ (2)
What I say in our discussions rarely has much effect.	True ☐ (1) False ☐ (2)
I feel put down in our discussions of key issues.	True ☐ (1) False ☐ (2)
I can't really be myself in this marriage.	True ☐ (1) False ☐ (2)
I often think that my partner is manipulating me.	True ☐ (1) False ☐ (2)
Sometimes I think that my spouse doesn't care about my feelings.	True ☐ (1) False ☐ (2)
My partner rarely makes a real effort to change.	True ☐ (1) False ☐ (2)
There are some basic faults in my partner's personality that he or she will not change.	True ☐ (1) False ☐ (2)
My partner disregards my fundamental needs.	True ☐ (1) False ☐ (2)
Sometimes I feel that my values don't matter to my spouse.	True ☐ (1) False ☐ (2)
When we discuss our issues, I feel I am right and my partner is wrong.	True ☐ (1) False ☐ (2)

THE FOUR HORSEMEN

Read each statement and place a check mark in the appropriate TRUE or FALSE box.

WHEN WE DISCUSS OUR MARITAL ISSUES:	RESPONSE
I feel attacked or criticized when we talk about our disagreements.	True ☐ (1) False ☐ (2)
I usually feel like my personality is being assaulted.	True ☐ (1) False ☐ (2)
In our disputes, at times, I don't even feel like my partner likes me very much.	True ☐ (1) False ☐ (2)
I have to defend myself because the charges against me are so unfair.	True ☐ (1) False ☐ (2)
I often feel unappreciated by my spouse.	True ☐ (1) False ☐ (2)
My feelings and intentions are often misunderstood.	True ☐ (1) False ☐ (2)
I don't feel appreciated for all the good I do in this marriage.	True ☐ (1) False ☐ (2)
I often just want to leave the scene of the argument.	True ☐ (1) False ☐ (2)
I get disgusted by all the negativity between us.	True ☐ (1) False ☐ (2)
I feel insulted by my partner at times.	True ☐ (1) False ☐ (2)
I sometimes just clam up and become quiet.	True ☐ (1) False ☐ (2)
I can get mean and insulting in our disputes.	True ☐ (1) False ☐ (2)
I feel basically disrespected.	True ☐ (1) False ☐ (2)
Many of our issues are just not my problem.	True ☐ (1) False ☐ (2)
The way we talk makes me want to just withdraw from the whole marriage.	True ☐ (1) False ☐ (2)
I think to myself, "Who needs all this conflict?"	True ☐ (1) False ☐ (2)
My partner never really changes.	True ☐ (1) False ☐ (2)
Our problems have made me feel desperate at times.	True ☐ (1) False ☐ (2)
My partner doesn't face issues responsibly and maturely.	True ☐ (1) False ☐ (2)
I try to point out flaws in my partner's personality that need improvement.	True ☐ (1) False ☐ (2)
I feel explosive and out of control about our issues at times.	True ☐ (1) False ☐ (2)
My partner uses phrases like "you always" or "you never" when complaining.	True ☐ (1) False ☐ (2)
I often get the blame for what are really our problems.	True ☐ (1) False ☐ (2)
I don't have a lot of respect for my partner's position on our basic issues.	True ☐ (1) False ☐ (2)
My spouse can be quite selfish and self-centered.	True ☐ (1) False ☐ (2)
I feel disgusted by some of my spouse's attitudes.	True ☐ (1) False ☐ (2)

WHEN WE DISCUSS OUR MARITAL ISSUES:	RESPONSE			
My partner gets far too emotional.	True	☐ (1)	False	☐ (2)
I am just not guilty of many of the things I get accused of.	True	☐ (1)	False	☐ (2)
Small issues often escalate out of proportion.	True	☐ (1)	False	☐ (2)
Arguments seem to come out of nowhere.	True	☐ (1)	False	☐ (2)
My partner's feelings get hurt too easily.	True	☐ (1)	False	☐ (2)
I often will become silent to cool things down a bit.	True	☐ (1)	False	☐ (2)
My partner has a lot of trouble being rational and logical.	True	☐ (1)	False	☐ (2)

FLOODING

Read each statement and place a check mark in the appropriate TRUE or FALSE box.

STATEMENT	RESPONSE			
Our discussions get too heated.	True	☐ (1)	False	☐ (2)
I have a hard time calming down.	True	☐ (1)	False	☐ (2)
One of us is going to say something we will regret.	True	☐ (1)	False	☐ (2)
My partner gets too upset.	True	☐ (1)	False	☐ (2)
After a fight, I want to keep my distance.	True	☐ (1)	False	☐ (2)
My partner yells unnecessarily.	True	☐ (1)	False	☐ (2)
I feel overwhelmed by our arguments.	True	☐ (1)	False	☐ (2)
I can't think straight when my partner gets hostile.	True	☐ (1)	False	☐ (2)
I think to myself, "Why can't we talk more logically?"	True	☐ (1)	False	☐ (2)
My partner's negativity often comes out of nowhere.	True	☐ (1)	False	☐ (2)
There's often no stopping my partner's temper.	True	☐ (1)	False	☐ (2)
I feel like running away during our fights.	True	☐ (1)	False	☐ (2)
Small issues suddenly become big ones.	True	☐ (1)	False	☐ (2)
I can't calm down very easily during an argument	True	☐ (1)	False	☐ (2)
My partner has a long list of unreasonable demands.	True	☐ (1)	False	☐ (2)

EMOTIONAL DISENGAGEMENT AND LONELINESS

Read each statement and place a check mark in the appropriate TRUE or FALSE box.

STATEMENT	RESPONSE			
I often find myself disappointed in this marriage.	True	☐ (1)	False	☐ (2)
I have learned to expect less from my partner.	True	☐ (1)	False	☐ (2)
I find myself quite lonely in this relationship at times.	True	☐ (1)	False	☐ (2)
It is hard for my deepest feelings to get much attention in this marriage.	True	☐ (1)	False	☐ (2)
I often try to avoid saying things I will later regret.	True	☐ (1)	False	☐ (2)
I feel like I have to be so careful, it is like walking on eggshells.	True	☐ (1)	False	☐ (2)
Suddenly, once again, I find I have said the wrong thing.	True	☐ (1)	False	☐ (2)
There is not much intimacy in this marriage right now.	True	☐ (1)	False	☐ (2)
Our marital problems are not really solvable.	True	☐ (1)	False	☐ (2)
Sometimes our marriage feels empty to me.	True	☐ (1)	False	☐ (2)
This marriage is not quite what I expected, and I feel let down by it.	True	☐ (1)	False	☐ (2)
We are pretty separate and unconnected emotionally.	True	☐ (1)	False	☐ (2)
We don't really talk very deeply to each other.	True	☐ (1)	False	☐ (2)
There is not enough closeness between us.	True	☐ (1)	False	☐ (2)
I sometimes think I expect too much and should settle for less in my marriage.	True	☐ (1)	False	☐ (2)
I am coping with a lot of marital stress, but it will be okay eventually.	True	☐ (1)	False	☐ (2)
I have adapted to a lot in this marriage, and I am not so sure it's a good idea.	True	☐ (1)	False	☐ (2)
There's certainly not much romance in this relationship.	True	☐ (1)	False	☐ (2)
I can't really say that we are very good friends right now.	True	☐ (1)	False	☐ (2)
I am often lonely in this marriage.	True	☐ (1)	False	☐ (2)

INNOCENT VICTIM AND RIGHTEOUS INDIGNATION SCALE

Fill out this scale while thinking about your last argument with your partner.

During our last discussion:

1. I felt hurt.
   Yes   No

2. I felt misunderstood.
   Yes   No

3. I thought, "I don't have to take this."
   Yes   No

4. I felt innocent of blame for this problem.
   Yes   No

5. I thought to myself, just get up and leave.
   Yes   No

6. I was scared.
   Yes   No

7. I was angry.
   Yes   No

8. I was worried.
   Yes   No

9. I felt disappointed.
   Yes   No

10. I wanted my feelings to get some attention here.
    Yes   No

11. I felt injustly accused.
    Yes   No

12. I thought, "My partner has no right to say those things."
    Yes   No

13. I felt let down.
    Yes   No

14. I felt sad.
    Yes   No

15. I was frustrated.
    Yes   No

16. I felt personally attacked.
    Yes   No

17. I wanted to strike back.
    Yes   No

18. I felt like I was warding off a barrage.
    Yes   No

19. I felt like getting even.
    Yes   No

20. I wanted to protect myself.
    Yes   No

21. I knew I was right.
    Yes   No

22. I had a pretty low opinion of my partner's personality at the time.
    Yes   No

Scoring

1. Tally the number of "yes" responses to statements 1, 2, 4, 5, 6, 8, 11, 13, 14, 16, 18, and 20. A score of 4 or more suggests you tend to have an innocent-victim reaction during negative times in your marriage.

2. Tally your "yes" responses to statements 1, 2, 3, 7, 9, 10, 12, 15, 17, 19, 21, 22. A score of 4 or more suggests you tend to have a righteous-indignation reaction during negative times in your marriage.

SHARED MEANINGS QUESTIONNAIRE: HONORING EACH OTHER'S DREAMS

We want you to think about how well you and your partner have been able to create a sense of shared meaning in your lives together. When people get married, they create a new culture, and some marriages also involve the union of two very different cultures. But even if two people are coming from the same regional, cultural, ethnic, and religious background, they will have been raised in two very different families, and their merging involves the creation of a new culture.

YOUR RITUALS	RESPONSE			
We see eye-to-eye about the rituals that involve family dinnertimes in our home.	True	☐ (1)	False	☐ (2)
Holiday meals (like Thanksgiving, Christmas, Passover) are very special and happy times for us.	True	☐ (1)	False	☐ (2)
Reunions at the end of each day in our home are generally special times in my day.	True	☐ (1)	False	☐ (2)
We agree about the role of TV in our home.	True	☐ (1)	False	☐ (2)
Bedtimes are generally good times for being close.	True	☐ (1)	False	☐ (2)
During weekends we do a lot of things together that we enjoy and value.	True	☐ (1)	False	☐ (2)
We have the same values about entertaining in our home (having friends over, parties, etc.).	True	☐ (1)	False	☐ (2)
We both value special celebrations (like birthdays, anniversaries, family reunions).	True	☐ (1)	False	☐ (2)
When I become sick, I feel taken care of and loved by my spouse.	True	☐ (1)	False	☐ (2)
I really look forward to and enjoy our vacations and the travel we do together.	True	☐ (1)	False	☐ (2)
The mornings together are special times for me.	True	☐ (1)	False	☐ (2)
When we do errands together, we generally have a good time.	True	☐ (1)	False	☐ (2)
We have ways of becoming renewed and refreshed when we are burned out or fatigued.	True	☐ (1)	False	☐ (2)

YOUR ROLES	RESPONSE			
We share many similar values in our roles as husband and wife.	True	☐ (1)	False	☐ (2)
We share many similar values in our roles as mother and father.	True	☐ (1)	False	☐ (2)
We have many similar views about what it means to be a good friend to others.	True	☐ (1)	False	☐ (2)
My partner and I have compatible views about the role of work in one's life.	True	☐ (1)	False	☐ (2)

YOUR ROLES RESPONSE

My partner and I have similar philosophies about balancing work and family life.	True	☐ (1)	False	☐ (2)
My partner supports what I would see as my basic mission in life.	True	☐ (1)	False	☐ (2)
My partner shares my views on the importance of family and kin (sisters, brothers, moms, dads) in our life together.	True	☐ (1)	False	☐ (2)

YOUR GOALS RESPONSE

We share many of the same goals in our life together.	True	☐ (1)	False	☐ (2)
If I were to look back on my life in very old age, I think I would see that our paths in life had meshed very well.	True	☐ (1)	False	☐ (2)
My partner values my accomplishments.	True	☐ (1)	False	☐ (2)
My partner honors my very personal goals, unrelated to my marriage.	True	☐ (1)	False	☐ (2)
We share many of the same goals for others who are important to us (children, kin, friends, and community).	True	☐ (1)	False	☐ (2)
We have very similar financial goals.	True	☐ (1)	False	☐ (2)
We tend to have compatible financial disaster scenarios (ones we both want to avoid).	True	☐ (1)	False	☐ (2)
Our hopes and aspirations, as individuals and together, for our children, for our life in general, and for our old age are quite compatible.	True	☐ (1)	False	☐ (2)
Our life dreams tend to be similar or compatible.	True	☐ (1)	False	☐ (2)
Even when different, we have been able to find a way to honor our life dreams.	True	☐ (1)	False	☐ (2)

YOUR SYMBOLS RESPONSE

We see eye-to-eye about what "home" means.	True	☐ (1)	False	☐ (2)
Our philosophies of what love ought to be are quite compatible.	True	☐ (1)	False	☐ (2)
We have similar values about the importance of "peacefulness" in our lives.	True	☐ (1)	False	☐ (2)
We have similar views about the meaning of "family."	True	☐ (1)	False	☐ (2)
We have similar views about the role of sex in our lives.	True	☐ (1)	False	☐ (2)
We have similar views about the role of love and affection in our lives.	True	☐ (1)	False	☐ (2)
We have similar values about the meaning of being married.	True	☐ (1)	False	☐ (2)
We have similar values about the importance and meaning of money in our lives.	True	☐ (1)	False	☐ (2)

YOUR SYMBOLS	RESPONSE
We have similar values about the importance of education in our lives.	True ☐ (1) False ☐ (2)
We have similar values about the importance of "fun" and "play" in our lives.	True ☐ (1) False ☐ (2)
We have similar values about the significance of "adventure."	True ☐ (1) False ☐ (2)
We have similar values about "trust."	True ☐ (1) False ☐ (2)
We have similar values about personal "freedom."	True ☐ (1) False ☐ (2)
We have similar values about "autonomy" and "independence."	True ☐ (1) False ☐ (2)
We have similar values about sharing "power" in our marriage.	True ☐ (1) False ☐ (2)
We have similar values about being "interdependent," of being a "we."	True ☐ (1) False ☐ (2)
We have similar values about the meaning of "having possessions," of "owning things" (like cars, nice clothes, books, music, a house, land).	True ☐ (1) False ☐ (2)
We have similar values about the meaning of "nature" and of our relationship to the seasons.	True ☐ (1) False ☐ (2)
We are both sentimental and tend to reminisce about things in our past.	True ☐ (1) False ☐ (2)
We have similar views about what we want in retirement and old age.	True ☐ (1) False ☐ (2)

Appendix C
The Basic Interviews

The Oral History Interview was developed over a period of more than a year by Lowell Krokoff (initially in collaboration with John Gottman). It began as an interview that lasted many hours and was pared down to one to two-and-a-half hours. It is a semi-structured interview, which means that you will memorize the questions. It is absolutely essential that you actually memorize the questions and make sure that you do not make up your own versions of the questions or follow the principles of *clinical* interviewing. However, the subjects may answer Question 10 as they are answering Question 2, and that is okay in a semi-structured interview. The important thing is to get answers to all the questions, but the order is not important. You will go with the natural course of conversation and try to get the subjects to be as expansive and involved as possible.

A good interviewer makes sure to get into the subjective world of the people being interviewed. For example, suppose that a couple describe a period in their relationship when he went to college but she stayed in high school one more year to finish. She says that she visited him a few times during this year. A good interviewer wonders about the inner experience of this period. Was the situation one in which he was embarrassed by her visits, viewing her as a kid or a yokel, and she felt the rejection? If so, how did they cope with these feelings? Or, was this a situation in which he felt great showing her the world of college and she was proud and excited? We want to know about these inner experiences.

Here are some major themes to look for:

- *We-ness.* You will find some couples who emphasize we-ness in these interviews, while others do not. Sometimes one person will be talking about the "we" while the other is emphasizing separateness and difference.

- *Glorifying the struggle.* Some couples will express the philosophy that marriage is hard, that it is a struggle, but that it is worth it.

- *Gender differences.* See if you can identify differences between spouses that relate to gender differences in emotional expression, responsiveness, and role.

- *Conflict-avoiding versus conflict-engaging.* Some couples minimize the emotional side of their marital interactions, whether positive or negative. They tend to avoid disagreements. They tend to speak about the events of the day in terms of errands rather than feelings. Self-disclosure is minimized. Their roles tend to be fairly stereotyped and prescribed by cultural norms.

This appendix includes:

1. Oral History Interview
2. Meta-Emotion Interview
3. Meanings Interview

ORAL HISTORY INTERVIEW

Part I: History of the Relationship

Question 1. Why don't we start from the very beginning. Let's discuss how the two of you met and got together. Do you remember the time you met for the first time? Tell me about it. Was there anything about your wife (husband) that made her (him) stand out? What were your first impressions of each other?

Question 2. When you think back to the time you were dating, before you got married, what do you remember? What stands out? How long did you know each other before you got married? What do you remember of this period? What were some of the highlights? Some of the tensions? What types of things did you do together?

Question 3. Tell me about how the two of you decided to get married. Of all the people in the world, what led you to decide that this was the person you wanted to marry? Was it an easy decision? Was it a difficult decision? Were you ever in love? Tell me about this time.

Question 4. Do you remember your wedding? Tell me about your wedding. Did you have a honeymoon? What do you remember about it?

Question 5. When you think back to the first year you were married, what do you remember? Were there any adjustments to being married?

Question 6. What about the transition to becoming parents? Tell me about this period of you marriage. What was it like for the two of you?

Question 7. Looking back over the years, what moments stand out as the really good times in your marriage? What were the really happy times? What is a good time for you as a couple? Has this changed over the years?

Question 8. Many of the couples we've talked to say that their relationships go through periods of ups and downs. Would you say that this is true of your marriage?

Question 9. Looking back over the years, what moments stand out as the really hard times in your marriage? Why do you think you stayed together? How did you get through these difficult times? What is your philosophy about how to get through difficult times?

Question 10. How would you say your marriage is different from when you first got married? (*Lots of people have losses here; they have stopped doing things that once gave them pleasure. Explore these with the couple.*)

Part II. Your Philosophy of Marriage

Question 11. We're interested in your ideas about what makes a marriage work. Tell me about why you think some marriages work while others don't. Think of a couple you know who has a particularly good marriage and one that you know who has a particularly bad marriage. Decide together which two couples these are. What is different about these two marriages? How would you compare your own marriage to each of these couples?

Question 12. Tell me about your parents' marriages. What was their marriage like? Would you say it's very similar or different from your own marriage?

Question 13. Make a map of the history of your marriage, its major turning points, ups and downs. What were the happiest times for you and your partner? How has your marriage changed over the years?

Question 14. Tell me what you currently know about your partner's major worries, stresses, hopes, and aspirations. How do you stay in touch with one another on a daily basis? What are your routines for staying in emotional contact?

Scoring the Oral History Interview

Therapist's Rating Form:
Critical Dimensions on Which to Rate the Couple

Rate the Couple on the Following Items:

Love Maps or cognitive room. How much did the couple recall about specific times in their marriage? This relates to how much cognitive room you think that they are allocating in their brains to this relationship and to knowing their partner's inner world. To evaluate this, we find that when asked about some aspect of their lives together, some event, or about their spouse, some people have a lot to say, and give lots of detail, whereas some people seem to not have stored very much information in their brains about this. This is related to whether or not there is a kind of "cognitive map" about the spouse's world and the relationship. Circle which best represents this couple (1 indicates *very little;* 9 indicates a *lot*).

Husband:

1   2   3   4   5   6   7   8   9

Wife:

1   2   3   4   5   6   7   8   9

Fondness and Admiration System. Were there spontaneous expressions of fondness and admiration expressed about the partner? When they talked about past events, did they spontaneously think of admirable and adorable qualities of the spouse that emerged during these times? Circle which best represents them.

Husband toward wife:

1   2   3   4   5   6   7   8   9

Wife toward husband:

1   2   3   4   5   6   7   8   9

Disappointment and negativity. Were there spontaneous expressions of, or memories about, feeling disappointment in the marriage or in the partner? Circle which best represents them.

Husband:

1   2   3   4   5   6   7   8   9

Wife:

1   2   3   4   5   6   7   8   9

We-ness. In the interview did you find that the two of them emphasized words like "we" and "us" as opposed to just talking about themselves as separate individuals, set apart from one another? Did they wind up finishing each other's sentences? Or did you find that one was talking about the "we," while the other was emphasizing separateness and difference? Circle which best represents them.

Husband:

1   2   3   4   5   6   7   8   9

Wife:

1   2   3   4   5   6   7   8   9

Glorifying the struggle. This dimension refers to how much they believe as a couple that they can be effective at solving their marital problems. Some people call it "couple efficacy." Some couples express the philosophy that marriage is hard, that it is a struggle, but that it is worth it. Do the two of them feel this way? Some couples have the opposite expectation, that even before their conversation about an issue, they will get nowhere. Have they expressed in their marriage that struggling through a problem was a potentially constructive experience? Do they have the expectation that the two of them can indeed get through a problem and solve it? Circle which best represents them.

Husband:

1   2   3   4   5   6   7   8   9

Wife:

1   2   3   4   5   6   7   8   9

Chaos. Do they feel that negative things in life "just happen" to the two of them and that they have very little control over this state of affairs? Would you describe their lives together as chaotic and out of control? Circle which best represents them.

As a Couple:

1   2   3   4   5   6   7   8   9

Husband:

1   2   3   4   5   6   7   8   9

Wife:

1   2   3   4   5   6   7   8   9

Stereotypic roles, traditionality. Do differences between the two of them relate to gender differences in emotional expression, or emotional responsiveness, and their roles as spouses and parents? How traditional is their marriage in terms of gender roles, where 1 is totally egalitarian and 9 is totally traditional?

As a Couple:

1   2   3   4   5   6   7   8   9

Husband:

1   2   3   4   5   6   7   8   9

Wife:

1   2   3   4   5   6   7   8   9

Conflict-avoiding versus conflict-engaging couples. Some couples minimize the emotional side of their marital interaction, particularly conflict. They tend to avoid disagreements. They also often minimize how intense their interaction is, and they keep a lot of personal things private. To what degree does a conflict-avoiding style characterize this marriage? Circle which best represents them.

As a Couple:

1   2   3   4   5   6   7   8   9

Husband:

1   2   3   4   5   6   7   8   9

Wife:

1   2   3   4   5   6   7   8   9

META-EMOTION INTERVIEW

In our Meta-Emotion Interview, we interview each person alone (although we have done this interview conjointly), and we ask people about their own family history with the emotions: anger, fear, sadness, pride, and love. We ask them if, as a child, they could tell that their father was angry, and what that experience was like for them. We ask about all these emotions, for both parents. (For example, we ask, "How did your parents show you that they were proud of you?" "How did your parents show you that they loved you?"). Then we ask about what things were like when they, as children, expressed these emotions. We continue through their lives, asking them about the history of their experience with these emotions. We ask them whether people can tell if they are having these emotions, what it is like for them to have each of these emotions, and what their philosophy about emotions is. In this interview we elicit stories (encouraging them, "Tell me the story of that"), metaphors, and narratives about these emotions in their lives. We ask about emotions that are most difficult for them to cope with having, and how they deal with these.

Then we ask them how they have arranged their marriage around these emotions. For example, many couples view anger as a dangerous emotion, and they have designed ways of dealing with anger so it does not hurt the marriage. Ask about this.

We also ask about how they deal with these emotions with their children, what they do when their child is sad, for example, and we ask for examples they can recall. We ask what they are trying to teach their children about each emotion.

MEANINGS INTERVIEW

We start with these instructions to the couple: "In this interview, we want to get to know you and your family and hear the stories about your family and both of the families you grew up in. We think that when people get married they create a new culture, and some involve the union of two very different cultures also. But even if two people are coming from the same regional, cultural, ethnic, and religious background, they will have been raised in two very different families, and their merging involves the creation of a new culture."

Rituals

Around rituals, explore areas of agreement and disagreement between the spouses. Are there conflicts in this area?

Tell us about family dinnertime in your home. What does eating together mean to you? What are family meals like? What were they like growing up for each of you? What about special meals? Thanksgiving, Christmas, Passover? What do these events mean to you, if anything? What is the role of food in your family?

Tell us about reunions at the end of each day in your home. What is the reunion like? What goes on? What is important when you all get together at the end of the day? What about TV?

Tell us about bedtime in your home.

Tell us about the weekends. What goes on during the weekends?

Tell us about the rituals you have around finances. How do you view money? Why?

Tell us about entertaining in your home, having friends over, parties, and so on. What typically goes on? What is important to you about these events? What atmosphere are you trying to create?

What are especially good times for you as a couple, and for your family together? Give us some recent examples. What was important to you about these times?

What are typical things you celebrate? Birthdays? Anniversaries? Family reunions? Any special holidays (religious or others like Thanksgiving, Valentine's Day, Halloween, New Year's)? How do you celebrate them? Tell me about recent events. What do these events mean?

What are typical things that happen around someone in the family being sick? What do these things mean to you?

Tell me about vacations and travel in your life. What are these events like typically [find out about one] and what do they mean?

Explore rituals that may surround other times, such as the mornings, fun and play times, marital dates and getaways, weekends, time with friends, time with kin, birthdays, holidays, sports events, movies and TV viewing, religious festivals and holidays, adventure, travel, vacations, and other things they like doing together (collecting things, going to garage sales, driving around, picnics, outings, shopping, singing, making music, arts and crafts, etc.).

How do you do things like running errands? Do you do errands together on Saturdays or Sundays, or split up? What is this time like?

How do you guys get renewed and refreshed when you are burned out or fatigued?

Roles

Around roles, explore areas of agreement and disagreement between the spouses. Are there conflicts in this area?

Tell me about your own personal view of what being a wife [husband, mother, father] means to you. How do you think of yourself in this role? What is important to you? What are you trying to accomplish in this role?

What kinds of events go along with being a good wife [good husband, good mother, good father] that would help me understand how you see this role?

Tell me about the role of your life work/occupation [expand this worker role to the more specific ones of "scientist," "physician," "craftsman," "carpenter," "lawyer," "artist," "musician," "actor," "builder," "architect," "mason," "homemaker," and so on] and what it means to you. What is your life mission in your work?

How do you balance work and other roles [mother, father, son, daughter, brother, sister, friend] with your role as a wife [husband]? What limits do you set on each of these roles and why?

What about other roles you play, such as provider, protector, nurturer, educator, mentor, friend, religious and philosophical person? Are any of these roles important to you? How do you see yourself?

Goals

Around goals, explore areas of agreement and disagreement between the spouses. Are there conflicts in this area?

What would you say that your life goals are for yourself? If you were to look back on your life in very old age, what would you like to be able to say about your life? What accomplishments would please you?

What are some of your very personal goals, unrelated to your marriage?

What are your goals for others who are important to you [your children, your spouse, kin, friends, and your community]? What would you like to see happen for them, and what role do you think you play in making these things happen?

What are your financial goals? What are your financial disaster scenarios you want to avoid?

What are your hopes and aspirations, as individuals and together, for your children, for your life in general, for your old age?

What are your life dreams? Why do you have these goals, and where do they come from in your lives?

Did your parents have similar or different goals?

What would you say is your life "mission," what do you hope to accomplish in your life, what is really important to you?

What is your common ground? What discrepancies between the two of you exist in this area? How satisfied are you with this area of your lives? To what extent do you feel that you are actually accomplishing important goals in your lives?

Symbols

Around symbols, explore areas of agreement and disagreement between the spouses. Are there conflicts in this area?

What does a "home" mean to you? What have you tried to create in your home together? It will mean very different things to different people.

What does "love" mean to you? How is this manifest in your lives?

What does being a "provider" mean to you?

What is the meaning of "peacefulness"?

What is the meaning of "family"?

What is the meaning of being married?

What does money mean to you? How is this evident in your life?

What does education mean to you?

What does "fun" or "play" mean to you? What role should it play in a person's life?

What is the meaning to you of "trust"?

What is the meaning to you of "freedom," of "autonomy," "independence," and "power"?

What is the meaning of being "interdependent," of being a "we"?

What is the meaning of "having possessions," of "owning things" (like cars, nice clothes, books, music, a house, and land)?

What is the meaning of "nature" to you, your relationship to the seasons?

What do you reminisce about?

What does it mean to be a [person's last name here]? Are there any stories you can tell me that go along with what it means to be a [person's last name here]?

Photo Albums

We have asked you to bring in your photo albums (childhood pictures as well) so we can get a good idea of what your family is like, and what is important to your family. [Take some time to put the MACRO lens on the camera and photograph the family albums on video-tape]. Please give us a tour of the main characters and events in your life growing up, and in your lives together.

Spirituality

Around spirituality, explore areas of agreement and disagreement between the spouses. Are there conflicts in this area?

Religion and spiritual growth play a role in some families and not in others. Can you share with us what your own views are about a spiritual life, and how you have created or tried to create shared meaning in this area of your lives?

What does it mean to you to be a good [Quaker, Christian, Jew, Moslem, Buddhist, Taoist, Hindu, etc.]?

What, if anything, is the meaning of religion and/or God in your lives?

What is the meaning of such concepts as "education," "learning," "peace," "commitment," "solidarity," "charity," and "community"?

What is your common ground?

What discrepancies between you exist in these areas?

How satisfied are you with these areas of your lives?

Appendix D
Intervention Tools

Here we include:

1. Aftermath of Failed Bids Questionnaire
2. The Resistance Interview
3. Internal Working Model of Relationships Questionnaire: I (D) [Depression]
4. Internal Working Model of Relationships Questionnaire: II (A) [Antisocial]

AFTERMATH OF FAILED BIDS QUESTIONNAIRE

This form is a guide for processing and evaluating what happened when one of you felt that the friendship in your marriage was not working well, when perhaps one of you felt alienated and lonely, while the other may have felt a great need for autonomy, independence, or being alone. This form is designed to try to increase understanding between the two of you. The idea here is that there is no absolute "reality" when two people miss each other in turning toward one another, or turning away, but only two "subjective realities." This form is designed to help you get at these, and to ease these situations in the future.

Answer each item, filling out the form individually. Then discuss with your partner how you filled out each item.

How did you feel?

1. During this week I felt defensive.	A Great Deal	Definitely	A Little	Not at All
2. During this week my feelings got hurt.	A Great Deal	Definitely	A Little	Not at All
3. I felt excluded.	A Great Deal	Definitely	A Little	Not at All
4. I felt angry.	A Great Deal	Definitely	A Little	Not at All
5. I felt sad.	A Great Deal	Definitely	A Little	Not at All
6. I felt misunderstood.	A Great Deal	Definitely	A Little	Not at All
7. I felt criticized.	A Great Deal	Definitely	A Little	Not at All
8. I felt like my partner didn't even like me.	A Great Deal	Definitely	A Little	Not at All
9. I was afraid.	A Great Deal	Definitely	A Little	Not at All
10. I was worried.	A Great Deal	Definitely	A Little	Not at All
11. I felt I was right and my partner was wrong.	A Great Deal	Definitely	A Little	Not at All
12. I felt out of control.	A Great Deal	Definitely	A Little	Not at All
13. I felt righteously indignant.	A Great Deal	Definitely	A Little	Not at All
14. I felt unfairly picked on.	A Great Deal	Definitely	A Little	Not at All
15. I felt unappreciated.	A Great Deal	Definitely	A Little	Not at All
16. I felt unattractive.	A Great Deal	Definitely	A Little	Not at All
17. I felt neglected.	A Great Deal	Definitely	A Little	Not at All
18. I felt disgusted.	A Great Deal	Definitely	A Little	Not at All
19. I was disapproving.	A Great Deal	Definitely	A Little	Not at All
20. I was morally outraged.	A Great Deal	Definitely	A Little	Not at All
21. I felt taken for granted.	A Great Deal	Definitely	A Little	Not at All
22. I felt like leaving.	A Great Deal	Definitely	A Little	Not at All
23. I was overwhelmed with emotion.	A Great Deal	Definitely	A Little	Not at All
24. I felt excluded.	A Great Deal	Definitely	A Little	Not at All
25. I felt powerless.	A Great Deal	Definitely	A Little	Not at All
26. I felt like I had no influence.	A Great Deal	Definitely	A Little	Not at All

27. I felt like my opinions didn't even matter.	A Great Deal	Definitely	A Little	Not at All
28. I had no feelings at all.	A Great Deal	Definitely	A Little	Not at All
29. I had no idea what I was feeling.	A Great Deal	Definitely	A Little	Not at All
30. I felt lonely.	A Great Deal	Definitely	A Little	Not at All
31. I felt alienated.	A Great Deal	Definitely	A Little	Not at All

Other feelings (write in):

What were the triggers?

Events Related to Inclusion

1. I felt excluded.	A Great Deal	Definitely	A Little	Not at All
2. No one was interested in me.	A Great Deal	Definitely	A Little	Not at All
3. I was being ignored.	A Great Deal	Definitely	A Little	Not at All
4. I was not important to my spouse.	A Great Deal	Definitely	A Little	Not at All
5. I felt cold toward my spouse.	A Great Deal	Definitely	A Little	Not at All
6. My partner was not happy to see me.	A Great Deal	Definitely	A Little	Not at All

Others (write in):

Events Related to Affection

1. I felt no affection from my partner toward me.	A Great Deal	Definitely	A Little	Not at All
2. My partner was cold toward me.	A Great Deal	Definitely	A Little	Not at All
3. I definitely felt rejected.	A Great Deal	Definitely	A Little	Not at All
4. I was criticized.	A Great Deal	Definitely	A Little	Not at All
5. I felt no affection toward my partner.	A Great Deal	Definitely	A Little	Not at All
6. I felt that my partner was not attracted to me.	A Great Deal	Definitely	A Little	Not at All

Others (write in):

Events Related to Influence

1. I had no power in this discussion.	A Great Deal	Definitely	A Little	Not at All
2. I felt helpless to affect how the conversation went.	A Great Deal	Definitely	A Little	Not at All
3. I felt there was a lack of respect toward me.	A Great Deal	Definitely	A Little	Not at All
4. My sense of dignity was being compromised.	A Great Deal	Definitely	A Little	Not at All
5. My partner was being domineering.	A Great Deal	Definitely	A Little	Not at All
6. I could not persuade my partner at all.	A Great Deal	Definitely	A Little	Not at All

Others (write in):

Do these feelings relate to your past?

Some self-examination is necessary here to identify where the triggers come from in your own past. What issues are you particularly sensitive about, and what is the origin of these sensitivities?

When people are under prolonged periods of stress, old patterns of thought and behavior can emerge, old sensitivities can become heightened, and the fighting in the marriage is a symptom of older patterns. This section is designed to help you see what potential past events may have set the conditions for the turning away from one another.

How I have been responding lately when stressed, what sensitivities, thoughts and feelings have I had lately in my marriage:

They come from the way I was treated in my family growing up (explain):

They come from a previous relationship (explain):

They come from past injuries I suffered (explain):

They come from really hard times I endured (explain):

They come from traumas I experienced (explain):

They come from basic fears and insecurities I have (explain):

They come from things and events I have not yet resolved or put aside (explain):

They come from unrealized hopes I have (explain):

They relate to ways I was treated in the past by other people (explain):

They relate to things I have always thought about myself (explain):

They relate to old "nightmares" or "catastrophes" I have worried about (explain):

Other (explain):

Summarize in writing your own subjective reality about closeness and autonomy during this week. What was the subjective reality for you? Share these subjective realities and try to see how your partner's subjective reality might make sense, given your partner's perspective.

Try to communicate (in writing here) your understanding of your partner's subjective reality about closeness and autonomy during this week.

It is essential that each of you attempts to give some credence to the other's subjective reality. Try to do that right now in your mind. In finding the right balance for both of you in connection (closeness) and individual autonomy (separateness), there is a need to first understand YOUR part in all of this.

How can you change the way you express your needs?

It is natural for each of us to make the fundamental error that it is all our partner's fault. Actually, because it is all a cycle, it is the *fault* of neither. What is necessary is to be able to move BOTH of you out of a defensive pattern into a more productive pattern. This starts by EACH OF YOU admitting some role (however slight at first) in creating this distance and loneliness.

- How did you (or your partner) express the needs for closeness or for dealing with loneliness?

- How did you (or your partner) express the need to be separate, autonomous or independent, or the feelings of being swamped and overwhelmed by your partner's needs?

Admitting your role. It is essential that you each take some responsibility for what happened. That cannot happen easily unless you have first calmed yourself down physiologically. Recall the five steps of self-soothing: Breathing evenly and deeply, tensing and then relaxing muscle groups, making the muscle groups heavy, making the muscle groups warm, and, finally, summarizing all of this in a personal image of tranquility and peace. Second, you have to let go of thoughts that maintain the distress, thoughts of feeling misunderstood and of either righteous indignation or innocent victimhood. Take some time, allowing at least 20 minutes for this to happen. Then fill out the rest of this form.

Calmer?   YES   NO

If NO, go back and calm down some more.

If YES, you are calmer, now try to admit to yourself what role you may have had this week.

1. I have been very stressed and irritable lately.	YES, DEFINITELY	MAYBE A LITTLE
2. I have not expressed much appreciation toward my spouse lately.	YES, DEFINITELY	MAYBE A LITTLE
3. I have taken my spouse for granted.	YES, DEFINITELY	MAYBE A LITTLE
4. I have been overly sensitive lately.	YES, DEFINITELY	MAYBE A LITTLE
5. I have been overly critical lately.	YES, DEFINITELY	MAYBE A LITTLE
6. I have not shared very much of my inner world.	YES, DEFINITELY	MAYBE A LITTLE
7. I have not been emotionally available.	YES, DEFINITELY	MAYBE A LITTLE
8. I have been more typically turning away.	YES, DEFINITELY	MAYBE A LITTLE
9. I have been getting easily upset.	YES, DEFINITELY	MAYBE A LITTLE
10. I have been depressed lately.	YES, DEFINITELY	MAYBE A LITTLE
11. I would say that I have a chip on my shoulder lately.	YES, DEFINITELY	MAYBE A LITTLE
12. I have not been very affectionate.	YES, DEFINITELY	MAYBE A LITTLE
13. I have not made time for good things between us.	YES, DEFINITELY	MAYBE A LITTLE
14. I have not been a very good listener lately.	YES, DEFINITELY	MAYBE A LITTLE
15. I have not asked for what I need.	YES, DEFINITELY	MAYBE A LITTLE
16. I have been feeling a bit like a martyr.	YES, DEFINITELY	MAYBE A LITTLE
17. I have needed to be alone.	YES, DEFINITELY	MAYBE A LITTLE
18. I have not wanted to take care of anybody.	YES, DEFINITELY	MAYBE A LITTLE

19. Other:

Overall, my contribution to this mess was:

How can you make this better in the future?

What one thing could your spouse do, and what one thing could you do next time to avoid this problem?

     It's easier to start here, so we will. What one thing could your spouse do differently?

     It's harder to do this, but try it. What one thing could you do differently?

Now share your form with your spouse and talk about the week without starting the pattern of increasing distance and loneliness again.

RESISTANCE INTERVIEW

I. Love Maps

1. What does it mean to this client to know someone?

2. What does it mean to this client to be known by someone?

II. Fondness and Admiration System

1. What does it mean to this client to be thought of with fondness and admiration by another?

2. What does it mean to this client to think of someone else with fondness and admiration?

III. Turning toward rather than away

1. What does it mean to this client to turn toward another characteristically and want to be with that one person, to be consistently attracted to that person, to be interested in that person, care about what that person has to say?

2. What does it mean to this client to have someone turn toward this client characteristically and want to be with this client, be attracted to this client, be interested in this client, care about what this client has to say?

IV. Having enough positive sentiment that it can override negativity

1. What does it mean to this client to have enough positive sentiment toward another that it can override that person's being negative?

2. What does it mean to this client to have someone else trust this client enough so that the client's negativity is overridden by positive feelings?

V. Dialogue with perpetual problems

1. What does it mean to this client to be able to accept someone else, despite his/her shortcomings, and be amused by his/her failings rather than enraged by them?

2. What does it mean to this client to be able to believe that he/she is accepted by someone else, despite his/her own shortcomings, and have that person be amused by the client's failings rather than enraged by them?

VI. How complaints are raised

1. What does it mean to this client to be able to raise a complaint with softened gentleness?

2. What does it mean to this client to be able to respond to another's gentleness?

VII. Accepting influence

1. What does it mean to this client to be able to influence someone else, be persuasive, but also yield to win?

2. What does it mean to this client to be able to accept influence from another?

VIII. Being able to repair an interaction

1. What does it mean to this client to be able to offer a repair when the interaction with the spouse isn't going very well?

2. What does it mean to this client to accept the spouse's attempt at repairing things when the interaction isn't going very well?

IX. Being able to de-escalate and calm down

1. What does it mean to this client to be able to self-soothe?

2. What does being able to soothe one's partner mean to the client?

X. Being able to compromise

1. What does it mean to this client to be able to propose a compromise solution to a marital problem?

2. What does it mean to this client to be able to accept another's compromise solution?

XI. Creating shared meaning

1. What does it mean to this client to accept and support the partner's dreams, even if they are different from the client's own?

2. What does it mean to this client to have the client's own dreams and develop them within the context of the relationship? [This is true individuation.]

INTERNAL WORKING MODEL OF RELATIONSHIPS: I (D)

Consider each statement made below, and see it fits something you yourself believe. Circle SA if you strongly agree with the statement. Circle A if you just agree with the statement. Circle N if you neither agree nor disagree with the statement. Circle D if you disagree with the statement. Circle SD if you strongly disagree with the statement.

1. It is scary to know someone intimately because then I might find out that I really am worthless.	SA	A	N	D	SD
2. If my partner gets to know me well, he (she) will discover that most people are better than me in some way.	SA	A	N	D	SD
3. When I get close to someone, I am afraid that they will find out the true me and not like me.	SA	A	N	D	SD
4. I expect rejection if I get too close.	SA	A	N	D	SD
5. If someone finds out the real me, that person will choose another.	SA	A	N	D	SD
6. I don't believe it when people pay me a compliment.	SA	A	N	D	SD
7. I have rarely believed it when someone is proud of me.	SA	A	N	D	SD
8. No one will value my being proud of them.	SA	A	N	D	SD
9. If I showed my partner I admired him (or her), he (or she) would just make fun of me.	SA	A	N	D	SD
10. I don't want to keep giving because it probably will turn him (or her) off.	SA	A	N	D	SD
11. My partner will find me repulsive if I keep being too nice.	SA	A	N	D	SD
12. I don't believe that I will ever be truly loved for who I am.	SA	A	N	D	SD
13. I don't think that anyone can really find me attractive.	SA	A	N	D	SD
14. I don't think that anyone can really find me interesting.	SA	A	N	D	SD
15. I don't think anyone really truly cares about me.	SA	A	N	D	SD
16. I always expect people to revert to true selfishness; that's human nature.	SA	A	N	D	SD
17. As soon as my partner is nasty, I have trouble remembering all the past nice things he (or she) did.	SA	A	N	D	SD
18. No matter how much you do for your spouse, they will always want more.	SA	A	N	D	SD
19. As soon as I am in a bad mood and show it, my partner's love for me will disappear.	SA	A	N	D	SD
20. I tend to focus on people's flaws.	SA	A	N	D	SD
21. I see mostly the dark side of human nature.	SA	A	N	D	SD
22. I find it hard to believe that someone will overlook my faults.	SA	A	N	D	SD
23. No one has really ever truly accepted me.	SA	A	N	D	SD

24. When I get upset, I find it hard to be gentle.	SA	A	N	D	SD
25. I usually come on too harshly with my complaints.	SA	A	N	D	SD
26. When my partner complains in a nice way, I find it hard to respond.	SA	A	N	D	SD
27. I don't believe it when my partner is upset and is still being nice.	SA	A	N	D	SD
28. I am never very good at persuading my partner that I am right.	SA	A	N	D	SD
29. Why try to be persuasive when you will only fail?	SA	A	N	D	SD
30. I find it hard to give in once I have made up my mind.	SA	A	N	D	SD
31. I can be very stubborn, but I think it's necessary.	SA	A	N	D	SD
32. I am not good at being able to make things better between us once they have gone sour.	SA	A	N	D	SD
33. When I am upset, I can't think of how to make it better.	SA	A	N	D	SD
34. When I am in a bad mood, it's hard for me to let someone try to make things better.	SA	A	N	D	SD
35. My partner's attempts to repair things between us usually seem hollow to me.	SA	A	N	D	SD
36. I have a lot of trouble calming down when I am upset.	SA	A	N	D	SD
37. I can nurse a bad mood or grudge for a long time and can't get myself out of it.	SA	A	N	D	SD
38. When my spouse is upset, I am no good at calming him (or her) down.	SA	A	N	D	SD
39. I am not good at creating peace once it is gone.	SA	A	N	D	SD
40. I am not very likely to think of some way of compromising.	SA	A	N	D	SD
41. When we disagree, I find myself sticking to my guns.	SA	A	N	D	SD
42. When someone suggests compromise, I get even more stubborn.	SA	A	N	D	SD
43. When my partner suggests that I give in a little if he (she) will, I simply refuse to budge.	SA	A	N	D	SD
44. If my partner wants things in life that are different from what I want, I feel lonely and abandoned.	SA	A	N	D	SD
45. I think it's a bad sign if you and your partner are different in what you want out of life.	SA	A	N	D	SD
46. I want my marriage to support my interests even if they are not my spouse's interests.	SA	A	N	D	SD
47. I think it's healthy to develop my own dreams and interests in life, different from my spouse's.	SA	A	N	D	SD

Total Score: For each item tally SA = 4, A = 3, N = 2, D = 1, SD = 0. A score of 62 or above indicates that the low self-esteem internal working model is active in this person's mind.

INTERNAL WORKING MODEL OF RELATIONSHIPS: II (A)

Consider each statement made below, and see it fits something you yourself believe. Circle SA if you strongly agree with the statement. Circle A if you just agree with the statement. Circle N if you neither agree nor disagree with the statement. Circle D if you disagree with the statement. Circle SD if you strongly disagree with the statement.

1. It is important to know about someone else because that knowledge is power.   SA   A   N   D   SD

2. If you really can read someone, you can usually get what you want from them.   SA   A   N   D   SD

3. If my partner gets to know me well, she (he) will use it to manipulate me toward her (his) ends.   SA   A   N   D   SD

4. When I get close to someone, I am afraid they will know too much about me.   SA   A   N   D   SD

5. When people pay me a compliment, I wonder what they want.   SA   A   N   D   SD

6. When someone is proud of me, I think they are out to get something from me.   SA   A   N   D   SD

7. I think most people's accomplisments are usually real hype and phony.   SA   A   N   D   SD

8. If I showed someone I admired him (her), I'd be making myself too vulnerable.   SA   A   N   D   SD

9. I don't want to spend too much time with any one person.   SA   A   N   D   SD

10. When I am being very nice, I am usually after something.   SA   A   N   D   SD

11. I don't believe that anyone ever truly loves me for who I am.   SA   A   N   D   SD

12. When someone finds me interesting, I feel like I have the upper hand.   SA   A   N   D   SD

13. In this world usually no one really truly cares about anyone else.   SA   A   N   D   SD

14. I expect people to be selfish because that's what I would do.   SA   A   N   D   SD

15. As soon as someone starts becoming nasty, I turn against them.   SA   A   N   D   SD

16. When you do things for others, they will take advantage of you.   SA   A   N   D   SD

17. I put on bad moods sometimes just to throw people off guard.   SA   A   N   D   SD

18. Everyone in this world is mostly out to get what they can.   SA   A   N   D   SD

19. I can't tolerate too much closeness to people.   SA   A   N   D   SD

20. I am basically a loner.   SA   A   N   D   SD

21. I am not all that fond of people.   SA   A   N   D   SD

22. No one will ever overlook my faults, so I try to
    keep them hidden.   SA   A   N   D   SD

23. No one has really ever truly accepted me, and I
    don't blame them.   SA   A   N   D   SD

24. When I get upset, I come on like a ton of bricks
    because of the element of surprise attack.   SA   A   N   D   SD

25. If I didn't come on strong, people would walk
    all over me.   SA   A   N   D   SD

26. When my partner complains in a nice way, I see it
    as a weakness.   SA   A   N   D   SD

27. People have their uses when you need something.   SA   A   N   D   SD

28. When my partner is upset and still trying to be nice,
    I know I have the upper hand.   SA   A   N   D   SD

29. I can always persuade people that I am right.   SA   A   N   D   SD

30. I always try to be persuasive, since it is so easy.   SA   A   N   D   SD

31. If you don't control others, they will try to control you.   SA   A   N   D   SD

32. I am not going to let my spouse influence or control
    me in any way.   SA   A   N   D   SD

33. I can be very stubborn, but that's because I can't let
    anyone walk all over me.   SA   A   N   D   SD

34. Once things have gone sour between us, I just couldn't
    care less.   SA   A   N   D   SD

35. When I am upset, I come on strong so that I will be
    in charge.   SA   A   N   D   SD

36. It's hard for me to let my spouse try to make things
    better between us, unless he (or she) gives in.   SA   A   N   D   SD

37. My partner's attempts to repair things between us are
    never going to work.   SA   A   N   D   SD

38. I don't usually get really upset, but I like to act upset
    for the effect it has.   SA   A   N   D   SD

39. I can put on a show of being in a bad mood just to
    get the upper hand.   SA   A   N   D   SD

40. When my spouse is upset, I wouldn't even bother
    calming him (or her) down.   SA   A   N   D   SD

41. I am good at creating upset in my partner if it helps
    me stay in control.   SA   A   N   D   SD

42. I believe, "Why compromise if you don't have to,"
    and I usually don't have to.   SA   A   N   D   SD

43. When we disagree, I become impatient and just
    want to win the argument.   SA   A   N   D   SD

44. When my partner suggests a compromise, I get mad and stubborn.   SA   A   N   D   SD

45. I don't have too much respect for rules.   SA   A   N   D   SD

46. When my partner suggests that I give in a little if he (she) will, I see that as an attempt to manipulate me.   SA   A   N   D   SD

47. If my partner wants things in life that are different from what I want, it's fine with me, as long as it doesn't cost me any of my freedom.   SA   A   N   D   SD

48. Unless they are the same as mine, I don't much care about my partner's goals in life.   SA   A   N   D   SD

49. I demand that my marriage support my interests even if they are not my spouse's interests.   SA   A   N   D   SD

50. My own dreams and interests in life have got to be central in my marriage.   SA   A   N   D   SD

51. I don't have too much respect for the law.   SA   A   N   D   SD

Total Score: For each item tally SA = 4, A = 3, N = 2, D = 1, SD = 0. A score of 68 or above indicates that the antisocial internal working model is active in this person's mind.

Appendix **E**

Products Available from the Gottman Institute

A SCIENTIFICALLY-BASED MARITAL THERAPY™
MATERIALS AVAILABLE

☐ *A Scientifically-Based Marital Therapy*™   **$295 for the set**
The Video Package

    A Scientifically-Based Marital Therapy™ is now available on video tape. Includes 12
hours of instruction by John Gottman, Ph.D., as he conducts recent training sessions
with counseling professionals. Complete with all marital assessment tools and
necessary exercises and materials for couples' intervention. Includes lecture notes from
workshop. Also includes time indexing guide for referral to specific topics. Packaged
with 125-page workshop handbook and 300-page workshop manual. (plus shipping
& handling)

☐ *A Scientifically-Based Marital Therapy*™, **The Video**   **$175 for the video**
for Clinicians Attending Marital Therapy Workshop

    This 12-hour video cassette instruction featuring John Gottman, Ph.D., is a valuable
reference. Includes 12 hours of instruction by John Gottman, as he conducts recent
training sessions with counseling professionals. Use it to review and learn about
A Scientifically-Based Marital Therapy™. Includes time indexing guide for referral to
specific topics. Use with resource materials received at the workshop. (plus shipping
& handling)

☐ **Clinical Manual for Marital Therapy**   **$105 for the manual**
A Scientifically-Based Marital Therapy™

    The *Clinical Manual for Marital Therapy,* written by Dr. John Gottman, is the workshop man-
ual used throughout the two-day training workshop for clinicians. Now available for those
unable to attend the workshop. The 350-page manual is complete with all marital assessment tools and necessary exercises and materials for couples' intervention. Includes all
materials from the workshop and 15 pages of references. Makes an ideal desk reference.
(plus shipping & handling)

☐ *The Heart of Parenting*™ **Video**   **$29.95 for the video**

    An in-depth video based on Dr. John Gottman's book, *The Heart of Parenting*™. The
video shows why emotion coaching is important and gives parents all the tools they
need to become an emotion coach. Video covers emotion coaching for kids, how to
talk to children, role playing, step-by-step explanation of 5 stages. (plus shipping
& handling)

☐ **The Gottman Love Map Exercise**™   **$24.95 for the exercise**

    Use this fun exercise to help couples develop a "Love Map" of their partner's world—
their history, concerns, preferences, and current issues. Includes "Love Map" and
"Opportunity" cards and Love Map instruction sheet. (plus shipping & handling)

☐ *Why Marriages Succeed or Fail™*, Audio Cassette   **$9.95 for the cassette**

> In this valuable 45-minute recording, John Gottman, Ph.D., discusses: four warning signs of a marriage in trouble and what you can do about it; the five common myths about marriage that sometimes stand in the way of progress; how you can build an emotional bank account and draw against it in tense or troubled times to build your relationship. (plus shipping & handling)

☐ *Repair Checklist and Four Horsemen of the Apocalypse™*,   **$4.95 for the card**
Reference Card

> This useful reference card is given to couples at the Gottmans' Marriage Survival Kit™ Workshops. The Repair Checklist reminds couples of options for "repair attempts" during emotional discussions. The reverse side of the card lists the Four Horsemen of the Apocalypse: criticism, contempt, defensiveness, and stonewalling. They are encased within the "anti" sign, the circle with the diagonal slash. This card is designed to post on one's refrigerator or on the bathroom mirror. Couples have found the Repair Checklist to be particularly helpful. (plus shipping & handling)

Books Written by John Gottman, Ph.D.

Available in your local bookstore or order through:
University Bookstore, Seattle, WA (206) 634–3400

1. *Why Marriages Succeed or Fail . . . . And How You Can Make Yours Last*
   Published by Simon & Schuster   ISBN 0-684-80241-4

   > For general audiences and for couples, this book describes the Gottman findings on divorce prediction and their implications for making marriages last.

2. *A Couples Guide to Communication*
   Published by Research Press   ISBN 0-87822-127-1

   > This book is the basis of the Markman PREP program. It contains the materials used in intervention studies done by the Gottman group (including some of Cliff Notarius's work) and by the Markman group. It is written for couples.

3. *What Predicts Divorce?*
   Published by Erlbaum   ISBN 0-8058-1402-7

   > This book describes the Gottman divorce prediction research. It is primarily for technically trained audiences, researchers and professionals. It contains the data and summary statistics that justify the conclusions of *Why Marriages Succeed or Fail*.

4. *Meta-Emotion: How Families Communicate Emotionally*
   Published by Erlbaum   ISBN 0-8058-1995-9

   > This book describes the research findings on the longitudinal study of meta-emotion in families. This work links marital and parent-child to child-child interactive systems. It is primarily for technically trained audiences, researchers and professionals. It contains the data and summary statisticis that justifies the conclusions of *The Heart of Parenting*.

5. *The Heart of Parenting: Raising an Emotionally Intelligent Child*
   Published by Simon & Schuster   ISBN 0-684-80130-2

   For general audiences and parents, this book describes the results of the Gottman finding on emotion coaching and meta-emotion. Buffers for protecting children from the negative consequences of ailing and dissolving marriages are also described.

6. *Web Site: To obtain the latest products and workshop schedules for clinicians and couples:*

   www.Gottman.com

7. *To order materials, call 888–523–9042.*

References

Achtenberg, J. (1985). *Imagery in healing: Shamanism and modern medicine.* Boston: Shambhala.

Ackerman, N. (1966). *Treating the troubled family.* New York: Basic Books.

Adelman, P.K., Chadwick, K., & Baerger, D.R. (1996). Marital quality of Black and White adults over the life course. *Journal of Social and Personal Relationships, 13,* 361–384.

Albee, E. (1962). *Who's afraid of Virginia Woolf?* New York: Dramatists Play.

Appel, M.A., Holroyd, K.A., & Gorkin, L. (1983). Anger and the etiology and progression of physical illness. In L. Temoshok, C. Van Dyke, & L.S. Zegans (Eds.), *Emotions in health and illness: Theoretical and research foundations,* (pp. 73–87). New York: Grune and Stratton.

Averill, J. (1982). *Anger and aggression.* New York: Springer Verlag.

Axelrod, J., & Reisine, T.D. (1984). Stress hormones: Their interaction and regulation. *Science, 224*(4648), 452–459.

Azrin, N.H., Naster, B.J., & Jones, R. (1973). Reciprocity counseling: A rapid-learning based procedure for marital counseling. *Behavior Research and Therapy, 11,* 365–382.

Bakeman, R., & Gottman, J. (1997). *Observing interaction: An introduction to sequential analysis (2nd ed.).* New York: Cambridge University Press.

Bakeman, R., & Quera, V. (1995). *Analyzing interaction: Sequential analysis with SDIS and GSEQ.* New York: Cambridge University Press.

Ball, F.L.J., Cowan, P., & Cowan, C.P. (1995). Who's got the power? Gender differences in partners' perception of influence during marital problem-solving discussions. *Family Process, 34,* 303–321.

Balswick, J., & Avertt, C.P. (1977) Differences in expressiveness: Gender, interpersonal orientation, and perceived parental expressiveness as contributing factors. *Journal of Marriage and the Family, 39,* 121–123.

Bank, L., Dishion, T., Skinner, M., & Patterson, G.R. (1990). Method variance in structural equation modeling: Living with glop. In G.R. Patterson (Ed.), *Depression and aggression in family interaction* (pp. 247–280). Hillsdale, NJ: Lawrence Erlbaum.

Barbach, L. (1984). *For each other: Sharing sexual intimacy.* New York: Signet.

Bardwick, J. (1979). *In transition: How feminism, sexual liberation, and the search for self-fulfillment have altered America.* New York: Harcourt Brace.

Barker, R.G. (1942). The social interrelations of strangers and acquaintances. *Sociometry, 5,* 169–179.

Barnett, R.C., Biener, L., & Baruch, G.K. (Eds.) (1987). *Gender and stress.* New York: The Free Press.

Bateson, G., Jackson, D.D., Haley, J., & Weakland, J. (1956). Toward a theory of schizophrenia. *Behavioral Science, 1,* 251–264.

Baucom, D.H. (1982). A comparison of behavioral contracting and problem-solving/communication training in behavioral marital therapy. *Behavior Therapy, 13,* 162–174.

Baucom, D.H., & Epstein, N. (1990). *Cognitive-behavioral marital therapy.* New York: Brunner/Mazel.

Baucom, D.H., Epstein, N., Rankin, L.A., & Burnett, C.K. (1996). Assessing relationship standards: The Inventory of Specific Relationship Standards. *Journal of Marriage and the Family, 10,* 72–88.

Baucom, D.H., & Hoffman, J.A. (1986). The effectiveness of marital therapy: Current status and application to the clinical setting. In N. Jacobson & A. Gurman (Eds.), *Clinical handbook of marital therapy* (pp. 597–620). New York: Guilford.

Baucom, D.H., & Lester, G.W. (1986). The usefulness of cognitive restructuring as an adjunct to behavioral marital therapy. *Behavior Therapy, 17,* 385–403.

Beck, A.T., Steer, R.A., Ball, R., & Ranier, W.F. (1996). Comparison of Beck Depression Inventory IA and II in psychiatric outpatients. *Journal of Personality, 67,* 588–597.

Bell, G.B., & French, R.L. (1950). Consistency of individual leadership position in small groups of varying membership. *Journal of Abnormal and Social Psychology, 45,* 764–767.

Belsky, J., & Kelly, J. (1994). *The transition to parenthood. How a first child changes a marriage: Why some couples grow closer and others apart.* New York: Dell.

Belsky, J., & Pensky, E. (1988). Marital change across the transition to parenthood. *Marriage and Family Review, 12*(3–4), 133–156.

Belsky, J., Spanier, G.B., & Rovine, M. (1983). Stability and change in marriage across the transition to parenthood. *Journal of Marriage and the Family, 45*(3), 567–577.

Bem, S.L. (1993). *The lenses of gender.* New Haven: Yale University Press.

Bergin, A.E., & Jasper, L.G. (1969). Correlates of empathy in psychotherapy: A replication. *Journal of Abnormal Psychology, 74,* 477–481.

Berkman, L.F., & Breslow, L. (1983). *Health and the ways of living: The Alameda County study.* New York: Oxford University Press.

Berkman, L.F., & Syme, S.L. (1979). Social networks, host resistance, and mortality: A nine-year follow-up study of Alameda County residents. *American Journal of Epidemiology, 109,* 186–204.

Berley, R.A., & Jacobson, N.S. (1984). Causal attributions in intimate relationships: Toward a model of behavioral marital therapy. In P. Kendall (Ed.), *Advances in cognitive-behavioral research and therapy: Vol. 3.* (pp. 2–90). New York: Academic Press.

Bernard, J. (1982). *The future of marriage.* New Haven, CT: Yale University Press.

Biglan, A., Rothlind, J., & Hops, H. (1989). Impact of distressed and aggressive behavior. *Journal of Abnormal Psychology, 98*(3), 218–228.

Birchler, G., Weiss, R., & Vincent, J. (1975). Multi-method analysis of social reinforcement exchange between maritally-distressed and non-distressed spouse and stranger dyads. *Journal of Personality and Social Psychology, 31,* 349–360.

Blier, M.J., & Blier, W.L.A. (1989) Gender differences in self-rated emotional expressiveness. *Sex Roles, 21,* 287–295.

Bloom, B., Asher, S., & White, S. (1978). Marital disruption as a stressor: A review and analysis. *Psychological Bulletin, 85,* 867–894.

Bloom, B., Hodges, W.F., Caldwell, R.A., Systra, L., & Cedrone, A.R. (1977). Marital separation: A community survey. *Journal of Divorce, 1,* 7–19.

Boegner, I., & Zielenbach-Coenen, H. (1984). On maintaining change in behavioral marital therapy. In K. Hahlweg & N.S. Jacobson (Eds.), *Marital interaction: Analysis and modification* (pp. 27–35). New York: Guilford Press.

Bohrenstein, M., & Cohen, J. (1988). *Statistical power analysis: A computer program.* Hillsdale, NJ: Lawrence Erlbaum Associates.

Booth, A., & White, L. (1980). Thinking about divorce. *Journal of Marriage and the Family, 42,* 605–616.

Bowen, M. (1978). *Family therapy in clinical practice.* New York: Aronson.

Bower, G.H. (1981). Mood and memory. *American Psychologist, 36,* 129–148.

Bradbury, T.N. (1998). *The developmental course of marital dysfunction.* New York: Cambridge University Press.

Bray, J.H., & Jouriles, E.N. (1995). Treatment of marital conflict and prevention of divorce. *Journal of Marital and Family Therapy, 21*(4), 461–473.

Brazelton, T.B., & Nugent, J.K. (1995). Neonatal assessment as an intervention. In R. Hellgard (Ed.), *Psychobiology and early development: Advances in psychology, No. 46* (pp. 215–229). Amsterdam, Netherlands: North-Holland.

Broderick, C.B. (1993). *Understanding family process.* Newbury Park, CA: Sage.

Broderick, C.B., & Schrader, S. (1991). The history of professional marriage and family therapy. In A.S. Gurman & D.P. Kniskern (Eds.), *Handbook of family therapy II* (pp. 3–40). New York: Brunner/Mazel.

Brown, E.M. (1991). *Patterns of infidelity and their treatment.* New York: Brunner/Mazel.

Brown, P.C., & Smith, T.W. (1992). Social influence, marriage and the heart: Cardiovascular consequences of interpersonal control in husbands and wives. *Health Psychology, 1*(2), 88–96.

Buchanan, C.M., Maccoby, E.E., & Dornbusch, S.M. (1991). Caught between parents: Adolescents' experience in divorced homes. *Child Development, 62,* 1008–1029.

Buehlman, K., Gottman, J.M., & Katz, L. (1992). How a couple views their past predicts their future: Predicting divorce from an oral history interview. *Journal of Family Psychology, 5,* 295–318.

Buongiorno, J., & Notarius, C. (1992). *Wait time until professional treatment in marital therapy.* Unpublished master's thesis, Catholic University of America, Washington, DC.

Burgess, E.W., & Wallin, P. (1953). *Engagement and marriage.* Chicago, IL: Lippincott.

Burman, B., & Margolin, G. (1992). Analysis of the association between marital relationships and health problems: An interactional perspective. *Psychological Bulletin, 112,* 39–63.

Capaldi, D., & Patterson, G.R. (1987). An approach to the problem of recruitment and retention rates for longitudinal research. *Behavioral Assessment, 9,* 169–177.

Carlson, J.G., & Hatfield, E. (1992). *Psychology of emotion.* New York: Harcourt Brace Jovanovich.

Carlson, J., & Sperry, L. (1993). Extending treatment results in couples therapy. *Individual Psychology: Journal of Adlerian Theory, Research & Practice (Special Issue: Marriage and Couples Counseling), 49,* 450–455.

Carrère, S., Gottman, J.M., & Ochs, H. (1996). *The beneficial and negative influences of marital quality on immune function.* Paper presented at the thirty-sixth annual Society for Psychophysiological Research Meeting, Vancouver, B.C.

Carstensen, L.L. (1992). Social and emotional patterns in adulthood: Support for socio-emotional selectivity theory. *Psychology and Aging, 7,* 331–338.

Carstensen, L.L. (1995). Evidence for a life-span theory of socio-emotional selectivity. *Current Directions in Psychological Science, 4,* 151–156.

Carstensen, L.L., Gottman, J.M., & Levenson, R.W. (1995). Emotional behavior in long-term marriage. *Psychology and Aging, 10,* 140–149.

Carstensen, L.L., & Turk, C.S. (1994). The salience of emotion across the adult life span. *Psychology and Aging, 9,* 259–264.

Cherlin, A.J. (1981). *Marriage, divorce, and remarriage.* Cambridge, MA: Harvard University Press.

Christensen, A. (1987). Detection of conflict patterns in couples. In K. Hahlweg & M.J. Goldstein (Eds.), *Understanding major mental disorder: The contribution of family interaction research* (pp. 250–265). New York: Family Process Press.

Christensen, A. (1988). Dysfunctional interaction patterns in couples. In P. Noller & M.A. Fitzpatrick (Eds.), *Perspectives on marital interaction* (pp. 31–52). Avon, England: Multilingual Matters.

Christensen, A. (1990). Gender and social structure in the demand/withdraw pattern of marital conflict. *Journal of Personality and Social Psychology, 59,* 73–81.

Christensen, A. (1991, Nov.). The demand/withdraw pattern in marital interaction. Paper presented at the annual meeting of the Association for the Advancement of Behavior Therapy, New York.

Christensen, A., & Heavey, C.L. (1990). Gender and social structure in the demand/withdraw pattern of marital conflict. *Journal of Personality and Social Psychology, 59,* 73–82.

Cleary, P.D. (1987). Gender differences in stress-related disorders. In R.C. Barnett, L. Biener, & G.K. Baruch (Eds.), *Gender and stress* (pp. 39–72). New York: Free Press.

Cleek, M.G., & Pearson, T.A. (1985). Perceived causes of divorce: An analysis of interrelationships. *Journal of Marriage and the Family, 47,* 179–183.

Cohen, R.S., & Christensen, A. (1980). A further examination of demand characteristics in marital interaction. *Journal of Consulting and Clinical Psychology, 48,* 121–123.

Coie, J., Watt, N., Hawkins, S., Ramey, S., Markman, H.J., Long, B., & West, S. (1991). Prevention research: Conceptual model of strategies and procedures. Paper presented at the National Prevention Conference, Washington, DC.

Cook, J., Tyson, R., White, J., Rushe, R., Gottman, J., & Murray, J. (1995). The mathematics of marital conflict: Qualitative dynamic mathematical modeling of marital interaction. *Journal of Family Psychology, 9,* 110–130.

Cookerly, J.R. (1974a). The reduction of psychopathology as measured by the MMPI clinical scales in three forms of marriage counseling. *Journal of Marriage and the Family, 36,* 332–335.

Cookerly, J.R. (1974b). Comparative results of six major forms of marriage counseling. *Dissertation Abstracts International, 35, 01, Section A,* 184.

Cookerly, J.R. (1980). Does marital therapy do any lasting good? *Journal of Marital and Family Therapy, 6,* 393.

Consumer Reports Study on Psychotherapy. *Consumer Reports,* November, 1995, pp. 734–739.

Covey, S.R., Merrill, A.R., & Merrill, R.R. (1995). *First things first.* New York: Simon & Schuster.

Cowan, P.A., & Cowan, C.P. (1987). Couple's relationships, parenting styles and the child's development at three. Paper presented at the Society for Research in Child Development. Baltimore, MD.

Cowan, P.A., & Cowan, C.P. (1990). Becoming a family: Research and intervention. In I. Sigel & A. Brody (Eds.), *Family research*. Hillsdale, NJ: Lawrence Erlbaum.

Cowan, C.P., & Cowan, P.A. (1992). *When partners become parents*. New York: Basic Books.

Cowan, C.P, Cowan, P.A., Heming, G., & Miller, N.B. (1991). Becoming a family: Marriage, parenting and child development. In P.A. Cowan & M. Hetherington (Eds.), *Family transitions*. Hillsdale, NJ: Lawrence Erlbaum.

Crosbie, J. (1993). Interrupted time-series analysis with brief single-subject data. *Journal of Consulting and Clinical Psychology, 61*(6), 966–974.

Cummings, E.M., & Davies, P. (1994). *Children and marital conflict: The impact of family dispute resolution*. New York: Guilford Press.

Damasio, A.R. (1994). *Descartes' error: Emotion, reason and the human brain*. New York: Putnam.

Davidson, R.J. (1984). Affect, cognition, and hemispheric specialization. In C.E. Izard, J. Kagan, & R. Zajonc (Eds.), *Emotions, cognition, and behavior* (p. 320). New York: Cambridge University Press.

Davidson, R.J. (1992). Anterior cerebral asymmetry and the nature of emotion. *Brain and Cognition, 20*, 125–151.

Davidson, R.J. (1994a). Temperament, affective style, and frontal lobe asymmetry. In G. Dawson & K.W. Fischer (Eds.), *Human behavior and the developing brain* (pp. 518–536), New York: Guilford.

Davidson, R.J. (1994b). Asymmetric brain function, affective style, and psychopathology: The role of early experience and plasticity. *Development and Psychopathology, 6*, 741–758.

Davidson, R.J., & Fox, N.A. (1982). Asymmetrical brain activity discriminates between positive versus negative affective stimuli in human infants. *Science, 218*, 1235–1237.

Davidson, R.J., & Tomarken, A.J. (1989). Laterality and emotion: An electrophysiological approach. In F. Boller & J. Grafman (Eds.), *Handbook of neurophysiology* (vol. 3, pp. 419–441). Amsterdam: Elsevier.

Dawson, G. (1994). Development of emotional expression and emotion regulation in infancy: Contributions of the frontal lobe. In G. Dawson & K.W. Fischer (Eds.), *Human behavior and the developing brain* (pp. 346-379). New York: Guilford.

Dawson, G., Klinger, L.G., Panagiotides, H., Speiker, S., & Frey, K. (1992). Infants of mothers with depressive symptoms: Electrophysiological and behavioral findings related to attachment status. *Development and Psychopathology, 4*, 67–80.

Deal, J.E., Hagan, M.S., & Anderson, E.R. (1992). The marital relationship in remarried families. In E.M. Hetherington & W.G. Clingempeel (Eds.), *Coping with marital transitions: A family systems perspective* (pp. 73–93). *Monographs of the Society for Research in Child Development*, Serial No. 227, *57*, Nos 2–3.

Dickstein, S., & Parke, R.D. (1988). Social referencing in infancy: A glance at fathers and marriage. *Child Development, 59*, 506–511.

DiPietro, J.A., & Porges, S.W. (1991). Relations between neonatal states and eight-month developmental outcome in pre-term infants. *Infant Behavior and Development, 14*, 441–450.

Dizard, J. (1968). *Social change and the family*. Chicago, IL: University of Chicago, Family and Community Study Center.

Doherty, W.J. (1997). *The intentional family: How to build family ties in our modern world*. Reading, MA: Addison-Wesley.

Dreyfus, N. (1992) *Talk to me like I am someone you love: Flash cards for real life.* Berkeley, CA: Celestial Arts.

Duncan, S.D. Jr., & Fiske, D.W. (1977). *Face-to-face interaction: Research methods and theory.* Hillsdale, NJ: Lawrence Erlbaum Associates.

Dunn, R.L., & Schwebel, A.I. (1995). Meta-analytic review of marital therapy outcome research. *Journal of Family Psychology 9*(1), 58–68.

Dutton, D. (1988). *The domestic assault of women.* Boston: Allyn & Bacon.

Dutton, D. (1995a). *The batterer.* New York: Basic Books.

Dutton, D. (1995b). *The domestic assault of women.* (2nd Edition). Vancouver: UBC Press.

Easterbrooks, M.A. (1987). Early family development: Longitudinal impact of marital quality. Paper presented at the Meeting of the Society for Research in Child Development, Baltimore, MD.

Ekman, P. (1984). Expression and the nature of emotion. In K.R. Scherer & P. Ekman (Eds.), *Approaches to emotion* (pp. 319–344). Hillsdale, NJ: Lawrence Erlbaum Associates Press.

Ekman, P., & Friesen, W.V. (1978). *Facial action coding system.* Palo Alto, CA: Consulting Psychologist Press.

Ekman, P., Friesen, W.V., & Simons, R.C. (1985). Is the startle reaction an emotion? *Journal of Personality and Social Psychology, 49,* 1416–1426.

Ekman, P., Levenson, R.W., & Friesen, W.V. (1983). Autonomic nervous system activity distinguishes among emotions. *Science, 221,* 1208–1210.

Emery, R.E. (1982). Interparental conflict and the children of discord and divorce. *Psychological Bulletin, 92,* 310–330.

Emery, R.E. (1988). *Marriage, divorce, and children's adjustment.* Newbury Park, CA: Sage.

Emery, R.E., & O'Leary, K.D. (1982). Children's perceptions of marital discord and behavior problems of boys and girls. *Journal of Abnormal Child Psychology, 10,* 11–24.

Esler, M., Julius, S., Zweiffer, A., Randall, O., Harburg, E., Gardiner, H., & DeQuattro, V. (1977). Mild high-renin essential hypertension: Neurogenic human hypertension? *New England Journal of Medicine, 296,* 405–411.

Faber, A., & Mazlish, E. (1980). *How to talk so kids will listen and listen so kids will talk.* New York: Avon.

Field, T., Fox, N.A., Pickens, J., & Nawrocki, T. (1995). Relative right frontal EEG activation in 3-to-6-month-old infants of "depressed" mothers. *Developmental Psychology, 31,* 358–363.

Fiese, B. (1997). Family context in pediatric psychology from a transactional perspective: Family rituals and stories as examples. *Journal of Pediatric Psychology, 22,* 183–196.

Fincham, F.D., Bradbury, T.N., & Scott, C.K. (1990). Cognition in marriage. In F.D. Fincham & T.N. Bradbury (Eds.), *The psychology of marriage* (pp. 118–149). New York: Guilford.

Fisher, H. (1992). *The anatomy of love.* New York: W.W. Norton.

Fitzpatrick, M.A. (Ed.) (1988). *Between husbands and wives.* Beverly Hills: Sage.

Floyd, F., Markman, H.J., et al. (1995). Preventive intervention and relationship enhancement. In N.S. Jacobson & A.S. Gurman (Eds.), *The clinical handbook of couples therapy.* New York: Guilford Press.

Forehand, R., Brody, G., Long, N., Slotkin, J., & Fauber, R. (1986). Divorce/divorce potential and inter-parental conflict: The relationship to early adolescent social and cognitive functioning. *Journal of Adolescent Research, 1,* 389–397.

Forehand, R., & McMahon, R. (1981). *Helping the noncompliant child: A clinician's guide to parent training*. New York: Guilford.

Fowers, B.J., & Olson, D.H. (1986). Predicting marital success with PREPARE: A predictive validity study. *Journal of Marriage and Family Therapy, 12*, 403–413.

Fox, N.A. (1989). The psychophysiological correlates of emotional reactivity during the first year of life. *Developmental Psychology, 25*, 364–372.

Fox, N.A. (Ed.) (1994). The development of emotion regulation. *Monographs of the Society for Research in Child Development, 59* (No. 240.).

Fox, N.A., & Davidson, R.J. (1989). Taste-elicited changes in facial signs of emotion and the asymmetry of brain electrical activity in human newborns. *Neuropsychologia, 24*, 417–422.

Fox, N.A., & Field, T.M. (1989). Individual differences in preschool entry behavior. *Journal of Applied Developmental Psychology, 10*, 527–540.

Fraiberg, S. (1959). *The magic years*. New York: Scribner's.

Frankl, V.E. (1983). *The doctor and the soul*. New York: Vintage.

Frankl, V.E. (1984). *Man's search for meaning*. New York: Washington Square Press.

Frankl, V.E. (1988). *The will to meaning*. New York: Meridian (Penguin).

Frankl, V.E. (1997a). *Victor Frankl recollections*. New York: Plenum.

Frankl, V.E. (1997b). *Man's ultimate search for meaning*. New York: Insight Books (Plenum).

Freedman, J., & Combs, G. (1996). *Narrative therapy: The social construction of preferred realities*. New York: Norton.

Friedman, H.S., Tucker, J.S., Schwartz, J.E., & Tomilson, K.C. (1995). Psychosocial and behavioral predictors of longevity: The aging and death of the "Termites." *American Psychologist, 50*, 69–78.

Frodi, A., Macaulay, J., & Thome, P.R. (1977). Are women always less aggressive than men? A review of experimental literature. *Psychological Bulletin, 84*, 634–660.

Frymer-Kensky, T. (1992). *In the wake of the goddesses: Women, culture, and the biblical transformation of pagan myth*. New York: Fawcett-Columbine.

Furedy, J.J., Heselgrave, R.J., & Scher, H. (1992). T-wave amplitude utility revisited: Some physiological and psychophysiological considerations. *Biological Psychiatry, 33*, 241–248.

Fuster, J.M. (1989). *The prefrontal cortex*. New York: Raven.

Fuster, J.M. (1997). *The prefrontal cortex: Anatomy, physiology, and neuropsychology of the frontal lobe* (3rd ed.) New York: Lippincott-Raven.

Gianino, A., & Tronick, E.Z. (1988). The mutual regulation model: The infant's self and interactive regulation and coping and defensive capacities. In T.M. Field, P.M. McCabe, & N. Schneiderman (Eds.), *Stress and coping across development* (pp. 47–70). Hillsdale, NJ: Lawrence Erlbaum.

Gigy, L., & Kelly, J.B. (1992). Reasons for divorce: Perspectives of divorcing men and women. *Journal of Divorce and Remarriage, 18*, 169–187.

Ginott, H. (1965). *Between parent and child*. New York: Avon.

Glass, S.P., & Wright, T.L. (1997). Reconstructing marriages after the trauma of infidelity. In W.K. Halford & H.J. Markman (Eds.), *Clinical handbook of marriage and couples interventions* (pp. 471–508). New York: Wiley.

Goleman, D. (1995). *Emotional intelligence*. New York: Bantam.

Goode, W.J. (1969). *Women in divorce*. New York: Free Press. (Originally published as *Divorce and after*, 1956, New York: Free Press.)

Gottman, J.M. (1979). *Marital interaction: Empirical investigations*. New York: Academic Press.

Gottman, J.M. (1980). The consistency of non-verbal affect and affect reciprocity in marital interaction. *Journal of Consulting and Clinical Psychology, 48,* 711–717.

Gottman, J.M. (1981). *Time-series analysis.* New York: Cambridge University Press.

Gottman, J.M. (1983). How children become friends. *Monographs of the Society of Research in Child Development, 48* (No. 201). Chicago, IL: University of Chicago Press.

Gottman, J.M. (1989). *The specific affect coding system, version 2.0: Real time coding with the affect wheel.* Unpublished manual, University of Washington, Seattle, WA.

Gottman, J.M. (1990). How marriages change. In G.R. Patterson (Ed.), *Depression and aggression in family interaction.* Hillsdale, NJ: Lawrence Erlbaum.

Gottman, J.M. (1993a). The roles of conflict engagement, escalation, or avoidance in marital interaction: A longitudinal view of five types of couples. *Journal of Consulting and Clinical Psychology, 61,* 6–15.

Gottman, J.M. (1993b). A theory of marital dissolution and stability. *Journal of Family Psychology, 7,* 57–75.

Gottman, J.M. (1994a). *What predicts divorce?* Hillsdale, NJ: Lawrence Erlbaum Associates.

Gottman, J.M. (1994b). *Why marriages succeed or fail.* New York: Simon & Schuster.

Gottman, J.M. (Ed.) (1996). *What predicts divorce?: The measures.* Hillsdale, NJ: Lawrence Erlbaum Associates.

Gottman, J.M., Coan, J., Carrère, S., & Swanson, C. (1998). Predicting marital happiness and stability from newlywed interactions. *Journal of Marriage and the Family, 60,* 5–22.

Gottman, J.M., & DeClaire, J. (1996). *The heart of parenting.* New York: Simon & Schuster.

Gottman, J.M., & Katz, L.F. (1989). The effects of marital discord on young children's peer interaction and health. *Developmental Psychology, 25,* 373–381.

Gottman, J.M., Katz, L., & Hooven, C. (1996). *Meta-emotion.* Hillsdale, NJ: Erlbaum.

Gottman, J.M., & Krokoff, L.J. (1989). The relationship between marital interaction and marital satisfaction: A longitudinal view. *Journal of Consulting and Clinical Psychology, 57,* 47–52.

Gottman, J.M., & Levenson, R.W. (1985). A valid procedure for obtaining self-report of affect in marital interaction. *Journal of Consulting and Clinical Psychology, 53,* 151–160.

Gottman, J.M., & Levenson, R.W. (1988). The social psychophysiology of marriage. In P. Noller & M.A. Fitzpatrick (Eds.), *Perspectives on marital interaction* (pp. 182–200). Clevedon, England: Multilingual Matters Ltd.

Gottman, J.M., & Levenson, R.W. (1992). Marital processes predictive of later dissolution: Behavior, physiology, and health. *Journal of Personality and Social Psychology, 63,* 221–233.

Gottman, J.M., Markman, H., & Notarius, C. (1977). The topography of marital conflict: A study of verbal and non-verbal behavior. *Journal of Marriage and the Family, 39,* 461–477.

Gottman, J.M., Notarius, C., Gonso, J., & Markman, H. (1976). *A couple's guide to communication.* Champaign, IL: Research Press.

Gottman, J., Notarius, C., Markman, H., Bank, S., Yoppi, B., & Rubin, M.E. (1976). Behavior exchange theory and marital decision making. *Journal of Personality and Social Psychology, 34,* 14–23.

Gottman, J.M., & Parker, J. (1986). *The conversations of friends.* New York: Cambridge University Press.

Gottman, J.M., & Porterfield, A.L. (1981). Communicative competence in the non-verbal behavior of married couples. *Journal of Marriage and the Family, 43,* 817–824.

Gottman, J.M., & Roy, A.K. (1990). *Sequential analysis: A guide for behavioral researchers.* New York: Cambridge University Press.

Gottman, J.M., Swanson, C., Murray, J., Tyson, R., & Swanson, K. (in press). *The mathematics of marital conflict.* Cambridge, MA: MIT Press.

Gray, J. (1989). *Men are from Mars, women are from Venus.* New York: Harper Collins.

Greenberg, L.S., & Johnson, S.M. (1988). *Emotionally focused therapy for couples.* New York: Guilford.

Greenburg, D., & O'Malley, S. (1983). *How to avoid love and marriage.* New York: Freundlich Books.

Griswold, R.L. (1993). *Fatherhood in America.* New York: Basic Books.

Gronlund, N.E. (1959). *Sociometry in the classroom.* New York: Harper & Brothers.

Gross, J.A., & Levenson, R.W. (1993). Emotional suppression: Physiological, self-report, and expressive behavior. *Journal of Personality and Social Psychology, 64,* 970–986.

Gruen, R.J., Folkman, S., & Lazarus, R.S. (1988). Centrality and individual differences in the meaning of daily hassles. *Journal of Personality, 56,* 743–762.

Guerney, B.G. (1977). *Relationship enhancement.* San Francisco: Jossey Bass.

Guerney, B.G., & Guerney, L. (1985). Marital and family problem prevention and enrichment programs. In L. L'Abate (Ed.), *Handbook of family psychology and therapy,* 1179–1217. Homewood, IL: Dorsey Press.

Gunnar, M.R., Connors, J., Isensee, J., & Wall, L. (1988). Adrenocortical activity and behavioral distress in human newborns. *Developmental Psychology, 21*(4), 297–310.

Gurman, A.S., & Kniskern, D.P. (1981). Family therapy outcome research: Knowns and unknowns. In A.S. Gurman & D.P. Kniskern (Eds.), *Handbook of Family Therapy,* 742–775. New York: Brunner/Mazel.

Gurman, A.S., Kniskern, D.P., et al. (1986). Research on the process and outcome of marital and family therapy. In S.L. Garfield & A.E. Bergin (Eds.), *Handbook of Psychotherapy and Behavior Change* (pp. 565–624). New York: Wiley.

Hafner, J., Badenoch, A., Fisher, J., & Swift, H. (1983). Spouse-aided versus individual therapy in persisting psychiatric disorders: A systematic comparison. *Family Process, 22,* 385–399.

Hahlweg, K., & Markman, H.J. (1988). Effectiveness of behavioral marital therapy: Empirical status of behavioral techniques in preventing and alleviating marital distress. *Journal of Consulting and Clinical Psychology, 56*(3), 440–447.

Hahlweg, K., Revenstorf, D., et al. (1984). Effects of behavioral marital therapy on couples' communication and problem-solving skills. *Journal of Consulting and Clinical Psychology, 52*(4), 553–566.

Hahlweg, K., Schindler, L., & Revenstorf, D. (1982). Treatment of marital distress: Comparing formats and modalities. *Advances in Behavior Research and Therapy,* 4(2), 57–74.

Hahlweg, K., Schindler, L., Revenstorf, D., & Brengelmann, J.C. (1984). The Munich marital therapy study. In K. Hahlweg & N.S. Jacobson (Eds.), *Marital interaction: Analysis and modification* (pp. 3–26). New York: Guilford Press.

Halford, W.K., & Markman, H.J. (Eds.) (1997). *Clinical handbook of marriage and couples intervention.* New York: Wiley.

Harburg, E., Julius, S., McGinn, N.F., McLeod, J., & Hoobler, S.W. (1964). Personality traits and behavioral patterns associated with systolic blood pressure levels in college males. *Journal of Chronic Disease, 17,* 405–414.

Harrell, J., & Guerney, B.G. (1976). Training married couples in conflict resolution skills.

In D.H. Olson (Ed.), *Treating relationships* (pp. 151–180). Lake Mills, IA: Graphic Publishing.

Haynes, S.N., Follingstad, D.R., & Sullivan, J.C. (1979). Assessment of marital satisfaction and interaction. *Journal of Consulting and Clinical Psychology, 47*, 789–791.

Heavey, C.L., Layne, C., & Christensen, A. (1993). Gender and conflict structure in marital interaction: A replication and extension. *Journal of Consulting and Clinical Psychology, 61*, 16–27.

Hendrix, H. (1988). *Getting the love you want.* New York: Henry Holt.

Henry, J.P., & Stephens, P.M. (1977). *Stress, health, and the social environment.* New York: Springer Verlag.

Hetherington, E.M. (1988). Coping with family transitions: Winners, losers and survivors. *Child Development, 60*, 1–14.

Hetherington, E.M., & Clingempeel, W.G. (1992). Coping with marital transitions. *Monographs for the Society for Research in Child Development, 57* (No. 227, 1–242).

Hetherington, E.M., Cox, M., & Cox, R. (1978). The aftermath of divorce. In J.H. Stevens, Jr., & M. Matthews (Eds.), *Mother-child, father-child relations.* Washington, DC: National Association for the Education of Young Children.

Hetherington, E.M., Cox, M., & Cox, R. (1982). Effects of divorce on parents and children. In M. Lamb (Ed.), *Non-traditional families* (pp. 233–288). Hillsdale, NJ: Erlbaum.

Hochschild, A.R. (1989). *The second shift: Working parents and the revolution at home.* New York: Viking.

Hofheimer, J.A., & Lawson, N. (1988). Neurophysiological correlates of interactive behavior in pre-term newborns. *Infant Behavior and Development, 11*, 143.

Holmes, T.H., & Rahe, R.H. (1967). The social readjustment rating scale. *Journal of Psychosomatic Research, 11*, 213–218.

Holtzworth-Munroe, A., & Jacobson, N.S. (1985). Causal attributions of married couples: When do they search for causes? What do they conclude when they do? *Journal of Personality and Social Psychology, 48*, 1398–1412.

Holtzworth-Munroe, A., Jacobson, N.S., Deklyen, M., & Whisman, M.A. (1989). Relationship between behavioral marital therapy outcome and process variables. *Journal of Consulting and Clinical Psychology, 57*(5), 658–662.

Hooven, C., Rushe, R., & Gottman, J. (1996). The play-by-play manual. In J. Gottman (Ed.), *What predicts divorce: The measures* (pp. im1–im26). Hillsdale, NJ: Erlbaum.

Hops, H., Biglan, A., Sherman, L., & Arthur, J. (1987). Home observations of family interactions of depressed women. *Journal of Consulting and Clinical Psychology, 55*(3), 341–346.

Howes, P., & Markman, H.J. (1989). Marital quality and child functioning: A longitudinal investigation. *Child Development, 60*, 1044–1051.

Huffman, L.C., Bryan, Y.E., Pederson, F.A., & Porges, S.W. (1988). *Infant temperament: Relationships with heart rate variability.* Unpublished manuscript, National Institute of Mental Health, Rockville, MD.

Huffman, L.C., Bryan, Y.E., Pederson, F.A., & Porges, S.W. (1992). *Autonomic correlates of reactivity and self-regulation at twelve weeks of age.* Unpublished manuscript, National Institute of Mental Health, Rockville, MD.

Hugdahl, K. (1995). *Psychophysiology: The mind-body perspective.* Cambridge, MA: Harvard University Press.

Huston, T.L., & Houts, R.M. (1998). The psychological infrastructure of courtship and marriage: The role of personality and compatibility in romantic relationships. In T.N.

Bradbury (Ed.), *The developmental course of marital dysfunction* (pp. 114–151). New York: Cambridge University Press.

Iverson, A., & Baucom, D.H. (1990). Behavioral marital therapy outcomes: Alternate interpretations of the data. *Behavior Therapy, 21,* 129–138.

Jacob, T. (Ed.) (1987). *Family interaction and psychopathology.* New York: Plenum.

Jacobs, S., & Ostfeld, A. (1977). An epidemiological review of the mortality of bereavement. *Psychosomatic Medicine, 39,* 344–357.

Jacobson, N.S. (1977). Problem solving and contingency contracting in the treatment of marital discord. *Journal of Consulting and Clinical Psychology, 45*(1), 92–100.

Jacobson, N.S. (1978). Specific and nonspecific factors in the effectiveness of a behavioral approach to the treatment of marital discord. *Journal of Consulting and Clinical Psychology, 46*(3), 442–452.

Jacobson, N.S. (1984). A component analysis of behavioral marital therapy: The relative effectiveness of behavior exchange and communication/problem-solving training. *Journal of Consulting and Clinical Psychology, 52*(2), 295–305.

Jacobson, N.S. (1991). Behavioral versus insight-oriented marital therapy: Labels can be misleading. *Journal of Consulting and Clinical Psychology, 59*(1), 142–145.

Jacobson, N.S., & Addis, M.E. (1993). Research on couple therapy: What do we know? Where are we going? *Journal of Consulting and Clinical Psychology, 61*(1), 85–93.

Jacobson, N.S., & Christensen, A. (1996). *Integrative couple therapy: Promoting acceptance and change.* New York: Norton. (Paperback edition: *Acceptance and change in couple therapy.* New York: Norton, 1997)

Jacobson, N.S., Follette, V.M., Follete, W.C., Holtzworth-Munroe, A., Katt, J.L., & Schmaling, K.B. (1985). A component analysis of behavioral marital therapy: One-year follow-up. *Behavior Research and Therapy, 23,* 549–555.

Jacobson, N.S., & Follette, W.C. (1985). Clinical significance of improvement resulting from two behavioral marital therapy components. *Behavior Therapy, 16*(3), 249–262.

Jacobson, N.S., Follette, W.C., & Revenstorf, D. (1984). Psychotherapy outcome research: Methods for reporting variability and evaluating clinical significance. *Behavior Therapy, 15*(4), 336–352.

Jacobson, N.S., Follette, V.M., et al. (1985). A component analysis of behavioral marital therapy: One-year follow-up. *Behavior Research and Therapy, 23*(5), 549–555.

Jacobson, N.S., & Gottman, J.M. (1998). *When men batter women.* New York: Simon & Schuster.

Jacobson, N.S., Gottman, J.M., Waltz, J., Rushe, R., & Babcock, J. (1994). Affect, verbal content, and psychophysiology in the arguments of couples with a violent husband. *Journal of Consulting and Clinical Psychology, 62*(5), 982–988.

Jacobson, N.S., & Gurman, A.S. (Eds.). (1995). *Clinical Handbook of Couple Therapy.* New York: Guilford.

Jacobson, N.S., & Margolin, G. (1979). *Marital therapy.* New York: Brunner/Mazel.

Jacobson, N.S., & Revenstorf, D. (1988). Statistics for assessing the clinical significance of psychotherapy techniques: Issues, problems, and new developments. *Behavioral Assessment, 10,* 133–145.

Jacobson, N.S., Schmaling, K., & Holtzworth-Munroe, A. (1987). Component analysis of behavioral marital therapy: Two-year follow-up and prediction of relapse. *Journal of Marital and Family Therapy, 13*(2), 187–195.

Johnson, S.M., & Greenberg, L.S. (1985). Differential effects of experiential and problem-solving interventions in resolving marital conflict. *Journal of Consulting and Clinical Psychology, 53*(2), 175–184.

Kagan, J., Reznick, J.S., & Snidman, N. (1988). The physiology and psychology of behavioral inhibition in children. *Annual Progress in Child Psychiatry and Child Development*, pp. 102–127. New York: Brunner Mazel.

Kahn, J.R., & London, K.A. (1991). Premarital sex and the risk of divorce. *Journal of Marriage and the Family, 53,* 845–855.

Karney, B.R., & Bradbury, T.N. (1995). The longitudinal course of marital quality and stability: A review of theory, method, and research. *Psychological Bulletin, 118,* 3–34.

Karney, B.R., & Bradbury, T.N. (1997). Neuroticism, marital interaction, and the trajectory of marital satisfaction. *Journal of Personality and Social Psychology, 72,* 1075–1092.

Katz, L.F., & Gottman, J.M. (1991a). Marital discord and child outcomes: A social psychophysiological approach. In K. Dodge & J. Garber (Eds.), *The development of emotion regulation and deregulation.* New York: Cambridge University Press.

Katz, L.F., & Gottman, J.M. (1991b, April). *Marital interaction processes and preschool children's peer interactions and emotional development.* Paper presented at the meeting of the Society for Research in Child Development, Seattle, WA.

Kelly, L.E., & Conley, J.J. (1987). Personality and compatibility: A prospective analysis of marital stability and marital satisfaction. *Journal of Personality and Social Psychology, 52,* 27–40.

Keyes, R. (Ed.). (1992). *Sons on fathers.* New York: HarperCollins.

Kiecolt-Glaser, J.K., Fisher, B.S., Ogrocki, P., Stout, J.C., Speicher, C.E., & Glaser, R. (1987). Marital quality, marital disruption, and immune function. *Psychosomatic Medicine, 49,* 13–33.

Kiecolt-Glaser, J.K., Kennedy, S., Malkoff, S., Fisher, L., Speicher, C.E., & Glaser, R. (1988). Marital discord and immunity in males. *Psychosomatic Medicine, 50,* 213–229.

Kiecolt-Glaser, J.K., Malarkey, W.B., Cacioppo, J., & Glaser, R. (1994). Stressful personal relationships: Immune and endocrine function: In M.R. Glaser & J.K. Kiecolt-Glaser (Eds.), *Human stress and immunity* (pp. 321–339). San Diego: Academic Press.

Kitson, G.C., & Sussman, M.B. (1982). Marital complaints, demographic characteristics, and symptoms of mental distress in divorce. *Journal of Marriage and the Family, 44,* 87–101.

Koch-Nielsen, I., & Gundlach, L. (1985). Women at divorce. In L. Cseh-Szombathy, I. Koch-Nielsen, J. Trost, & I. Weda (Eds.), *The aftermath of divorce: Coping and family change* (pp. 99–121). Budapest: Akademiai Kiado.

Komoravsky, M. (1962). *Blue collar marriage.* New York: Random House.

Koop, R. (1995). *Metaphor therapy.* New York: Brunner/Mazel.

Krokoff, L. (1987). Anatomy of negative affect in working class marriages. *Dissertation Abstracts International, 45,* 7A. (University Microfilms No., 84–22 109).

Kurdek, L.A. (1993). Predicting marital dissolution: A five-year prospective longitudinal study of newlywed couples. *Journal of Personality and Social Psychology, 64,* 221–242.

Lakoff, G. (1993). The contemporary theory of metaphor. In A. Ortony (Ed.), *Metaphor and thought* (pp. 202–251). New York: Cambridge University Press.

Lakoff, G., & Johnson, M. (1980). *Metaphors we live by.* Chicago: University of Chicago Press.

Langer, E.J. (1992). Matters of mind: Mindfulness/mindlessness in perspective. *Consciousness and Cognition, 1,* 289–305.

Langer, E.J., & Newman, H.M. (1979). The role of mindlessness in a typical social psychology experiment. *Personality and Social Psychology Bulletin, 5,* 295–298.

Langer, E.J., Perlmutter, L., Chanowitz, B., & Rubin, R. (1988). Two new applications of mindlessness theory: Alcoholism and aging. *Journal of Aging Studies, 2,* 289–299.

Langer, E.J., & Piper, A. (1987). The prevention of mindlessness. *Journal of Personality and Social Psychology, 53,* 280–287.

Larson, M.C., Gunnar, M.R., & Hertsgaard, L. (1991). The effects of morning naps, car trips, and maternal separation on adrenocortical activity in human infants. *Child Development, 62*(2), 362–372.

Lawson, A. (1988). *Adultery: An analysis of love and betrayal.* New York: Basic Books.

Leakey, R. (1994). *The origins of humankind.* New York: Basic Books.

Leakey, R., & Lewin, R. (1992). *Origins reconsidered: In search of what makes us human.* New York: Anchor.

Lederer, W.J., & Jackson, D.D. (1968). *The mirages of marriage.* New York: W.W. Norton.

LeDoux, J.E. (1993). Emotional memory systems in the brain. *Behavioral Brain Research, 58,* 1–2, 69–79.

LeDoux, J.E. (1997). *The emotional brain.* New York: Simon & Schuster.

Levant, R.F. (1986). An overview of psychoeducational family programs. In R.F. Levant (Ed.), *Psychoeducational approaches to family therapy and counseling* (pp. 1–51). New York: Springer Publishing Co.

Levenson, R.W. (1992). Autonomic nervous system differences among emotions. *Psychological Science, 3,* 23–27.

Levenson, R.W., Carstensen, L.L., Friesen, W.V., & Ekman, P. (1991). Emotion, physiology, and expression in old age. *Psychology and Aging, 6,* 28–35.

Levenson, R.W., Carstensen, L.L., & Gottman, J.M. (1993). Long-term marriage: Age, gender and satisfaction. *Psychology and Aging, 8,* 301–313.

Levenson, R.W., Carstensen, L.L., & J.M., Gottman, (1994). The influence of age and gender on affect, physiology and their interrelations: A study of long-term marriages. *Journal of Personality and Social Psychology, 67,* 56–68.

Levenson, R.W., Ekman, P., & Friesen, W.V. (1990). Voluntary facial action generates emotion-specific autonomic nervous system activity. *Psychophysiology, 27*(4), 363–384.

Levenson, R.W., Ekman, P., Heider, K., & Friesen, W.V. (1992). Emotion and autonomic nervous system activity in the Minangkabau of West Sumatra. *Journal of Personality and Social Psychology, 62*(6), 972–988.

Levenson, R.W., & Gottman, J.M. (1983). Marital interaction: Physiological linkage and affective exchange. *Journal of Personality and Social Psychology, 45,* 587–597.

Levenson, R.W., & Gottman, J.M. (1985). Physiological and affective predictors of change in relationship satisfaction. *Journal of Personality and Social Psychology, 49*(1), 85–94.

Levenson, R.W., & Ruef, A.M. (1992). Empathy: A physiological substrate. *Journal of Personality and Social Psychology, 63,* 234–246.

Lewis, J. (1997). *Marriage as a search for healing.* Bristol, PA: Brunner Mazel.

Lewis, M., & Haviland, J.M. (Eds.). (1993). *Handbook of emotions.* New York: Guilford.

Linnemeyer, S.A., & Porges, S.W. (1986). Recognition memory and cardiac vagal tone in six-month-old infants. *Infant Behavior and Development, 9,* 43–56.

Loeb, J. (1966). The personality factor in divorce. *Journal of Consulting Psychology, 30*(6), 562.

Loftus, E.F., Banaji, M.R., Schooler, J.W., & Foster, R.A. (1987). Who remembers what? Gender differences in memory. *Michigan Quarterly Review, 26,* 64–85.

LoPiccolo, J., & Steger, J. (1974). The sexual interaction inventory: A new instrument for assessment of sexual dysfunction. *Archives of Sexual Behavior, 3,* 585–595.

Maccoby, E.E. (1990). Gender and relationships: A developmental account. *American Psychologist, 45*(4), 513–520.

Mace, D.R. (1976). Marital intimacy and the deadly love-anger cycle. *Journal of Marriage and Family Counseling, 2,* 131–137.

Malarkey, W.B., Kiecolt-Glaser, J.K., Pearl, D., & Glaser, R. (1994). Hostile behavior during marital conflict alters pituitary and adrenal hormones. *Psychosomatic Medicine, 56,* 41–51.

Mandler, G. (1975). *Mind and emotion.* New York: Wiley.

Margolin, G., & Weiss, R.L. (1978). Comparative evaluation of therapeutic components associated with behavioral marital treatments. *Journal of Consulting and Clinical Psychology, 46*(6), 1476–1486.

Markman, H.J. (1977). *A behavior exchange model applied to the longitudinal study of couples planning to marry.* Unpublished doctoral dissertation, Indiana University, Bloomington.

Markman, H.J., Floyd, F.J., Stanley, S.M., & Storaasli, R.D. (1988). Prevention of marital distress: A longitudinal investigation. *Journal of Consulting and Clinical Psychology, 56,* 210–217.

Markman, H.J., & Hahlweg, K. (1993). The prediction and prevention of marital distress: An international perspective. *Clinical Psychology Review, 13*(1), 29–43.

Markman, H.J., Renick, M.J., Floyyd, F.J., Stanley, S.M., et al. (1993). Preventing marital distress through communication and conflict management training: A four- and five-year follow-up. *Journal of Consulting and Clinical Psychology, 61*(1), 70–77.

Markman, H., Stanley, S., & Blumberg, S.L. (1994). *Fighting for your marriage.* San Francisco: Jossey Bass.

Martin, T.C., & Bumpass, L. (1989). Recent trends in marital disruption. *Demography, 26,* 37–51.

Matthews, L.S., Wickrama, A.S., et al. (1996). Predicting marital instability from spouse and observer reports of marital interaction. *Journal of Marriage and the Family, 58,* 641–655.

McCarter, L.M., & Levenson, R.W. (1996). *Sex differences in physiological reactivity to the acoustic startle.* Paper presented at the Society for Psychophysiological Research, Vancouver, BC.

McCrady, B., Stout, R., Noel, N., Abrams, D., & Nelson, H. (1991). Comparative effectiveness of three types of spouse-involved alcohol treatment: Outcomes 18 months after treatment. *British Journal of Addiction, 86,* 1415–1424.

McCrae, R.R., & Costa, P.T., Jr. (1997). The NEO personality scale: Personality trait structure as a human universal. *American Psychologist, 52,* 509–516.

McManus, M. (1995). *Marriage savers.* Grand Rapids, MI: Zondervan.

Mehlman, S.K., Baucom, D.H., et al. (1983). Effectiveness of co-therapists versus single therapists and immediate versus delayed treatment in behavioral marital therapy. *Journal of Consulting and Clinical Psychology, 51*(2), 258–266.

Michael, R.T., Gagnon, J.H., Laumann, E.O., & Kolata, G.B. (1995). *Sex in America.* New York: Warner.

Millon, T., & Davis, R.D. (1997). The MCMI: III. Present and future directions. *Journal of Personality, 68,* 69–85.

Mirsky, A.F. (1996). Disorders of attention: A neuropsychological perspective. In R.G. Lyon & N.A. Krasnegor (Eds.), *Attention, memory, and executive function* (pp. 71–95). Baltimore: Paul H. Brookes.

Mirsky, A.F., Anthony, B.J., Duncan, C.C., Ahearn, M.B., & Kellam, S.G. (1991). Analysis of the elements of attention: A neuropsychological approach. *Neuropsychology Review, 2,* 109–145.

Murray, J. (1989). *Mathematical biology.* New York: Springer Verlag.

Murstein, B.I., Cerreto, M., & MacDonald, M.G. (1977). A theory and investigation of the effect of exchange-orientation on marriage and friendship. *Journal of Marriage and the Family, 39,* 543–548.

Newcomb, M.D., & Bentler, P.M. (1980). Assessment of personality and demographic aspects of co-habitation and marital success. *Journal of Personality Assessment, 44*(1), 11–24.

Noller, P. (1980). Gender and marital adjustment level differences in decoding messages from spouse and strangers. *Journal of Personality and Social Psychology, 41,* 272–278.

Noller, P. (1984). *Non-verbal communication and marital interaction.* New York: Pergamon.

Notarius, C.I., Benson, P.R., Sloane, D., Vanzetti, N.A., & Hornyak, L.M. (1989). Exploring the interface between perception and behavior: An analysis of marital interaction in distressed and non-distressed couples. *Behavioral Assessment, 11,* 39–64.

Notarius, C., & Herrick, L. (1988). Listener response strategies to a distressed other. *Journal of Social and Personal Relationships, 5,* 97–108.

Notarius, C., & Johnson, J. (1982). Emotional expression in husbands and wives. *Journal of Marriage and the Family, 44,* 483–489.

Notarius, C., & Levenson, R. (1979). Expressive tendencies and physiological response to stress. *Journal of Personality and Social Psychology, 37,* 1204–1210.

Notarius, C., & Markman, H. (1993). *We can work it out: Making sense of marital conflict.* New York: G.P. Putnam.

Notarius, C., Wemple, C., Ingraham, L., Burns, T., & Kollar, E. (1982). Multichannel responses to an interpersonal stressor: The interrelationships between facial display, heart rate, self-report of emotion, and threat appraisal. *Journal of Personality and Social Psychology, 43,* 400–408.

Obrist, P. (1981). *Cardiovascular psychophysiology.* New York: Plenum.

O'Farrell, T.J., & Rotunda, R.J. (1997). Couples interventions and alcohol abuse. In W.K. Halford & H.J. Markman (Eds.), *Clinical handbook of marriage and couples interventions* (pp. 555–588). New York: Wiley.

Oggins, J., Veroff, J., & Leber, D. (1993). Perceptions of marital interaction among Black and White newlyweds. *Journal of Personality and Social Psychology, 65,* 494–511.

O'Leary, K.D., & Beach, S.R.H. (1990). Marital therapy: A viable treatment for depression and marital discord. *American Journal of Psychiatry 147*(2), 183–186.

O'Leary, K.D., & Smith, D.A. (1991). Marital interactions. *Annual Review of Psychology, 42,* 191–212.

O'Leary, K.D., & Turkewitz, H. (1978). Marital therapy from a behavioral perspective. In T.J. Paolino & B.S. McCrady (Eds.), *Marriage and Marital Therapy* (pp. 240–297). New York: Brunner/Mazel.

Olson, D.H., & Ryder, R.G. (1970). Inventory of marital conflicts (IMC): An experimental interaction procedure. *Journal of Marriage and the Family, 32,* 443–448.

Orbuch, T.L., House, J.S., Mero, R.P., & Webster, P.S. (1996). Marital quality over the life course. *Social Psychology Quarterly, 59*(2), 162–171.

Ortony, A., Clore, G.L., & Collins, A. (1988). *The cognitive structure of emotions.* New York: Cambridge University Press.

Osgood, C.E., Suci, G.J., & Tannenbaum, P.H. (1957). *The measurement of meaning.* Urbana: University of Illinois Press.

Panksepp, J. (1998). *Affective neuroscience.* New York: Oxford University Press.

Papero, D.V. (1995). Bowen family systems and marriage. In N.S. Jacobson & A.S. Gurman (Eds.), *Clinical handbook of couple therapy* (pp. 11–30). New York: Guilford.

Papp, P. (1998). *The process of change.* New York: Guilford.

Parke, R.D. (1996). *Fatherhood.* Cambridge, MA: Harvard University Press.

Parrott, L., & Parrott, L. (1995). *Becoming soul mates: Cultivating spiritual intimacy in the early years of marriage.* Grand Rapids, MI: Zondervan Publishing House.

Patterson, G.R. (1982). *Coercive family process.* Eugene, OR: Castalia.

Peterson, J.L., & Zill, N. (1986). Marital disruption, parent-child relationships, and behavior problems in children. *Journal of Marriage and the Family, 48,* 295–307.

Pinsof, W.M. (1995). *Integrative problem-centered therapy: A synthesis of family, individual, and biological therapies.* New York: Basic Books.

Pinsof, W.M., & Wynne, L.C. (1995). The effectiveness of marital and family therapy: An empirical overview, conclusions and recommendations. *Journal of Marital and Family Therapy, 21,* (4), 341–343.

Pittman, F. (1989). *Private lies: Infidelity and the betrayal of intimacy.* New York: W.W. Norton.

Pittman, F.S., & Wagers, T.P. (1995). Crises of infidelity. In N.S. Jacobson & A.S. Gurman (Eds.), *Clinical handbook of couple therapy* (pp. 231–246). New York: Guilford.

Polefrone, J.M., & Manuck, S.B. (1987). Gender differences in cardiovascular and neuroendocrine responses to stressors. In R.C. Barnett, L. Biener, & G.K. Baruch (Eds.), *Gender and stress* (pp. 13–38). New York: The Free Press.

Popenoe, D. (1996). *Life without father.* New York: The Free Press.

Porges, S.W. (1972). Heart rate variability and deceleration as indices of reaction time. *Journal of Experimental Psychology, 92,* 103–110.

Porges, S.W. (1973). Heart rate variability: An autonomic correlate of reaction time performance. *Bulletin of the Psychonomics Society, 1,* 270–272.

Porges, S.W. (1991a). Autonomic regulation and attention. In B.A. Campbell, H. Hayne, & R. Richardson (Eds.), *Attention and information processing in infants and adults* (pp. 201–223). Hillsdale, NJ: Lawrence Erlbaum Associates.

Porges, S.W. (1991b). Vagal tone: An autonomic mediator of affect. In J. Garber & K.A. Dodge (Eds.), *The development of emotion regulation and dysregulation* (pp. 111–128). New York: Cambridge University Press.

Porges, S.W. (1994, October). *Orienting in a defensive world: A poly-vagal theory of our evolutionary heritage.* Presidential address, Society for Psychophysiological Research.

Porges, S.W., Arnold, W.R., & Forbes, E.J. (1973). Heart rate variability: An index of attentional responsivity in human newborns. *Developmental Psychology, 8*(1), 85–92.

Porter, B., & O'Leary, K.D. (1980). Marital discord and childhood behavior problems. *Journal of Abnormal Child Psychology, 8,* 287–295.

Porter, F.L., Porges, S.W., & Marshall, R.E. (1988). Newborn pain cries and vagal tone: Parallel changes in response to circumcision. *Child Development, 59,* 495–505.

Price, R.H. (1992). Psychosocial impact of job loss on individuals and families. *Current Directions in Psychological Science, 1,* 9–11.

Rasmussen, K.L.R., Fellowes, J.R., Byrne, E., & Suomi, S.J. (1988). Heart rate measures associated with early emigration in adolescent male rhesus macaques (Macaca mulatta) [abstract]. *American Journal of Primatology, 14,* 439.

Raush, H.L., Barry, W.A., Hertl, R.K., & Swain, M.A. (1974). *Communication, conflict, and marriage.* San Francisco: Jossey-Bass.

Redl, F. (1965). *When we deal with children.* New York: The Free Press.

Richards, J.E. (1985). The development of sustained visual attention in infants from fourteen to twenty-six weeks of age. *Psychophysiology, 22,* 409–416.

Richards, J.E. (1987). Infant visual sustained attention and respiratory sinus arrhythmia. *Child Development, 58,* 488–496.

Robinson, E.A., & Price, M.G. (1980). Pleasurable behavior in marital interaction: An observational study. *Journal of Consulting and Clinical Psychology, 48,* 117–118.

Rowell, L. (1986). *Human circulation: Regulation during physical stress.* New York: Oxford.

Rubin, L.B. (1976). *Worlds of pain.* New York: Basic Books.

Rutter, M. (1971). Parent-child separation: Psychological effects on the children. *Journal of Child Psychology and Psychiatry, 12,* 233–260.

Sanday, P.R. (1981). *Female power and male dominance: On the origins of sexual inequality.* New York: Cambridge University Press.

Schaap, C. (1982). *Communication and adjustment in marriage.* The Netherlands: Swets & Feitlinger.

Schacter, S., & Singer, J.E. (1962). Cognitive, social and physiological determinants of emotional state. *Psychological Review, 69,* 379–399.

Schindler, L., Hahlweg, K., et al. (1983). Short- and long-term effectiveness of two communication training modalities with distressed couples. *American Journal of Family Therapy, 11*(3), 54–64.

Schnarch, D. (1991). *Constructing the sexual crucible.* New York: W.W. Norton.

Schneirla, T.C. (1959). An evolutionary and developmental theory of biphasic processes underlying approach and withdrawal. In M.R. Jones (Ed.), *Nebraska symposium on motivation* (pp. 1–42). Lincoln: University of Nebraska Press.

Schwartz, P. (1994). *Peer marriage.* New York: The Free Press.

Seligman, M.E.P. (1995). The effectiveness of psychotherapy: The *Consumer Reports* study. *American Psychologist, 50,* 965–974.

Shadish, W.R., Montgomery, L.M., et al. (1993). Effects of family and marital psychotherapies: A meta-analysis. *Journal of Consulting and Clinical Psychology, 61*(6), 992–1002.

Shadish, W.R., Ragsdale, K., et al. (1995). The efficacy and effectiveness of marital and family therapy: A perspective from meta-analysis. *Journal of Marital and Family Therapy, 21*(4), 345–360.

Shapiro, A.F., Gottman, J.M., & Carrère, S. (unpublished). *Buffers against divorce after the first baby arrives.* University of Washington, Department of Psychology, Seattle, WA 98195.

Shaw, D.S., & Emery, R.E. (1987). Parental conflict and other correlates of the adjustment of school-age children whose parents have separated. *Journal of Abnormal Child Psychology, 15,* 269–281.

Siegel, J. P. (1992). *Repairing intimacy.* New York: Jason Aronson.

Simmons, D.S., & Doherty, W.J. (1995). Defining who we are and what we do: Clinical practice patterns of marriage and family therapists in Minnesota. *Journal of Marital and Family Therapy, 21,* 3–16.

Smith, T.W., & Brown, P.C. (1991). Cynical hostility, attempts to exert social control, and cardiovascular reactivity in married couples. *Journal of Behavioral Medicine, 14*(6), 581–592.

Snyder, D.K., & Wills, R.M. (1989). Behavioral versus insight-oriented marital therapy:

Effects on individual and interspousal functioning. *Journal of Consulting and Clinical Psychology, 57*(1), 39–46.

Snyder, D.K., Mangrum, L.F., et al. (1993). Predicting couples' response to marital therapy: A comparison of short- and long-term predictors. *Journal of Consulting and Clinical Psychology, 61*(1), 61–69.

Snyder, D.K., Wills, R.M., & Grady, F.A. (1991). Long-term effectiveness of behavioral versus insight-oriented marital therapy: A four-year follow-up study. *Journal of Consulting and Clinical Psychology, 59*(1), 138–141.

Spring, A., & Spring, M. (1996). *After the affair.* New York: Harper Collins.

Steinberg, L., & Silverberg, S.B. (1987). Influences on marital satisfaction during the middle stage of the family life cycle. *Journal of Marriage and the Family, 49,* 751–760.

Stenberg, C.R., Campos, J.J., & Emde, R.N. (1983). The facial expression of anger in seven-month-old infants. *Child Development, 54,* 178–184.

Stifter, C.A., & Fox, N.A. (1990). Infant reactivity: Physiological correlates of newborn and five-month temperament. *Developmental Psychology, 26,* 582–588.

Stifter, C.A., Fox, N.A., & Porges, S.W. (1989). Facial expressivity and vagal tone in five- and ten-month-old infants. *Infant Behavior and Development, 12,* 127–137.

Straus, M.A. (1979). Measuring intrafamily conflict and violence: The Conflict Tactics Scales (CTS). *Journal of Marriage and the Family, 41,* 75–88.

Straus, M.A. (1999). *Child-report and adult-recall versions of the revised Conflict Tactics Scales.* Durham, NH: Family Research Laboratory, University of New Hampshire.

Straus, M.A., Hamby, S.L., Boney-McCoy, S., & Sugarman, D.B. (1996). The revised Conflict Tactics Scales (CTS2): Development and preliminary psychometric data. *Journal of Family Issues, 17*(3), 283–316.

Straus, M.A., Hamby, S.L., Finkelhor, D., Moore, D.W., & Runyan, D. (1998). Identification of child maltreatment with the parent-child Conflict Tactics Scales: Development and psychometric data for a national sample of American parents. *Child Abuse and Neglect, 22,* 249–270.

Stuart, R.B. (1980). *Helping couples change* (pp. 309–315). New York: Guilford.

Subotnik, R., & Harris, G. (1994). *Surviving infidelity.* Holbrook, MA: Adams Publishing.

Sullivan, K.T., & Bradbury, T.N. (1997). Are premarital prevention programs reaching couples at risk for marital dysfunction? *Journal of Consulting and Clinical Psychology, 65*(1), 24–30.

Tavris, C. (1982). *Anger: The misunderstood emotion.* New York: Simon & Schuster.

Terman, L.M., Buttenweiser, P., Ferguson, L.W., Johnson, W.B., & Wilson, D.P. (1938). *Psychological factors in marital happiness.* Stanford, CA: Stanford University Press.

Tharp, R.G. (1963). Psychological patterning in marriage. *Psychological Bulletin, 60,* 97–117.

Thibaut, J.W., & Kelly, H.H. (1959). *The social psychology of groups.* New York: Wiley.

Thorne, B. (1993). *Gender play: Girls and boys in school.* New Brunswick, NJ: Rutgers University Press.

Thurner, M., Fenn, C.B., Melichar, J., & Chiriboga, D.A. (1983). Socio-demographic perspectives on reasons for divorce. *Journal of Divorce, 6,* 25–35.

Van Dyke, C., & Kaufman, I.C. (1993). Psychobiology of bereavement. In L. Temoshok, C. Van Dyke, & L.S. Zegans (Eds.), *Emotions in health and illness: Theoretical and research foundations* (pp. 37–50). New York: Grune and Stratton.

Vansteenwegen, A. (1996). Who benefits from couple therapy? A comparison of successful and failed couples. *Journal of Sex and Marital Therapy, 22*(1), 63–67.

Verbrugge, L.M. (1979). Marital status and health. *Journal of Marriage and the Family, 41*(2), 267–285.

Verbrugge, L.M. (1985). Gender and health: An update on hypotheses and evidence. *Journal of Health and Social Behavior, 26,* 156–182.

Verbrugge, L.M. (1986). Role burdens and physical health of women and men. *Women and Health, 11*(1), 47–77.

Verbrugge, L.M. (1989). The twain meet: Empirical explanations of sex differences in health and personality. *Journal of Health and Social Behavior, 30,* 282–304.

Veroff, J., Kulka, R.A., & Douvan, E. (1981). *Mental health in America: Patterns of help seeking from 1957 to 1976.* New York: Basic Books.

Vincent, J.P., Friedman, L.C., Nugent, J., & Messerly, L. (1979). Demand characteristics in observations of marital interaction. *Journal of Consulting and Clinical Psychology, 47,* 557–566.

von Bertalanffy, L. (1968). *General system theory.* New York: George Braziler.

Vygotsky, L.S. (1962). *Thought and language.* Cambridge: MIT Press.

Walker, L.E. (1984). *The battered woman syndrome.* New York: Springer.

Watzlawick, P., Beavin, J.H., & Jackson, D.D. (1967). *Pragmatics of human communication: A study of interactional patterns.* New York: W.W. Norton.

Weiss, R.L. (1975). Contracts, cognition, and change: A behavioral approach to marriage therapy. *Counseling Psychologist, 5,* 15–26.

Weiss, R.L. (1980). Strategic behavioral marital therapy: Toward a model for assessment and intervention. In J.P. Vincent (Ed.), *Advances in family intervention, assessment and theory* (Vol. 1, pp. 229–271). Greenwich, CT: JAI Press.

Weiss, R.L., & Cerreto, M.C. (1980). Development of a measure of dissolution potential. *American Journal of Family Therapy, 8,* 80–85.

Weiss, R.L., & Summers, K.J. (1983). Marital Interaction Coding System-III. In E. Filsinger (Ed.), *Marriage and family assessment.* Beverly Hills, CA.: Sage.

Wetzel, J.W. (1994). Depression: Women at risk. *Social Work in Health Care, 19*(3-4), 85–108.

White, L.K., & Booth, A. (1991). Divorce over the life course. *Journal of Family Issues, 12,* 5–21.

Whitehead, L. (1979). Sex differences in children's responses to family stress. *Journal of Child Psychology and Psychiatry, 20,* 247–254.

Wile, D.B., (1992). *Couples therapy: A nontraditional approach.* New York: Wiley.

Wile, D.B. (1993). *After the fight: A night in the life of a couple.* New York: Guilford.

Williams, E., & Gottman, J.M. (1981). *A user's guide to the Gottman-Williams time series analysis programs.* New York: Cambridge University Press.

Williams, R.B., et al. (1980). Type A behavior, hostility, and coronary atherosclerosis. *Psychosomatic Medicine, 42,* 539–549.

Williams, R., & Williams, V. (1994). *Anger kills.* New York: Harper Perennial.

Wills, T.A., Weiss, R.L., & Patterson, G.R. (1974). A behavioral analysis of the determinants of marital satisfaction. *Journal of Clinical and Consulting Psychology, 42,* 802–811.

Wilson, G.L., Bornstein, P.H., et al. (1988). Treatment of relationship dysfunction: An empirical evalution of group and conjoint behavioral marital therapy. *Journal of Consulting and Clinical Psychology, 56*(6), 929–931.

Winch, R.F. (1958). *Mate selection: A study of complementary needs.* New York: Harper & Row.

Winkler, I., & Doherty, W.J. (1983). Communication styles and marital satisfaction in Israeli and American couples. *Family Process, 22,* 229–237.

Yerkes, R.M., & Dodson, J.D. (1908). The relation of strength of stimulus to rapidity of habit formation. *Journal of Comparative Neurological Psychology, 18,* 459–482.

Zeiss, A.M., Zeiss, R.A., et al. (1980). Sex differences in initiation of and adjustment to divorce. *Journal of Divorce, 4*(2), 21–33.

Zilbergeld, B. (1993). *The new male sexuality.* New York: Bantam.

Zillmann, D. (1979). *Hostility and aggression.* Hillsdale, NJ: Lawrence Erlbaum.

Index